Post-Cold War Defense Reform

Lessons Learned in Europe and the United States

♦ ♦ ♦

POST-COLD WAR DEFENSE REFORM

Lessons Learned in Europe and the United States

István Gyarmati and Theodor Winkler, *Editors*

Marc Remillard and Scott Vesel, *Associate Editors*

Foreword by

Lord Robertson, *Nato Secretary-General*

Potomac Books

An imprint of the University of Nebraska Press

Library of Congress Cataloging-in-Publication Data

Post-Cold War defense reforms : lessons learned in Europe and the United States / István Gyarmati and Theodor Winkler, editors ; Marc Remillard and Scott Vesel, associate editors.—1st ed.
   p. cm.
  ISBN 1-57488-577-4 (CL)—ISBN 1-57488-578-2 (PB)
   1. Europe—Armed Forces—Reorganization. 2. United States—Armed Forces—Reorganization. 3. World politics—1989– I. Gyarmati, István.
II. Winkler, Theodor.
UA646 .P673 2002
355′.03304—dc21   2002008603

First Edition

Contents

Foreword   vii
Lord Robertson, NATO Secretary-General

Introduction   ix
István Gyarmati and Theodor Winkler

1. Defense Reform in Switzerland   1
   Christian Catrina

2. The European Dimension of Defense Reform: From the
   WEU to the EU's New Defense Role   19
   Andrew Cottey

3. Reform Realities   36
   Chris Donnelly

4. Defense Sector Reform: The French Case Study   44
   Alain Faupin

5. Implementing a Revolution in Military Affairs: The U.S.
   Quest for Military Reform   61
   Dennis M. Gormley

6. Ukraine's Military Reform Efforts: Lessons Learned   78
   Anatoliy Grytsenko

7. Continuity, Restructuring, or Development from Scratch?
   Dilemmas of Slovenian Defense Reform, 1991–2001   111
   Ljubica Jelušič

8. Defense Reform in Turkey   135
   Ali L. Karaosmanoğlu and Mustafa Kibaroğlu

9. Defense Reform in Poland, 1989–2000   165
   Andrzej Karkoszka

10. Defense Reform and NATO   189
    George Katsirdakis

11. Reforms in Finnish Defense   205
    Mika Kerttunen

12. The *Bundeswehr* on Its Way into the Twenty-First Century   224
    Policy Planning and Advisory Staff of the German Ministry
    of Defense

13. U.S. Defense Reform in a Decade of Change   247
    Eric V. Larson

14. Defense Reform in Hungary: A Decade of Strenuous
    Efforts and Missed Opportunities   269
    Zoltán Martinusz

15. Greece Ventures onto New Ground: The New Greek
    Security and Defense Policy, 2000–2015   297
    Margarita Mathiopoulos

16. Defense Reform in Romania: An Ongoing Process   305
    Liviu Mureşan

17. The Restructuring of the Swedish Armed Forces after the
    Cold War   315
    Karlis Neretnieks

18. Creating Defense: The Estonian Case Study   330
    Andrus Öövel

19. Norwegian Defense Reforms of the 1990s   356
    Jonny M. Otterlei

20. Defense Reforms in the Postsocialist States: The Experience
    of Latvia   372
    Jan Arveds Trapans

21. Defense Reform in the Czech Republic   391
    Marie Vlachova

22. Defense Reform in the Netherlands   408
    Peter M. E. Volten

About the Contributors   427

Foreword

The last decade of the twentieth century was a period of fundamental change in Euro-Atlantic security. Now the threat of a massive war in Europe has faded and, with it, the need for Cold War forces. Today, we face different challenges and different missions—regional or civil wars, humanitarian emergencies, peacekeeping operations, and responding to terrorism and the use of weapons of mass destruction.

As a result, today's armed forces must be more flexible and more mobile than in the past, able to deploy quickly to trouble spots. They must have the right equipment for the challenges they face. And they must have the logistical support and appropriately trained personnel to stay in theater for extended periods of time. In modern operations, militaries from around the world must work together seamlessly. We can see this in the Balkans, where troops from Europe, North America, Africa, Latin America, and even Asia are operating under the same command. In today's operations, interoperability is key.

To meet these challenges, our nations are undergoing fundamental defense and military reform. This reform is the essential foundation for building the modern forces and defense capabilities that we need—and it remains a challenge of considerable proportions. After all, defense reform is about serious, structural, long-term change within very large and very expensive organizations. As all nations operate under resource constraints, defense reform has to be protected against many competing demands on state budgets. Last, but not least, defense reform carries with it both political and social implications.

No two nations have the same defense organization; hence, there can be no single model for defense reform. Yet our defense establishments feature enough similarities to benefit from each other's experiences. This volume provides us with twenty-two such distinct national reform experiences, from a wide variety of countries. And while appreciating the uniqueness of each case, the reader will also note the similarities of the lessons learned. These lessons are timely. They should ensure that this volume arouses not only the interest of the academic but, above all, the practitioner.

Lord Robertson
NATO Secretary-General

Defense Reforms in the Trans-Atlantic Region: Lessons (Not) Learned

Ambassador István Gyarmati and
Ambassador Theodor Winkler

After the landslide political changes in Europe, politicians and military planners started to think about the possible consequences of the change on military postures. The conflicts in the Balkans accelerated this process. The notion that military forces could be necessary and useful, especially for peace enforcement, gained ground. More and more frequently, the question was asked whether the military should be seen as an important instrument to defend and promote interests. Another question also arose: Is there a need to rethink the military postures amid shrinking budgets and indefinable threats? The European Union also started to recognize that Common Foreign and Security Policy might remain a paper tiger without some force supporting it, and came up with the concept of a sixty thousand-troop force and adequate command and logistical support to be created by 2003. NATO also felt the need to give some thought to emerging new needs.

This led to an attempt in almost all of the countries in the transatlantic region to review their military posture. In certain cases, as in the United Kingdom, this review produced significant results. In many countries, conscription was eliminated in the process. However, in most countries, reforms went unenforced due to lack of political will and, consequently, lack of money; the resistance of the conservative military; and no real pressure arising from any clear and present danger or threat against the countries concerned.

September 11 was portrayed in many cases as a wake-up call—and one that was rather loud and clear, but that nonetheless did not elicit a clear response. Even in the United States, where recognition of the need for defense reform was the strongest early this year, real defense reform seems to be yet another casualty of the September 11 attacks.

The good news is that there are signs of an emerging debate about the future of military forces, the revolution in military affairs, and the future of NATO and European Security and Defense Cooperation. As of today, however, it is uncertain whether these initial discussions will lead to real strategic thinking, threat analysis, and, finally, to a meaningful strategic review. The editors of this publication hope it will serve as a timely contribution to the debate on determining what lessons have, and have *not*, been learned—while suggesting possible courses for the way ahead.

CHAPTER ONE

Defense Reform in Switzerland

Christian Catrina

THE REFORM "ARMED FORCES XXI"

Like many, if not most, other European countries, Switzerland has embarked on a reform of its armed forces and its Department of Defense, Civil Protection and Sports (for the purpose of this paper, abbreviated to Department of Defense, or DOD). This paper focuses on the armed forces' reform, but some aspects of the DOD reform are mentioned where useful and appropriate.

PARAMETERS

The main objective of the reform is to transform the current Swiss armed forces with a full-mobilization strength of 350,000 to a smaller and more flexible force, with improved training and equipment—while fully respecting the parameters discussed below.

The Missions Provided for by the Federal Constitution "The armed forces serve to prevent war and contribute to the maintenance of peace. They support the civilian authorities in the defense against serious threats to the internal security and in the management of other extraordinary situations. The law can assign further tasks."[1] The missions, spelled out in more detail in the *Swiss Government Report on Security Policy* of 7 June 1999, include contributions to international peace support and crisis management; area protection and defense; and subsidiary operations to prevent and manage existential dangers (for example, natural disasters, threats to domestic peace and stability that cannot be coped with by civilian means alone).[2]

The Militia System as Stipulated by the Federal Constitution "Switzerland has armed forces. These are in principle organized according to the militia principle."[3] This implies that the proportion of professional armed forces must remain small and that the majority of conscripts do their military service not in one period, but in one basic training period, followed by several refresher courses spread out over several years.

Permanent Armed Neutrality   Neutrality is not an objective in itself, but an instrument. In the Federal Constitution, neutrality is mentioned only in two instances, in connection with the rights and duties of Parliament and government: "The Federal Assembly . . . takes measures to maintain the external security, independence and neutrality of Switzerland," and, "The Federal Council takes measures to maintain the external security, independence and neutrality of Switzerland."[4]

Although formally speaking not a parameter, but in practical terms of similarly decisive nature, are the financial resources available to the Swiss armed forces. In real terms, they dropped by about one-third over the past ten years, to a level of 4.3 billion Swiss Francs per year. Defense expenditures, which include additional outlays of approximately five billion Swiss Francs linked to the personnel of the DOD as well as expenditures of the Federal Office for Civil Defense, now account for slightly less than 10 percent of the federal budget and 1.3 percent of the Swiss gross domestic product (GDP). Admittedly, the full costs of Swiss defense are higher, since some costs are borne by cantons, municipalities, and the private sector (especially in the form of continuing to pay full salaries to employees serving temporarily in the armed forces, even though the state reimburses less than full salary). Even taking into account these costs, Switzerland's defense expenditures are less than 2 percent of GDP. The Armed Forces XXI have to be realized without an increase in the defense budget, including modernization of training and equipment and, thus, the required investment in facilities and arms procurement. Therefore, operating costs must be reduced.

MAIN FEATURES

QUANTITATIVE STRENGTH
The Swiss armed forces consist of the General Staff, the Ground Forces, and the Air Force. They currently have (that is, before the reform, "Armed Forces XXI") a strength of 350,000 when fully mobilized. A mere thirty-seven hundred of these are professional officers or noncommissioned officers (NCOs). The remainder are temporarily active armed

forces, that is, soldiers, NCOs and officers who are activated only period-
ically, for refresher courses or training necessary for new functions or
higher ranks. With "Armed Forces XXI," the personnel strength will be
reduced to 140,000 for the professional and the temporarily active part
combined, supplemented by about eighty thousand in a newly introduced reserve. The 140,000 temporarily active forces include about
twenty thousand conscripts in basic training. The professional component will be increased to about fifty-five hundred. In keeping with the
provisions of the Federal Constitution, professional officers, NCOs, and
soldiers can be used only for tasks requiring either a permanent high
readiness (not achievable with conscripts) or a particularly advanced
technical skill (again, not effectively achievable with conscripts, for
example, pilots for the F/A-18 combat aircraft).

In the unlikely case that a military threat calling for larger armed
forces should materialize in the future, generation of additional forces
would require amendments to the current laws to increase length of
service.

CONSCRIPTION

As a consequence of the reduction in armed forces (and, to some extent,
as a driving factor of this reduction), the age range of Swiss males obliged
to serve in the armed forces (with the exception of those unfit for health
reasons and conscientious objectors) will be reduced. At present, service
obligation starts at the age of twenty and ends at the age of forty-two for
soldiers; in the future, it will still start at the age of twenty but conclude
at the age of thirty. The "standard" model of service in Armed Forces
XXI will consist of an initial training period for each conscript of 139
days at the age of twenty, followed by annual refresher courses of nineteen days each from age twenty-one to twenty-six, and four years' assignment to the reserve, with no training obligation there. Since there is
universal conscription in Switzerland, the only way of reducing the
armed forces is by cutting the service age. The annual intake of conscripts is about twenty thousand and, hence, a force of eleven annual
cohorts numbering about 220,000, less attrition, but plus officers serving
beyond the age of thirty. The idea of permitting a free choice between
service in the armed forces or in civil defense was floated in 1999, but
was unable to find the necessary consensus. However, another novelty
will be introduced: On a voluntary basis, some of the conscripts—up to
about three thousand, which means about 15 percent of the intake—can

accomplish their whole service duty of three hundred days in one period at the age of twenty. (They are then assigned to the reserve until age thirty.) This new feature, called single-term soldiers, is meant to increase the number of soldiers immediately deployable, for example, in case of natural disasters.

Reducing the numerical strength of the armed forces was not the only reason for reducing the length of service duty. In a militia system, it is imperative to take into account the needs, not only of the armed forces, but also of the economy and society at large. The obligation of ensuring that the militia system remains viable falls not only on society, but also on the armed forces: They must adapt their demands on the militia so that they can be reconciled with the demands of professional life. A shorter time of service, with more front-loading, reduces the problems caused by considerable and repeated absences from work for militia beyond the age of twenty-six. For NCOs and officers, the burden also will be alleviated by increasing professional support for the preparation and conduct of training.

STRUCTURE

In Armed Forces XXI, the ground forces will include eight training commands, eight brigades (two tank brigades, four infantry brigades, and two mountain infantry brigades), and four territorial regions, the last of which will have no troops permanently assigned to them. The Air Force will consist of several wings of combat aircraft, helicopters, and transport aircraft; airfield formations; and anti-aircraft battalions.

In principle, the Armed Forces XXI will be structured in a modular fashion, with battalions being the basic modules. The levels of corps, divisions, and regiments will be abolished. In the basic structure, battalions will be grouped into eight brigades, but these brigades may—and will—be adapted if it comes to operations. Theoretically, a straightforward approach would be to subordinate all battalions to the training commands and assign them to brigades only when an operation is due. This was proposed first by the armed forces, but proved to be not viable politically.

GRADUATED READINESS

Another feature of the reform is creation of a system of gradual readiness. Such a system will ensure a sufficient number of forces available within hours (for example, for assistance in case of disasters) and, at the same time, obviate the need to keep too large a number at an unnecessarily high—and costly—state of readiness. The number of armed forces personnel immediately available will be increased to about twenty-three hundred (consisting of a professional component of about fourteen hundred and about nine hundred single-term soldiers), up from the present level of about six hundred. Within days, it will be possible to deploy additional forces that happen to attend refresher courses and, within weeks, additional units of the temporarily active part of the armed forces could be called up. Deploying the reserve component as an effective force would require months.

COOPERATION AND INTEROPERABILITY
Reflecting long-standing Swiss policy and practice, and a strict interpretation of neutrality during the Cold War, the Swiss security policy and the armed forces have been geared so far to autonomous defense of Switzerland. International cooperation, at least until the end of the Cold War, was essentially confined to procuring arms abroad and sending a limited number of officers abroad for training. The new Swiss security policy (*Security through Cooperation*) indicates a shift of emphasis, which will be reflected in the Armed Forces XXI as well. The security policy is based on the recognition that threats, dangers, and risks are increasingly cutting across international borders, and that international cooperation is necessary to cope effectively with most of them. The armed forces have to cooperate internationally in several respects:

Arms Procurement All major weapons systems have to be procured abroad, since production of such systems has not been economically viable in Switzerland for some time. There is a defense industry in Switzerland, but it is limited to smaller systems, assembly of foreign-designed systems, and maintenance.

Participation in Peace Support Operations During the 1990s, Switzerland has increased its commitment to peace support operations, taking part, with unarmed contingents, in the United Nations Transition Assistance Group (UNTAG) (Namibia, 1989–90) and the United Nations Mission for the Referendum in Western Sahara (MINURSO) (Western Sahara, 1991–94), supporting the Organization for Security and Cooperation in Europe (OSCE) Mission to Bosnia and Herzegovina from 1996 to 2000 with a Headquarters Support Unit ("Yellow Berets"), and providing a Swiss logistics company to KFOR in the Multinational Brigade South since 1999. In addition, Switzerland provides about twenty military observers to United Nations (UN) missions. In addition, since 1953, Switzerland has been a party to the Neutral Nations Supervisory Commission in Korea, with a contingent that numbered ninety-three officers at one time, but has dwindled to five.

Along with the main reform of the armed forces, a popular vote on 10 June 2001 enabled the Swiss government to arm Swiss peace support units, if and when this should be necessary to protect the armed forces and enable them to carry out their missions. Although heavily contested, this proposal, approved by a 51 percent majority, facilitates cooperation in peace support operations.

Training Cooperation In the past, the Swiss armed forces have posted officers to foreign military training institutions. In addition, the Air Force—and, more rarely, the Ground Forces—have used foreign training ranges. This cooperation will be intensified, primarily because Switzerland is small and densely populated, so all necessary training cannot be conducted at home. In a public vote on 10 June 2001, the Swiss government was authorized to conclude status-of-forces agreements facilitating such cooperation.

In addition—and as somewhat of a departure from past policy, at least in terms of explicitness—the Swiss armed forces will also build up a capability for cooperation with foreign armed forces in defense operations proper. The government's *Report on Security Policy* of 1999 ruled out joining a military alliance (that is, The North Atlantic Treaty Organization [NATO]) as militarily unnecessary and politically unfeasible. The Swiss armed forces should aim for significant autonomous defense capability, but, at the same time, build up, through interoperability, a fallback option of common defense, should this become necessary, for example, in case of a military attack and a possible subsequent abrogation of neutrality. In the same report, the old Swiss strategy of deterrence, of "dissuasion" in Swiss parlance, was dropped.

International cooperation requires—or is at least facilitated by—interoperability. Conversely, such cooperation is a means to build up interoperability. The Armed Forces XXI are charged with building up interoperability, for peace support operations in the short term, and for defense in the longer term.

ARMED FORCES LEADERSHIP
Currently, the Chief of the General Staff is "first among equals" among the leadership of the armed forces. He has the rank of Lieutenant Gen-

eral, like the chiefs of the Ground Forces and the Air Force and the commanders of the four Army Corps. As part of the reform, a new post of Chief of the Armed Forces will be created. This individual will be the chief interlocutor for the Swiss Defense Minister on military matters. The creation of a full-fledged Commander-in-Chief (and full General) in peacetime is anathema in Switzerland. Therefore, the Chief of the Armed Forces will have the rank of Lieutenant General, the same as the commanders of the Ground Forces and the Air Force. With the reform, the number of general-rank officers will be reduced from more than seventy to fewer than sixty, due primarily to elimination of the corps and divisions. There will still be four major generals, in spite of eliminating the division level. The four territorial regions to be created will be commanded by such division-level officers. This deviation from a pure model of brigades is dictated by two considerations: First, under some circumstances, the territorial regions may be assigned one or several brigades, and, second, these territorial commands are the prime military interlocutors for the cantons, so it was appropriate to give them as high a rank as possible.

REFORM OF THE DEPARTMENT OF DEFENSE

The reform of the armed forces is accompanied by a reform of the Defense Department. The future Department of Defense, Civil Protection and Sports will consist of six units: a General Secretariat with primarily supporting functions (such as personnel, finance, legal affairs); a Directorate for Security Policy; the Defense part (armed forces); Procurement and Technology; Civil Protection; and Sports. This also will replace the former Board of the Department, consisting predominantly of corps commanders (seven out of ten members), with a management board chaired by the Defense Minister and including the heads of the six units mentioned above. Even though the power of decision has always rested with the Defense Minister (and not with majority voting in the Board of the Department), this underscores the democratic and political control over the Swiss armed forces.

PROCEDURE

It takes time to change things in Switzerland; this is particularly true for such a large national institution as the armed forces. The basic procedure consists of the government issuing a new *Report on Security Policy* and, subsequently, new Armed Forces Guidelines, accompanied by proposals for the necessary legislative changes.

THE STUDY COMMISSION ON STRATEGIC ISSUES

The sequence mentioned above was followed for this reform as well, but an additional initial step was inserted: creation, by then Swiss Defense Minister Adolf Ogi, of a "blue ribbon" commission in the fall of 1996, which presented its proposals for development of Swiss security policy in February 1998. This commission, chaired by former State Secretary Edouard Brunner, consisted of forty-two eminent individuals, including members of Parliament from different parties, representatives of the economy, journalists, students, and even the single Swiss astronaut. The commission came up with fairly progressive suggestions, and only one member dissented from their findings (National Councillor Christoph Blocher, who was also among those most fiercely opposed to arming Swiss peace support troops).[5] One rationale behind creating this ad hoc commission was to identify areas of consensus and, as in the manner of a snowplow, open up avenues for developing of official Swiss policy.

THE REPORT ON SWISS SECURITY POLICY

The Report on Swiss Security Policy was submitted for broad public consultation. Based on an analysis of the comments it elicited, in September 1998, the Swiss government formulated guidelines for drafting a formal government report on Swiss security policy. A project team, which included representatives from most federal departments and was headed by the DOD, started in the fall of 1998 to draft this report. In January 1999, the government examined a draft and gave further instructions on a number of controversial issues. From mid-February to mid-April, the cantons, political parties, trade unions, employers organization, and numerous associations were invited to comment on the draft. After an additional revision, the paper was adopted by the Federal Council on 7 June 1999 and submitted to Parliament, which took note of it, with approval, in December 1999 (National Council) and March 2000 (Council of States). The title of this government report indicates the general thrust of Swiss security policy: *Security through Cooperation*.

ARMED FORCES GUIDELINES

The Armed Forces Guidelines describe the armed forces' missions, doctrine, organization, structure, and training system. Their initial drafting was undertaken by the General Staff, based on a number of more detailed studies of specific issues. The General Staff also was involved in subsequent redrafts, proposing language taking into account the necessary modifications and generally supporting the civilian side with military and technical expertise.

An initial draft was ready by late 2000, and, on 21 December, the Swiss government discussed the draft and fixed some basic parameters.

As the new Defense Minister, Federal Councillor Samuel Schmid, assumed office in January 2001, he decided that the draft language should be improved as should the draft's attention to politically sensitive issues. This was done in February within the civilian part of the DOD. The resulting second draft was submitted to the Swiss government and, subsequently, discussed informally with representatives of the cantons, the private sector, the trade unions, the Swiss Officers Society, and the NCO associations. The refined draft was submitted to the formal consultation required by law from May through July 2001.

This consultation elicited very divergent views. Among the four parties in the Swiss government, two dissented fundamentally from the proposal: The Social-Democratic Party argued for much smaller and more professional armed forces; the Swiss People's Party, for larger armed forces and strictly autonomous national defense. These views not only were contradictory, but they could not be accommodated within the general direction of Swiss security policy laid out two years earlier in the government's *Report on Security Policy*. The Swiss government had to choose a middle ground, hoping to garner sufficient support for this position in Parliament and, if it came to that, in a national referendum.[6]

After a partial redrafting, the Armed Forces Guidelines finally were adopted by the Swiss government on 24 October 2001 and forwarded to Parliament. The first chamber takes up this subject in March 2002, the second one, in June. Differences between the chambers should be settled in September, after which the hundred days start running during which fifty thousand signatures can be collected to force a public referendum.

OBJECTIVES

The general objectives of defense reform in Switzerland can be stated quite simply: The armed forces have to be adapted to the politico-military situation in Europe and to the changes in society. The reform must respect the militia system, neutrality, and the armed forces missions as laid down in the Federal Constitution, and, at the same time, get a sufficiently broad political consensus. The reform also should make the Swiss armed forces fit for current and future security challenges and should be capable of permanent adaptation, to some extent obviating the need for additional reform later.

An additional objective is to arrive at armed forces that fit within the constraints of a budget of about 4.3 billion Swiss Francs annually—about one-third less, in real terms, than a dozen years ago. Given this budget, and assuming it will remain flat for the foreseeable future, the armed forces nevertheless should be able to improve training and modernize their equipment and armament. This calls for a significant cut in numerical strength and operating costs to generate the financial means necessary for modernization that would keep the Swiss armed forces at a comparable technological level to that of other European states—not Great Britain and France and certainly not the United States.

The strengthening of democratic control of the armed forces was not a major objective, since, in essence, such control is not under challenge in Switzerland. The militia system, providing for conscription over a considerable number of years for all able-bodied male citizens, provides one check on the armed forces. Direct democracy, with fairly frequent votes on military issues, provides another. Added to this is, of course, the authority of Parliament to decide on the military budget, including procurement. However, certain elements of the reform help to strengthen democratic control, in particular, the appointment of a Chief of the Armed Forces and the DOD reform, which eliminates the numerical preponderance of the military in the DOD management board.

PROBLEMS AND CHALLENGES

Taking into account the conditions that have to be observed in any defense reform in Switzerland—militia system, neutrality, federalism, and a very inclusive, and hence rather time-consuming, decision-making process—reform has gone reasonably well so far. The sequence of steps was logical, from the more general to the more specific: from security policy to the armed forces. At virtually every stage, consultation was a main feature, often resulting in compromise, and establishing an ad hoc commission as a forerunner to the government reports also turned out to be a useful device, enhancing the likelihood of finding a sustainable political basis for the proposed changes.

MISSING YARDSTICK FOR DEFENSE CAPABILITIES

From the point of view of someone involved in this reform on the civilian side of the DOD, there were a number of difficulties in this project. Some of them arose from the fact that conventional military aggression against Switzerland is highly unlikely and is expected to remain so unless there are truly fundamental changes in the politico-military situation around Switzerland. This means that the Swiss armed forces are unlikely, in the foreseeable future, to be employed in military defense, their core mission and the decisive mission in terms of resources, training, and equipment. Of course, a conventional military attack on Switzerland cannot be ruled out entirely. The residual risk of such an attack is the main reason for maintaining the armed forces.

The very low probability of a military attack on Switzerland has several consequences. For one, this means that there is no objective standard to determine the armed forces' necessary size and defense capabilities. During the Cold War there were also many uncertainties (some of which were cleared up when the archives of former Warsaw Pact member states were opened up), but it was still possible to derive reasonably realistic scenarios that indicated the capabilities necessary for Swiss defense. This changed with the end of the Cold War. It would take a considerable stretch of the imagination to identify any state in Europe that now or in the foreseeable future might launch a military attack against Switzerland. Moreover, Switzerland is surrounded almost completely by NATO member countries—states that can hardly be considered as potential military adversaries and that would have to be overrun before an aggressor could launch a ground attack on Swiss territory.

DIVERGENCES AMONG THE GOVERNMENT PARTIES

With a low likelihood of the armed forces needing to be employed to defend Switzerland against military attack, and in the absence of reliable criteria for determining the size and capabilities required of the armed forces, there is a temptation to make defense policy—and defense reform—an issue of party politics. If a conventional military threat to Switzerland were more likely, there would be pressure on all major political parties to minimize their differences with respect to the armed forces and establish a common ground.

As it happened, during the formal consultation period of the Armed Forces Guidelines in the summer of 2001, the Christian-Democratic Party generally supported the whole the Swiss government's draft; the

Radical Party called for some revisions and supplementary explanations; the Social-Democratic Party argued for radically smaller and more professional armed forces; and the Swiss People's Party wanted a large force, with a low-to-medium level of technology, but able to defend Switzerland in full autonomy against any adversary. These are just the parties represented in the Swiss government. The demands of the Social-Democratic Party and the Swiss People's Party not only were mutually contradictory, but, moreover, they were not reconcilable with the government proposal supported, though with some reservations, by the other two parties. In this situation, the Swiss government decided to stick to the basic lines of its draft, while improving it in some cases. The Swiss government hopes that, in Parliament, a certain number of representatives from both dissenting parties will support the government proposal.

PRIORITIES OF ARMED FORCES MISSIONS

In response to these issues, suggestions were made to amend the order of the armed forces' missions. In both the government's *Report on Security Policy* (1999) and the draft Armed Forces Guidelines, these missions were enumerated as follows:

- peace support and crisis management;
- area protection and defense; and
- subsidiary support for civilian authorities (for example, in case of disasters).

The Swiss People's Party and, somewhat less insistently, the Radical Party, requested that this order be changed, with area protection and defense coming first and peace support and crisis management last. All government papers indicated that the order was not especially important (or entitled to resource allocation), but they preferred that the two missions where the army would have operational responsibility should come first, then the subsidiary operations. In addition, the first two were ordered according to the likelihood of operations actually taking place. The government stuck to its order in the end, supported by the fact that in much earlier, agreed-on papers (the *Report on Security Policy* of 1990 and the Armed Forces Guidelines 1995, elaborated in 1992) peace support was first on the list of missions.

AGREEMENT IN GENERAL, DISAGREEMENT ON SPECIFICS

Usually, general policy is considerably easier to agree on than concrete issues, especially if the latter touch on economic interests. This is a familiar international phenomenon, for example, judging from the reactions to U.S. government proposals to close down that country's military bases. Formulating the general strategy of *Security through Cooperation* was not without difficulties, but these were minor compared to reform of the armed forces.

One example of successful pressure by interest groups is the government's decision to maintain—though in significantly reduced numbers—packhorses in the Swiss armed forces. From a military point of view, their utility is low if at exists at all; therefore, the draft Armed Forces Guidelines proposed abolishing their use—a preliminary decision that subsequently was reversed. In contrast, the government's proposal to abolish bicycle troops did not encounter any fierce objection, so it was sustained.

SUBORDINATION OF BATTALIONS

A point of contention among those considering reform was the subordination of the battalions. The military planners argued that the battalions should be subordinated to the training command, in keeping with true modularity. The battalions would be assigned to a brigade for operations only and, every few years, for training in the framework of a brigade. The cantons and other groups (with the notable exception of the Swiss Officers Society), however, argued in favor of their subordination to the combat brigades. To understand this controversy, one must realize that the training commands are led by professional military, while the brigade staffs are manned almost exclusively by militia officers. To satisfy the proponents of a strong militia, it was decided in the end to subordinate the battalions to the brigades, even though this may not be the best solution in terms of pure military efficiency and efficacy.

A related issue was limiting the military careers of militia officers. Even if the armed forces leadership intended, at one time, to limit the career possibilities of militia officers to the level of captain or, perhaps, major, this line was not pursued because it would have been hopeless politically. As it turned out, even the possibility of militia officers commanding brigades was maintained, though tempered by the provisions that they not only had to have the necessary qualifications, but also had to be able to devote the time necessary for such office. In practice, a militia officer appointed head of brigade would have to devote at least half of his work time to commanding the brigade.

LENGTH OF THE INITIAL TRAINING PERIOD

In its draft of May 2001, the Swiss government proposed extending the initial training period (the recruit school at the age of twenty) from the currently fifteen weeks to twenty-four. With twenty-four weeks, it would be possible to train at the level of reinforced company, or even battalion—training that had been neglected. At the same time, twenty-four weeks would allow conscripts to be trained so that one conscript could fulfill functions that currently required several individuals. Last, front-loading military service (145 days out of a total of 280 days) right at the beginning would lessen the demands of the military on conscripts later on, when such demands are more likely to conflict with their professional lives.

The proposal of twenty-four weeks ran into heavy opposition, with many consulted cantons, parties, and organizations arguing for eighteen weeks. A twenty-four-week recruit school, they claimed, would cause university students to lose a full year. In response, the government proposed an initial training period of twenty-one weeks, a compromise between the needs of the military and those of professional life. The "loss" of three weeks from the government's original proposal would not be compensated for by an additional refresher course; the number of days a conscript has to serve consequently dropped from 280 to 262. It remains to be seen whether Parliament will accept this proposal or come up with an amendment.

INTRODUCTION OF SINGLE-TERM SOLDIERS

As part of the reform, the government proposes to offer part of the conscripts the option of doing their entire military service in one single term of three hundred days when they are twenty years old. This ensures that forces are immediately available at any time (for example, for immediate response to natural disasters). The armed forces would like to have about three thousand single-term soldiers per year (out of a total annual intake of about twenty thousand), but it remains to be seen whether enough conscripts are willing to choose this option. The original proposal to compel conscripts to single-term service, if necessary, was abandoned in the face of almost unanimous opposition.

From some, even introducing the single-term option on a voluntary basis was—and continues to be—opposed on the grounds that it undermines the militia system and paves the way toward professional armed forces. It is indeed characteristic of the Swiss militia system that conscripts do their military service in several installments (recruit school and a number of refresher courses), but limited deviation from this rule is in accordance with the Federal Constitution, as long as it is necessary on military grounds and is not offered to anywhere near a majority of the conscripts.

COORDINATION WITHIN A SYSTEM OF DOMESTIC SECURITY
Together with the cantons, the Swiss government is reexamining the Swiss system of internal security. This concerns, above all, police, and the police force is, in principle, still a cantonal issue. (There is a Federal Office for Police, but no federal police force.) Given the broad range of issues involved—including federalism and finances—this reexamination is a complex and rather protracted process. At any rate, it is expected to produce results within years, rather than months. Whatever the results, they will have a bearing on the armed forces, whose mission includes subsidiary operations in support of civilian authorities, for example, protecting international conferences, organizations, and embassies in times of increased risk.

Coordination between the police and the armed forces would have been facilitated if the outlines of the future Swiss system of internal security had been known when the Armed Forces Guidelines were drafted. However, the timetables of the two projects were too far apart. Still, within the next several years, the armed forces should be able to make the necessary adjustments.

LESSONS LEARNED

START OFF WITH BOLD PROPOSALS
One lesson—perhaps not a particularly original one—is that the armed forces, the DOD, and the government have to start off with bold proposals if reform is intended to be indeed substantial. Their proposals are always watered down, especially in a political system like Switzerland's, with its emphasis on broad and repeated consultation.

TEMPER TECHNOCRATIC APPROACHES
Without any reflection on the abilities of the military planners, it must be said that the most challenging part of the Swiss defense reform was not to define solutions to military problems, but to steer the proposals through the political arena without compromising too much of the logic behind the original plans.

Any country's armed forces are a large national institution. In Switzerland, with its militia system, the armed forces—and, even more, any changes to them—are permanently a matter of public interest. The fact that the large majority of male Swiss are serving, or have served, in the armed forces for a considerable part of their lives has the additional effect of inducing a not always justified conviction that they are in a good position to judge all military issues. This is, for better or worse, not fertile ground for technocratic approaches. The fact that changes in the law concerning the armed forces may be subject to a popular vote (if so demanded by fifty thousand citizens) means that widespread dissatisfaction is not just a passing problem, but may well spell disaster for the whole reform.

CONSULT BROADLY AND REPEATEDLY
It might be tempting in such a situation and political system—at any rate, for technocratically minded planners and bureaucrats—to cut down on the number of consultations. However, this would carry a fatal risk in Switzerland. This is a state and society built on the painstaking, and sometime tedious, search for consensus. The solutions arrived at may not be best from a professional point of view, but they have the overriding benefit of being politically sustainable. This is true even if many views and requests cannot be accommodated; the very act of soliciting the most diverse views contributes to acceptance, if not enthusiastic support.

THE MILITARY ADVISE—THE POLITICIANS DECIDE
Obviously, defense reform has to be directed by democratically legitimized political leadership. The role of the armed forces is to present the plans and requirements based on their professional judgment and to adapt them to political decisions. The armed forces may point out the consequences of different political choices, but they have to continue their work loyally, as they did in the case of Swiss defense reforms.

DON'T INSIST ON A MILITARY DOCTRINE IF THE PREREQUISITES ARE MISSING
One of the criticisms directed against the draft Armed Forces Guidelines was that they contain no military doctrine. The reason for this is simple: In the absence of any reliable indicator of the identity and nature of a military aggressor, and given the very low probability of such an aggression occurring within the foreseeable future, it would have been intellec-

tually dishonest to come up with a full-fledged military doctrine. In response to the call for military doctrine, some fragments of such a doctrine finally were included in the Armed Forces Guidelines, but they fall well short of a proper military doctrine, for good reasons.

LESSONS LEARNED THAT ARE RELEVANT FOR OTHERS

Most of the lessons drawn from the Swiss experience are probably applicable to other countries, with the possible exception of the extremely strong emphasis on consultation deriving from the special nature of the Swiss political system.

POLICY FIRST

Defense reforms must be grounded in an overall policy or strategy that includes determining the objectives of security policy and the missions of each instrument of security policy, thus also delineating what are—and, equally important, what are not—the missions of the armed forces. Given the size and overall capabilities of Switzerland's armed forces, they have to be ready to take part in noncore missions (for example, relief operations in case of disasters, reinforcing the police in particularly high-risk situations), but using armed forces within the country has to be approached very carefully, and must be limited to situations where there is clear need.

COOPERATION, BUT NO MUTUAL USURPATION OF ROLES

The armed forces, the civilian part of the DOD, the government and Parliament, have to cooperate in defense reforms, each playing its proper role and not trying to usurp roles properly assigned to others. A purely military-technocratic approach is unlikely to be sustainable because it is likely to omit crucial political, economic, and social aspects. This may detract from military efficiency and efficacy, thereby frustrating military planners, but it is a prerequisite for sustainable armed forces.

FINANCIAL RESOURCES DETERMINE WHAT IS POSSIBLE

Financial resources are an important factor; they determine what armed forces a country can, or is willing to, afford. Particularly when armed forces are based fully or in part on conscription, it is necessary to include external costs, that is, costs borne by other agencies, other political levels (cantons, municipalities), or the private business sector in the overall picture.

CONSULTATION, COOPERATION, AND COMPROMISE

Finally, it seems appropriate to stress the three Cs—"consultation, cooperation, and compromise." The Swiss system may grant them particular importance, but other countries certainly would be well advised to observe them, too. Security policy is *not* party politics, but enhances the security of the whole population, and the armed forces are not an instrument of government, but of a state and its citizens.

ENDNOTES

1. *Federal Constitution of Switzerland*, Article 58, paragraph 2.

2. *Security through Cooperation*—Report of the Federal Council to the Federal Assembly on the Security Policy of Switzerland, as of 7 June 1999, pp. 43–48.

3. *Federal Constitution of Switzerland*, Article 58, paragraph 1.

4. *Federal Constitution of Switzerland*, Article 173, paragraph 1a; Article 185, paragraph 1.

5. Report of the Study Commission on Strategic Issues, issued by the Swiss Federal Department of Defense, Civil Protection and Sports, 26 February 1998.

6. Technically speaking, the Armed Forces Guidelines are not subject to parliamentary approval, much less a referendum. However, the accompanying proposals for changes in the law concerning the armed forces are subject to debate and possible amendments in Parliament, and a referendum is necessary if demanded by fifty thousand citizens. Without the changes in legislation, the Armed Forces XXI proposed in the Armed Forces Guidelines cannot be realized.

CHAPTER TWO

The European Dimension of Defense Reform: From the WEU to the EU's New Defense Role

Andrew Cottey

Over the last decade, there has been much debate about a "European"—as distinct from transatlantic/North Atlantic Treaty Organization (NATO)—contribution to defense.[1] For much of the 1990s, however, major Western European countries were divided over whether, how far, and how to proceed down this road. As a consequence, they agreed on a compromise formula whereby the Western European Union (WEU)—rather than the European Union (EU)—would act as the institutional framework for European defense cooperation but its use would be limited to crisis management operations (the so-called Petersberg tasks) rather than to defend national territory. In practice, NATO remained the primary body for collective defense planning. When the Western European countries and the United States decided to undertake military action in the former Yugoslavia, they turned first to the United Nations and then to NATO rather than to the WEU. For the new democracies of Central and Eastern Europe, NATO—through the Partnership for Peace (PfP)—rapidly became the primary institutional interlocutor in the defense field. Operational cooperation with NATO in the peace support operations in the former Yugoslavia reinforced this relationship. Nevertheless, the Central European states also developed a distinctive relationship with the WEU in the 1990s and a much more limited defense dimension to their ties with the EU.

Since 1998–99, a dramatic new impetus has been given to European defense by establishment of the Common European Security and Defense Policy (CESDP) within the EU framework. The EU's 1999 Cologne and Helsinki European Council decisions to develop by 2003 the capability to deploy a rapid reaction force of fifty thousand to sixty thousand troops, and to establish the political and military institutions necessary to support that force, were a major step on the road to giving the Union a defense role and an operational military capability for the first time in its history. At the same time, the EU and NATO are engaged in processes of enlargement into Central and Eastern Europe that will have important implications for Western defense cooperation with these countries. The EU is engaged in membership negotiations with twelve Central and South Eastern European states, with up to ten of these states considered likely to become full members of the Union in 2004 or 2005. The Czech Republic, Hungary, and Poland joined NATO in 1999, and, at its Prague summit in November 2002, the Atlantic Alliance was expected to issue further membership invitations to up to nine other Central and Eastern European states. As of early 2002, it remains to be seen exactly how the CESDP will develop, which countries will join the EU and NATO over the next few years, and how the interrelationships between the Europeanization of defense and the enlargement of the EU and NATO will evolve.

Against this background, this chapter reviews the evolution of the European—specifically the WEU and EU—contribution to defense reform in Central and Eastern Europe since the early 1990s. The first part of the chapter examines the limited role of the WEU and the EU in supporting defense reform in postcommunist Europe in the 1990s. The second part addresses the issue of how the countries of Central and Eastern Europe may be integrated into the EU's emerging defense policy. The concluding sections explore the lessons that may be learned from the experience of the 1990s; the possible future role of a distinctively European, EU-led, contribution to defense reform in the new democracies; and the potential contribution of these states to European defense.

Europe's Limited Contribution to Defense Reform in the East in the 1990s

Europe's role in addressing the challenge of defense reform in Central and Eastern Europe is largely the story of a negative. In the decade after the end of the Cold War, neither the WEU nor the EU considered promoting defense reform in the new democracies to be part of its goals or primary responsibilities. This reality reflected a number of factors. The WEU was generally a weak and underused organization that had never carried out a defense operation or even a live exercise; its small military

Planning Staff had no slack for educational duties.[2] Some WEU members were particularly averse to its doing anything that might compete with NATO, in this instance, with the Alliance's Partnership for Peace. In any case, the WEU only had competence for the "Petersberg tasks," that is, tasks of military crisis management, not "real" or comprehensive defense.[3] For its part, the EU did not claim any competence or responsibility for military matters, nor did it have any organs equipped to deal with them, until the launch of the CESDP in 1998–99.

It will be some time before history can judge whether this was a wasted opportunity. On the face of it, the pulling power of EU membership—which has led Central and Eastern European candidates to make so many serious system changes and real sacrifices in the hope of entry—might have offered a lever for defense reform as well, and a forum for discussing those aspects of it (financial, social, human rights) less easily grasped by NATO. The motivating force of enlargement was shown by the serious efforts Central and Eastern European countries made, as Associate Partners of the WEU, to use that body as a stage for impressing both NATO and the EU with their good behavior. Russia also might have found it easier to discuss some aspects of the issue with Europeans alone than with the United States present in NATO. Nevertheless, NATO's continuing centrality in defense affairs, and the desire of both long-standing members and new partners to the east to use it as the primary framework for security and defense cooperation, meant that the Alliance—through the Partnership for Peace (PfP)—assumed the largest role in this area.

The Western European Union

Although the WEU's ties with the new democracies of Central and Eastern Europe remained very much secondary to Central and Eastern European States' relations with NATO, the WEU nevertheless did develop close cooperation with these countries.[4] In 1992, the WEU established a Forum for Consultation with those countries that had Association (or "Europe") Agreements with the EU and, hence, were recognized as candidates for EU membership. In 1994, the members of the Forum were offered the status of Associate Partner of the WEU, which was taken up by all ten Central and Eastern European countries recognized as applicants to the EU. After the 1999 accession of the Czech Republic, Hungary, and Poland to NATO, these three states became Associate

Members of the WEU (along with the other European countries that were members of NATO but not the EU—Iceland, Norway, and Turkey). This left seven Associate Partners: Bulgaria, Estonia, Latvia, Lithuania, Romania, Slovakia, and Slovenia. The WEU also developed separate dialogue relationships with Russia and Ukraine, involving both political discussion and practical cooperation.

All Associate Partners maintained delegations at the WEU's headquarters in Brussels, in practice double-hatted with their NATO delegations, and including both civilians and military representatives. Over the years, these nations were admitted to an increasingly wider range of WEU meetings, including the Council at least every second week, the majority of meetings of the Politico-Military Group, and (especially in the late 1990s) certain Military Committee and Military Working Group meetings. In practice, however, they never got involved in armaments work or in the obscure sub-bodies discussing various concrete aspects of military harmonization, and they were never allowed to send officers to the WEU Military Staff. Nonetheless, the discussions they attended were substantial and difficult enough (especially when relating to the albeit limited operations the WEU did take on) to offer Central and Eastern European military personnel something of a crash course in defense-related diplomacy and, particularly, in the tensions and dynamics of a Europeans-only group. A speciality of the WEU was that it never used interpretation, so the military personnel involved had to understand at least both its working languages—English and French. Overall, one of the defining features of the WEU, as it developed from the early 1990s, was that most of its meetings, discussions, and activities took place among the entire WEU "family" of twenty-eight states—that is, full Member States, Associate Members, Associate Partners, and Observers (the last being the European neutral or nonaligned states, Austria, Finland, Ireland, and Sweden, plus NATO member Denmark, which chose not to adopt the status of Associate Member). For the Central and Eastern European states, this meant that, although their ties with the WEU generally were less significant than their ties with NATO or the EU, these ties nevertheless offered them status closer to full membership—and the experience of cooperating as virtual full members in most circumstances—than was available to them in the NATO or EU contexts.

The Associate Partners were involved in a number of specific WEU activities that may have had some impact—however indirectly or unconsciously—on their thinking about defense reform:

- The development of the 1995 paper, "European Security: A Common Concept of the twenty-seven WEU Countries": the Associate Partners were fully involved in drafting this paper, which at least in broad and abstract terms offered a framework for defining the goals of defense policy in a new era (Slovenia only became a WEU Associate Partner in 1996, when its Association Agreement with the EU came into effect, so the EU "family" consisted of twenty-seven states before then).[5]
- The nonmilitary operations carried out by the WEU in the mid- to late 1990s, notably the Multinational Advisory Police Element (MAPE) police training mission in Albania and the small WEU Demining Assistance Mission (WEUDAM) mine-clearance training team in Croatia: The former included personnel from the military police and border guards of several Associate Partners, and the latter a Bulgarian military officer. On a miniature scale, these gave the Central and Eastern European states some experience with Western standards and approaches to operational organization as well as the very difficult issues of mission management and budgeting. (MAPE itself was, of course, an intervention directly aimed at postcommunist reform in Albania, but it affected only the police sector, not the defense reform issues addressed in this volume.)
- The drafting of WEU doctrinal and policy papers on issues such as Civil-Military Cooperation (CIMIC), Host Nation Support, and medical support for operations, in which Central and Eastern European states' diplomatic and military representatives took a full and equal part: The specific interest of WEU work on this subject was that it reflected a purely "European" standard and synthesis independent of U.S. views. The Associate Partners also were given copies of other papers drafted by WEU's West European participants alone (for example, on the Legal Framework for Petersberg Operations).
- WEU and WEU/NATO headquarters exercises, which typically focused on the various phases of decision making and development of command structures for Petersberg operations: Associate Partners participated enthusiastically in these and used them as opportunities to try out domestic mechanisms for coordinating decision making and rapid response. Most of them were able to identify and volunteer troop contributions for the hypothetical peacekeeping missions faster than some of the EU participants.

- Activities of the WEU Institute for Security Studies in Paris (WEU-ISS): Associate Partners were free to attend the Institute's seminars, several of which dealt with defense modernization. However, their themes were chosen overwhelmingly with Western preoccupations (such as equipment collaboration) in mind, and those events consciously aimed at the Central and Eastern European partners tended to have a more general security policy focus. There was also discussion about whether the WEUISS could or should be converted into a "European defense academy" where officers of different countries would receive joint instruction, at least on the European aspects of defense, but this, too, was seen by its proponents primarily as a vehicle for closer West-West cooperation, and there was never sufficient consensus (or money) to get the idea even as far as the drawing board.
- The WEU Assembly in Paris accepted observers from Associate Partner countries and from some countries (such as Croatia) that did not have that status, plus Russia and Ukraine: Because the Assembly's deliberations—especially in committee—covered a wider range of topics than the Council's activities (including many military-technical questions), it offered a good education for those who were able to take advantage of it, on both the policy substance and parliamentary dimension of defense reform. At least some Associate Partner parliamentarians felt they had gained valuable background for running defense committees in their own national Parliaments.

The WEU did address the question of its nations' defense structures and planning in a very limited way, through an annual review, conducted with NATO's help, of their capabilities suited to Petersberg operations. This produced at least some general pointers, for example, on the lack of "ilities" (sustainability, flexibility, and mobility) and the need to build up national or collective assets especially relevant to deployments on foreign territory—such as strategic air- and sealift capabilities; command, control, communications, and intelligence (C3I) infrastructure; and chemical and biological warfare (CBW) protection. Supplementing this was some rather tentative and delicate work on guidelines for "multinationalizing" the European military headquarters that might be needed for such operations. This work was limited, however, to the WEU nations that also belonged to NATO and/or the EU. Only at the very end of the WEU's existence in 2000–2001 were the results of some work shared with Central and Eastern European partners, and there was no time left to embark on any meaningful probe of the partners' relevant capabilities. At no stage did the WEU have any meaningful independent capacity to deduce performance targets for individual countries, and even less to enforce them.

The one-time only WEU "Audit" of 1999 was the organization's most serious attempt to probe its collective military capabilities for crisis management and to identify and prioritize areas for improvement. The Audit was carried out with the prospect of an EU takeover consciously in mind and, for this as well as other reasons, looked at the capabilities of "the twenty-one" only (that is, all European NATO and EU members, but not the Associate Partners). The Audit served its purpose in providing a military analytical background and precooking some policy content for the Headline Goal adopted by the EU in December 1999 (see below). But it was only copied to the Central and Eastern European states after completion, and no attempt was made to look at any challenges of military deficiency and transformation particular to these states.

The WEU's dialogue with Russia and Ukraine included occasional meetings with the WEU Council where these countries' NATO ambassadors briefed on and debated issues, including their countries' defense reform plans and development of their forces to deal with crisis management. Though always interesting and conducted in a civilized fashion, these discussions were not given any practical follow-up for lack of suitable machinery (including the absence of an independent analytical capacity within the WEU). There were some signs that the Russians and Ukrainians would have liked to have gone further in this direction—for example, through targeted seminars with military participation—had WEU resources allowed. They certainly showed real interest in the briefings they were offered on WEU crisis management exercises.

THE EUROPEAN UNION

From 1994 onward, the EU developed a Common Foreign and Security Policy (CFSP) dialogue with its Central and Eastern European partners but, like the CFSP itself, this discussion dealt only with "soft" aspects of security policy (including arms control, disarmament, regional cooperation, and the like) rather than "hard" defense. There would have been particularly strong objections from some Member States to extending this work into any field that would have overlapped with NATO and/or implied giving an EU "second opinion" on matters handled in the Alliance. Similarly, the negotiating process for EU enlargement could only cover matters within EU competence, so it did not address defense issues.

The closest the EU came to involvement in Central and Eastern European defense reform was in the field of PHARE (the French acronym for Poland and Hungary Assistance to Economic Restructuring, the Union's aid program for the candidate countries) assistance for development and reform of state structures. After some hesitation, the EU was prepared from the mid-1990s onward to grant PHARE money to support English-language teaching in the defense forces as well as other areas of administration; for broader civil service training programs, which could include ministry of defense officials; and for seminar- and research-type activities with the Central and Eastern European states extending to comprehensive security and even defense topics. Delivery of this training, however, was in the hands of national or nongovernmental agencies and experts hired by the EU rather than the EU's own staff. Thus, one cannot speak of an EU "doctrine" or "model" being conveyed (and performance measurement processes to determine exactly what had been conveyed were flimsy at best).

EUROPEAN DEFENSE AND EU ENLARGEMENT

The adoption of the CESDP, and the parallel process of EU enlargement, means that for the first time the Union is engaging directly with the Central and Eastern European candidate states on defense issues. As was noted at the beginning of this chapter, at the Cologne and Helsinki European Councils in June and December 1999, the EU agreed to develop by 2003 the capability to deploy a rapid reaction force of fifty thousand to sixty thousand troops and establish the political and military institutions necessary to support such a force. The requirements for the military force were laid down in a Headline Goal, adopted at the Helsinki summit, that defined a requirement not only for a corps-level force of up to fifteen brigades or fifty thousand to sixty thousand troops, but also for the necessary supporting infrastructure (command and control, logistics, air and naval elements, and additional forces to provide replacements for the initial forces) to deploy and sustain the force for at least a year.[6]

As EU leaders have made clear, this new force will not be a "European army," but rather a European force based on national contributions from member states operating under the political and operational control of those states within the framework of the Union. Agreement also was reached on establishing an ambassadorial-level Political and Security Committee (PSC, or COPS in its French acronym) to provide overall direction and control of the CESDP, and an EU Military Committee (EUMC) and EU Military Staff (EUMS) to provide military advice and an operational military command and control capacity. These institutions became operational on an interim basis in March 2000 and permanently in the first half of 2001.

To meet the Headline Goal, the EU has put in place mechanisms to identify the required forces and to enable states to agree to supply those forces. A Capabilities Commitment Conference was held in November 2000, at which EU member states committed themselves to provide forces to meet the Headline Goal and identified shortcomings in their collective military capabilities. A further Capability Improvement Conference was held a year later, in November 2001, at which states revised their national contributions and agreed on a European Capability Action Plan to meet the Headline Goal.[7] At the Laeken European Council in December 2001, the EU announced that it was now capable of conducting some crisis management operations and, on the basis of the revised national contributions, "should be able to carry out the whole range of Petersberg tasks by 2003."[8] It thus appears that the EU will have in place the national contributions of forces and the political and military institutions necessary to meet the Helsinki Headline Goal and declare its new rapid reaction force fully operational by 2003. The effectiveness of that military force, and the political and military institutions for its control, of course, remain to be tested in the real world.

The establishment of the EU's CESDP raised the difficult question of how non-EU members, including the Central and Eastern European candidate states, would relate to the Union's new military role. The issue was complicated, and controversial, for a number of reasons. First, the EU has emphasized repeatedly the need to maintain the "autonomy" of its own decision making (that is, that no nonmember should have a veto over EU decisions, especially in the sensitive area of defense and military intervention), but the Union also has an interest in accepting offers of military contributions from nonmembers that might strengthen the Union's overall military capability. Second, nonmembers—and especially those countries seeking membership in, or a close political relationship with, the Union—have sought to maximize their involvement in the CESDP. Third, the various nonmembers have different relations with both the EU and NATO, so these states fall into different categories. Specifically, these include the non-EU European members of NATO

(Iceland, Norway, Turkey, and, since 1999, the Czech Republic, Hungary, and Poland—a group informally referred to as "the six"); the candidates for EU membership that are not (as of early 2002) members of NATO (Bulgaria, Estonia, Latvia, Lithuania, Romania, Slovakia, and Slovenia from Central and Eastern Europe, plus Cyprus and Malta— [these nine states, together with "the six," are referred to as "the fifteen"]); plus countries a little farther afield that nevertheless have important relationships with the EU (Russia, Ukraine, and the former Yugoslav republics, plus smaller North American NATO member Canada). The picture is complicated further because, depending on the enlargement decisions made at the November 2002 Prague NATO summit, and by the EU over the next few years, these various overlapping membership patterns will shift in important ways by the mid-2000s.

The EU's relationship with NATO is also important in this context because plans for the CESDP involve two possible types of EU military operations: those involving only EU assets and capabilities, and those involving NATO assets and capabilities (such as NATO planning infrastructure or command and control facilities). In the latter case, NATO (and, hence, its non-EU members) will retain a veto over access to Alliance resources. Here, Turkey's position—an important member of NATO, a state seeking membership in the EU but unlikely to achieve the goal in the short to medium term and a country with significant national interests in areas on the EU's periphery where the Union is most likely to deploy its new military force—is crucial. As of early 2002, Turkey's insistence on full participation in EU defense decision making, and the EU's opposition to such an infringement of its "autonomy," was preventing agreement on modalities for the provision of NATO resources to possible future EU military operations.

The EU has faced a difficult task in balancing the autonomy of its own decision making, the need to secure an agreement with NATO (including the non-EU NATO members, especially Turkey) on access to Alliance assets, and the need to integrate nonmembers, especially "the fifteen," into its emerging defense policy. Integrating "the fifteen" into the EU's emerging defense policy has involved two areas: first, agreement on modalities for their participation in any EU military operations, and, second, establishment of institutions for their involvement in the broader development of the CESDP. Key in both areas has been the EU's establishment of inclusive structures encouraging all of "the fifteen" to participate, as well as development of a slightly closer relationship with the non-EU NATO members ("the six")—because their membership in NATO gives them a de facto veto over provision of Alliance assets to EU operations and a presumed right to participate in EU operations that use NATO assets—than with the remaining nine EU candidates. At the December 1999 Helsinki European Council, the EU committed itself in general terms to consult with "the fifteen" (and other partners) on CESDP and defined the basic terms for participation by "the fifteen" (and other interested states) in future EU military operations (see box). As can be seen, a distinction is drawn between the non-EU European NATO members, which "will participate *if they so wish*, in the event of an operation requiring recourse to NATO assets and capabilities" and the other nine EU candidates, which "*may also be invited* by the Council to take part in EU-led operations."

At the Feira European Council in June 2000, the EU agreed to establish a "single inclusive structure" for "dialogue, consultation and cooperation" with "the fifteen," with additional meetings with the six non-EU European NATO members on matters relating to EU-NATO issues.[9] The PSC was given the leading role in developing this EU + 15 (and EU + 6) relationship, but meetings in this framework quickly developed at all levels (including foreign and defense ministers, political directors of foreign ministries, and military experts). The EU also invited "the fifteen" to offer contributions to the developing rapid reaction force, and they attended the November 2000 Capabilities Commitment Conference and the November 2001 Capabilities Improvement Conference, where they made offers of specific force contributions. "The fifteen" have been involved in the follow-up mechanism designed to enable the EU to meet the 2003 Headline Goal and, more generally, to enhance its military capabilities. "The fifteen's" national military contributions to the CESDP have thus been assessed in the same way as those of the full EU members. In addition, they have appointed representatives from their EU missions to follow CESDP and act as interlocutors with PSC, have accredited officers to the EU Military Staff and have been invited to participate in or observe EU military exercises (as part of the EU Exercise Policy adopted at the June 2001 Göteborg European Council). At a further remove, Russia and Ukraine also have been involved in political dialogue with the EU on CESDP.

The overall consequence of these developments is that the Central and South Eastern European candidates for EU membership (plus the other three non-EU European NATO members, Iceland, Norway, and Turkey)

European Council, Helsinki, 10–11 December 1999

Presidency Progress Report to the Helsinki European Council
on Strengthening the Common European Policy
on Security and Defense

Consultation and cooperation with non-EU countries and NATO

The Union will ensure the necessary dialogue, consultation and cooperation with NATO and its non-EU members, other countries who are candidates for accession to the EU as well as other prospective partners in EU-led crisis management, with full respect for the decision-making autonomy of the EU and the single institutional framework of the Union.

With European NATO members who are not members of the EU and other countries who are candidates for accession to the EU, appropriate structures will be established for dialogue and information on issues relating to security and defense policy and crisis management. In the event of a crisis, these structures will serve for consultation in the period leading up to a decision of the Council.

Upon a decision to launch an operation, the non-EU European NATO members will participate if they so wish, in the event of an operation requiring recourse to NATO assets and capabilities. They will, on a decision by the Council, be invited to take part in operations where the EU does not use NATO assets.

Other countries who are candidates for accession to the EU may also be invited by the Council to take part in EU-led operations once the Council has decided to launch such an operation.

Russia, Ukraine and other European States engaged in political dialogue with the Union and other interested States may be invited to take part in the EU-led operations.

All States that have confirmed their participation in an EU-led operation by deploying significant military forces will have the same rights and obligations as the EU participating States in the day-to-day conduct of such an operation.

In the case of an EU-led operation, an ad hoc committee of contributors will be set up for the day-to-day conduct of the operation. All EU Member States are entitled to attend the ad hoc committee, whether or not they are participating in the operation, while only contributing States will take part in the day-to-day conduct of the operation.

---

have been integrated quite rapidly and closely into the EU's emerging defense policy. The EU's emphasis on maintaining the "autonomy" of its decision making (in particular, that decisions on the initiation and overall political parameters of any EU military operation be made only by full members), and the fact that "the fifteen's" new defense relationship with the EU is in some respects more removed than their old relationship with the WEU (where, as noted above, most activity involved the entire WEU "family"), has prompted some resentment. However, except in the case of Turkey, this has been relatively limited in nature.

The impact of this emerging East European-EU relationship on the defense policies of the Central and Eastern European states and their approaches to military reform remains to be seen. Nevertheless, a number of initial observations may be made. First, just as for full EU members, establishment of the CESDP has generated important political pressure for Central and Eastern European states to contribute to the EU's emerging military capabilities. Second, and again, just as for full EU members, the new CESDP institutions designed to facilitate achievement of the Headline Goal provide a significant means of assessing Central and Eastern European military capabilities and suggesting ways in which those national capabilities may be enhanced and/or contribute more effectively to the EU's overall defense capability. Third, the practical day-to-day political and military cooperation emerging in the EU + 15 framework is likely to reinforce the more general "Westernization" of Central and Eastern European security and defense policies and the development of political and military interoperability with the EU (and, more generally, with the West). Overall, therefore, the new East European-EU defense relationship is likely to reinforce the trend in Central and Eastern Europe toward smaller, more professional armed forces focused on peacekeeping and enforcement operations.

A number of caveats should be added to this broad argument, however. First, while it can be argued that establishment of the CESDP may generate significant political and institutional pressure for military reforms designed to enhance European power projection capabilities and, thereby, have a powerful impact in the longer term on national defense policies and overall European military capabilities, critics suggest that other factors—reluctance to increase defense spending, the absence of a direct external military threat to most European states, and the inevitable inefficiencies of what may remain fifteen (and more in the future) *national* defense policies—will severely constrain development of the EU's military role. Which of these pressures and trends will prove more powerful remains to be seen, but the outcome of the tension between them will have a fundamental impact on the long-term success or failure of the CESDP. Second, for the Central and Eastern European states, it is not yet clear how the CESDP will interact with (and reinforce or contradict) the "message" they receive from NATO on defense reform. Third, while integration with the CESDP may encourage the Central and Eastern European states to develop armed forces capable of making greater contributions to peacekeeping and enforcement operations outside their national borders, these countries also face particular constraints in reforming their armed forces. The broader problems of postcommunist economic development mean that, even with increases in defense spending, the resources the countries of Central and Eastern Europe will be able to devote to military reform—and especially to the expensive business of developing power projection forces—will be limited. The relatively small size of most Central and Eastern European states also means that what they can contribute to EU (and NATO) power projection capabilities inevitably will be limited.

The ongoing processes of EU and NATO enlargement also will alter the nature of the EU-Eastern European defense relationship. As of early 2002, the EU is discussing a relatively big enlargement, whereby up to ten states (Cyprus, Czech Republic, Estonia, Hungary, Latvia, Lithuania, Malta, Poland, Slovakia, and Slovenia) may join the Union by 2004–2005. As full EU members, these states then would become equal participants in the CESDP, with all of the attendant rights and responsibilities. After taking in the Czech Republic, Hungary, and Poland in 1999, NATO formally recognized nine states (Albania, Bulgaria, Estonia, Latvia, Lithuania, Macedonia, Romania, Slovakia, and Slovenia) as candidates for membership. Again, by early 2002, it appeared that NATO also might opt for a big enlargement, offering membership to up to seven of these states (the likely exceptions being Albania and Macedonia) at its November 2002 Prague summit—with those states likely to join the Alliance formally in 2004. By the mid 2000s, therefore, the majority of Central and Eastern European states may be full members of both the EU and NATO, and the institutions for integrating nonmembers into the EU's CESDP may assume less importance. The EU and its CESDP also may assume more importance, however, as a means of engaging in dialogue on defense reform with other neighboring states (in particular, the former Yugoslav republics, but also perhaps the southern Mediterranean states).

The likelihood of an enlarged EU that has achieved the Helsinki Headline Goal by the mid-2000s raises important questions about the CESDP's longer-term direction. Although significant, the military capability envisaged in the Helsinki Headline Goal—a rapid-reaction force of fifty thousand to sixty thousand troops—is also limited. The currently envisaged rapid-reaction force might allow the EU to take on operations of the size and scale of the current NATO-led peacekeeping operations in Bosnia and Kosovo (although even this is likely to depend on some NATO assets and capabilities). More demanding peace enforcement or war-fighting operations may remain beyond the capability of the EU, at least in the short to medium term. By way of comparison, for example, the United States deployed approximately half a million troops during the 1991 Gulf War—ten times the size of the currently planned EU rapid-reaction force. From this perspective, more serious discussion of the long-term defense role of the EU is needed—what types of missions it may take on, what forces will be required, whether this will require increased defense spending, and how further integration can contribute to these goals (for example, in sensitive areas such as armaments production). The nature and outcome of this longer-term debate may have a significant impact on military reforms in Central and Eastern Europe. As small and medium-size members of the EU and NATO, for example, the Central and Eastern European states may face particular pressures to undertake military role specialization, development of supranational military units, and joint procurement.

CONCLUSION

This chapter has examined the "European" contribution—in terms of the distinctive role of the two institutions of Europe integration, the EU and the WEU—to addressing the challenge of defense reform in post-communist Europe. As has been seen, for most of the 1990s, the role of the WEU and the EU in addressing this challenge was limited, whereas NATO took the lead in this area (although it also should be noted that much substantive activity has taken place within the framework of the national defense outreach programs of individual NATO members rather than the multilateral NATO/PfP context). Nevertheless, during the 1990s, Central European states did develop a unique and close relation with the WEU, which helped to socialize their political and military elites into the norms of Western security and defense cooperation, as well as to explore in general terms some defense reform-related issues.

Establishment of the EU's CESDP has given a new and important momentum to the European dimension of defense reform. As detailed above, the Central and Eastern European states are now engaging directly with the EU on defense issues in a political context which makes military reform a key issue for both the Union and the candidate countries. In particular, the Central and Eastern European states have been actively encouraged to contribute forces to the EU's new rapid-reaction capability. Their involvement with the EU's new defense institutions means that their armed forces are now coming under the same Union purview and review mechanisms as those of full EU members. In addition, within in a few years the Central and Eastern European states will participate in the CESDP as full members of the EU. All of this is likely to encourage the Central and Eastern European states to develop smaller, more professional armed forces oriented toward participation in peace-keeping and enforcement operations. The EU, therefore, may become an important driver of defense reform in postcommunist Europe. As argued above, however, more serious debate is needed on the long-term defense role of the EU and the implications of that role for member states' armed forces and national defense policies.

The EU's new CESDP also raises the defense dimension of the Union's relations with neighboring states beyond the current candidates, in particular, Russia, Ukraine and the former Soviet republics, the former Yugoslav republics, and the southern Mediterranean states. To the extent that the EU plays the leading role in promoting stability in Europe and its "near abroad" and is developing a substantive role in defense, and the United States is refocusing its attention on global challenges such as terrorism, there is a case that the Union should take on a growing—and perhaps even leading—role in supporting defense reform in these areas. To the extent that NATO has the institutions, resources, and track record in this area—and the direct involvement of the United States is considered important—a case may be made that the Alliance still may be best suited to this task. The time is ripe for a review of a decade of defense reform efforts, and Western support for those efforts, in postcommunist Europe and for a new discussion of the relative roles and priorities of NATO and the EU in this area.

ENDNOTES

1. The author wishes to acknowledge a special debt of gratitude to Ambassador Alyson Bailes in developing this chapter. The contents, however, are entirely the author's responsibility.

2. On the WEU's role, see G. Wyn Rees, *The Western European Union at the Cross-roads: Between Trans-Atlantic Solidarity and European Integration*, Boulder, CO: Westview Press, 1998; Anne Deighton (ed.), *Western European Union 1954–1997: Defense, Security, Integration*, Oxford: European Interdependence Research Unit, St. Anthony's College, 1997.

3. The Petersberg tasks were adopted by the WEU in 1992 and defined as

"humanitarian and rescue tasks; peacekeeping tasks; [and] tasks of combat forces in crisis management, including peacemaking." Western European Union, Council of Ministers, Bonn, 19 June 1992, Petersberg Declaration, Part II: On Strengthening WEU's Operational Role.

4. Rees, op cit., Chapter 6, "The Enlargement of the WEU," pp. 96–113; Stuart Croft, John Redmond, G. Wyn Rees, and Mark Webber, *The Enlargement of Europe*, Manchester: Manchester University Press, 1999, Chapter 4, "The Enlargement of the WEU," pp. 89–111.

5. Western European Union, *European Security: A Common Concept of the 27 WEU Countries*, WEU Council of Ministers, Madrid, 14 November 1995.

6. European Council, Helsinki, 10–11 December 1999, Annex IV: Presidency Reports to the Helsinki European Council on "Strengthening the Common European Policy on Security and Defense" and on "Non-Military Crisis Management of the European Union," in Maartje Rutten, *From St-Malo to Nice—European Defense: Core Documents*, Chaillot Paper 47, Paris: Institute for Security Studies Western European Union, May 2001, p. 85.

7. 2386th Council Meeting, General Affairs, Brussels, 19–20 November 2001 (13802/01 [Presse 414]).

8. Presidency Conclusions, European Council Meeting in Laeken, 14–15 December 2001 (SN 300/1/01 REV 1) para 6, Annex II Declaration on the Operational Capability of the Common European Security and Defense Policy, and Report from the Presidency on ESDP (15193/01).

9. European Council, Santa Maria da Feira, 19–20 June 2000, Presidency Conclusions and Annex I: Presidency Report on Strengthening the Common European Security and Defense Policy in Rutten, op cit., pp. 120, 23, 124, 127–30.

CHAPTER THREE

Reform Realities

Chris Donnelly*

Over the past ten years, the armed forces of every country in Central and Eastern Europe have undergone drastic transformation and downsizing. Brought about by the end of the Cold War and the changing nature of the threats to national security, this is an ongoing process. The countries of Central and Eastern Europe differ in terms of size, economic capability, geostrategic situation, and the nature of their relationships with the European Union (EU) and the North Atlantic Treaty Organization (NATO). However, notwithstanding the corresponding differences in size and composition of their armed forces, the path of military reform has followed a remarkably similar pattern everywhere.

The first stage was characterized by a loss of rationale and ideology, and by massive force reductions brought on by the change in geostrategic, economic, and political circumstances. This was attended by a loss of Communist Party and governmental control mechanisms that were not replaced by any corresponding mechanisms for democratic control. New governments everywhere lacked military expertise and had no adequate civilian mechanisms to make military policy or to direct the course of military affairs and the development of their armed forces. Where mechanisms existed, they were crude and amounted to little more than establishing ever lower financial ceilings for defense expenditure. In many countries, internal power struggles resulted in authority over the armed

*Chris Donnelly is NATO's special adviser for Central and Eastern European affairs. His office has given its consent to the Geneva Centre for Democratic Control of the Armed Forces (DCAF) and the EastWest Institute (EWI) for this article to be included in the background papers provided to the Federal Republic of Yugoslavia (FRY) government. It was originally published on the Web-based edition of *NATO Review*, 49–No. 3 (Autumn 2001): 13–15.

forces either being divided among many ministries and agencies, including some that would not normally have expected to have responsibility over troops, or being moved from one branch of the executive to another, such as from the government to the president, or vice versa. In some countries, politicians sought to use the military directly in power struggles, which further reduced the degree of real political control over the armed forces.

The second stage in the process saw the armed forces' leaderships rally to protect and preserve their military systems, striving to retain as much of the old force structure and infrastructure as possible. This was influenced by a combination of motives in which vested interests undoubtedly played a part. But sincere conviction, based on patriotism and a strong belief in the validity of the former system, and reinforced by the lack of competence and expertise of new civilian governments, was the driving factor. This was exacerbated by the militaries' lack of exposure to alternative professional views and by the naturally cohesive qualities found in all effective military systems.

The effects were felt quickly. Trying to maintain a massive but obsolete structure at a time of rapid social change and economic decline proved to be disastrous. As Central and Eastern European countries moved painfully toward a real cash economy, resources available for the military began to dry up. In most countries, this was not immediately obvious because the military establishment had traditionally been able to draw on resources in kind rather than in cash and had its own means of generating income and consumable resources. Exploiting these assets allowed the core of the military to survive, despite the lack of government funding.

After more than four, and in some cases seven, decades of a command economy, all Central and Eastern European countries lacked appropriately trained accountants and effective accounting procedures. Moreover, neither police nor judiciary were equipped to monitor and control financial irregularities. This was particularly the case in defense establishments, where the need for military secrecy further impeded transparency. As a result, the defense sector in Central and Eastern Europe was slow to set up proper budgetary systems, and corruption became endemic in some instances. The uncontrollable sale or distribution of military material, lack of guidelines on officers using their positions and forces under their command for personal purposes, hiring out of soldiers by officers, straightforward theft, and other corrupt practices—all highly destructive of military discipline—proliferated. This led to a rapid decline in training standards and then in living standards, both for conscripts and for those officers and senior noncommissioned officers who lacked the rank or position to control marketable resources, or who were simply honest (the majority).

In the third stage, the procurement system broke down. Defense industries, deprived of a tied domestic market, generally tried to avoid restructuring and reorientation, taking refuge in the fiction that arms sales abroad would save them. In the event, as a result of corruption, of an unwillingness to reform and a lack of expertise in market economic realities, Central and Eastern European defense industries missed what might have been a window of opportunity in the early 1990s to seize a share of the world market. With this export opening lost, and with domestic demand collapsèd, defense industries looked to governments to bail them out. Defense factories soaked up massive state subsidies but used the money to keep large numbers of idle workers on subsistence pay, rather than to restructure the industry. In the long term, no country can maintain the quality and cost benefits that make for attractive exports without the security of a good home market. The ability to draw on vast reserves of fundamental, scientific research, and the existence of military research and development, has enabled industries to survive in their obsolete form and avoid painful reform. But these reserves are running out now, and defense industries in Central and Eastern Europe that have not restructured face near-total collapse. Reform today will be far more difficult and painful than if it had been undertaken ten years ago.

The impact of these myriad problems was felt first in almost all countries among conscripts, whose training and living standards disintegrated. The failure of the military establishment in some countries to change with society meant the young were no longer willing to serve, and the breakdown of the established system meant they no longer could be compelled to do so. The system of universal conscription decayed rapidly and, with it, any preservice military training in schools and universities. Henceforth, only a fraction of the eligible age groups would serve in the military. Legal exemption, the ineffectiveness of the draft, and bribery would ensure that the better-off and better-educated would never have to serve in the ranks.

With the disintegration of national service, the concept of a "socialist nation-in-arms" died. Moreover, it could not be restored because the social basis from which it had sprung, and on which it had depended, had gone forever. In retrospect, this seems obvious. But, at the time, in the early to mid-1990s, it was not appreciated by decision makers who had been brought up in a very different system, so the decline continued. The fall in the number and quality of conscripts, the endemic problem of physical abuse of conscripts by senior soldiers and officers, the catastrophic decline in training, and the consequent collapse of the armed forces' prestige next took its toll on the ranks of young officers, many of whom resigned. Meanwhile, standards of entry to officer training colleges dropped. Moreover, many cadets, having received a good technical education, decided not to enter the army and left on or just before graduation. This completed the destruction of the old system.

The armed forces of the Soviet Union and Warsaw Pact, working to a common Soviet model, had relied on young officers to conduct all the junior command and training tasks at unit level that, in most Western armies, are carried out in depots or by regular professional, long-service noncommissioned officers. The lack of young officers accelerated the steady downward spiral of training. A vicious circle had become established: training standards fell, equipment broke down and was not replaced, poor treatment of soldiers increased, the gap between the command and the soldier grew, recruitment of young officers became more difficult, and morale fell and, with it, public respect. The result was declining competence, accompanied by a steady command and administrative drain, as officers left their posts at all levels and the force structure crumbled. When this process was accompanied by military action, such as affected the Russian Army in the first Chechen War, the results of the decay were instantly visible.

As armies shrank, their officer corps became grossly top-heavy, and this itself created an obstacle to reform. But attempts to reduce the officer ranks drastically were also harmful. The sight of the government discharging unwanted senior officers without thanks, without proper pensions or social security, and with little chance of taking up a new career led those who were not qualified for other employment to do everything in their power to stay in the armed forces. It also demoralized younger officers and deterred many young men from considering a military career.

The deterioration of the armed forces did not take place at the same speed everywhere, and the pace differed even within the armed forces of the same country. In general, problems have been worse in Russia and some new countries of the former Soviet Union than in most of Central

Europe. But many experiences are common to most countries. Successive ministers and chiefs of defense attempted to rationalize their shrinking armies, and they succeeded, to differing degrees. In units and formations with exceptional commanders, competence and combat capabilities were retained. By concentrating efforts and resources on a small number of units—regiments, squadrons, or ships—some of these have been maintained at a reasonable standard of military readiness.

But, in the main, the decline was not halted. As a result, during the 1990s, none of the armed forces of countries in the former Soviet Union or its former Central and Eastern European allies managed to reconstruct an effective and sustainable military system along modern lines. Indeed, a point was reached in most Central and Eastern European countries where the situation got so dire that the armed forces became desperate. Their plight was obvious, and the only way they could pursue reform was to seek more money from the state.

A thorough military reform program is expensive. However, experience in Central and Eastern Europe has shown that, when money was made available to defense establishments in advance of reforms, it tended to be spent not on reform but on keeping the old system on life support. Cosmetic improvements were made, but essential, fundamental reform was actually put off, and the situation only worsened. Indeed, reform became more difficult because the money stiffened resistance.

The "NATO factor" has played a role in this process in many Central and Eastern European countries. In some countries keen to get into NATO, the military command has proposed on occasion the procurement of unnecessary and often unaffordable equipment, arguing that: "It will be needed to get us into NATO." At a time when the political leadership and their civilian staffs, as well as parliamentarians and journalists, did not know enough about military issues, this argument could sound persuasive. Moreover, Western arms manufacturers often peddled the same line. In other countries, governments sometimes used NATO "demands" as the excuse for pushing for defense reform because they lacked the self-confidence to tackle this issue on their own authority. Both approaches have damaged civil-military relationships and eroded public confidence.

In Russia, the "NATO factor" has been used differently. Maintaining a perception of a military threat from NATO has been used to justify preservation of much of the old military infrastructure. This in turn has distracted attention and siphoned off money from real defense reform.

The final element in the "NATO factor" has been the readiness of Central and Eastern European governments and militaries alike to look to the West for models of military organization and reform. NATO members have different military systems, while Central and Eastern European countries have widely differing requirements for defense reform or for building forces anew. Therefore, Central and Eastern European countries have found it exceptionally difficult to evaluate successful models, to work out which elements are relevant for their own development, and to find reliable, unbiased advice. Governments and armies have gone from the one extreme of rejecting any Western influence to the other of rushing to embrace Western ideas, such as professionalization, without any real understanding of what it involves—or what it costs.

Many efforts to reform from below failed. At one stage, advocates of reform hoped young officers would be able to rejuvenate the system and bring in new ideas from the bottom up. Indeed, this approach did have some temporary successes. However, in the end, there were too few energetic young officers to create sufficient momentum for reform. They failed, either because they could not overcome the inertia of the mid-level structures or because they were undermined by superiors who viewed them as a threat.

The story is similar with officers sent for training and education abroad, most frequently to Canada, France, the United Kingdom, and the United States. These individuals were expected to return home and infuse their military systems with new ideas. In practice, however, this proved to be a false hope as, all too often, the military establishment closed ranks to protect itself. In some Central European countries, even as late as 2000, every single officer who had been sent abroad on training courses was, on return, dismissed, demoted, or sent to serve in a dead-end post in some military backwater. In another country, although all senior officers had received training abroad, their lead was ignored by the mass of colonels beneath them, who obstructed implementation of orders from on high. "Democratic control of the armed forces" is usually taken to mean the generals will obey the politicians. But democratic control also can fail if colonels do not obey generals.

A further common failing has been the inability of defense ministries in Central and Eastern Europe to implement an effective budgetary and planning system. Such implementation is extremely difficult because it requires converting the mentality of the military collective. Militaries traditionally have wished to retain the existing system, while modernizing weapons and improving conditions for soldiers. As a result, they have pushed for the resources for such a vision, refusing to accept that economic realities make excessive defense spending unjustifiable and that social and economic changes necessitate reform. Western armies, by contrast, approach defense planning from the perspective of the budget, working out what that pot of money will buy and prioritizing on the basis of current threat assessments.

Linked to this common failing is the almost total absence of an honest and open system for evaluating the abilities and qualifications of officers. In the absence of such a system, it is almost impossible to develop a proper promotion and posting process. Without this, defense ministers will never be able to institutionalize reform because they will not be able to identify officers with the qualities needed to create a new kind of army, or put them into positions where they can transform words into action.

Much attention has been given in Central and Eastern European countries to democratic control of armed forces, but a frequently neglected aspect of democratic control is whether the government is actually competent to decide on and implement a defense policy and direct the course of military reform. This is a common failing, with frequently disastrous results. The fact is that Central and Eastern European countries have not yet been able to develop the civilian expertise in defense issues needed to ensure balance and to provide dispassionate advice. The rapid turnover of governments in Central and Eastern European compounded this lack of expertise. When governments rely on the military for advice on defense issues, it is the armed forces, not the government, that decides policy. This state of affairs still persists in some Central and Eastern European countries, despite the existence on paper—and in law—of what otherwise would be adequate mechanisms for democratic control.

In recent years, the situation in some Central and Eastern European countries has begun to change, however. The decline has been halted, and prospects for rebuilding a new kind of armed forces appear to be good. Countries that have faced up to the fundamental nature of their problems are now poised to take the plunge, do away with the remaining elements of the old system, and rebuild anew. But this is not true everywhere. In some countries, such as Russia, the fundamental problems are yet to be faced.

In those Central and Eastern European countries where reform has taken root and is now capable of flourishing, it has been led by a few senior officers of vision, courage, determination, and technical knowledge. They have been able to inspire subordinates to follow them and to draw on external experts to help them. Moreover, they also have been fortunate to have strong political backing to protect and encourage them, and to organize public information campaigns to ensure popular support. The reform processes now underway in several Central and Eastern European countries will take a long time to see through, but they are being spurred on by the growing realization that, were they to be postponed even further, reform would be even more difficult in the future.

CHAPTER FOUR

Defense Sector Reform: The French Case Study

Alain Faupin

INTRODUCTION

For a sixty-year-old French retired officer who began his life during World War II bombings and his military career at war in Algeria, for a man who went through the Cold War and any number of crises before ending his career in a rather peaceful and stabilized Europe, how can I not be amazed by the unprecedented collapse of so many organizations, states, and coalitions? Although many places are still torn by conflict, and many regions of the world are still prone to crises, this general improvement can be attributed to the defense planning efforts made by mature nations, more eager to prevent war than to declare it. These nations have based their policy on the overall protection of human rights, as stated in the 1789 *Declaration des Droits de l'Homme et du Citoyen*.[1] No doubt recent events in the United States are further incentive to adjust to the global needs of defense security while adhering to the same basic and enduring principles.

Planning defense, restructuring forces and organizations, and reforming the defense sector are essential to balancing ends and means. What follows is the French solution to a French equation. The process is interesting in that France resisted its national inclination to change things by revolution rather than by a steady and planned evolution. So far, the feeling in France is that we have succeeded. A new system is replacing the former one, and it already works. This major undertaking, which has taken several years already and will continue until 2015, has proved to be extremely complex and demanding. It has been neither simple nor exempt from flaws, miscalculations, or surprises. But it has proved to be indispensable.

This chapter focuses first on the changes that have occurred in the strategic environment, followed by a review of the twenty-year-old French defense concept, and then concludes with a discussion of the process leading to the decision to restructure the entire French defense sector.

BACKGROUND

Field-Marshall Ferdinand Foch, the first Supreme Allied Commander in Europe, from 1917 until the end of World War I, used to welcome his visitors with a single question, always the same, calling for a precise, intelligent, timely, and responsible answer: "What is your problem?" In so doing, he forced his commanders, and the politicians with whom he had to work, to solve their part of the problem before coming to him. To answer such a question one has to understand precisely the meaning of the words and the concepts. Within any democratic coalition, this question is even more crucial.

Another point: one cannot simply adapt to the new era and the new conditions if one does not agree, willingly, to change one's former habits and mind-set. In other words, and using a familiar image, "Sacred cows make the best hamburgers." Let us also quote Frederick the Great, warning the reformers of his army not to be overly ambitious: "He who attempts to defend too much defends nothing." Conversely, a nation should not think it has resolved the reform problem just by drawing down its forces and equipment and closing its military bases. Such a process is only one face of the coin. According to General Gordon Sullivan, former Chief of Staff of the U.S. Army (199–95) "Smaller is not better, better is better," by which he meant that, in addition to drawing down any organization, a nation also has to make sure it is improving its effectiveness as well.

French defense sector reform began significant change in 1997, after four years of preparation. The reform effort intended to achieve an entirely new armed forces structure at the end of its first phase in 2002. So far, so good. A strong and focused political will, and a close to complete consensus across the board, has supported this reform effort with a steady budget. Conscription is now over; bases have been closed in France, abroad, and overseas; and most of the military and *Gendarmerie* forces have already been relocated, reassigned, and retasked, and reequipping is underway. The first objective of the three-phase, fifteen-year plan has almost been reached, with the unfaltering support of the nation.

EVOLUTION SINCE 1990

So, we are now in the midst of an evolution. The starting point was the end of the Cold War: a prolonged end, because its consequences will continue to be felt over at least one generation, especially economically, socially, and culturally.[2]

Operation Desert Storm was the other benchmark of our evolution. For the first time since World War II, France took part in the most formidable show of force ever, altogether a mandated operation, a test bed for high-tech, a coalition of the willing. It was for France, as well as for many other participants, the mirror of the nation's weaknesses, flaws, and shortcomings. In short, the Gulf War provided a major lesson and a turning point, revealing the need for a strategic review and corrections and adaptations.

The undertaking began in 1992. No one knew then exactly what the endgame should be, but everybody knew it had to be a drastic, global, and long-term change. One date was fixed—2015, as were the dates for the two intermediate steps: 2002, 2008.

We drew our conclusions from the following changes in the strategic environment: For the first time in centuries, our borders, and those of the European Union, were not threatened, so we no longer had to invest in a broad national defensive organization. However, we felt that only our nuclear arsenal of strategic weapons would deter the few lethal threats still hanging over our country. The reemergence of a major nuclear threat could not be disregarded totally; therefore, we needed to keep this major tool in existence and credible.

We did not feel that our vital and primary interests were solely confined to Europe. As a permanent member of the United Nations (UN) Security Council, and physically, politically, and culturally present, in full sovereignty, on other continents and oceans, France had to remain involved in world affairs. Not only as a nation, but also as an important member of a broad, wealthy, and powerful Union, we should remain capable of intervening, whenever and wherever required in the world, and in space.

LESSONS LEARNED FROM DESERT STORM

The Gulf War experience brought to light France's lack of a command and control instrument tailored to the requirements of the new strategic context. In addition to the lessons learned about the new and important pattern of international and joint operations, it became obvious that the suddenness and number of simultaneous crises required a joint, multinational approach that would give conventional forces a role of their own. The same goes for information warfare and strategic intelligence. This recognition had to allow for precise, updated, and continuous threat assessments that are the baseline for any planning process.

In addition, Desert Storm demonstrated clearly the need to turn our conscription forces into an all-volunteer body. All of these considerations led, in 1992, to the creation of a Joint Military Intelligence Agency, a Joint Special Operations Command, and a Joint Planning Staff, all of which have been instrumental in the later stages of the reform of our defense sector and in recent crises.

REVIEW OF THE FRENCH DEFENSE CONCEPT

While participating in Desert Storm, France had several other deployments going on in Africa, the Middle East, and as part of several UN peacekeeping operations. Therefore, she therefore had to maintain forces in many places around the world, for sovereignty purposes or to fulfill ongoing bilateral defense agreements. France had no choice then but to undertake a complete review of her defense concept. At this stage it was necessary to assess what capabilities we needed to tackle the whole range of situations we were likely to face in the future.

A "Strategic Committee" comprising representatives of nine ministerial departments and several agencies convened and assembled a "White Paper on Defense" intended to lay down the basic principles of a major defense sector reform. It took almost a year and a half to write, have approved, and publish. This was, by all means, a consensus paper issued by the government, and on which the Parliament agreed informally. The paper detailed, through six different scenarios, the different capabilities we should maintain, create, and develop, and it stated clearly a new set of four missions. Furthermore, it depicted the new framework of engagement and defined, for the first time, the four strategic postures we should be able to handle simultaneously. Last but not least, it set a three-phase time frame for completion of reform: 2002, 2008, and 2015.

Let us look back for a minute at the scenarios. It is probably not the wisest thing in defense planning to leave open an option that could indeed lead to further shortcomings and catastrophes. For example, an armored thrust through the Ardennes was ruled out by the French political planners in the 1930s and that decision resulted in a major German breakthrough in May 1940; the same assumption made by U.S. planners in 1944 resulted in a near-catastrophe at Bastogne. Therefore, the six scenarios of the White Paper have been drafted in a very generic manner and remain general enough to encompass all possible situations.[3] They are intended to assist in drafting the capabilities the armed forces should have to face all the challenges of the new strategic environment.

Brainstorming meetings on capabilities were carried out by specialized "Strategic Committees and sub-Committees," followed by experts' assessments, and backed up by analyses and recommendations by defense institutes. This resulted in the definition of new missions and force requirements that were submitted to the Prime Minister and the President, who had to make difficult choices among different options.

These missions and force requirements were then translated into force structure, manpower policy, and procurement requests, after which the budget people took over to propose appropriation bills over a six-year period. Politicians in the Parliament then had their say, on the plan as a whole, and then each year until the Strategic Committees reconvened for the next phase. Plans for reconvening for the next phase (2003–2008) are underway, and a special expert group is looking at the long term (2030). The consensus reached in the earlier phase has prevented any erroneous and unplanned political decisions.

The differences between the new missions and the old ones reflect strategic changes and new goals. For example, Europe and the Mediterranean are mentioned specifically because they are part of France's vital interest areas. Our armed forces are to carry out their missions in well-defined frameworks of engagement that have a strong impact on the force structure.

The different defense and security organizations, including the French Ministry of Defense (MOD), play different roles and have different requirements for type of forces, armaments, missions, and doctrine. Their ultimate goals may not be the same, even if the search for peace and stability remains a common ground. Varying goals calls for versatility of soldiers, units, and headquarters; highly adaptable—therefore very sophisticated—equipment; and, of course, forces and power projection assets.

Aside from the new set of four missions, and the depiction of four different frameworks of engagement (North Atlantic Treaty Organization [NATO], European Union [EU], United Nations [UN], Organization for Security and Cooperation in Europe [OSCE]), four strategic postures were recommended: deterrence, prevention, protection, and protection.[4]

DETERRENCE

Deterrence, a major security and political instrument, is strictly national, although it benefits our friends, allies, and neighbors. It remains the key and fundamental element of France's defense strategy, so nuclear strategic forces have been streamlined over the last few years to be consistent with the disappearance of major threats in Europe and signing of non-proliferation treaties.[5]

In deterrence, conventional forces play a much smaller role than before. Conversely, these forces are used in the rest of the world more than they were in the past, but their nature has changed. The new forces clearly call for professional soldiers and enhanced command, control, and deployment/projection assets.

PREVENTION

The second strategic posture or function, crisis prevention, is probably the least costly way to maintain peace and stability, not only in Europe but throughout the world. Diplomacy now takes the lead, but diplomats, no matter how clever, cannot do much without the backing of a strong and uncompromising political will that could take the shape of military force in readiness and economic sanctions.

Intelligence is another major asset in crisis prevention. High technology helps immensely, but is not enough; the role human intelligence plays in crisis prevention is irreplaceable. It is not surprising, therefore, that under these conditions France has decided, along with some European partners, to establish a space observation program, Helios 1, 2, and 3, using European high technology, the French Guyana space facility, and the Ariane 4 and 5 launch vehicles.

The third element needed in crisis prevention is the presence of pre-positioned forces at or in the vicinity of a possible theater of operations. Combined with our defense and cooperation agreements, these forces have often played a deterring and crisis-defusing role, especially when used to back up diplomatic negotiations.

PROTECTION

France is now able to make available thirty thousand ground troops, a naval air carrier group, and one hundred aircraft for the Air Force at short notice, and to deploy in one theater of operation, while at the same time capable of tackling other minor crises simultaneously, at any time, and with lesser forces (three thousand to five thousand soldiers).

PROTECTION

Protection of the national territory remains the enduring and ultimate mission of the armed forces, wherever they are deployed. However, the new and various threats to the integrity, the stability, the institutions, and the well-being of the state demand more of a security than a defense answer. This requires the combined efforts of police, customs, *Gendarmerie*, and, occasionally, special forces.

Terrorism might be used as a lever to curb our national resolve. In addition, we owe the national community collective protection against weapons of mass destruction. We need to protect our lines of communication, airspace, borders, laws, culture, and order. We also have to provide the population with relief in case of civil emergencies.

In today's European context, national needs merge with those of the rest of Europe, not only in our minds but also in an increasing number of bi- and multilateral arrangements.

LESSONS FROM EXPERIENCE

Considering the combination of different tasks that are incumbent upon the defense establishment in response to the four strategic postures mentioned earlier, the question is: "What command structure, if any, will ever be able to coordinate this large array of missions?"

The French have come up with an answer that emphasizes the joint character of any given deployment and stresses the need to think in terms of modularity and ad hoc task forces. A permanent reservoir of available, trained, and ready forces and a reservoir of command elements have replaced the traditional divisional structure. Besides, nothing is ever undertaken without consulting with global and regional security and defense organizations; whether they take the lead or not, the emphasis on liaisons and political military training has been stressed as well.

CHALLENGES FOR THE FUTURE: ALL VOLUNTEER, RESERVES, PROCUREMENT

The chart attached as Annex 2 shows the figures before the reform, in 1995, and on completion of reform, in 2015. But the goals, in terms of

strength and structures, will be reached as soon as 2002. The force reduction has been important: At least one-fourth of the French forces, the
bulk of them belonging to the Army, have disappeared: lighter but
tougher!

The next two phases of reform will see improvement of the overall
functioning of this new arrangement, especially in the reserve component, as well as in fielding of weapons programs—those initiated in the
1990s, those under current examination, and those yet to come. New patterns in education, training, and career management are to be introduced
and implemented.

The success of this reform relies essentially on correct and timely execution of the first phase, aimed at restructuring the forces and making
them more professional. One can take for granted that the French armed
forces will have been restructured, wherever they are stationed—in
France, Europe, and the world—and that almost no conscripts will be
called to service by the end of 2002. To that end, we must meet five challenges:

BUILDING A RESERVE FORCE
The first challenge is to construct a Reserve Force from scratch, which
will take a lot of time and of effort, but still may become a weakness of
our system. The reserves cannot ignore the ongoing change. Indeed, the
reduced size and structures of the French Defense Forces correspond to
current strategic assessments and to the foreseeable future. But unfore-
seen events could create a need for military reinforcements.

In the past, thanks to conscription, France had a considerable number
of would-be reservists, although they were difficult to manage and to
train. Our choice, from now on, is to have only trained and ready reservists, along the lines of the excellent model developed by our British
friends. Though our traditions are different on different sides of the
Channel, we share the same concept of operational effectiveness, and we
will follow the same lines:

- a *first reserve*, comprising fifty thousand deployable soldiers and an
  additional fifty thousand to protect the national territory (under the
  lead of *Gendarmerie*), and
- a *second reserve* of roughly the same number, not totally trained and
  ready but clearly volunteer and available to be used as an additional
  reservoir of forces.

PROFESSIONALIZATION

Second, we must end the National Military Service gradually, not abruptly, over a five-year transition period. To this end, national service is halted, though registration remains mandatory, through a one-day information session, which is compulsory for all young people, male and female, on their eighteenth birthday. Named Defense Preparation Call, this very short session is intended to offset the deficit created by the end of conscription after more than a hundred years of continuous existence. The goal of this new process, starting in school, is to make the younger generation aware of the necessities of defense and to encourage them to make a personal commitment to the reserve or even volunteer for full-time military service (twenty-seven thousand slots remain open for this program).

Improving the Officer/Soldier Command Ratio We also seek to improve the command ratio among officers, noncommissioned officers (NCOs), and the rank and file. Our units were understaffed and still are, so this component requires a dynamic recruiting policy and, probably, a drastic change in the education and training of the elite as well as in career patterns.

Reassigning Nonmilitary Tasks to Civilians We must hand over all trades that are not purely military to civil employees to refocus professional soldiers on their own specific business: operations.

Recruiting Last, we need to develop a carefully targeted and well-financed recruitment program to attract and retain the best people available through innovative, proactive, and reliable policy and intelligent incentives. The aim should be to fit the enlistees' skills and capabilities to the needs of the different forces, which need a broad array of specialists.

PRIORITIES FOR THE FUTURE

The following domains are France's *main priorities* for the fifteen coming years; they are consistent with the main lines of our defense sector reform and are intended to meet the capabilities demanded by the new world order in which we and the next generation will live:

- intelligence,
- power projection,

- strategic mobility, and
- C4 (command, control, communication, and computers).

Counterterrorist and internal security forces, in high demand since the September 11 attacks, are included under these headings; they cannot be created overnight, and they need be planned for well in advance while remaining under strict political control.

French defense reform is supported by an enduring national consensus and sustained by a strong and constant political, bipartisan will. This restructuring and defense planning effort has a price, of course; however, we managed to stretch the cost over a period of eighteen years. This cost is commensurate with our expectations and remains reasonable in the eyes of the politicians and the general public. However, it is also true that when it comes to budgetary matters, priorities generally go where short-term political (and/or electoral) emergencies are or seem to be.

RECOMMENDATIONS

It is always difficult to convince people, whether in government, Parliament, or the public, that investing in the first phase of development of an obscure weapon system not to be fielded until 2013 is more important than, or equally important as, appropriating money for an urgent, visible, and politically rewarding social program. Whatever the incentives for a reform plan, the process should answer four basic requirements:

- A period of prudent maturation to make sure that the changes that have occurred in the national and international environment are long-lasting; this period also should allow for refinement of the strategic assessment and the study of different solutions, examples, and models.
- A deliberately collective, interdepartmental, and interagency venture, animated by the highest level in the state with the will to include all the components of the nation as deeply and as completely as possible.
- A detailed and deliberate process, with distinct and identifiable steps, such as issuing a White Paper on defense, a major and binding decision on the type of force structure and military service (draft versus career), and passing a defense law.
- The will to set up an inclusive and all-encompassing project in the spirit of the national constitution and to have it applied with flexi-

bility but firmness (in the case of France, through passage through Parliament of a six-year defense law).

The participants in this process should be numerous and diverse: the defense ministry is only one of the major players. For instance, the first phase (a White Paper on defense policy) should be headed by a high-ranking civil servant from an independent, nongovernmental state agency (*Conseil d'État*, for example), assisted by executives from all concerned ministerial departments and by well-known members of academic and other research institutes.

Even in the other phases in which the Ministry of Defense plays a major role, it is necessary to keep these participants active and involved. The overall organization of the process is quite arduous, given the need to break the topics down and distribute them to many different groups, each presenting a diverse blend of people, expertise, talents, and opinions, with different approaches and agendas. Very special attention should be devoted to the secretariats, which are the key elements of such working groups. Two challenges have to be met: mastering the complexity of the problems and guaranteeing independent thinking and free expression. These are two prerequisites to any new proposals submitted for approval to the political authorities.

It is obvious that, whenever a large national sector has to undergo a major reform, it is confronted immediately with immense methodological difficulties. The reform's natural complexity is exacerbated by the need for continued operation. One cannot shut the door to carry out the renovation. Any evolution in these circumstances becomes a perilous exercise. In addition, what makes it even more difficult is the cultural diversity of the working group members. Some may be reluctant to recommend or support a much-needed reform that could put their power, career, or interests in jeopardy. But that is the price to pay in terms of efforts, time, and negotiation to reach a common understanding encompassing the different layers of the national community. Under these conditions, the final document directing the project will stand as the founding act of the evolution.

No mention has been made so far of the role of Parliaments. Depending on their degree of influence over the executive branch—weak in France, stronger in Great Britain and Germany, and very strong in the United States—they should be included early on in the different stages of the process. This creates an additional guarantee of consensus, but it also risks having the issues politicized before they are assessed properly. However, when the time comes to adopt the reform program and fund it, it will certainly prove advantageous to have had the members of parliaments associated with it throughout its development. A subtle balance should be found between cultural habits and effectiveness.

Within a given phase, all of the issues need to be studied simultaneously. For instance, to define a new type of armed forces, the focus should be on more than just the armed forces themselves; the development process is progressive, iterative, repetitious, and simultaneous in all the fields related to defense, such as defense policy, general military strategy, operational concepts, military capabilities, European Headline Goal, collective security arrangements, balance among the different services and components, personnel policy (status, recruiting, education and training, return to civilian life, etc.), technical and industrial capabilities, budget, cultural aspects (language, traditions, religions), communications and public relations, etc.

The first task of the working group in charge of reorganizing land forces would be to define basic principles on significant points such as a new logistic system for the operational command, a new combatant system, a new pattern of procurement, etc. The group then would build on this strong base a series of intermediate "mock-ups" technically tailored to meet the required capabilities. This technical responsibility should rest with the military staffs, whereas the definition of an Army model is, in essence, a political act because it involves the expenditure of resources.

Conclusion

It is still too early to say how effective the French defense reform will be. It has to succeed, even if adjustments and amendments have to be made to the initial plans to comply with changes in a realistic way. No model fits all. Every nation is unique and needs a unique solution to its unique set of problems and circumstances. However, nations contemplating major reforms certainly would benefit from the experience and examples of other nations.

That was the aim of this chapter.

Annex 1

Toward a New Force Structure

The days of planning for massive armored clashes in the Fulda Gap are behind us. Today, we need forces that can move fast, adjust quickly to changing requirements, hit hard, and then stay in theater for as long as it takes to get the job done: This means that today military forces must be mobile, flexible, effective at engagement, and sustainable in theater.

—Lord Robertson, 31 January 2000

Recent experiences have made it obvious that the traditional structure of large all-arms units, such as army corps and divisions, is outdated. The need is now for highly trained and ready forces, available at short notice, deployable, and task-organized to fulfill, on request, one specific mission. Therefore, the French defense reform establishes four specific forces that constitute—with dedicated training, equipment, and units—four such reservoirs of forces from which to draw for our contingency units.

Each of these forces corresponds roughly to a NATO division: fifteen thousand soldiers. One is an armored force, another is mechanized, a third is a rapid-reaction light-armor force, and the fourth is an infantry air assault force. Each force can provide for an operational and deployable headquarters, able to run a division-size contingency operation.

The differences among these forces stems from the kind of mission they will have to carry out and from the mode of recruiting, training, and managing the manpower, staff, and equipment. These forces are to be combined with one another to answer the operational requirements of a given crisis.

To this end, the French Army is undergoing the greatest transformation in its several-centuries-long history. In less than ten years, it has lost more than one hundred battalion-size units, ending up with but eighty-six regiments. Its overall strength has been reduced from 330,000 in 1990 to an expected 136,000 military and thirty-four thousand civilians in 2002, which represents the first leg of reform.

This drastic reduction elicited a lot of discontent among the local authorities where the garrisons were located. They were vexed by the huge base closure program that had nothing to do with "the peace dividends of the Cold War." On the contrary, the defense budget increased to pay for these costly reductions and to beef up the quality of the people and of the equipment: "Smaller is not better, better is better. . . . "

Quite a few weapons system programs, launched in the early 1990s, allowed us to reequip the four newly designed forces and brought about, in the wake of our own revolution in military affairs:

- a better balance between light and heavy equipment;
- a drastic improvement of the tank-helicopter tandem;
- a major increase in the range and accuracy of all firing arms; and
- a computerized battle management system that is interoperable with NATO's.

The French Navy had to lose some weight as well. It has been decreased from an estimated 350,000 tons in the early 1990s to an anticipated figure of 235,000 tons by 2002. The number of sailors will be reduced in a couple of years, from sixty-five thousand in 1996, to about forty-five thousand, but the number of civil employees will grow to eleven thousand, from only about seven thousand four years ago.

The Navy is structured primarily around a "Strategic Sea Force" comprising a Naval Air Group associated with all combat surface support and service support ships, plus, of course, nuclear-powered attack submarines. I also mention here the six surface-to-surface ballistic missile (SSBM) nuclear submarines that belong to the Strategic Nuclear Forces Command.

As is the case for the Army, smaller did not mean weaker: on the contrary. The first French nuclear-powered aircraft carrier, the *Charles de Gaulle*, enters active duty this year, and the multirole Navy *Rafale* fighters are being "fielded." Our amphibious force has been reshuffled and augmented to cope more efficiently with the requirements of our deployable land forces.

The French Air Force will include sixty-three thousand military and seven thousand civilians (they were eighty-five thousand and five thousand, respectively, in 1996). Here again, a lot of cuts have been made, but they have been compensated by a far better cost-efficiency ratio due to the fielding of new and technically advanced assets (*Rafale*, special ammunition, space).

The combat force will include approximately three hundred fighters of the latest generation—the *Rafale*—capable of delivering the most advanced weapon systems.

The French Air Force did well during the Kosovo Air Operation, with more than a hundred aircraft permanently committed to flying almost one-third of the missions tasked to the Europeans. It is currently striving to correct the flaws and shortcomings that have appeared, especially in some high-tech weapons systems.

Military air transport will be modernized, it is hoped, as part of a European venture, beginning in 2003. In-flight refueling capabilities also will improve to provide the French forces with indisputable capability force projection.

One component of the French Air Force is dedicated to the Nuclear Strategic Command, and quite a few air and space assets to strategic intelligence.

Last but not least, the National Military Police Force, referred to in France since the sixteenth century as *Gendarmerie Nationale*, has been strengthened. The overall strength of this "corps" will amount to ninety-eight thousand men and women, including two thousand civilians and a few remaining voluntary draftees. The *gendarmerie* is the second-ranking service, in terms of strength, after the Army. This force is well equipped because it requires a heavy degree of interoperability with the military forces and with the civilian authorities. It also must be well protected against any possible terrorist attack and ready to react rapidly to any terrorist activity. Units of the *Gendarmerie Nationale* are disseminated widely throughout the country, and their reaction time is designed to be very short. These forces are on permanent alert.

This professional but rather static category of forces has been given this mission of territorial defense under the recent reform, thus allowing professional soldiers to concentrate on deployments and operational missions abroad. The *Gendarmerie*'s theater of operation includes French territory, Europe, and the overseas territories. It is also in charge of the legal aspect of all operations in which the French forces are involved and routinely answers requests from other ministerial departments, namely Justice and Interior, to enforce law and order.

Annex 2

Armed Forces, 2015

French Force Structure

		1995	2015
Army	Military manpower	239,000	136,000
	Heavy-armored tanks	927	420
Navy	Military manpower	63,000	45,500
	Ships (without SSBN)	101	81
Air Force	Military	89,200	63,000
	Combat aircraft	405	300
Gendarmerie	Military	92,230	95,600
Common Service	Military	18,130	12,600
Total	Military	502,460	352,700
	Civilians	74,500	81,300
	Total	577,360	434,000

ENDNOTES

1. The guarantee of the human and civil rights calls for a public force: this force is instituted for everyone's benefit and in no way to serve the interests of those in charge of it.

2. The end of the bipolar world brought an immediate change in the strategic environment in three ways: First, the conventional threat over Europe had vanished. We have to remain alert, however, and, at the same time, pursue a policy of close cooperation in security, defense, culture, and economy with the former "communist" Europe.

Second, proliferating media educate more people about events taking place around the world than ever before.

Third, we have this vision, dating back to the 1950s, that we share with most of the European nations of a wealthier, safer, more competitive, more generous Europe. It already exists and functions economically: Nations have invested part of their sovereignty in it with the advent of the Euro, but they have to invest still more in defense. One of the aims of our reform plan is to coordinate European defense identity more closely with NATO.

3. The six scenarios read as follows:

- regional conflict with no vital interests involved;
- regional conflict threatening our vital interests;
- aggression against our overseas territories;
- implementation of our defense agreements and bilateral treaties; and
- peace operations in support of international law.

4. Each one of them somehow overlaps the other three; the best way to represent them is by four "Olympics" secant circles.

5. And it is totally consistent with the Comprehensive Test Ban Treaty and other international agreements (Rarotonga, etc.). Smaller has proved to be better.

CHAPTER FIVE

Implementing a Revolution in Military Affairs: The U.S. Quest for Military Reform

Dennis M. Gormley

THE ORIGINS OF AMERICAN MILITARY REFORM

Although the intellectual foundation of current American efforts to institute significant military reform took root nearly fifteen years ago, not until 1997 did signs become evident that both senior civilian and military officials grasped why military transformation had become imperative. Muted recognition came in the form of rhetorical encouragement of military transformation in the 1997 Quadrennial Defense Review (QDR), which is conducted every four years to review underlying military strategy supporting force procurement. A more vociferous call for transformation came a few months later in the report of the National Defense Panel, which grew out of a congressional mandate to provide a "second opinion" in regard to the QDR's strategy and recommendations. It seems fair to say that not much of substance—aside from the creation of several perfunctory Pentagon bureaucratic entities having nominally if not substantively to do with transformation—came from these initial appeals for military reform. It would remain the job of the new Bush administration to take up the challenge of true military reform.

As for the intellectual roots of American military transformation, they originated not only from analyses of U.S., British, and German military history between 1918 and 1939, but also from detailed assessments of debates within the Soviet military press commencing in the late 1970s and continuing right up to the demise of the Soviet state. Andrew W. Marshall, Director of the Pentagon's Office of Net Assessment, commissioned these assessments in the mid-1980s.[1] In regard to the Soviet case, senior military analysts perceived nascent revolutionary changes, the product of innovative military electronics—including computers, sensors, and communications systems—tied conceptually and organizationally to long-range conventional weapons. These analysts foresaw a qualitative change in conventional warfare, in that non-nuclear military means eventually would approach the effectiveness of low-yield nuclear weapons.[2] A key dimension of the Soviet debate was the importance of conceptual and organizational change, without which revolutionary improvements were problematical. American proponents of the military reform, most notably Marshall and his acolytes, emphasized the notion that transformation was highly unlikely based on technology alone. To underscore this proposition, the Marshall assessments turned the Soviet notion of a "military technological revolution" into a "revolution in military affairs," or the now widely used appellation, RMA.

What constitutes an RMA? Perhaps the best way to illustrate it lies in associating its key components with a historical example. Using the case of German tank warfare circa 1940, an RMA is said to occur when new technologies (for example, the internal combustion engine, radios) are incorporated into a sufficient number of militarily significant systems (for example, main battle tanks), which are then combined with innovative operational concepts (for example, blitzkrieg tactics) and novel organizational adaptation (for example, creation of Panzer Divisions) to produce quantum improvements in military effectiveness.

To be sure, the 1991 war in the Persian Gulf showed signs of revolutionary changes in warfare. The best example comes from a brief comparison of nonprecision and precision attacks taken from the Gulf War Air Power Survey.[3] In the nonprecision case, twelve representative aircraft sorties (F-111s delivering unguided Mark 82 bombs) covered two targets using 168 bombs, producing a target/sortie ratio of 1:6. By comparison, twelve representative sorties (F-117s and F-111s delivering laser-guided bombs) covered twenty-six precision targets with twenty-eight bombs, achieving a target/sortie ratio of 2:1. Thus, the differential between the precision and nonprecision cases was 13:1, or more than an order of magnitude improvement in effectiveness. That said, however, it is important to note that all of these targets were fixed, well-known points. By comparison, the coalition had no confirmed kills in the so-called Scud hunt, in spite of using nearly 15 percent of its total air sorties against Iraqi missile launchers. Detecting and attacking mobile targets, particularly ones armed with weapons of mass destruction, arguably represents the paramount challenge against which to judge truly revolutionary transformation in military capability.[4] The truth is that virtually all the weapons used during the 1991 war in the Gulf were decades old; moreover, there was no evidence of any dramatic doctrinal or organizational adaptations reflected in the overall campaign, however successful it proved to be.

A decade after the Gulf War, the American quest for military reform continues. One hears fewer references today to implementing an RMA, which perhaps underscores the excessive hype and fruitless debate that has occurred over what truly constitutes an RMA. Instead, transformation rather than revolution has become the American quest, reflecting the strong probability that change inevitably will be evolutionary and will occur over a decade, if not two.

THE CURRENT STATE OF MILITARY TRANSFORMATION

Two primary reasons animate the American transformation quest. The first is the stark reality that nearly the entire stock of military hardware in the hands of today's U.S. military forces will need to be replaced over the next two decades or so.[5] In a sense, this reality offers the American military an opportunity to enhance its effectiveness while reducing overall numbers of military personnel. Naturally, substituting improved military hardware for labor has its inherent limitations, particularly for such missions as peacekeeping and combat in urban and jungle settings, which will continue to depend on manpower, not just technology.[6]

Beyond this opportunity lies the necessity, which comprises the second animating reason behind transformation, of coping with the downside risks of today's globalization of advanced information technology. To be sure, the civilian commercial economy, not government-sponsored military research and development, has largely driven the technology underlying America's opportunity for military transformation.[7] Information technology is having a profound impact on transformation as it shapes new doctrinal development, experimentation, and military systems, especially sensors for precision targeting and attack operations. But there is an ominous side to the information technology revolution. Because it is commercially driven, advanced information technology is readily within the grasp of potential adversaries, too. Of course, what distinguishes the American and European exploitation of information technology from potential adversaries in the developing world is the capacity to bring outstanding systems integration and engineering skills to the task of creating advanced military systems. For the most part, these skills are glaringly few in the nonindustrialized world. Still, both nonstate and state actors eventually could take advantage of these new technologies to produce, however selectively, new military capabilities that could threaten both homeland and overseas American interests.

The emerging threat implications of the commercially driven technology revolution are most profoundly the case with weapons of mass destruction (WMD) and their means of delivery.[8] These developments imply that future American forces may, eventually, no longer be able to deploy over long ranges into increasingly vulnerable air bases, ports, and large-signature logistical facilities in proximity to the enemy. The increasing vulnerability of fixed targets also suggests to American planners the need for a much greater capacity to deploy forces rapidly with much smaller logistical footprints, in some cases from intercontinental ranges. Most important, the American military must find ways to cope with WMD threats, not merely through greatly improved missile defenses, but through improvements in intelligence and surveillance, counterforce targeting, and passive defenses as well.[9]

METHODS FOR IMPLEMENTING REFORM

With the inauguration of a new President, George W. Bush, in January 2001, new emphasis was assigned to implementing military reform. The Clinton administration's approach had been largely rhetorical, including occasional references to the RMA by Clinton's secretary of defense and the creation of what proved to be token bureaucratic attention to programs that qualified as revolutionary in their potential to transform warfare. Naturally, the military services characterized virtually every new program as meeting the definition of revolutionary. During his election campaign, Bush raised the prospect of "skipping a generation" of military procurement to exploit new information technologies as a means to implement true transformation of military capabilities against new, uncertain future threats.

With the selection of Donald Rumsfeld as his secretary of defense, President Bush seemed truly interested in turning rhetoric into reality. Rumsfeld immediately set out to create roughly twenty independent review panels, which essentially excluded the military services and the U.S. Congress from substantive participation and, in some cases, even knowledge of what was transpiring. The panels variously focused on different aspects of U.S. military strategy, organization, weapon systems, budget requirements, and other matters to help fashion a new defense strategy. To long-time advocates of defense reform, the opaque Rumsfeld approach, relying heavily on experts outside the Department of Defense, meeting behind closed doors, represented "the most far-reaching and significant review of the U.S. military in years." Outside experts were relied on heavily because "If the reviews were left to the military services, [they] would be used to justify the current approach to transformation."[10] Quite naturally, those with a substantial stake in the US$325 billion defense budget for 2002, not to speak of the stakes associated with the long-term impact on defense strategy and congressional-industrial interests, found Rumsfeld's closed-ended approach unacceptable.

The key Rumsfeld elements or tools for implementing military reform, which together comprise what some might call a transformation strategy, can be culled from developments to date. Six factors seem to have become crucial in measuring the success of the Rumsfeld-led transformation initiative, including:

- a future vision of warfare;
- the selection of senior leaders willing to implement military reform;
- a willingness to fund so-called leap-ahead technologies;
- the creation of sufficient organizational slack to foster innovation and institutional change;
- the reform of procurement strategy; and
- a divestment strategy that frees up funding for transformational systems.

First, and most important, is a future warfare vision that will give meaning to transformation efforts. The most salient work in this regard lies in the development of new joint warfare concepts and experimentation at the Joint Forces Command (JFCOM) in Norfolk, Virginia. One of nine unified commands, JFCOM has both functional (joint concept development and experimentation) and geographic (Atlantic theater and homeland defense support) responsibilities.[11] JFCOM will be at the forefront of efforts to develop a vision that expands on the U.S. military's *Joint Vision 2020*, its current visionary representation of future warfare concepts.[12]

Equally important in implementing reform is the selection of senior leaders based on their willingness and ability to effect transformational change. Rumsfeld has inserted himself into promotional activities of each of the military services to meet this goal.

A third element of the emerging transformation strategy is the willingness to fund so-called leap-ahead technologies that can be subjected to sustained experimentation and detailed lessons learned to extract implications for new operational concepts and organizational entities. This, by necessity, dictates a substantial increase in research and development accounts, which have suffered over the last eight years because of unanticipated increases in operations, maintenance, and readiness accounts. As for experimentation, JFCOM will play the primary role as far as joint efforts are concerned, while each of the military services will continue to hold dearly onto its respective training and experimentation responsibilities.

A fourth feature of the emerging U.S. transformation strategy is a desire to create enough organizational slack to foster innovation and institutional reform within the Department of Defense, the military services, and the defense industrial base. Given the conservative approach of the affected stakeholders, in many respects this goal will be the most difficult to implement.

A fifth element of American transformation strategy is creation and implementation of a procurement strategy in the near and mid-term that emphasizes limited production runs of a whole new range of capabilities. Accompanying this would be a willingness to extend the service life of legacy systems through product improvements and upgrades. Procurement reform is a long-standing quest, particularly as it relates to joint requirements for major systems, as the latter responsibility lies squarely in the hands of each of the military services rather than in any joint authority. Title 10 of the U.S. Code gives procurement authority to each service for major military systems. If this element of transformation strategy is to succeed, methods for working around this constraint must be found.[13]

Finally, if transformation is to succeed, supporters argue that a divestment strategy must be implemented to eliminate capabilities that fit poorly with the emerging strategic environment. Perhaps the most notable example is the existing requirement to procure three new tactical fighters (the F-22, FA-18, and Joint Strike Fighter) at a time when transformation advocates are calling for greater attention to uninhabited combat air vehicles (UCAVs), such as the X-45A, which is designed to attack air defense sites. Elimination of one of these three tactical fighter programs would free up resources to support transformation initiatives.

THE AMERICAN VISION OF TRANSFORMATION

Although the Rumsfeld approach to implementing military reform creates enormous friction among key stakeholders, many agree with the underlying vision and broad objectives driving the quest for transformation. The core factors shaping the current transformation vision include the challenges of projecting power in an antiaccess environment that will likely include WMD and difficult operating environments (not least urban and jungle terrain); defending the homeland against new threats (a notable requirement even before the events of September 11); and ensuring space and information superiority to support these diverse challenges. The events of September 11 also have given new resonance to an overarching question posed by many transformation advocates: Why can't the sole military superpower exploit its dominant military advantage more effectively? Transformation advocates answer this rhetorical question by noting that American dominance is manifested largely in airpower improvements, which are best suited to the defeat of well-known fixed targets and exposed enemy forces in regular wars. American military strengths produce very uncertain advantages in highly asymmetric conflicts. Moreover, U.S. capacity to deter and defeat threats consisting of significant missile forces armed with WMD is uncertain. America's current war against terrorism, particularly the challenges of bringing forces rapidly to bear on the ground in harsh operating environments and identifying and protecting against bioterrorist threats, exemplifies the kinds of new challenges against which current U.S. strengths are suspect.

Rapid and agile response to emerging threats is a key thematic element in America's transformation vision. The intellectual seeds of this theme were first evident in Roberta Wohlstetter's 1962 book, *Pearl Harbor: Warning and Response*, which introduced the notion that, because warning of conflict will always be ambiguous, the United States needs an array of response options that are repeatable, affordable, and appropriate to the threat.[14] A contemporary reflection of the importance of rapid response to emerging threats became evident with the publication in June 2001 of one of the twenty or more Rumsfeld-commissioned reports in briefing form. General James McCarthy (U.S. Air Force, ret.)

headed a "Transformation Study," that focused on providing the secretary of defense with new concepts and approaches to transform the military. The featured new concept was rapid response, including projecting force both rapidly and potently to halt aggression, combining precision with speed, and undertaking more parallel, continuous, and seamless operations (compared with sequential, scheduled, and segmented ones).[15]

The vision of providing rapid, virtually instantaneous response to threats stands in decided contrast to the lengthy build-up phases that have preceded each and every U.S and coalition military engagement since the end of the Cold War. To give meaning to this vision, the 2001 Quadrennial Defense Review called for examination of several Standing Joint Task Forces (SJTFs), most prominently one earmarked to execute "unwarned, extended-range conventional attack against fixed and mobile targets at varying depths."[16] This SJTF would focus on a major shortcoming in U.S. defense capability: the ability to continuously locate and track mobile targets at any range and attack them rapidly with precision.[17] To give practical meaning to this vision would require enhanced intelligence capabilities, including a space-based radar system, more human intelligence resources on the ground, and improved airborne systems, all of which would be netted together to locate and track critical mobile targets and provide actionable strike information to attack resources in near-real time. Creating such an SJTF is seen as furnishing the "vanguard" for a transformed American military. Besides offering immediate operational benefits once it became available, it would provide a test bed for experimenting with new operational concepts, organizational changes, and the incorporation of new technologies, not just in new organizational entities, but in the legacy forces as well. Thus, the SJTF would become the "tip of the spear," thereby permitting legacy forces a longer effective life.[18]

PROBLEMS AND CHALLENGES IN THE TRANSFORMATION PROCESS

On reflection, the efforts of Secretary of Defense Donald Rumsfeld to institute defense reform can be viewed as a preemptive attempt to overtake the normal bureaucratic process within the Pentagon and impose rapid change from atop the bureaucracy. Transformation advocates believed that success in this regard could occur only if the initial strategic reviews were completed quickly and then subsequently exploited to reshape the fiscal year 2001 defense budget, with more substantive changes, including divestiture of some major weapons programs and force structure changes, in the 2002 and 2003 defense budgets.[19] Instead, the review process grew out of hand, expanding to more than twenty separate study groups, most of which comprised experts from outside the military's Joint Staff and service staffs. The review process grew longer and remained shrouded in mystery, a fact that many affected stakeholders argued was similar in nature to the much maligned closed-review process of health care policy headed by First Lady Hilary Clinton during her husband's presidency. The Congress became increasingly concerned about the future direction of defense policy and the impact of such opaque decision making on the individual stakes of particular members of the Senate and House. By early summer, 2001, it had become evident that Rumsfeld's preemptive strategy would not succeed.

The 2001 report of the Quadrennial Defense Review, coming less than three weeks after the terrorist attacks on the World Trade Center and the Pentagon, reflected little of the original intent to institute a major transformation program. To be sure, much of the new transformation vision, including the possibility of standing up a joint task force to focus on the most difficult military challenges, made it into the QDR. Also of note is the replacement of the two-war strategy with a broad set of policy goals designed to give military leaders more flexibility in shaping the future force structure, and the institution of a capabilities-based versus an old threat-based process for determining new military requirements. The latter reflects the fact that the United States must contend less with who and where the adversary might be than with how the adversary will fight. But aside from these modest shifts in strategy, the QDR produced little in the way of substantive change, particularly as measured against the elements or tools for implementing military reform outlined earlier. A brief assessment of what went well and what turned out to be difficult to implement illustrates the challenges of instituting rapid, top-down reform.

As noted above, a good deal of the reformers' vision of the future American military made it into the QDR. The events of September 11 also served to underscore the need for considerably greater flexibility in configuring forces to respond quickly to a variety of diverse contingencies, not just major regional campaigns. Indeed, the capabilities implied in the Standing Joint Task Force concept reflect precisely the kind of response options required to cope with the absence of solid warning, the fleeting nature of targets, and the need for instantaneous action. But the SJTF concept begs many questions, not the least of which include how would such a task force be organized and implemented (which components of each military service, for example), and what new leap-ahead technologies are required to support the daunting needs of real-time detection and tracking of fleeting targets and the provision of a supporting command, control, communications, computer, and intelligence (C4I) support capability to orchestrate this complex military mission.

The second measure of transformation success is the selection of key senior military leaders who are willing to foster such reform. Time will tell how successful the Rumsfeld Pentagon will be in this regard, but there is already a certain irony in the selection of a new Chairman of the Joint Chiefs of Staff, Air Force General Richard Myers. The outgoing Chairman, Army General Henry Shelton, came from the Army Special Operations Forces, which arguably makes him eminently qualified to deal with the immediate challenge of rooting out terrorist cells in hostile environments. Myers, his replacement, has specialized in space warfare, an area that is favored for expansion by transformation advocates, but not one necessarily relevant to the crisis at hand. That said, Myers comes with a solid reputation, and only time will tell whether he promotes the careers of true transformation advocates.

The third transformation measure—willingness to fund leap-ahead technologies and foster sustained experimentation leading to new concepts, doctrine, and organizations—shows little if any progress.[20] This is because the 2001 QDR put off any decisions on major weapons programs or force structure changes that might have freed up significant resources to fund such new technologies. Moreover, the requirements associated with urgently implementing new homeland defense needs as well as funding required to support the war against terrorism further complicate this transformation measure. So, too, does the elevation of homeland defense as a primary responsibility of the newly reformulated Joint Forces Command. JFCOM now must balance the complicated demands of providing an experimental incubator for transformation ideas with the currently uncertain needs of fostering a new role for the military in homeland defense. Much depends not only on the level of funding for JFCOM experimentation, but equally as much on the extent to which such experimentation is grounded in operational realities, lessons learned from the past, and an emerging vision of future warfare.

The need for sufficient organizational slack to foster innovation within the military services, the Pentagon, and the industrial base will also be adversely affected by September 11's demanding events. Even under the most favorable conditions, innovation would be difficult. By their nature, bureaucracies are rarely innovative institutions. The mere fact that a new secretary of defense, supported by a well-meaning array of transformation advocates (mostly civilian acolytes), enters office with the primary goal of instituting reform within military institutions has marginal bearing on the outcome. Simply put, the military services, particularly their senior leadership, must accept the necessity of fundamental change. Absent bureaucratic acceptance within the institutions that must fight future wars, little hope exists for true military transformation. Once that acceptance settles in, innovation becomes far more acceptable to other critical institutional players, including those within the Pentagon hierarchy, the industrial base, and the U.S. Congress.

Procurement reform, the fifth measure of transformation success, will become increasingly more likely if and when the military services bureaucratically accept the transformation process. As noted earlier, under Title 10 of the U.S. Code, each military service has procurement responsibility for its major military systems. To the extent that the services remain wedded to service-centric compared with joint solutions to future warfare, obstacles to integrating modern information technology effectively into the force structure will remain in place.[21] Title 10 authority fosters a procurement bureaucracy adept at procuring major weapons platforms rather than information systems. Enormous financial resources are consumed to design, develop, and field these so-called Programs of Record,[22] many of which are now Cold War legacy systems. In most cases these legacy systems manifest hardware and software components that are multiple generations behind the commercial marketplace and whose custom military applications fail to address the real-world operational needs of today's—no less future—military requirements. There are several ways to work around Title 10's procurement limitations, however, and several of these alternative bureaucratic processes are being used today to foster innovation, or simply to meet urgent military needs.[23] The challenge facing Rumsfeld and future secretaries of defense is to broaden the workaround process to the point where its features become the standard operating process. But this is unlikely without broad bureaucratic acceptance of the underlying transformation goals.

The sixth and final measure of transformation success involves a divestiture strategy that eliminates major capital investment in military systems thought to fit poorly into America's new military strategy. The 2001 QDR demonstrated that the new Pentagon's civilian leadership found it impossible at the time to make these difficult choices. Instead, it constituted additional study panels to investigate future options for such divestiture and other critical matters.[24]

THE TRANSFORMATION BALANCE SHEET

On balance, it should come as no surprise that the new Pentagon leadership has found it difficult to institute reform in the brief period its members have been in office. If there is anything certain about the process of engendering innovation within any complex organizational setting—no less one like the American military that is so prone to caution and conventional reliability—it is that it inevitably will be messy and lengthy. Moreover, the history of military innovation suggests that such innovation is not subject to tight management control from atop the defense leadership, civilian or military.[25] Although Rumsfeld's desire to select senior leaders based on their willingness and ability to effect transformation is necessary, and perhaps his most important lever of change, it alone is not sufficient to foster long-term success.

More than anything else, changing military culture will lead to true military transformation. Much is made of the unbreakable links between so-called platform advocates, who represent key states and U.S. congressional districts with large workforces having enormous stakes in the continuation of large legacy systems. These advocates include senior military officers and layers of deeply rooted bureaucracy within the civil and military services, government research and development organizations, and the defense industrial base. All of this is true, but it doesn't really get at the source of the transformation challenge. The focus on large platforms and the maintenance of existing force structure will begin to change only when senior military leaders identify and select an increasing number of junior military officers who ultimately will comprise the basis for a reintellectualization of military thinking within the services. The roots of military strategy exist deep within the distinctive cultures of the American military services. Sadly, those cultures are dominated today by an emphasis on engineering management and administration rather than a study of new theories of warfare and new operational concepts for achieving victory.

LESSONS FOR OTHER NATIONS

Even if the goal is simple military reform rather than instituting a transformational leap in military capability, there are important lessons to be taken from the current American experience for other nations. More than anything else, the paramount lesson is that the distinctive cultures of military institutions must undergo fundamental change before truly substantive reform is likely to occur.

Military training institutions, supported by their national civilian leadership, need to invest in the underlying intellectual process that helps to formulate a vision of future warfare. Naturally, such a vision must be grounded in national goals as well as realistic operational conditions that dictate what can and cannot be achieved. These intellectual needs have profound implications for the kind and variety of military educational institutions and course work that furnish the intellectual environment for such pursuits. However important having sufficient engineering and project management skills might be, particularly in light of the growing importance of information technology, military institutions will do a disservice if they fail to provide the basis for a systematic study of the past. Studying the past is not just related to lessons learned from other national experiences with military reform and innovation. Its most important component is a systematic, indeed even ruthless appraisal of the one's own unique military experiences. As too often occurs in the American military experience, to the extent that any study of the past occurs, it is used simply the reassert the correctness of current operational, doctrinal, and technological approaches.[26] As noted earlier, it was Soviet military strategists and historians who first drew attention to the profound implications information technology would have on future warfare. Russian military analysts have continued these appraisals of foreign military experience. They and other military analysts in South Eastern European countries must turn their attention to appraising their own unique military experiences.

The nations of South Eastern Europe have woefully few resources to invest in the new technologies of modern warfare. That stark reality underscores the critical importance of linking the lessons learned from the past to a rigorous process of military experimentation that subjects newly derived operational concepts to real-world operational realities. The notion of joint combined operations is given much rhetorical attention in U.S. military experience but too little attention at the experimental level. If nations are to spend their limited resources in a reform-minded way, systematic experimentation is as important as the intellectual process that informs it.

Nations without America's resources should take heart from the fact that successful military innovation is rarely the product of money invested in military institutions. Small nations such as Sweden and Australia have achieved notable progress in systematically appraising the impact of new information technology, experimenting with new operational concepts, and implementing several incremental changes in military capabilities.[27] Yet, no matter whether enormous or very marginal financial resources are earmarked for military reform, neither civilian nor military leadership can dictate genuine innovation instantaneously. It will remain a seeming undisciplined and messy process, taking years to unravel in a frequently uncomfortable way. The only thing that is certain is that it will not occur without a vibrant intellectual process within military institutions and promotion of that process from atop by both the civilian and military leadership.

ENDNOTES

1. The author knows firsthand of these assessments of the Soviet military as he headed a research group at Pacific-Sierra Research Corporation that conducted several of them. See, for example, Notra Trulock III, *Soviet Military Thought in Transition: Implications for the Long-Term Military Competition*, Arlington, VA: Pacific-Sierra Research Corporation, May 1987. It is important to note that Marshall also sponsored a series of historical assessments of the period between World Wars I and II, when several revolutionary developments (blitzkrieg strategy, carrier aviation, amphibious warfare, strategic aerial bombardment) came to fruition. The best public treatment of these developments is Williamson Murray and Allan R. Millett (eds.), *Military Innovation in the Interwar Period*, Cambridge, UK: Cambridge University Press, 1996.

2. Despite severe limitations in military electronics, by the mid-1980s, the Soviet military had begun to experiment with rather innovative operational and organizational concepts, such as "maneuver by fire" as embodied in Operational Maneuver Groups. It seems reasonable to speculate that Marshall Nikolai Ogarkov, the strongest Soviet proponent of revolutionary change, probably ran afoul of the dominant traditionalists in the Soviet military hierarchy, who favored a much more evolutionary approach to military reform. Ogarkov was sacked as Chief of the General Staff in late 1984, though his successor, Marshall Sergei Akhromeyev, continued to challenge the military to plan not just for the last war.

3. Thomas A. Keaney and Eliot A. Cohen, *Gulf War Air Power Survey: Summary Report*, Washington: U.S. Government Printing Office, 1993, p. 243.

4. For a more detailed discussion of current limitations in U.S. conventional denial strategy, see Dennis M. Gormley and Thomas G. Mahnken, "Facing Nuclear and Conventional Reality," *Orbis* (Winter 2000): 109–25.

5. For a useful analysis of this dilemma, see Daniel Goure and Jeffrey M. Ranney, *Averting the Defense Train Wreck in the New Millennium*, Washington: The CSIS Press, 1999.

6. A point made in Paul K. Davis, "Transforming the Armed Forces: An Agenda for Change," in Stephen J. Flanagan, Ellen L. Frost, and Richard L. Kugler (eds.), *Challenges of the Global Century: Report of the Project on Globalization and National Security*, Washington: National Defense University, 2001, pp. 423–40.

7. See the author's anonymous essay, "Is There a Revolution in Military Affairs?" in *Strategic Survey 1995/96*, Oxford: The International Institute for Strategic Studies, 1996, pp. 29–40.

8. For an illustration of how this might play out in the case of land-attack cruise missiles, currently the exclusive domain of a few industrialized states, see Dennis M. Gormley, *Dealing with the Threat of Cruise Missiles, Adelphi Paper 339*, Oxford: Oxford University Press for IISS, 2001.

9. This paper deals with military solutions to WMD threats. America would also be well served to focus on improvements in the first line of defense against WMD—or nonproliferation policies. See ibid., chapter 5, for an elaboration of this point.

10. Or so argued Andrew Krepinevich, executive director of the Center for Strategic and Budgetary Assessments, who was a member of the National Defense Panel that critiqued the 1997 QDR. See Tom Canahuate, "U.S. Needs to Take Risks, Says Rumsfeld," *Defense News*, http://www.defensenews.com/pgt.php?htd = mf_story_330638.html&tty = qdr

11. See http://www.jfcom.mil/

12. See http://www.dtic.mil/jv2020/jvpub2.htm

13. Of course, the military services and their congressional supporters would argue that important benefits derive from procurement authority being in the hands of each individual service. Supporters argue that the services have long traditions and great expertise in research, development, training, and experimentation. See, for example, the discussion in Davis, op cit. For a contrasting view, see Admiral William A. Owens (with Ed Offley), *Lifting the Fog of War*, New York: Farrar, Straus and Giroux, 2000.

14. Roberta Wohlstetter, *Pearl Harbor: Warning and Response*, Stanford: Stanford University Press, 1962. Andrew Marshall, who worked at the Rand Corporation

with both Roberta and Albert Wohlstetter in the late 1950s, encouraged Wohlstetter's research that led to the Pearl Harbor book. Marshall went on to become head of Rand's Strategic Studies Division and to author a Rand Report in 1972, entitled "Long-Term Competition with the Soviets: A Framework for Strategic Analysis," that not only shaped Rand's research agenda but formed the basis of thinking about how best to compete strategically with one's adversaries.

15. General James McCarthy, U.S. Air Force, ret., Press Briefing, "Transformation Study," 12 June 2001 (mimeo).

16. *Quadrennial Defense Review Report*, Washington: U.S. Department of Defense, 30 September 2001, p. 34.

17. For an examination of these weaknesses, see Dennis M. Gormley and K. Scott McMahon, "Who's Guarding the Back Door? The Neglected Pillar of U.S. Theater Missile Defense," *International Defense Review*, vol. 29 (May 1996): 21–24.

18. See McCarthy, op cit., vugraph number 5, for a reference to the notion, "tip of the spear." This notion plays on the German creation of Panzer Divisions before World War II. Such divisions represented only a small fraction of overall German forces, which otherwise represented in many respects the legacy of World War I.

19. Based on author interviews with several transformation advocates in Washington, D.C., June 2001.

20. A notable exception is reinvigoration of a requirement for space-based radar surveillance. Canceled by Congress during the last year of the Clinton administration, the Discoverer II space-based radar program, jointly sponsored by the Defense Advanced Research Projects Agency, the Air Force, and the National Reconnaissance Office, set out to demonstrate the feasibility, utility, and effectiveness of space-based moving target detection via a series of experiments and demonstrations. This particular capability is crucial to the success of the SJTF concept for tracking and attacking fleeting targets.

21. A useful illustration is found today in the way in which each military individually rather than jointly approaches defending against land-attack cruise missiles. See Gormley, op cit., especially chapter 4.

22. "Program of record" is a bureaucratic term of art for a procurement effort that exists as a designated line item in the annual Department of Defense budget. Therefore, it is officially sanctioned and protected by senior military and civilian leadership.

23. Advanced Concept Technology Demonstrations (ACTDs), funded jointly by the Pentagon and a specific military user, are designed to inject new technologies quickly into a theater military setting (the most notable examples include the *Predator* and *Global Hawk* unmanned aerial vehicles). The U.S. Army's Warfighter Rapid

Acquisition Program and the U.S. Air Force's Warfighter Rapid Acquisition Process essentially mimic the ACTD process as the service level.

24. These include reviews of a transformation road map, intelligence, surveillance and reconnaissance operations, service unmanned aerial vehicle programs, funding levels for ongoing interoperability efforts for legacy systems, reduction of overhead costs and performance-based logistics, and modernization of the Pentagon's business practices and financial management systems.

25. For numerous examples, see Barry Watts and Williamson Murray, "Military Innovation in Peacetime," in Williamson and Millet, *Military Innovation in the Interwar Period*, pp. 369–415. It is at least conceivable that military innovation today, built around the notion of Network Centric Warfare, requires far more determined leadership from atop the civilian and military leadership than did military innovation during the interwar period. Network Centric Warfare strategies entail real-time and unprecedented collaboration among several military organizations comprising components, typically, from each military service. Because such military organizations are expected to be configured jointly, some even permanently maintained in peacetime, some analysts insist that strong top-down leadership—particularly from the Pentagon's civilian leaders—will be essential to convince the military services of the efficacy of such changes. That said, for innovation to succeed—as measured by the creation of new operational concepts and military organizations—bureaucratic acceptance within each of the military services is still fundamental to achieving true military reform. The author is grateful to Frank Hoffman, Marine Corps consultant and former staff member of the Hart-Rudman Commission, for bringing to his attention the possible distinction between the interwar years and today's reform challenges.

26. For example, the U.S. Air Force largely ignored the most profound implications of the *Gulf War Air Power Survey* conducted at the behest of the Secretary of the Air Force after the conclusion of the 1991 Gulf War. See *Gulf War Air Power Survey: Summary Report*, p. 411.

27. For a brief appraisal of the Swedish and Australian experiences, see "Military Transformation: A Report Card," in *Strategic Survey 2000/01*, Oxford: Oxford University Press for IISS, 2001, pp. 30–32.

CHAPTER SIX

Ukraine's Military Reform Efforts: Lessons Learned[1]

Anatoliy Grytsenko

INTRODUCTION

Back in 1989–91, an opinion that almost 780,000-strong military grouping stationed in Ukraine's territory would accept unhesitatingly the idea of separating from the Soviet Army and serving a young independent state seemed utopian even to many Ukrainians. In spite of that, by the end of 1991, the aforementioned Soviet military grouping had been converted peacefully, without a single shot, into the Armed Forces of Ukraine.

By and large, in 1991, Ukraine faced an extremely difficult task: first, to forge the national Armed Forces out of hypertrophied troops stationed in its territory; second, no established state institutions, no people— neither military nor civilian—capable of running the Armed Forces on their own; third, no military industry capable of producing weaponry autonomously and no nongovernment component of civilian control. In short, Ukraine had almost nothing but problems.

Notwithstanding, Ukraine started a full-scale build-up of its Armed Forces. The process of reform used to begin at individual agencies and spread "bottom-up," which corresponded to the realities of the time. On the one hand, military and political points of reference were unclear and became feasible only two or three years ago. It was impossible to set the course for reform without clear political aims. On the other hand, the fundamentals of reform were underestimated, especially the real condition of military units, assessment of their capabilities and limitations, and available resources, proceeding from the priorities of national progress. Finally, the fact that reform should be based on certain scientific principles (methods), detailed analysis, and concrete calculations, was not considered.

During Ukraine's ten years of independence, its military organization[2] has become established. Military formations are now capable of executing their basic functions. Nevertheless, they are still unable to defend Ukraine's sovereignty in the event of a serious military threat. The military organization, in its present structure and strength, will remain inefficient and costly for Ukraine, even after its country's economic revival.

This chapter analyzes the current state of Ukraine's military organization, the conditions that hampered Ukraine's military reform efforts, and proposals aimed at enhancing the effectiveness of military reform planning and implementation, which are applicable not only to Ukraine, but to other Central and Eastern European states as well. Although Ukraine's defense reform can hardly be considered a success story, Ukraine's lessons learned and experience could help other countries avoid typical mistakes.

CURRENT STATE OF UKRAINE'S MILITARY THROUGH A PRISM OF REFORM SHORTCOMINGS

Since 1991, Ukraine's military organization has gone through a complex period of evolution, from an unsystematic conglomerate of separate parts to a relatively workable integrated structure. On the other hand, the imbalance between what is desired and what is available is so evident that one cannot help but take notice. The following arguments prove that conclusion.

STRUCTURAL ISSUES

Until now, functions of military formations have not been properly defined.

Laws on military formations specify duties in different ways: those of the Civil Defense Troops, Border Troops, Internal Troops, and the Security Service are described more or less clearly, while the duties of the Armed Forces are presented too generally.[3] This hampers strategic planning, distribution of manpower and hardware, and drafting of operation plans. It is clear that a function, such as "Defense of Ukraine," allows for provision of a hundred thousand men and nine hundred thousand men with equal success; it is only a question of the military's imagination.

The military organization is structurally excessive.

Separate military formations are developing on their own, without proper national coordination. Each military formation creates its own subsystems of command and control, logistics, maintenance, military education and training, acquisition and defense research. Ukraine maintains two military fleets: the Navy (incorporated into the Armed Forces) and a naval component of the Border Troops. Both fleets operate in the same water area, and each of them has about a hundred ships and an air component. As a result, the two fleets lack funds even for fuel, let alone combat training. Each military formation maintains its own supply bases where almost identical stocks of fuel and materiel are stored. This results in extra budget expenses, excessive manpower, and suboptimal cargo movement. The structural excess of the military organization does not facilitate performance of its vital functions. Similar duties are performed by different military formations, while other duties are left to no one.

The serious disproportion in the development of military formations becomes evident.

To a certain extent, this situation may be explained. Indeed, the criminalization of society, organized crime, emergency situations, illegal migration, drug trafficking, and terrorism have become the most serious threat to Ukraine's national security. Large-scale external aggression against Ukraine seems improbable, which has influenced military priorities: the Security Service and Internal Troops are much better funded, Armed Forces and Civil Defense Troops are financed at a lower level, and Border Troops get what is left over.

The Army still operates a bulky command and control system inherited from the Soviet Army.

A total of 180,000 men are divided into thirteen divisional and five corps headquarters, whereas the U.S. Army, with its five hundred thousand members (three times bigger than the Ukrainian Army), is divided into only ten divisional and four corps headquarters.

FINANCIAL ISSUES

None of the military structures is funded according to the planned amounts.

Budget revenues are disrupted continuously. In Ukraine, this problem is especially acute, given the depth of economic crisis in 1990–2000.

The amount of red ink is comparable to the amount of allocated funds. For instance, the Armed Forces keep living on credit, and the imbalance between needs and available resources is disastrous. The yearly indebtedness of the Armed Forces reaches 90 percent of the Ministry of Defense (MoD) budget. And this is only the documented debt; the so-called accumulated debt is ten to fifteen times larger.[4] For several years, there has been a steady tendency to reduce the defense budget (see Figure 1). As a result, Ukraine allocates close to US$1,550 a year to maintain one serviceman, while Russia spends US$3,750 for this purpose; Turkey, US$12,700; Hungary, US$14,750; and Poland, US$18,350. And if we look at the developed Western countries, in France and Germany, this figure exceeds US$90,000; in Great Britain, US$170,000; and in the United States, US$190,000. Therefore, in contrast to Ukraine, those countries' governments managed to find a balance between defense needs and government support.

According to expert estimates, maintaining Ukraine's Armed Forces in their present strength (and in the strength approved for 2005) under North Atlantic Treaty Organization (NATO) standards

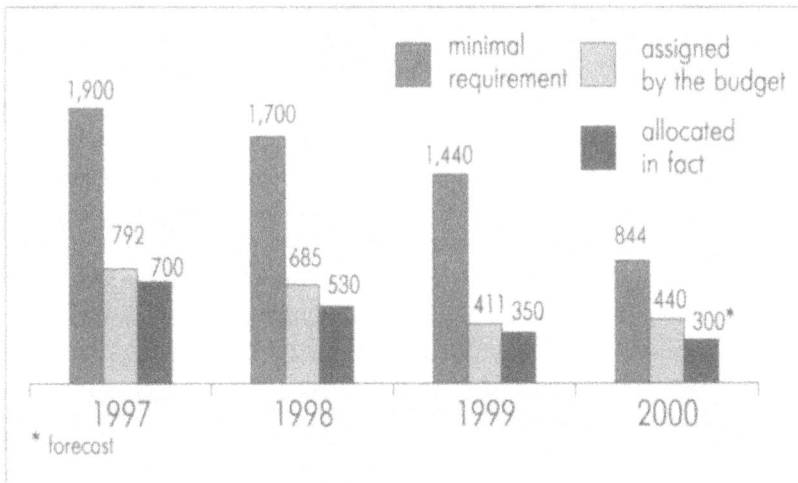

Figure 1
Funding of Ukraine's Armed Forces, US$ mln.

Source: Grytsenko et al., *National Security & Defense*, 2000, No. 11.

will cost US$5.5 billion to US$7.5 billion a year, comparable to Ukraine's total state budget. This means that cosmetic changes will not help; military reform must bring radical solutions in terms of both funding and reduction of manpower.

READINESS ISSUES

Combat readiness of military structures remains low.

The number of unready and partly ready units is not decreasing because of the poor condition of equipment and inadequacy of material resources. There are other reasons, too: commanders' efforts (and limited resources) often are channeled to arrange demonstrations, especially those conducted under international cooperation plans, rather than to ensure better combat training. Combat training is becoming more and more relative, exercises are held on maps and in classrooms, firing practice is conducted primarily from static positions. Ukraine operates more than eight hundred airplanes, but can hardly select a squadron able to perform combat missions at night, in bad weather conditions, at the level of NATO standards.

The condition of weapon systems is unsatisfactory.

Around 1997–98, Ukraine reached a critical point, where its weapons and equipment became inoperable. This happened in 1997–98. Today, 70 percent of weapon types require capital repair, and 40 percent to 50 percent of all equipment is obsolete. If weapon systems are not re-equipped at a rate of 4 percent to 5 percent a year, all talk of effective Armed Forces should be dropped. Given the present strength of military units, reequipment would mean purchasing forty-five aircraft, ten ships, hundreds of tanks and IFVs, and several thousand trucks a year. To maintain the fighting power of the Armed Forces in their present composition, at least US$2 billion to US$3 billion should be spent to purchase and maintain weapons and equipment annually.

Professionalization of the Armed Forces happens slowly and does not lead to an increase in combat effectiveness.

About thirty thousand men serve in the Armed Forces on a contract basis, and other military formations employ another eleven thousand such servicemen. Replacement of conscripts is not an easy task: Only

10 percent of contract soldiers occupy positions vital for combat effectiveness, such as squad leaders and tank and IFV crew commanders. Another 90 percent prefer to serve in more comfortable administrative and logistic positions.

PERSONNEL ISSUES

The military organization is overmanned.

Exact data on the total numerical strength of military formations is inaccessible. The fact that the White Book, *Ukraine's Defense Policy*, has not been published for more than four years seems symbolic: The President's instructions on its annual publication (beginning from 1997) were not carried out in 1997, nor in 1998–2001. The estimated manpower of the main military formations of Ukraine is presented in figures 2 and 3.

In general, according to expert estimates, one in fifty Ukrainian citizens is serving (is employed) in power structures, and most of them

**Figure 2
Dynamics of Personnel Reduction
in Ukraine's Armed Forces,**
thousand servicemen

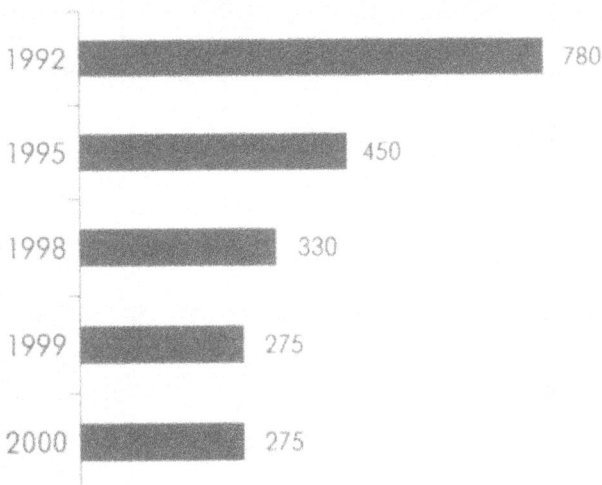

Year	Thousand servicemen
1992	780
1995	450
1998	330
1999	275
2000	275

Figure 3
Manpower of Ukraine's Military Structures

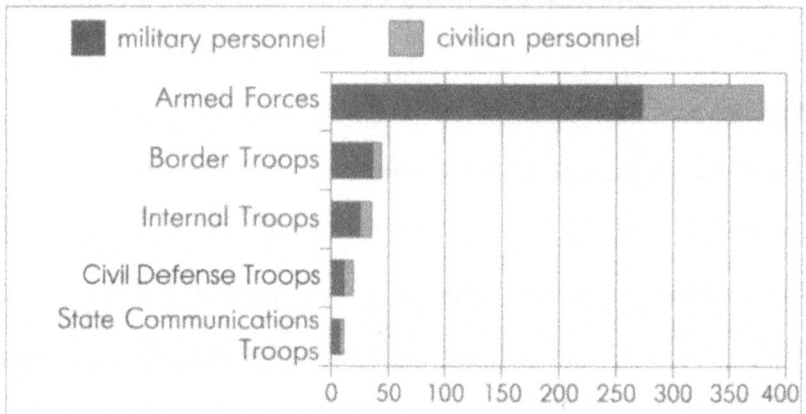

Source: Grytsenko et al., *National Security & Defense*, 2000, No. 1.

wear military uniform and bear arms. That is too many, and the situation should be corrected.

Ukraine's Armed Forces long ago turned into an army of workers and peasants.

The prestige of the active duty remains low, and the quality of recruits is deteriorating. Close to eighteen thousand men are evading military conscription, despite the fact that some 90 percent of conscripts are either released from duty or enjoy postponement rights. Out of fourteen professions mentioned in the questionnaire, respondents ranked the military tenth (see Figure 4). The military profession has surpassed only those specialities that do not require high qualification or education.

The low morale (see Figure 5) and poor psychological condition of servicemen may be explained by the impoverishment of their families and the absence of any chance to get an apartment in the next fifteen to twenty years. Monetary allowances do not allow officers to support their families, and they are forced to look for extra work. More than 80 percent of officers describe their families' living conditions as "below average" and "low." Cantonments and outstations house "a great many educated, qualified citizens—former servicemen and their dependents, and 60 percent of them are unemployed."[5]

Figure 4
Prestige of Different Professions among
Ukraine's Populace,
% of those polled

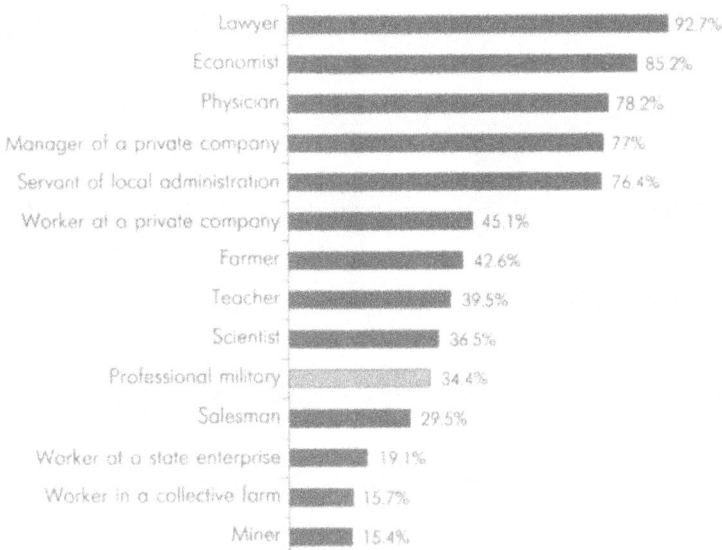

Profession	%
Lawyer	92.7%
Economist	85.2%
Physician	78.2%
Manager of a private company	77%
Servant of local administration	76.4%
Worker at a private company	45.1%
Farmer	42.6%
Teacher	39.5%
Scientist	36.5%
Professional military	34.4%
Salesman	29.5%
Worker at a state enterprise	19.1%
Worker in a collective farm	15.7%
Miner	15.4%

Source: Grytsenko et al., *National Security & Defense*, 2000, No. 11.

There is substantial disproportion in manning of power military formations.

The sharp reduction of manpower, ill-advised structural changes, and ungrounded introduction of higher ranks for most regular positions—all this leads to a serious imbalance. The proportion of officers in the Armed Forces of Ukraine (28 percent) is almost three times higher than the optimum figure (10 percent to 12 percent) for armies manned on the basis of conscription. The number of soldiers and sergeants in the Armed Forces is equal to the number of generals, officers, and warrant officers. There is one officer or warrant officer for every Ukrainian soldier (cadet) (see Figure 6). Such an army is inefficient, excessively consuming, and poorly controlled.

Another problem is a disproportion in the officers' corps: the number of junior officers (lieutenants through captains) should be much higher than that of senior officers (majors through colonels). In Ukraine, this pyramid is upside down: there are plenty of officers in

**Figure 5
The Assessment of Morale and Discipline in the Armed
Forces and Other Military Formations by the Populace
% of those polled**

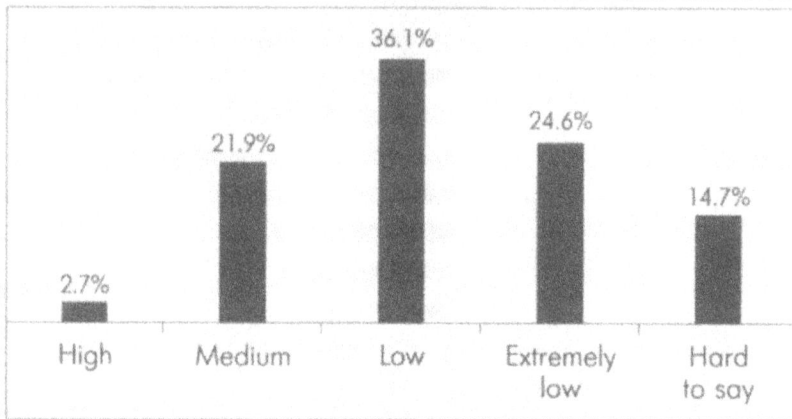

36.1%

24.6%

21.9%

14.7%

2.7%

High   Medium   Low   Extremely   Hard
                             low   to say

Source: Grytsenko et al., *National Security & Defense*, 2000, No. 11.

**Figure 6
Distriubition of Servicemen
in Ukraine's Armed Forces,
by categories**

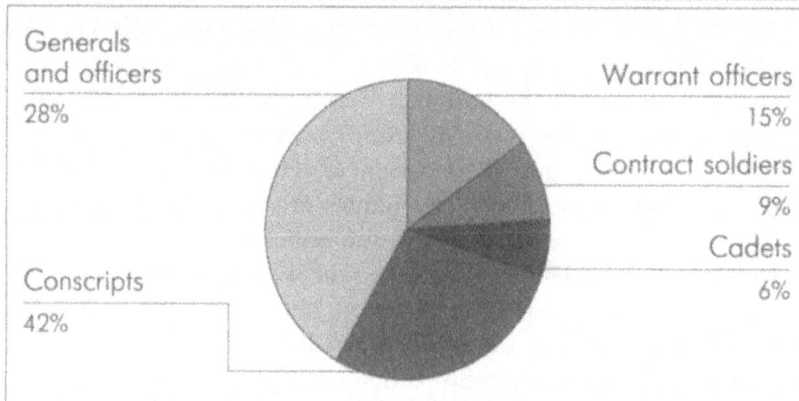

Generals
and officers

28%

Warrant officers

15%

Contract soldiers

9%

Cadets

6%

Conscripts

42%

Figure 7
Assessment of the Level of Social Security
of Servicemen by the Populace,
% of those polled

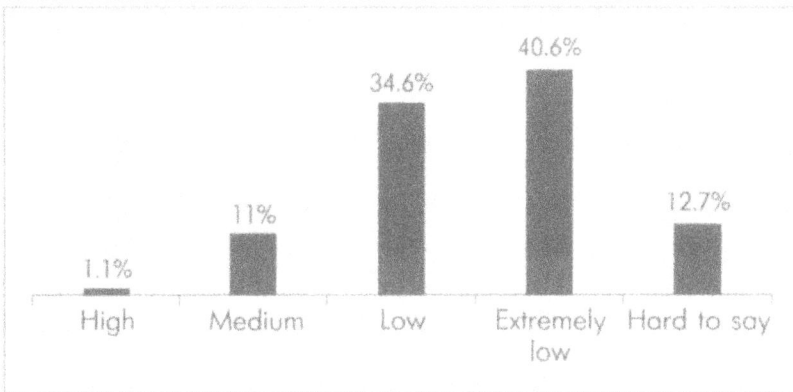

Source: Grytsenko et al., *National Security & Defense*, 2000, No. 1.

Ukraine (compared to soldiers and sergeants), but not enough (there is a 30 percent shortage of lieutenants in all military formations).

The system of officer training is ineffective.

The military education system employs about 10 percent of the total Armed Forces' manpower. Even educational institutions' minimum requirements account for 20 percent to 25 percent of the defense budget. A unified system of military training for all military formations has not been created; it exists on paper only.

The Armed Forces elite (Officers Corps) produces a generally negative assessment of the military service.

Officers account for 28 percent of the servicemen, but their role in reforming the Army is decisive. Sociological studies show that approximately 57 percent of officers and warrant officers describe their condition as close to apathy or depression, which is attributed to poor material status (39 percent), the situation in the Armed Forces (38 percent), and public attitude toward the Armed Forces (36 percent). Despite all of these difficulties, officers still hope for positive change and are willing to contribute to the reform of the Armed Forces. The proportion of

Figure 8
The Assessment of the Level of Servicemen
Training by the Populace,
% of those polled

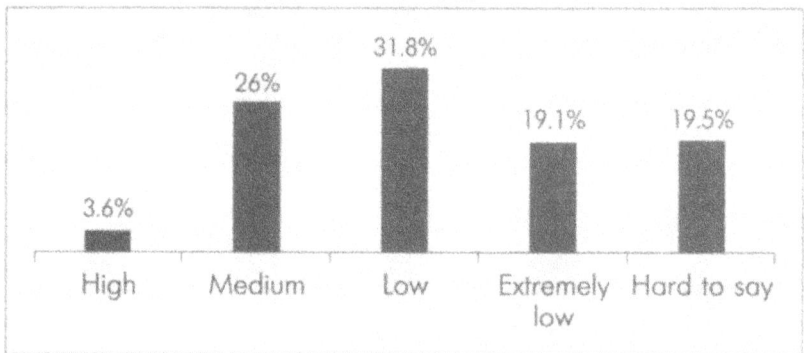

Source: Grytsenko et al., *National Security & Defense,* 2000, No. 11.

officers with no aspirations, but who intend to continue serving in the Armed Forces (so-called ballast), fortunately, is only 4.4 percent.

PUBLIC OPINION

The decline of the prestige of military service.

There are evident signs of alienation (the gap between the interests and the perception of social values) by the military and society. The Ukrainian Center for Economic and Political Studies (UCEPS) socio-logical surveys demonstrate a relatively high level of confidence of Ukraine's population in the Army (see Figure 9). However, this fact should not placate anyone. First, this level of confidence is indeed *relative*, that is, comparatively higher than the still lower indicators of public trust in other state and social institutions. If we look at the absolute figure (close to 30 percent), this indicator is neither high, nor sufficient for maintaining stable solidary relations between the Army and society. Second, over the last five years, the level of public trust in the Armed Forces has been falling slowly but methodically. According to Socis-Gallup, in 1996, the Army enjoyed complete trust of 40 percent of citizens; in 1997, this figure was 35 percent, and since the end of 1998, it has been fluctuating between 31 percent to 27 percent. At the same time, the proportion of people who "do not trust in the

Figure 9
The Level of Ukrainian citizenry Confidence
in Separate State Institutes,
% of those polled

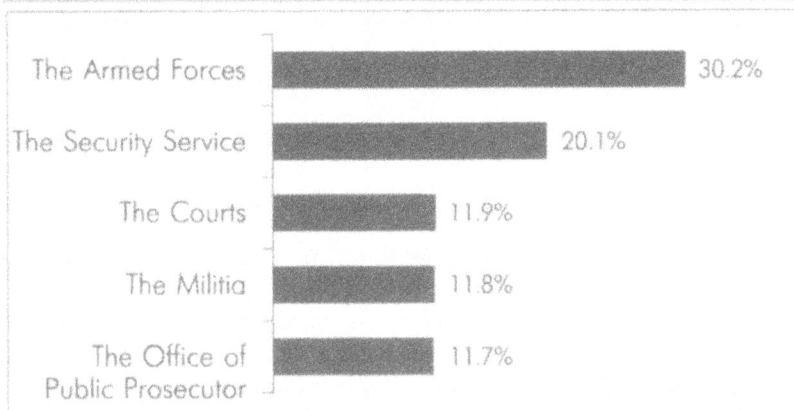

Institute	%
The Armed Forces	30.2%
The Security Service	20.1%
The Courts	11.9%
The Militia	11.8%
The Office of Public Prosecutor	11.7%

Source: Sociological Service of Razumkov Center.

Armed Forces at all" rose from 19 percent in 1996 to 27 percent by the end of 1998.

When polled, professional servicemen reveal negative assessments of the civilian population's attitude toward the military. The overwhelming majority (61 percent) of respondents believe the populace treats servicemen "indifferently," 15 percent are sure the populace "disrespects" servicemen, and 12 percent have found themselves in a situation where "their dignity was humbled." Only 8 percent of polled officers testified that the population treats them "with respect."

It is easy to see, therefore, why military service in Ukraine has lost much of its prestige. The level of public trust in the military, though relatively high, is decreasing gradually. In such a situation, it is hard to consider the effectiveness of civilian control of the military sector in Ukraine.

Public awareness of military reform efforts.

Poll results show that not only do experts know the outcome of military reform, ordinary Ukrainian citizens do as well. Only 4.4 percent of the citizens polled believe the changes in the Army present a "preplanned process of reforming" (see Figure 10); by contrast, two-thirds

**Figure 10
The Assessment of Changes Taking Place in
the Armed Forces by the Populace,
% of those polled**

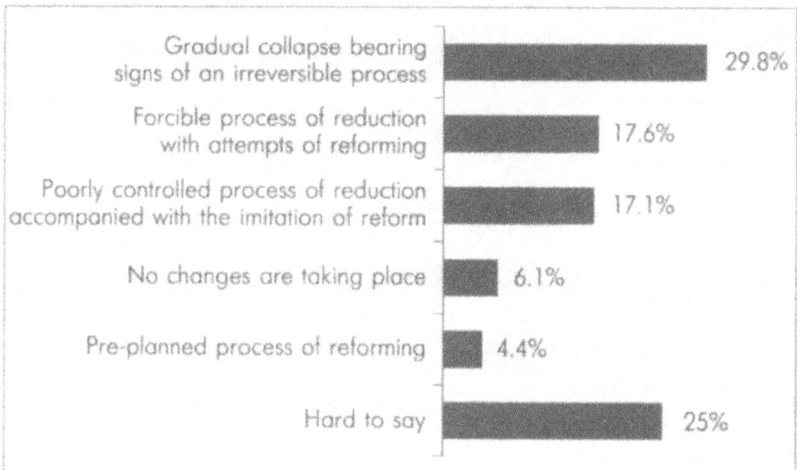

Assessment	Percentage
Gradual collapse bearing signs of an irreversible process	29.8%
Forcible process of reduction with attempts of reforming	17.6%
Poorly controlled process of reduction accompanied with the imitation of reform	17.1%
No changes are taking place	6.1%
Pre-planned process of reforming	4.4%
Hard to say	25%

Source: Grytsenko et al., *National Security & Defense*, 2000, No. 11.

of those polled tend to give negative assessments: 29.8 percent of citizens called the changes a "gradual collapse, which bears signs of an irreversible process"; roughly the same number of respondents said this was a "forcible process of reduction with attempts at reforming" (17.6 percent) and a "poorly controlled process of reduction accompanied with the imitation of reform" (17.1 percent).

All of these factors show that, despite rather persistent reform efforts, Ukraine's military organization is still in crisis, and, in its present condition, it is too expensive for the Ukrainian economy. Even in twenty or thirty years Ukraine won't be able to ensure an adequate level of combat readiness and equipment of such a large Army. Resolute and dynamic military reforms are needed, not cosmetic measures, which is why this essay focuses on the military sector's shortcomings and weaknesses, rather than on its successes.

Ukraine should define priorities to keep a balance between desired goals and available possibilities. The military organization should not be too strong, which would frighten its neighbors, exhaust the economy, and hamper social development. However, it should not be so weak as to provoke military conflicts. The Armed Forces should support the political, economic, and diplomatic mechanisms of Ukraine's national policy.

To a great extent, the overall success of reform will depend on a sound analysis of experience to determine the direction of reform and avoid repeating mistakes.

CONDITIONS HAMPERING MILITARY REFORM IN UKRAINE

Two conditions hamper achievement of the Ukrainian military's desired result: The first group has constrained military reform as far back as its development (concept) and drafting phase. The second includes factors that affected implementation of military reform.

PROBLEMS AT THE MILITARY REFORM PLANNING STAGE: POLITICAL AND LEGISLATIVE LIMITATIONS

No mechanisms existed for strategic planning, formulating the defense budget, and protecting national interests by military means. When Ukraine gained independence, it had no National Security and Defense Council, no Ministry of Defense, no General Staff, and no Armed Forces, or the systems that accompanied them. Nor did Ukraine have a scientific and analytical infrastructure to support strategic planning. Capabilities of the Ministry of Foreign Affairs, Ministry of Interior and the Security Service were limited, given their republican subordination (within the former Soviet Union) and the routine practice of sending the best specialists to Moscow.

National priorities were shifting as time passed.

Priorities shifted from controlling military formations and establishing formal signs of national sovereignty in 1991–92 to the nation's economic survival in the years that followed. If, in the first two years of independence, the military sector was among the main priorities, later, in the absence of a direct military threat, other sectors, such as political, economic, social, and energy, were the primary focus of the authorities and public. Polls showed that from mid-1994, personal welfare (76 percent), food prices (39 percent), and unemployment (22 percent) were the most pressing issues. Citizens no longer were concerned about the defense potential of the state: it occupied last, or second-to-last place, and was considered important only by 1 percent of respondents.

Foreign assistance was very limited.

Unlike other postcommunist countries, such as Poland, the Czech Republic, Hungary, Slovenia, Romania, Bulgaria, and the Baltic states, which began to reform their armies with active NATO assistance, Ukraine did not receive such assistance. For evident reasons, Russia was trying to hamper military construction in Ukraine. In 1991–92, the United States, Great Britain, and other NATO members viewed Ukraine, with its million-strong army and mighty nuclear potential, with caution. Ukraine's partners would go no further than to issue general declarations of support for its independence and demand immediate nuclear disarmament. And Ukraine was not ready to define its priorities, either.

There was lack of national legislative experience in Ukraine.

Acts adopted in the first years of independence were declarative, politicized, and sometimes naive. Elements of the military organization were not defined, even in principle, and the functions of the military formations forming it were not specified. The Military Doctrine, adopted in 1993, two years after Ukraine gained independence, reflected the euphoria and inexperience of that time. Instead of concrete, basic data, the Military Doctrine only contained general (acceptable for any state) tasks and a long list of good intentions and priorities unsupported by resources. What is the use of such provisions in that still valid document: "Priority should be given to precision guided weapons of increased power, intelligence, airspace defense, electronic warfare, missile forces, air force and air mobile units, advanced types of surface ships and submarines"? According to UCEPS experts, support for only those "priorities" would require US$80 billion to US$200 billion in budget funds.

The country's top leadership did not manage to initiate systematic reforms of Ukraine's military organization.

For years, the branches of government struggled for power and focused on the constitutional process. The military was not among the main priorities in this struggle for power; all activity was concentrated on subordinating military formations, rather than trying to reform the institution. Continuous distrust, and sometimes outright hostility, between legislative and executive authorities presented another political factor hampering reform. The possibility of Parliament blocking all attempts at military reform made the government search for roundabout ways of reforming that sector. As a result, the *Verkhovna Rada* actually was excluded from the reform process. The State Program of Armed Forces Construction and Development was adopted by Presidential Decree, but those who had engineered such a device (though legal) did not account for important legal and political consequences. The Program (as a file of papers) was formally approved, but the process meant nothing. Legal and material support was needed to implement it, but these were unavailable. The structure, manpower ceiling, and functions of the Armed Forces (the parameters of military reform) had to be approved exclusively by the *Verkhovna Rada*. Similarly, only Parliament is authorized to take final decisions about budget funding. The reforms skidded to a halt.

The programs of reforms were developed without concrete basic data, such as military-political, economic, and other targets and limitations.

The Constitution had not been adopted yet, and there was no concept of the national security of Ukraine. There was (and still is) no strategy for the military security of the state. Under such circumstances, the State Program of Armed Forces Construction and Development was deemed a failure, and the fate of the State Program for the Development of Weapons and Military Equipment, under development for so long and now being prepared for adoption, is in question.

The system of civilian control over the military has not been finalized.

State power bodies, public organizations, nongovernmental analytical centers, and mass media, all of which rank higher in importance than the military, exist in Ukraine, although their influence should be stronger. At the same time, another important element of the system, providing control from inside the Army, should be established. By this we mean hiring civil servants in responsible posts. Real changes may be expected only when (a) civilian administrators are well informed of the real situation in the Armed Forces; (b) they have mechanisms to influence the internal operation of military formations; (c) civilians' responsibility for development of power structures and their competence in military issues is established.

ORGANIZATIONAL LIMITATIONS

Nobody bore personal responsibility for reforming the military sector.

Each military formation was developing concepts and programs for itself; government involvement in the process was minimal. For instance, when the Interdepartmental Committee for Military Reform was finally established in 1996, it was headed not by the Prime Minister or by the Secretary of the National Security and Defense Council of Ukraine (as the essence of reform demanded, if reform really was to be interdepartmental), but by the newly appointed Defense Minister. No one else was willing (and ready) to assume responsibility for solving complex military problems.

Immaturity of the Armed Forces and the Defense Ministry as state institutions, in comparison with other armed structures.

In every country, the war office holds a leading place in the hierarchy of power of ministries. Things are somewhat different in Ukraine. The Ministry of Interior and the Security Service existed under different names and grew along with other structures. Naturally, over the years, their authority grew, and they have become part of the state mechanism. The MoD, however, did not exist at the level of republic: during the Soviet period, Ukraine, by law, did not have its own Armed Forces. They have been in existence only since 1992, and now they are experiencing great difficulties. The young Defense Ministry fights for its fair "share of the pie" in a rather competitive environment, being surrounded by other, more powerful, military structures. At present, all of these military structures lack the necessary resources, even to function at a minimal "survival" level. In addition, the Defense Ministry has been allocated budgetary funding whatsoever for development. Under these circumstances, it does not make sense to reform just the Armed Forces without redistributing functions and optimizing the military organization of the entire state.

Reforming the military organization lacked coordination at the national level.

The body entrusted with interdepartmental coordination—the National Security Council of Ukraine (renamed the National Security and Defense Council [NSDC] in 1996)—gained influence only in 1994. The General Military Inspection attached to the President of Ukraine became fully operational at the end of 1996.

There were some attempts to work out reform program in the narrow circle of experts within the framework of military formations.

The State Program of Armed Forces Construction and Development was drafted with the limited involvement of experts from other government agencies immediately related to national Defense. Most of the tasks relating to program development were entrusted to the Main Operational Directorate of the General Staff. This Directorate employed many qualified experts in strategic planning for the *application* of forces. Unfortunately, they had no experience with strategic planning for armed forces *development*. Furthermore, the Directorate continued to exercise its vast routine duties. As a result, the team did not (and was objectively unable to) work out a comprehensively supported program. The development of the State Program did not involve people's deputies of Ukraine and representatives of nongovernmental (public) organizations. For this reason, many constructive proposals and important ideas for improving the program were omitted. Moreover, at the implementation stage, the MoD failed to obtain proper and timely legislative support, so the people's deputies viewed the prepared documents with natural caution.

The legislation did not specify state programs' requirements, how to form them, and their coordination, adoption and funding mechanisms.[6]

The only regulatory document partly governing those issues was "Regulations of the State Scientific and Technical Programs."[7] However, these regulations are outdated. Due to the absence of defined requirements for the content and procedure of state programs, in most cases, administrators set unrealistic deadlines for their development, which has resulted in insufficient quality, poor substantiation, and further revision of projects. The State Program of Armed Forces Construction and Development was prepared in 1995–96, at which time unrealistic terms were set and then postponed several times.

Favorable conditions were not created for large-scale and responsible work relating to the development of state programs.

Normally, developers are not released from their principal duties, even when they are ineffectual. The effectiveness of their work often is limited by unsolved infrastructure problems (poor transportation facilities, communication, office machinery, information support, leisure conditions, etc.) that may seem minor, but determine results.

The experience of military reform in advanced countries was not taken into account.

Democratic countries have worked out effective mechanisms that could be useful models for Ukraine. Military reforms are engineered and implemented under the direct supervision of government's civilian leaders. Reforms are developed by small groups of skillful intellectuals, assisted by numerous support teams and leading research centers. The government regularly publishes the White Book on defense to ensure the public's (the taxpayers) support for reform. Regular open parliamentary hearings on military issues make legislators aware of the urgent problems of the army and encourage their help in solving those problems. Cyclic planning of budget expenditures on Defense (for example, on a five-year basis) also promotes the stability of military programs. This experience deserves the attention of Ukrainian reformers.

PROBLEMS AT THE STAGE OF MILITARY REFORM
IMPLEMENTATION

Despite all of its deficiencies, the State Program of Armed Forces Construction and Development became an important stage in Ukrainian nation building. If, compared to the Ministry of Defense, other ministries (including "civilian" ones) have far more modest results in strategic planning for their areas of responsibility, it must be acknowledged that the military produced the best results it was able to at that time. Unfortunately, this result proved to be insufficient to ensure successful reform. Cited below are the main factors that hampered military reform from implementing the approved programs.

Financial resources allocated from the state budget were insufficient even to sustain the Armed Forces, let alone reform them.

Indeed, this situation was expected and should have been taken into account at the program development stage (if resource limitations are not taken into account, a document cannot be termed a program). However, this was not done, and six months after the program was adopted, talk of its shifting terms began. The figures cited in Table 1 show that, in 1997–99 (the first stage of reform), the government substantially curtailed funding of the military sector. This complicated the situation further, and the MoD could only afford actions requiring few or no funds.

Table 1
Funding of Ukraine's Armed Forces

	1992	1993	1994	1995	1996	1997	1998	1999	2000
Defense budget, % of GDP	2.4%	1.6%	1.5%	1.8%	1.9%	1.3%	1.3%	1.4%	1.3%

Sources: Grytsenko et al., *National Security & Defense,* 2000, No. 1, 11; Razumkov Centre estimates.

The structure of the Defense budget did not correspond to reform requirements.
Analysis shows that funding reform was in no way accounted for in the budget: One can scarcely expect reforms when the government plans to spend more than 80 percent of the available funds just to sustain the Armed Forces. For instance, manpower reduction is an important element of military reform. According to MoD estimates, reducing the size of the Army costs 1.5 to two times more than sustaining the same number of personnel. Overall expenditures decrease only with time. However, no additional funds were allocated to reduce manpower; such expenditures were not even planned.

A comparative analysis of the structure of the defense budgets of Ukraine and of NATO countries (figures 11 and 12) demonstrates some trends as well.

First, Ukraine spends unjustifiably few funds (only 4 percent) on equipment acquisition. NATO countries allocate a four to five times larger share of their defense budgets for this purpose. Second, development of new weapon systems in Ukraine is underfunded: NATO countries spend some 10 percent of their defense budgets on research and development (R&D), on the average; Ukraine spends only 3 percent. Finally, Figure 13 shows that the Armed Forces of Ukraine are spending the military budget primarily on food: Personnel expenditures account for 70 percent of allocated funds. A serious approach to reform requires changing those proportions, irrespective of the budget value. What matters when defining reform priorities is not the expenses themselves, but their proportions.

At present levels of funding, Ukraine's Armed Forces will continue

**Figure 11
Typical Structure of NATO
Countries' Defense Budget**

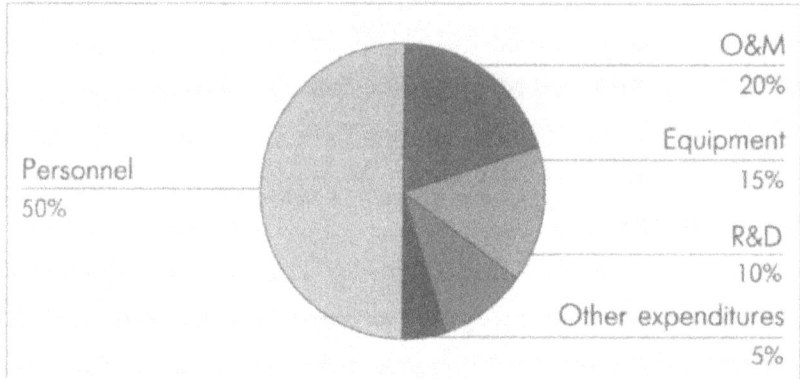

Personnel
50%

O&M
20%

Equipment
15%

R&D
10%

Other expenditures
5%

**Figure 12
Structure of Ukraine's Defense Budget**

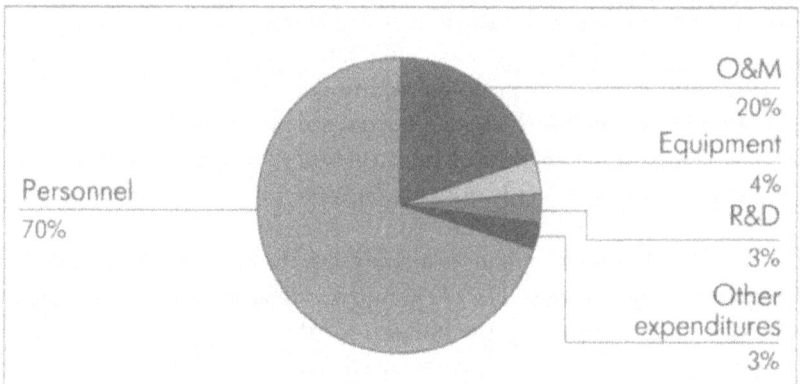

Personnel
70%

O&M
20%

Equipment
4%

R&D
3%

Other
expenditures
3%

Source: Grytsenko et al., *National Security & Defense*, 2000, No. 1.

to deteriorate. How can one hope for any improvement if a Ukrainian citizen can afford to spend only few dollars on defense per year? One should keep this in mind when considering possible "peace dividends" of Armed Forces' reduction (see Figure 13).

An absence of funds alone is sufficient evidence for the necessity of reform: "Opponents to military reform argue that there are no funds for reforming effectively. However, the lack of funds proves the need

Figure 13
1999 Defense Expenses Per Capita

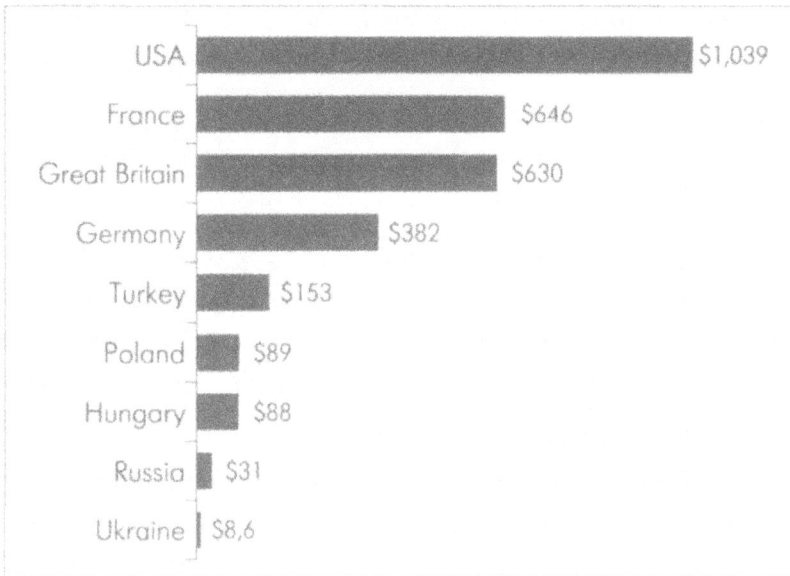

USA	$1,039
France	$646
Great Britain	$630
Germany	$382
Turkey	$153
Poland	$89
Hungary	$88
Russia	$31
Ukraine	$8,6

Source: Grytsenko et al., *National Security & Defense*, 2000, No. 1.

to reform the expensive 'machinery' of the Armed Forces. When funds are sufficient, there is no need for reform."[8]

Frequent replacement of the military heads had an adverse effect on reform.

It is worth noting that almost half of all officers (49 percent) see the lack of stability in the Armed Forces' command as a "factor hampering the process of reform." Over the eight years of Ukrainian independence, there have been four ministers of Defense, five chiefs of the General Staff, four ministers of internal affairs, five heads of the Security Service, and three heads of the State Border Security Committee. Such staff turnover did not encourage mastering official duties and long-term planning and made administrative continuity impossible.

Information support for and propaganda about reform were insufficient.

The State Program of Armed Forces Construction and Development was developed as a confidential document, and, after adoption, it was stamped "classified."[9] The experience of other countries proves the importance of information and propaganda support for reform. Unfortunately, limited information about reform plans and achievements, and the absence of broad public debate, led to a lack of interest in military reform among Ukrainians (see Figure 14). At the same time, reform of state structures cannot be successful without public support, because reforms require significant taxpayer funds. When the public is aware of the purpose and direction of reforms, and confident of their usefulness, even so-called unpopular steps may enjoy public support.

Ukraine did not consider the useful experience of modern armies.

A characteristic example is the formation of three operational commands in the Armed Forces. Indeed, international experience proves the credibility of regional operational commands. A similar command structure is used in the United States and NATO. Such a system has withstood the test of time and proved effective. The effectiveness of regional operational commands is, to a large extent, conditioned by their *joint* nature: they incorporate all services (land, air, and naval forces) necessary for conducting operations in the area of responsibil-

Figure 14
The Level of the Populace's Awareness
of the Situation in Ukraine's Armed Forces
and Other Military Formations,
% of those polled

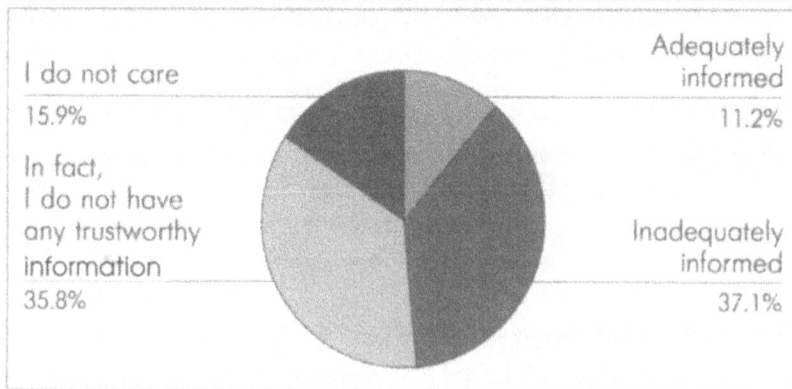

I do not care
15.9%

Adequately informed
11.2%

In fact, I do not have any trustworthy information
35.8%

Inadequately informed
37.1%

Source: Grytsenko et al., *National Security & Defense,* 2000, No. 11.

ity. At first, Ukraine seemed to be going the same way, but later it returned to its former system. As a result, operational commands in Ukraine never became joint. Moreover, they were subordinated, not to the General Staff (or the Minister of Defense, as in the United States), but to the Army command. This makes no sense: there will be no separate army operations in modern warfare. The worst thing to happen is the loss of control over forces for a more or less lengthy period when hostilities start. The Armed Forces command will have to introduce a new system of command and control, and it will be done not in a calm, measured manner, but under conditions of war. More attention should be paid to the experience of advanced countries, and improper decisions should be corrected promptly.

All in all, there is no reason to expect any serious military reform in Ukraine, unless the nation recovers its economy and accumulates a "critical mass" of people with the vision, courage, political will, and support needed to make tough choices in the defense sphere. Otherwise, the government can only keep the Army at its minimal "survival" level, slightly reducing the number of personnel every year. Resolute actions of civilian authorities need to be aimed at further reductions of manpower in the military, provision of desperately needed funds, strict priority setting, and enhancement of civilian control over the military.

How to Avoid Mistakes in the Course of Military Reform

Well-thought-out and sustainable military reform effort should be based on certain methodological principles. UCEPS experts have developed such a methodology for forming state construction and development programs for Ukraine's military organization, which includes the following: (a) analysis of the national experience of the establishment and reformation of power structures in 1991–2000; (b) analysis of the experience of strategic and defense planning in more than twenty countries; and (c) familiarization with Ukrainian and foreign studies in the field of systems analysis and goal-oriented planning acceptable for the implementation in Ukraine. The main two elements of this methodology are the principles and algorithm of military reform planning and implementation presented below.

PRINCIPLES OF MILITARY REFORM

Proceeding from Ukraine's own lessons learned and world experience in the sphere, military reform in Ukraine should be based on the following principles:

- *Use nonforcible means for conflict resolution.* Hostilities are easy to start but difficult to end. Most problems cannot be solved by military means at all. Priorities may include strengthening the political, diplomatic, and economic components of state policy; military strength presents the last argument. The functions of the power structures should not be excessively great.

- *Strengthen democratic civilian control over the military sector,* an important precondition for effective use of budget funds, protection of human rights within military formations, and, generally, steady social progress. The military needs a mechanism for presenting its problems to government officials and legislators, while it continues to concentrate on purely military issues. The present situation, military commanders spending 70 percent to 90 percent of their time solving supply and funding problems, is abnormal; their main duty is combat training.

- *Reject gigantomania and stereotypes of the past,* and adopt realistic assessments of military threats, available resources, effectiveness of international confidence-building measures, reliability of partner states, and the country's real influence on European processes.

- *Economic acceptability* of the military organization, which should not turn into an insurmountable obstacle to the country's economic development.

- *Give priority to developing capabilities designed to identify threats and contain conflicts early on.* Given the limited combat readiness of troops and their low mobilization capabilities, development priorities for Ukraine's Armed Forces should include an increase in the potential of military intelligence and development of rapid-deployment forces capable of inflicting unacceptable losses on the enemy, thereby containing any escalation of aggression. A full-fledged air mobile brigade, capable of fighting in border areas within forty-eight hours (or attacking targets on enemy territory, if necessary), would be more useful than a "dwarf" Army corps short of resources.

- *Avoid structural excessiveness.* Liquidation of duplicate structures makes it possible to reduce budget expenses and increase the effectiveness of the command and control system.

- *Make full use of manpower and equipment.* Most military structures should be entrusted with several functions, which helps to save budget funds.[10]
- *Ensure adequate manpower and equipment for the execution of functions.* Military formations should not be reduced below the level where they would be unable to perform assigned functions, even when accounting for a multiplicity of functions.
- *Preserve effective military units and avoid any decrease in troops' combat effectiveness in the course of reform.* First, there should be as little reorganization as possible, and, second, reorganization should be so planned in such a way that, at each stage of reform, the combat effectiveness of military formations rises (or, at least, does not fall).
- *Channel any assets released as a result of the reduction of ineffective units toward the completion of priority tasks.* For instance, decommissioning and sale (even for scrap) of costly and obsolete Navy ships makes it possible to strengthen coastal missile units and the marines.
- *Coordinate results at each stage of reform.* Unless reform programs are coordinated properly (balanced), the desired results will not be achieved. What is the use of acquiring (leasing) new helicopters for an air mobile brigade if there are no trained pilots, technicians, or ground equipment to support their sorties?
- *Make the build-up of mobilization potential an important precondition for reducing the regular armed forces' manpower.* Without effective reserves, one can scarcely hope for victory in a prolonged military conflict.
- *Make more effective use of the Armed Forces' potential in peacetime.* Generations invested billions in the construction of Ukraine's Army; it would make little sense to use its potential in wartime only. The unique capabilities of the Armed Forces would help Ukraine's government solve many problems in peacetime. For this purpose, the internal functions of the Army should be fixed legislatively.
- *Implement world experience applicable to Ukraine.* Only a few aspects of the development of Ukraine's Armed Forces are unique, and require unique approaches; applying foreign experience would save time and money.
- *Gradually provide interoperability with the armed forces of partner countries*, which would be necessary for conducting joint peacekeeping, search and rescue, humanitarian, and other military operations.
- *Review alternative options.* Only in some exceptional cases is a solu-

tion evident and requires no additional substantiation. Meanwhile, reform planning generally requires brainstorming more or less equal alternatives and comparing them according to established criteria to reach a consensus-derived solution.

Obviously, most of these principles of military reform planning and implementation are applicable not only to Ukraine, but to other Central and Eastern European states facing similar problems.

Annex

Algorithm of Military Reform

The second element of the methodology is the generalized algorithm[11] of military reform in Ukraine, presented below. The main conclusions drawn on the basis of an analysis of this algorithm are as follows.

1. The reason for military reform (the starting point of the algorithm) may be explained by one of the following factors (see Figure 15): a change in the strategic goals of nation building and the political priorities of the country's leadership; severe resource limitations; the emergence (forecast) of new military threats; development of new types of weapons and methods of combat operations; a change in the balance of forces in the region (military blocs, allies, etc.); an inability to accomplish basic functions and missions with present forces; and the accelerated outdating of weapon systems.

2. Today, most countries begin military reform to reduce the defense budget and channel budget funds toward solving economic and social problems. In many European countries, armed forces are being reformed in connection with the transition to a volunteer force (not only because of military, but also economic and social, reasons). Many democratic states regularly undertake a thorough (top-down) analysis of their military structures to check on the efficiency of the use of budget funds, assess the combat effectiveness of the army, and identify problem areas. Normally, this is done when new leadership takes power. In the postcommunist countries of Central and Eastern Europe, reforms envisage a gradual reduction of manpower, and bringing it's structure and the level of training into compliance with NATO standards.

3. Several directions of reform may be combined, as shown in Figure 15: "top-down"—when new political goals and priorities are formulated, and doctrinal principles change; "bottom-up"—when the effectiveness of present forces is increased by means of organizational

Figure 15
ALGORITHM OF MILITARY REFORM IN UKRAINE

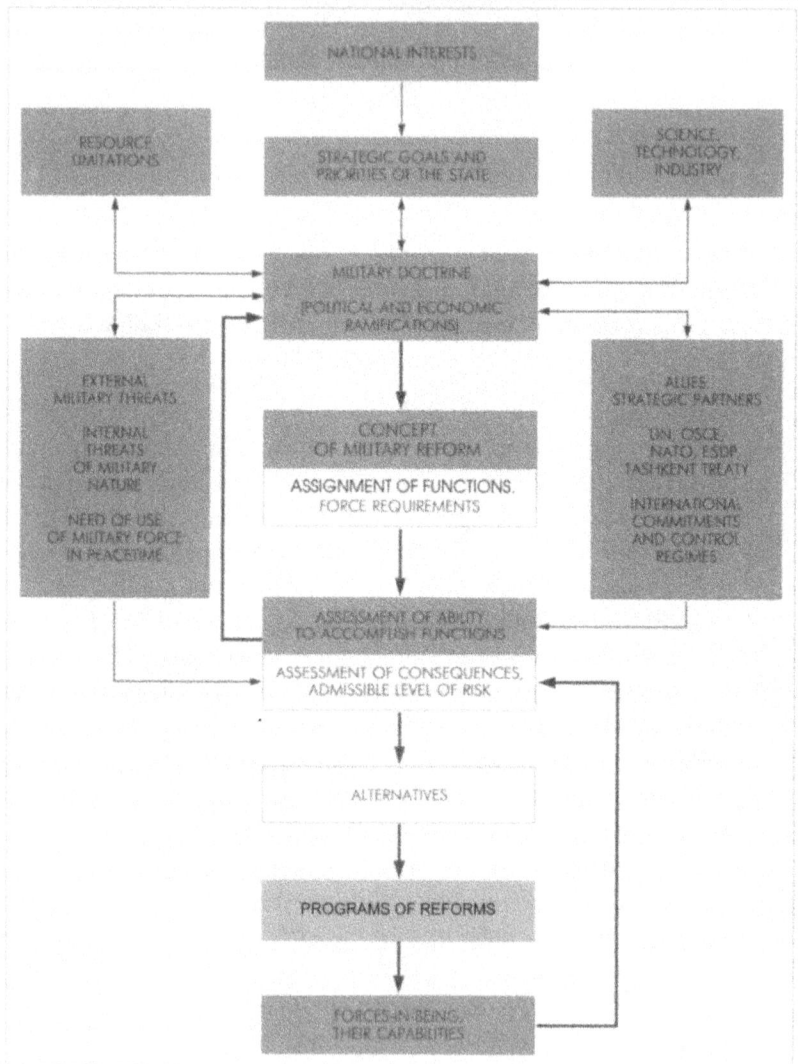

arrangements, without a considerable increase in expenditures; "budget-driven"—when the Army is reduced because of pressure from economic problems; "threat-oriented"—when the structure, composition, and numerical strength of the Army change to protect national interests from new threats.

4. Even brief acquaintance with the algorithm is sufficient to see that it is impossible to work out a concept (and especially a program) of military reform without first analyzing national development priorities; identifying concrete limitations and targets (manpower ceiling, funding limits); and assessing ability to accomplish basic functions and missions with available manpower and equipment, threat assessment, etc. Unfortunately, those obvious things were not understood in Ukraine; their importance was called into question both in 1992, when Ukraine's Armed Forces were being created from the ruins of the Soviet Army, and in 1995–96, when the State Program of Armed Forces Construction and Development was drafted. After adoption of the Constitution and the National Security Concept of Ukraine, the top segment of the algorithm became more or less clear, at which time the threat assessment, the potential of national science and the military-industrial complex, the economic situation, and the effectiveness of international security mechanisms became more realistic.

5. At different stages of the reform (balancing of the system presented in Figure 15), the problem of choosing among several alternative decisions arises. At the highest political level, the choice lies in how priorities and strategic goals of the state are determined; the search for possible allies and strategic partners; definition of the directions and the degree of cooperation with international organizations in the field of security; manpower ceilings for the entire military organization and each military formation; and the scope of budget funding and logistic support. Such background data for conducting military reforms are to be approved by the political leadership, because these issues are beyond the competence of the military. The concept of military reform cannot be worked out, and reasonable amendments to military doctrine cannot be prepared, without these data. Ukraine learned this lesson as far back as 1996. The problem of choice arises at the level of the military formation, too, when it appears (see Figure 15) that certain functions will not be accomplished. If the consequences could be serious (the risk is high), changes are required; in this case, alternatives should be generated.

Of course, the choice would be simpler after making the necessary calculations and defining criteria for comparison.

6. Figure 15 shows that military reform preparation is an interactive process. It suggests feedback for adjustment: If the required level of combat effectiveness cannot be provided within the set limits, adjustment may be performed at different levels. At the military formation level, there should be a search for more effective options for force development (new proposals for structure, manpower, command and control system, methods of training, etc.). At the doctrine level, the balance between what is desired and what is available may be regained by introducing new doctrines, acceding to military blocs, obtaining essentially new weapon types, removing resource limitations, settling conflicts primarily by political or diplomatic means, etc. If all those measures fail to ensure the protection of national interests against military threats, a decision may be made at the top political level to change strategic goals and state priorities. Normally, such feedback is rarely workable (primarily only during a period of deep social transformation, in the event of war, or a if there is a cardinal change in the international situation).

7. Assessment of military formations' capability to perform assigned functions; assessment of the risk of not performing them and the consequences thereof; choosing among alternatives and substantiating modifications—all of these actions envisage obligatory calculations. This does not mean exclusion of qualitative assessments and substantiation of obvious things. The point is that reforming a huge structure (hundreds of thousand people, tens of thousands of units of costly hardware, hundreds of cantonments, etc.) cannot be based on the verbal opinion of several experts. The cost of erroneous decisions is too high; that is why national leaders should not set unrealistic terms for drafting military reform.

Experience shows that even in developed countries, such as Great Britain, the Netherlands, the United States, and France, under conditions of stability and in the absence of radical changes, it takes six to eight months to work out a sound concept of military reform. Creating the corresponding program (balanced with resources) takes another ten to twelve months. There is no reason to hope that any other country would be able to engineer its military reform much more quickly, although it is possible to reduce this period by learning from the mistakes of others.

BIBLIOGRAPHY

Anatoliy Grytsenko, "Civil-Military Relations in Ukraine: A System Emerging from Chaos," Harmonie Paper No. 1, Groningen, The Netherlands: Centre for European Security Studies, 1997. Available at http://odur.let.rug.nl/cess/hp/hp1.htm

Anatoliy Grytsenko, "Defense Reform in Ukraine: Defining Strategic Goals and Military Functions of the Armed Forces," UCEPS paper, Kyiv, Ukraine, 1999. Available at http://www.uceps.com.ua/eng/all/publications/publicat_1022_eng.pdf

Anatoliy Grytsenko, "Ukraine's Defense Sector in Transition: Impacts on Foreign and Security Policy," in Kurt R. Spillmann, Andreas Muller, and Derek Muller (eds.), *Foreign and Security Policy of Independent Ukraine*, Bern: Lang, 1999, pp. 95–119. Available at http://www.uceps.com.ua/eng/all/publications/publicat_1021_eng.pdf

Anatoliy Grytsenko, "Reforming the Military in States of Transformation: The Case of Ukraine," European Fellowship Program Working Paper No. 3, Groningen, The Netherlands: Center for European Security Studies, 1999.

Anatoliy Grytsenko, "Is it Possible for the Ukrainian Armed Forces to Perform Internal Functions?" in *Zerkalo Nedeli* (29 January 2000): 1, 4. Available at http://www.uceps.com.ua/eng/all/journal/2000_1/html/48.shtml

Anatoliy Grytsenko et al., "Military Reform in Ukraine: The Start, or Another False Start?" *National Security and Defense*, No. 1 (2000): 2–39. Available at http://www.uceps.com.ua/eng/all/journal/2000_1/html/2.shtml

Anatoliy Grytsenko, "Civil-Military Relations in Ukraine: On the Way from Form to Substance," NATO fellowship paper, 2000. Available at http://www.nato.int/acad/fellow/98-00/grytsenko.pdf

Anatoliy Grytsenko et al., "Military Reform in Ukraine: Expert Opinion Poll," *National Security and Defense*, No. 2 (2000): 31–39. Available at http://www.uceps.com.ua/eng/all/journal/2000_2/html/31.shtml

Anatoliy Grytsenko et al., "Democratic Civilian Control over the Military in Ukraine: The Path from Form to Substance," *National Security & Defense*, No. 11 (2000): 2–45. Available at http://www.uceps.com.ua/eng/all/journal/2000_11/html/2.shtml

ENDNOTES

1. This paper is based on several in-depth studies conducted by the author and his colleagues—Leonid Polyakov and Mykola Sungurovskyi—from the Ukrainian Center for Economic and Political Studies (UCEPS). A complete listing of these articles is included in the Bibliography section.

2. According to Ukraine's National Security Concept (1997), "Military organization of the state, including Ukraine's Armed Forces, Security Service, Internal

Troops, bodies and units of the Ministry of Interior, Border Troops, military units of the Ministry for Emergency, other military units established in accordance with Ukraine's Constitution, shall ensure the Defense of Ukraine, protection of its sovereignty, territorial integrity and inviolability of its borders, counteract external and internal military threats, and fight organized crime; ensure protection of population in case of catastrophes, natural disasters, dangerous social conflicts, epidemics, etc." In fact, the manpower of the Armed Forces is estimated to be less than half of the total numerical strength of Ukraine's military.

3. Functions of Ukraine's Armed Forces are too general: they encompass the defense of Ukraine, protection of its sovereignty, and the territorial integrity and inviolability of its borders. In Great Britain and Canada, those functions are defined more precisely. For instance, the White Book of the Canadian government determines their character (containment of a low- or high-intensity conflict), composition of allocated manpower and equipment (number and classes of ships, warplanes, regiments, and brigades), deployment readiness (twenty-four hours, three weeks), duration of combat operations without reinforcements, etc. So, the Canadian military gets concrete initial information for planning. Those same indices serve as a basis to control the Armed Forces, which raises the responsibility of both military and civilians for budget funds.

4. This refers to delayed terms of reequipment, housing for the military, curtailment of reservist training, etc.

5. Extract from the Defense Minister's report at a Congress of officers of the Armed Forces of Ukraine, 13 July 1999. Updated data are not available.

6. The Law "On State Programs" was only adopted in 2000.

7. The Cabinet of Ministers Resolution No. 796 of 10 October 1995.

8. S. Rogov, "Security of the State and the Military Reform," *Krasnaya Zvezda* (23 November 1996): 3.

9. It is quite possible that the developers wanted to escape criticism this way. Such a possibility was mentioned by the military attaché of the Netherlands in Ukraine, G. Timmer: "I have got the impression that there is either no such plan, or its quality is very low. . . . The Dutch Army has no secrets from its people and from the international community. This may be one of the reasons why it took only eighteen months to make our Army professional." See V. Voroniuk, "Holland Stands for Greater Openness of Military Contacts with Ukraine," *Den'* (27 November 1999): 4.

10. Estimates exist demonstrating that if the multiplicity of functions were not adopted as a baseline principle of strategic planning in Great Britain, that country's defense budget would rise by 90 percent–100 percent.

11. Based on the results of R. Lloyd, "Strategy and Force Planning Framework," *Strategy and Force Planning*, Newport: U.S. Naval War College, 1995, pp. 1–14.

CHAPTER SEVEN

Continuity, Restructuring, or Development from Scratch? Dilemmas of Slovenian Defense Reform, 1991–2001

Ljubica Jelušič

INTRODUCTION—HISTORICAL BACKGROUND OF SLOVENIA'S INDEPENDENCE

On the geopolitical map of Europe, Slovenia is a new and relatively small country that, after winning its political independence in 1991, has been making its way slowly toward broader recognition by Europe and the world through many and increasingly extensive economic, scientific, cultural, sport, tourist, and political contacts. In fact, Slovenia existed long before the turmoil of 1991. For more than seventy-three years, it was part of Yugoslavia, and before then it belonged to the Austrian part of the Austro-Hungarian Empire. Yugoslavia existed in two incarnations: first as a kingdom generally referred to as Royal Yugoslavia, and second as a socialist republic (Socialist Federal Republic of Yugoslavia [SFRY]).

The second Yugoslavia that emerged out of World War II was a genuine attempt to reconcile the interests of all the countries' peoples. The system of governance was complex, but it was designed to be fair to all nations and national minorities within the state. The Yugoslavs managed to get along with each other, although there were major differences among Yugoslavia's regions: differences in concepts of development strategies; allocation of scarce resources; political freedoms; civilian control over the armed forces; and accession to Western European and world economic, financial, and security structures. These differences were not enough to break the historical bonds built up over more than seventy years. Many countries, with regimes far more despicable than Yugoslavia's ever was, nevertheless remain together.[1] Above all, the SFRY was the first socialist country to develop cooperation with the European Economic Community.

The central conflict that destabilized the SFRY was between the desire to create or consolidate a state in which one nation would be dominant and the perceived vulnerability of minorities (or smaller nations of the former Yugoslavia) in such a state. The inequality of nations was a step backward from the standard of political rights and freedoms achieved in the SFRY. In December 1990, Slovenians voted overwhelmingly to declare independence from Yugoslavia. The Slovenian Assembly confirmed the results of the December 1990 plebiscite in June 1991, when, on 26 June 1991, the Founding Charter of Independence was approved. During the evening ceremony on the same day, held to mark the approval of the Charter, some military units of the Yugoslav Peoples' Army (YPA) began marching across and into Slovenia. On 27 June 1991, military operations and armed conflict developed throughout Slovenia. The minor armed conflict lasted from 27 June 1991 until 6 July 1991, when the last cease-fire was agreed on between the opponents. It was followed on 7 July 1991 by the Brioni Declaration, which was meant to end hostilities, withdraw the Yugoslav military units from the field back to the barracks, and demobilize the Slovenian Territorial Defense and Police Forces. Under pressure of European Union (EU) mediators, Slovenia agreed to freeze independence activities for three months. The armed conflict became known as the "ten-day war" or "war for independence."

The YPA's intervention within national borders put an end to fictitious brotherhood and unity. The decision of the YPA to deploy classic military intervention instruments to bring the insubordinate inhabitants and politicians of Slovenia under central control was an intervention against the very people whose security the YPA was supposed to protect. As tanks and armored vehicles rolled in, Slovenian citizens and political leaders had to advance from declarations and ceremonies to more operational activities. They decided to mobilize all possible resources, including arms, of the territorial military units, called the Territorial Defense, and of the police as well to defy the militarily superior federal force. Both decisions (of the Yugoslav authorities and the YPA to intervene, and of Slovenian citizens and leaders to resist militarily) were a prelude to the war, which lasted from June 1991 until November 1995 (involving Slovenia, Croatia, Bosnia, and Herzegovina), and was reignited in 1999–2001 (involving Kosovo, Macedonia).

Defense Reforms in Slovenia after Independence

THE FOUNDATIONS OF THE DEFENSE REFORMS

Slovenia learned three important principles on its way to independence, which served as cornerstones for establishing the defense sector and transforming it further in the independent Slovenia during 1991–2001.

The first principle is the equilibrium of the armed forces' social and functional imperative.[2] The YPA had followed a functional imperative to keep the state together with all military means, but it failed to recognize the social expectations of the Slovenian population regarding its military and social functions. After the "ten-day war," the YPA lost the majority of its manpower in Slovenia (soldiers, noncommissioned officers [NCOs], and some lower-ranked officers left the garrisons or were captured as prisoners of war by Slovenian military units). This action revealed the absolute loss of legitimacy of the YPA within Slovenian society and the loss of authority within the military's rank and file. Slovenian politicians and civil society learned that to have an efficient and legitimate military, there must be certain equally fulfilled social and functional expectations.

The second principle for establishing the defense sector in Slovenia is rooted in the ten-day armed conflict perceived by the Slovenian population as a real war with radical consequences and related changes. The war and victorious independence that followed provide the elementary sources of defense legitimacy.

The third principle was the importance of relying on the country's own forces when subjected to outside aggression. Slovenia learned this lesson during World War II, when partisan units, together with progressive political and social forces, fought German, Italian, and Hungarian occupation. This proved valid again in 1991, when certain important international actors were prepared to tolerate the rapid and efficient intervention of the YPA with the aim of holding Yugoslavia together, no matter how totalitarian it might be.

In 1991, Slovenia was a postsocialist, newly established state that—at the beginning of its independence—had experienced war. Fighting the war meant nothing but putting into practice the total national defense measures learned in the times when a common total national defense system existed within the former Yugoslavia. Therefore, establishing Slovenia's defense sector incorporated the remedies of the past and, at the same time, the need for new solutions, and sometimes even countersolutions. The call for change was not always the result of rational choices, but merely the expression of dissatisfaction with the past. The best description of this first period would be "between continuity and transformation." Regardless of the decade of transformation in between, it is still possible to find the same dilemma in certain recent changes in the Slovenian defense sector.

PHASES OF DEFENSE SECTOR TRANSFORMATION IN SLOVENIA

Establishing the Defense System (1991–94) in a Trinity of Civil Defense, Rescue and Self-Protection, and Military Organization   Before declaring independence, the Slovenian political elite and public opinion were divided between those in favor of Slovenia's demilitarization (departure of all military units from Slovenia and closing down of all military infrastructure) and those in favor of establishing the Slovenian Armed Forces. This clash was very intense and had pushed the government into a stalemate, so the only working solution on the eve of the armed conflict in June 1991 was to continue the activities and mobilization of the Territorial Defense (which, as a second echelon of the Yugoslav armed forces, already existed, and was organized at the level of republics), and the Slovenian police (also organized at the republican level). In addition to these two actors, nearly all Slovenian citizens cooperated with violent and nonviolent means and methods in the ten-day war for independence. Until January 1992, Slovenia existed without any international recognition. During this period, it preserved the concept of defensive self-reliance inherited from the former Yugoslavia, but it had lost its nonaligned character. After international recognition in January 1992, the possibilities for guaranteeing its security changed considerably. Slovenia became a member of the United Nations (UN) and the Conference on Security and Cooperation in Europe.

The first phase of defense sector transformation in Slovenia took place between two historical events, the June–July 1991 war for independence, and 30 March 1994, when the Partnership for Peace (PfP) Framework Document was signed. The defense system of independent Slovenia was established as a continuation and counterimage of the former Yugoslavia's system of total national defense. Some characteristics of the former doctrine were preserved because that system had been very well developed. According to some evaluations, the Slovenian system of total national defense was one of the best of all the republics of the former

Yugoslavia. This system was victorious in the ten-day war for independence in 1991. Although its military component, the Territorial Defense Units, was very poorly equipped and armed, together with the police units, it was successful in armed resistance against the better-equipped and -trained YPA units. Slovenia's defense system, as established in 1991, comprised civil defense (the framework for all important national enterprises in national security, such as telecommunications, railway, energy, and other services, all of which supported the military organization and fulfilled their own defense-related obligations); rescue and self-protection (a system of organizations and individuals obliged to work in the event of natural and other disasters); and military organization, which continued under its former name, Territorial Defense, until 1994.

Some solutions in the newly established defense system were instituted to show the break with the former Yugoslavia. For instance, defense education was abolished immediately in primary, secondary, and high schools, compulsory military service was shortened to seven months (in the former YPA, it had been twelve months). These recruits served very close to their homes—whereas, in the YPA, recruits been sent very far from home, usually to the republic farthest away, for example, from Slovenia to Macedonia, from Kosovo to Slovenia, etc. Conscientious objection was allowed on a very broad basis, with only very poor checking of the sincerity of such requests. Alternative civil service was the same length as military duty and could be fulfilled within a wide range of organizations. In the former Yugoslavia, conscientious objection was not allowed until the very end, when military authorities finally recognized objections on a religious basis and established nonarmed military duty for objectors.

From the legislative point of view, Slovenia adopted a new Constitution in December 1991, of which Article 92 (war and state of emergency), Article 102 (functions of the President of the Republic), Article 123 (the duty to serve in the Defense Forces), and Article 124 (Defense of the State) concerned national security. The Defense Act (1991, amended in 1994) and the Act on Military Duty are the next most important legal documents. The basic doctrinal document is the Resolution on the Principles of National Security of the Republic of Slovenia, adopted by the National Parliament in December 1993.

The documents laying out the legal foundations for the state were created as a compromise among different influential political and social actors: political parties, civil society organizations, the public, the media, academic circles, and researchers. Academic experts from defense sciences were asked for their opinion in concluding the preparation phase of the defense documents; their opinions provided the final legitimacy for the documents' acceptance. Among other things, the documents codified the roles of the Parliament, the President, the government, and the military organization.

The National Parliament defines the national security policy of the state and exercises control over the armed forces, especially through committees, such as the Defense Committee, the Committee on Budget and Finance, the Committee for Control of the Intelligence Services, and the Committee for Control of the Realization of the National Security Resolution. Through the allocation of defense funding, the National Parliament supervises the development and equipping of the armed forces.

The government has an executive role in the defense sphere and is responsible for keeping the unity and concordance of the defense forces in line with national security and defense policy. The government is also responsible for exercising defense measures on the basis of decisions made by the National Parliament.

The President of the Republic is the Supreme Commander of the Defense Forces, that is, the Slovenian Army.

Pursuant to the Defense Act, the Slovenian Army's fundamental tasks are as follows:

- providing defense in the event of an attack on the country;
- complying with Slovenia's commitments to international organizations;
- training for defense purposes;
- providing an adequate level of combat readiness; and
- participating in civil emergency operations in the event of natural or other disasters.

Some articles of the documents were amended during further changes within the defense sector, but the primary ideas remained the same as in the establishment phase of the defense system. The rigidity of the basic documents and, in particular, the obstacles to the political process of changing them, created a gap between the reality of the defense sector, which has to follow the internal and international inputs, and the system's formal appearance.

The first phase of defense reforms was marked by creation of both the basic documents and the defense system's framework. Establishment of the defense sector was influenced by remnants of the former system in the SFRY, the internal Slovenian situation after becoming independent, and inputs from the neighboring international community (events in the Balkans). It is worth noting that there were many finished and unfinished defense sector reforms after the sector was established, but most of them did not affect the civilian component of the defense system. Although there were some discussions and tendencies to reestablish the subsystem of rescue and self-protection as a government agency independent of the defense sector, this has remained part of the defense system for ten years, with the likelihood of staying there in the near future as well. In later phases of defense reform, the main focus has been on military reform.

From the Balkans to Europe and the UN (1994–2000): The Prevalence of International Inputs   The Slovenian defense system's first period of development was occupied with preparations and measures to ensure security with regard to events in the Balkans. Two major wars were underway nearby: in Croatia and Bosnia-Herzegovina. Slovenia accepted some one hundred thousand refugees from both countries, with different national origins: Croats, Serbs, and Muslims. Refugee camps were set up in former military barracks, marking the first civilian use of the former military infrastructure.

The second phase of defense reform was influenced by international inputs that came from a much broader international environment than in the first phase. The substance of these reforms was connected to the possibility of Slovenia becoming a member of different international security agreements and mechanisms. Adaptation of the main legal documents, military reform, and the new doctrine of foreign relations all were marked by rapprochement with NATO (through the PfP program, in 1994), negotiations with the EU on possible accession, and the country's nonpermanent membership in the UN Security Council (1998–99). Parallel to national security reform, and involving a change of direction from the earlier self-reliance doctrine of total national defense to collective security and defense in international alliances, major reforms and restructuring of the military took place after 1994. The end of 1994 was marked by the amended Defense Act, which successfully passed through the parliamentary procedure. That changed the name of the Defense forces from the Territorial Defense into the Slovenian Army, from territorial guerrilla forces into a standing army.

Throughout 1993, the Slovenian Government began informal cooperation with the North Atlantic Treaty Organization (NATO), and, at the end of the year, the concept of seeking NATO membership became a doctrinal issue. In December 1993, the National Parliament adopted the Resolution on the Principles of National Security and, within that framework, formalized accession to NATO as one of the key goals of Slovenian foreign and defense policy. March 1994 brought the PfP document and, in July 1994, the Government of Slovenia presented NATO with its reasons for accession to the PfP program, implementation of measures for its realization, and planned military and civilian activities. The whole process shows Slovenia's gradual turning away from obsession with the Balkans and threats from the Balkans toward the wider world, the wider Europe, NATO, and international organizations. To be more prepared organizationally for international security activities and to establish a military organization on the principles of a standing army, Slovenia decided to increase its military professional corps, composed mainly of soldiers, NCOs, and officers. By the end of 1994, a special military unit was organized, the Tenth Battalion for International Cooperation, whose duty was to train and cooperate in international military exercises, in units of bilateral or multilateral military cooperation, such as peacekeeping operations. This was the first major military reform of the Slovenian defense sector.

In May 1995, the first individual partner program on cooperation between Slovenia and NATO was adopted, stressing adjustment of the defense system and military structure, education, military exercises, standardization, and civil-military relations, according to NATO's expectations. This document meant the beginning of Slovenia's path to NATO and the start of investment in NATO membership. When the NATO study on enlargement was presented to partner states in September 1995, the Slovenian political elite perceived Slovenia as being well prepared, according to prescribed conditions for NATO membership. Certain of being one of the best candidates to join NATO, the Slovenian Parliament decided to strengthen the country's desire for NATO membership by adopting the decision to ensure Slovenia's fundamental security interest within the framework of the collective defense system enabled by NATO membership. In April 1997, the newly elected National Parliament again confirmed Slovenia's willingness to become a NATO member by adopting the Declaration of Parliamentary Parties in Support of Slovenia's Integration into NATO. The declaration was a prerequisite for the

NATO Summit in Madrid 1997. When the Madrid NATO Declaration classified Slovenia as not yet an invited candidate for NATO membership, the country's failure to be invited to join had a sobering effect on Slovenian public opinion and the political elite, but it did not stop the active cooperation of the Slovenian Army in NATO activities. Furthermore, the Slovenian Army began cooperating in peacekeeping operations under NATO command (Stabilization Force [SFOR] in Bosnia-Herzegovina in October 1997 and continued in the Kosovo Force [KFOR] at Kosovo in 1999).

Slovenian soldiers' participation in peacekeeping operations in general dates from 1997. The first deployment was for the ALBA operation in Albania under Italian leadership (May–July 1997), where a medical unit participated as a battalion aid station and, after September 1997, larger numbers and units of service members were sent to the United Nations Peacekeeping Force in Cyprus (UNFICYP) operation. The Slovenian contingents participated as part of the Austrian battalion and, along with the withdrawal of Austrian troops from UNFICYP in June 2001, Slovenia also stopped sending its troops to Cyprus. Instead, the number of Military Police members sent to SFOR increased: from one platoon, which had participated in SFOR until 2001, participation increased to two platoons, deployed in 2001. Cooperation in SFOR also includes helicopter transport and a transport airplane, along with a military medical unit in Sarajevo. Since 1998, two officer-observers have been participating in the United Nations Truce Supervision Organization (UNTSO). From 1999 on, every six months, six officers are sent to KFOR in Kosovo. In November 2000, civilian police from Slovenia also participated in UNMIK (fifteen police officers), signaling another important shift in Slovenian national security policy as a whole. The international military cooperation of Slovenian defense forces is the most important result of restructuring in the second phase of defense sector reforms. In particular, cooperation in peacekeeping operations has helped to restore the decreasing military legitimacy and, together with the NATO Membership Action Plan, gave new motivation to the professional soldiers, NCOs, and officers of the Slovenian Armed Forces (SAF).

It is important to note that, in 1997, Slovenia was elected by a significant majority of the UN General Assembly to become a nonpermanent member of the UN Security Council. Slovenia fulfilled its duty in 1998–99 and proved to be highly instrumental in the peaceful solution of international armed conflicts. Slovenian politicians became aware of international security as a collective effort, and the Slovenian public finally realized that Slovenia is (like all other countries) responsible for peace everywhere in the world.

Professionalisation of the Defense Sector (2000–Present): From Growth to Development   The third important shift in Slovenian Defense reforms is connected with the new government elected in 2000. New Defense Minister Anton Grizold announced the professionalization and increasing level of defense expertise in his directives for the further development of the country's defense sector (February 2001). He stressed the fact that, in the past ten years, the Slovenian defense sector had increased in quantity, but not so much in quality. Moreover, after seven years of being a member of the PfP program, and six years after the parliamentary decision to seek NATO membership, the Slovenian political elite still was not sufficiently aware of the priority of military and defense restructuring to becoming a NATO member. The Defense Minister announced the focus would be on restructuring the size and structure of the Slovenian Armed Forces until 2003. The aims of the reforms are to create defense forces, which are small in size, but well-armed, -equipped, and -trained. The focus is on professional units, which need to recruit rank and file soldiers. The restructuring process should be complete with twenty-five thousand service members (including seven thousand professionals, five thousand recruits under compulsory military service, and the rest reserve soldiers). This plan aims for the biggest reduction of the armed forces' size in ten years, cutting back the mass army of fifty-six thousand soldiers in 1998 to less than half that number over a five-year period.

The announcement also initiated debates in autumn 2001 on doing away with compulsory military service, which were reopened in February 2002. To clarify the status of professional soldiers, the Defense Act has to be changed. The system of military education and training of draftees was altered radically in July 2001: The former system of dispersed education among twenty-two different battalions throughout Slovenia (which led to very different levels of military effectiveness) was replaced by a system of common basic education in four major training centers and advanced military education in different military units. The education reform aims to improve and make more uniform military education of recruits under compulsory military service, achieving a higher level of combat readiness of tactical units and a higher level of individual military skills. Better-trained draftees would have the opportunity to sign contracts as professional soldiers after finishing their compulsory military service.

According to the Defense Minister's directives, it is possible to conclude that commitments to peace support operations and international security organizations will become the main task of the professional, all-volunteer part of the Slovenian Army, and reserve units will continue homeland defense training.

The Membership Action Plan for NATO accession of October 2001 was evaluated as the best-prepared plan so far. It shows the preparedness of the Slovenian defense sector for realistic planning and for keeping the promises regarding participation in NATO activities. Slovenia is offering its professional units to European defense forces as well, which is part of its accession negotiations with the EU.

The developments of 2001 reveal the Slovenian decision to suspend the old total national defense's doctrine of self-reliance and to develop the ability to cooperate in common international security and defense mechanisms. The reality of the higher security level assured within the alliances is becoming part of Slovenian political and public opinion debate. There is also a significant amount of skepticism in society about Slovenia's membership in NATO. The Prague NATO Summit at the end of 2002 is another cornerstone in the attempts of postsocialist countries to be invited to join NATO. Slovenia is among these countries and is rated very well, but politicians and public opinion are now more realistic about NATO membership. The fact that Slovenia is an excellent candidate for membership is not enough to receive an invitation; the nineteen current member nations of NATO have to agree.

PROBLEMS AND CHALLENGES IN DEFENSE REFORM

THE NEED FOR A STRATEGIC VISION

One of the first challenges the Slovenian political elite faced after gaining independence was to decide on the country's main strategic interests and orientations. As part of the former Yugoslavia, Slovenia had a positive experience as part of a nonaligned federation. The former Yugoslavia had a somewhat intermediate geographical and political position between two blocs, the capitalist West and the socialist East, and their military-political alliances, NATO and the Warsaw Pact. There was a specific political orientation that viewed both alliances as negative factors of international politics. Yugoslavia found itself among the "founding fathers" of the Nonalignment Movement and of the Conference on Security and Co-operation in Europe. All of these processes formed and maintained Yugoslavia's political character as a nonaligned country with no external security guarantees. The value of independence in defense policy was esteemed among the country's values and was preserved in Slovenia during the ten-day war in 1991. This value was especially important as the basis for the will to fight in 1991, when Slovenians did not expect any foreign support in their attempt to declare and preserve independence. It stayed realistic during the conflict and respected the Brioni Declaration, although the document served to stymie Slovenian independence activities. Some European countries, among them Germany, showed more sympathy with the Slovenian struggle for independence, and members of the European Community (EC) recognized Slovenia as a state in January 1992. This was a turning point in Slovenian political culture; for the first time, Slovenians were seeing Western Europe as its main security and economic guarantee. At that time, NATO was not perceived as a promised alliance. In 1994, when the Slovenian political elite announced the possibility of becoming a NATO member more openly, the public was not sure how realistic such a desire might be.

Because their country is relatively small, Slovenians were eager to preserve their political and cultural individuality, which resulted in some public skepticism about NATO-. An additional ambiguity of the Slovenian political landscape creates ambivalence in political culture: the Slovenian political elite feels a psychological need to be recognized symbolically as belonging to "Europe" and to the West, and not as just part of the Balkans.

In 1991, the newly established state of Slovenia needed much new or amended legislation. The rights and duties of all individual subjects, comprising the security system and other subsystems of the state, needed to be explained in laws and legislative norms, starting with the Constitution and ending with military regulations and rules. Slovenia was somewhat dilatory in this respect. First, serious difficulties were accounted before reaching a clear and unambiguous agreement on the country's key security interests. The newly elected Slovenian multiparty elite from 1990 lacked the knowledge to prepare defense documents, one of the most necessary political skills. Former politicians were educated in defense matters so they could understand and lead defense issues. Second, the main strategic security documents were prepared by think tanks in Belgrade, at the federal level, and as top-down documents they were sent out for political debates at the lower political echelons. Therefore, the former Slovenian political elite (some of whom had survived the change from a one-party to a multiparty system in 1990) was more involved in debates on the documents and than in actually preparing them. Third, the Slovenian political landscape in 1991 was sharply divided into two groups on basic national security issues: One was in favor of demilitarization, and the other in favor of establishing armed forces. Due to this division, the defense sector lacked the political guidance to form the basic structures of the defense system. Some basic principles and structures were formed more under the influence of defense experts from autonomous, mainly university, circles, than according to political expectations. This lack of political guidance is one of the most dangerous inadequacies of postsocialist countries, because it can result in a lack of political control over the defense sector. The Slovenian political elite managed to reach a consensus on the main security issues (as shown in the case of the parliamentary declaration to join NATO in 1997), but there are still some open security issues that might divide the elites and cause a slowdown in military and defense reforms in Slovenia. One of these issues is the European-wide problem of the decline of mass armies, as elaborated and surveyed by Haltiner,[3] which, at the national policy level, tends to translate into abolishing compulsory military service.

The gap between the political and security culture of the citizens and politicians, and the expectations of the international community to reflect the new trends in security matters challenged the Slovenian defense sector. The political elite took the first step and had to work intensively to change public opinion. For instance, in 1994, the decision to ask for PfP membership and to sign the PfP program was a political initiative; the public was unaware that this was Slovenia's first investment in NATO membership. Some NATO skeptics, who led a media debate in summer 2001 against membership in NATO, were not aware of the country's seven-year investment in rapprochement with NATO. They still think the debate can start from scratch, but it is too late.

MILITARY SECTOR HAS EXPERIENCED TOO MANY (UNFINISHED) REFORMS

The social and functional imperatives of the armed forces reflect a basic contradiction of the past ten years of security development. According to public opinion polls from the former Yugoslavia (the period between

1982–90), the Slovenian public did not agree with the social imperative of the former YPA. There was a rise in expectations concerning the functional imperative, understood as resistance of the YPA to outside threats, successful military training, and help in natural disasters. On the other hand, the Slovenian public strove to reduce the social role of the military in domestic matters and to deny it the right to educate young males in a patriotic spirit. Slovenians were also against all possible forms of military engagement in defending the constitutionally decided political system. The Slovenian public, surprisingly, still has the same expectations of its own Slovenian armed forces. The main problem of the Territorial Defense (1991–94) lay in its ability to fulfill the social imperative better than expectations regarding the functional imperative. The discrepancies between the functional expectations of public opinion and the social role of the Territorial Defense Units led to a very slow process of modernization and transformation of the Territorial Defense into a standing army, and it was the source of lost military legitimacy. The military, exposed to decreasing legitimacy, decided to form some clearly professional units (1994–97), which tend to be the military elite in many respects (military police, Tenth Battalion for International Cooperation, armored units, air and marine units). These units claimed to fulfil the functional imperative better than others, which have to train military recruits or consist of a large number of reserve soldiers. This contradiction causes macho-militarism tendencies among professional units and the sense of being a less competent or second-class army among other units. Draftees, challenged by the less prestigious status of the roles they are supposed to play within the military, disobey and decide (in significant numbers) to escape military service.

The problem of insufficient political guidance led the Slovenian defense sector, and especially the military organization, to a few unfinished military reforms that involved a lot of financial, time, and motivational costs, but that did not meet the final aims. Usually, they occurred after a government change and after a change of Defense Minister. The position of Defense Minister is one of the least liked jobs in the Slovenian government, as shown by the seven different people who have filled the role in a ten-year period. Each minister tried to show his authority in mandating "significant" changes in the military sector. The real basis for their attempts was not to improve the military sector (which is urgently needed), but to promote their own political party within the military. Many of them understood political control over the armed forces as their political party's feud, in which they could use party sympathizers or realize personal ambitions.

There was no debate on the system of manning the armed forces in 1991, when Slovenia, being subject to the YPA's military intervention, mobilized the Territorial Defense Units. Continuation of compulsory military service was the only culturally accepted form of maintaining the massive forces needed in the case of any further YPA attacks (which the Slovenian public expected after the cease-fire of July 1991). Military service was much shorter than in the former Yugoslavia, which increased the motivation of young males to serve, and many of them were proud to serve in the victorious army of 1991. There were few requests for conscientious objector status (240 in 1991), even though the right to serve in the alternative civil service was equal to military service of the same length and such status was recognized in almost all cases. The recruits under compulsory military service served near their homes, and were able to spend nearly all their weekends with their families, outside the barracks. To illustrate the difference from the former YPA, discipline within the barracks was weak. Officers were very limited in the sanctions they could use against disobedient soldiers, and soldiers had a number of channels at their disposal through which they could claim inequality in the officer-soldier relations. Officers were forced to use the polite form of addressing soldiers (the "Sir" form), and they were afraid of causing any harm to the draftees and of the media, which would portray possible accidents involving draftees as a major social problem. This slowly changed the methods of training to very low intensity. They tried to avoid accidents, soldiers' complaints, and parent pressure to make exceptions for their sons. This process caused a degradation of military training, which was perceived by new generations of recruits under compulsory military service as a waste of time. They reacted with increasing refusals to carry out the compulsory service.

The number of requests for conscientious objector status increased, and were expected to reach three thousand out of fifteen thousand people eligible for service in 2001. There also has been a significant increase in those dropping out for medical reasons (16 percent of those eligible for service in 2000). The data show that there is no longer universal military service, but a very selective military service, where the most educated recruits apply for civil service or exemption, and those who serve are poorly educated or motivated recruits. Many of those who remain in service are serving under the pressure of the social values of their home region, or because they were not clever enough to find a way out of serving.

The problems in recruiting draftees forced the Ministry of Defense (MOD) to initiate surveys on the adequacy of military service for future soldier corps of the Slovenian Army and on possible future recruitment methods. The surveys, which took place in autumn 2001, are supposed to support the anticipated political decision to suspend compulsory military service in the future or transform it completely. Male compulsory military service is connected to the issue of inequality in burden sharing among the young population. First, women are excluded from military service, which is seen as incorrect because it ignores gender equality in civil society (but no politician has the courage to say publicly that women should also fulfill some kind of national service). Second, every third male is excluded from military service before even having any contact with the military (medical and conscientious objector dropouts). Third, those who do serve have no benefits; in fact, they experience losses in civil life because they have to spend seven months in the military (which takes them out of the civilian job market and education, and they receive no pension funds for the seven-month period involved).

Some observations and public debates constantly repeat the idea of conscientious objection being the precondition for military (in)effectiveness in Slovenia. The Constitution stipulates the general defense obligations of all male citizens and the right of conscientious objection, on religious, philosophical, and humanistic grounds, to contribute to the country's defense and security by other means than military service. It means that military service and alternative civil service are constitutionally equal ways of fulfilling the compulsory military duty. The number of conscientious objectors has increased rapidly in the past ten years, and a growing number of them are partly a consequence of ineffective military training. The surveys show the prevalence of postmodern values among the young in general. Therefore, objectors also reflect general social and value changes in society. In the case of the Slovenian Armed Forces, there is a trend toward training ineffectiveness in cases when some recruits under compulsory military service decide to ask for objector status while they are in service, which is possible, according to conscience objector regulations but frustrates the officers, NCOs, and other soldiers to the extent that many officers try to get rid of such people at the start of training. As a result, many recruits are sent out of their units in the first two weeks, usually to the military psychological unit, which proves the unpreparedness of a young man for the communitarian values of the military. Some commanders suggest a young man seek objector status to help him find a way out, and to help the unit get rid of unmotivated and disruptive individuals. In such cases, alternative civil service is a positive channel for excluding from the military disruptive soldiers (who might be overly educated for NCOs and officers, too critical of the military, unmotivated, unable to accept military responsibilities, or show some personal trauma, etc.).

Officers' professional socialization is the issue on which all military reforms are dependent. Slovenia has never had any kind of military academy; therefore, it lacks experience in educating military professionals. In 1991, Slovenia was challenged by its own lack of experience in this field; the changing nature of military officers in post-Cold War Europe; the changing balance between institutional and occupational characteristics of a modern officer[4]; and the perceived civilianization of military education in Western European countries. The government decided to educate military officers at civilian universities to have bachelor of arts-degree-level personnel to help with military education. There was the Officer's School, established in the framework of the Center of Military Schools, which lasts one year and gives specialized training in military skills and knowledge to participants.

The system of military education is partly convergent (theory of convergence-divergence of military education according to Caforio[5]) with other civilian professions (a bachelor of arts degree from a civilian university provides high school authority and a chance for conversion), and partly divergent (the Officer's School is not recognized as formal education, it only serves to get a military promotion). The education system seemed to be successful in socializing officers for the army of recruits under compulsory military service, but they are not sufficiently socialized militarily or trained to meet the challenges of an all-volunteer force. Many officers, now in units with a high percentage of volunteers, were sent to different military courses in foreign countries. Therefore, with the possible abolition of compulsory military service or the intended higher concentration on an all-volunteer force (AVF), Slovenia is forced to upgrade its military education system. One solution follows the experience with university defense studies designed twenty-six years ago to educate civilian experts for defense matters at Ljubljana University, where half of the courses offered are on defense or military topics. More military exercising, which should become part of the education of those defense studies students interested in military jobs, would improve the military socialization of future officers and shift the existed convergent system of education slightly to a more divergent one. It also would help to demobilize personnel.

All postsocialist armies are subject to a huge demobilization of officers, NCOs, and enlisted soldiers, a consequence of decreasing military threats after the end of the Cold War and shrinking defense budgets. Demobilization is a huge and sometimes dangerous process in war-affected areas, such as the Balkans. Demobilization and the ill treatment of veterans is one of the most critical issues in Croatian society, where veterans are in the forefront of many social movements and radical demonstrations. These processes did not affect Slovenia because it had to establish its armed forces from scratch, and officers of different origins were urgently needed to fill the ranks. The problem was that there were officers from the former YPA, reserve officers, officers educated at foreign military academies, and officers trained at the Slovenian Officer's Schools, all gathered together in the same officers' corps, but they did not develop any common professional culture. After ten years, they are still different factions of the same corps and view each other as competitors. Some were promoted rapidly to very high ranks without adequate advanced military education, which caused additional troubles. After ten years, some of them are poorly motivated to work with recruits or to do any kind of military job, and should be retired or transferred to civilian jobs as soon as possible to make room for fresh young officers and to exclude disruptive tendencies in the officers' corps. Successful conversion is possible if military officers hold a civilian degree. According to the experiences of 1991, an officer whose only occupation is "military officer" contends with huge difficulties, and some cannot even find appropriate jobs. Many officers who came back from the YPA and other Yugoslav republics to live in Slovenia after 1991 had to wait for a long time at the Employment Service, because, by virtue of having been an "officer of the YPA," it was nearly impossible for them to find a job. Aware of these conversion problems, Slovenia decided to have all officers obtain a civilian university degree before entering military schools. The civilian degree would help the officers to leave the military and seek jobs in the civilian market.

The Slovenian Armed Forces are facing the process of changing the main source of their legitimacy—the pattern of social representativeness—to that of social diversification. This means that all social strata should be presented within the military, but not proportionally. One problem in this regard is the issue of women in the army. In World War II, women played an important role in Slovenian resistance against occupiers. Many of them were included in armed units as combatants; many others were nurses and partisan medical officers. After the war, nearly all of them were demobilized. The culture of women able to fight against aggression remained one of the positive elements of the political socialization of Slovenian society. As women were excluded from the former YPA, the newly established army decided to differentiate itself from the YPA by including women in the rank and file. Some women already were included in armed conflict in 1991, where they showed their combat (and command) abilities. The large number of women integrated into the armed forces was proof of the military's progressive outlook, but this turned out to be a symbolic gesture in the initial stage of establishing the military organization. There is a tendency to push women into jobs they might have in civil society—education, motivation, logistic, communication. Because these jobs are not combat and operational ones, however, promotion opportunities are very limited. Women hold 13 percent of operational and nonoperational posts within the military organization, and many of them perceive the military job as a form of emancipation. Males in the military perceive them as competitors for the same jobs, which should be reserved for men (because, they feel, the military should be a male organization), and they are not particularly supportive of female desires for emancipation. Some male service members think female integration into the military is more about the capriciousness of feminists than any contribution to military combat effectiveness.

Postsocialist armies are challenged by ideological pluralism brought about by multiparty elections. Slovenian officers were prohibited from becoming party members but, at the same time, they, personally, and other strata of the military were exposed to different ideologies and patterns of thinking. They are exposed to the process of desecularization: Due to the division of state and church in socialism, religious practice was not allowed in the former YPA. Some members of the Slovenian Armed Forces expected to be allowed to practice their religion within the military service. Free expression of religion is one of the postulates of the Constitution, so, in trying to ensure motivated soldiers, the Slovenian Armed Forces introduced the military chaplaincy in 2001. Equality of all religious communities is carried over from civilian society to the military, and chaplains are supposed to care for all soldiers of all different religions. Moreover, they are prohibited from proselytizing soldiers to their own religion. The Slovenian Armed Forces are looking for a means to offer spiritual service for atheists as well.

POLITICAL (CIVILIAN) CONTROL OVER THE ARMED FORCES
Political control over the defense sector was one of the hot issues in dispute between former YPA General Staff and Slovenian civil society movements in the 1980s. The YPA and defense sector as a whole was dominated by the military, although the doctrine of total national defense presupposed the significant involvement of all political and economic organizations and institutions in defense matters. When establishing the defense system of the independent Slovenia, its creators tried to balance the three pillars of defense (civil defense, rescue and self-protection, and military organization) to exclude the tendency of the military to predominate. Control over the defense sector was institutionalized through a civil Defense Minister, the government, the President as Supreme Commander, and the Parliament and its special committees. The real problem was the effectiveness and understanding of control. Newly elected Members of Parliament (MPs) were educated in the former Yugoslav military, and many of them had no direct experience with the new Slovenian Army. Service members of the military were not allowed to join political parties; they are asked to be politically neutral. Many of them have accepted this and regard it as a good way to hide their political emotions. Due to their political nonalignment, however, some were more subject to political corruption from different party members.

The lack of defense and military expertise among politicians is one of the weakest points of the control system. Some civilian institutions developed in the former Yugoslavia might be able to develop expert control over the defense sector in general. The former Yugoslavia had a tradition of educating civilian experts for defense matters at civilian universities. These personnel, highly qualified to understand the needs of the military organization, also were educated to develop the preparedness of all organizations and institutions in society for defense. Five universities in the former Yugoslavia had defense studies programs in 1975: Belgrade University, Skopje University, Sarajevo University, Zagreb University, and Ljubljana University. Three of these programs survived the changes of 1991—Skopje, Sarajevo, and Ljubljana. In 2001, a National and International Security study program of was reestablished at the Faculty of Political Sciences in Zagreb. There is also some support for reestablishing the Faculty of Civil Self-Protection in Belgrade. According to experiences with Ljubljana's Defense Studies, the importance of the personnel educated there is growing. First, they are the basis for the recruitment of civil administration workers at the Defense Ministry. Second, they are inevitable in the process of defining the holistic defense system within the country. Third, due to their integration into international scientific networks of defense, security, war studies, and military sociology, they are able to put international findings into domestic defense practice in Slovenia. Fourth, and specific to Slovenia, they are forming the corps of career officers of the armed forces. Fifth, defense studies have developed research capabilities and have become the most important autonomous civil research center for defense and security-related issues in Slovenia. They survey the civilian environment and, on many occasions, serve as the most reliable research organization for internal issues of the defense system. Sixth, defense studies developed the methodology and subjects of defense at the scientific level and organized postgraduate defense sciences' courses where higher-level staff from the defense sector can obtain a master's degree or a doctorate. As civilian university studies, they offer military persons the opportunity to meet civilian public servants from other sectors of national security, and they offer the kind of education that helps military persons in particular prepare for possible conversion to civilian employment.

RELEVANT LESSONS LEARNED

ESTABLISHING AND STRENGTHENING THE CIVILIAN COMPONENT OF THE SECURITY SECTOR

According to trends in Western democracies, the military is one of the subsystems of national security, a security provider, yet not the predominant one. The perception of threat is changing, meaning that military threats are perceived as marginal, and other economic, ecological, or social threats have increasing significance in postsocialist countries. Therefore, security is perceived as a multidimensional system in which different mechanisms should be engaged. The key person to balance out the desires of the different parts of the defense system is the civilian defense minister. Defense ministers with weak ties to political parties are more effective in exercising political control over the armed forces but, on the other hand, as free riders, they are subject to short tenures. The political culture in the Balkans favored the top-down definition of the defense system, which is still possible in postsocialist times, where the structure of the Parliament changes with every election, and the newly elected MPs are unfamiliar with the internal reality of the defense system. The existence of civil defense experts is of great importance in these cases.

In countries where military traditions are very deeply rooted in the political culture, it takes some time to educate people not to confuse defense with the military and not to describe defense narrowly as just military defense. The military itself is the last segment prepared to accept a diminished role in the public eye, especially if its legitimacy is based on a recent victory. If the military is perceived as betraying the national interest (losing a war or armed conflict in recent times), the possibilities of installing it as one of the subsystems in the defense system are much higher. It also means that the civilian part of the defense system, whether civil defense and/or rescue and self-protection subsystems, needs to be developed.

One of the most important steps to civilianize the armed forces and to show that modern armed forces are able to respect human rights is recognition of conscientious objection. This could lead to overwhelming escapism from military service. Due to selective compulsory military service, which is now a reality, there are fewer people with direct experience in the military. Therefore, the military urgently needs someone to present it to the public, primarily to the media. The media mediate between the military and society, and serve as the main source of civilian control over the armed forces, especially in countries where the political elite is not strong enough to control the armed forces. Militaries are challenged by shrinking defense budgets, but requests to meet the new tasks are on the rise. This situation means that they have to do more with less money and fewer personnel. The rise of postmodernity has been observed among the young population, which threatens recruitment for armies with draftees as well as all-volunteer forces.

THE NEED TO BALANCE FULFILLMENT OF THE SOCIAL AND FUNCTIONAL IMPERATIVES

Equilibrium of fulfillment of social and functional expectations is needed to maintain the military's legitimacy. It is important to respect public needs concerning help in natural disasters or humanitarian catastrophes, although the military is not trained for disaster relief.

Cooperation in peace support operations is a new source of military legitimacy. Defense reform that involves the shift of military duties from homeland defense only to peace operations has proved to be one of the most important changes in military doctrine. International missions are a place for comparison with other militaries and the venue where soldiers learn about other cultures and train to use less force than is expected in training for one's homeland defense. The army should preserve the balance among defense of the homeland, peace support operations, and aid in natural disasters. According to public opinion, these three tasks are the top duties of modern Western European armies.

The reduced level of social representativeness in postsocialist militaries calls for social diversification as a new concept of public identity with the military. The female part of society, traditionally excluded from military service in socialist countries, should be invited in large proportions to the military's rank and file. Women in the armed forces are a symbol of the forces' progressiveness. They should be accepted and promoted more broadly than in the former Yugoslavia or other formerly socialist countries, and they should be encouraged to enter voluntary military service (as in Sweden, Finland, Switzerland) or professional units.

According to the recent trend in military education, most European countries are moving from divergent model of officers' education into a more convergent one.[6] For example, there are many new courses in military education that reflect the military's new tasks and missions, such as political science, international law, anthropology, and foreign languages, all of which help officers adapt to the requirements of peace support operations. The tendency to change the profession of officer into an occupation comparable to a civilian one initiates the process of deprofessionalization or deinstitutionalization.[7] Convergent systems of military education are among the most important defense reforms of postsocialist countries.

Another inevitable change in the officers' corps of postsocialist countries concerns the political neutrality of military professionals, a transitional characteristic that shows the change in officers devoted to (and controlled by) one party to officers able to serve under different political parties. However, it is impossible to stop people from thinking politically. Political engagement is a human right, suspended because of their military job. Official exclusion from political practice gives the impression that officers are public servants.

Since the end of the Cold War, postsocialist and other countries have been exposed to rapid decreases in manpower. The decline of mass armies in Europe initiated the debate on how and whether to continue compulsory military service, the main basis for mass recruitment. Universal compulsory military service has changed to selective after recognizing conscientious objectors and medical dropouts. Due to inequality in burden sharing among members of the young population, the debate on suspending obligatory military service is inevitable in postsocialist countries.

THE INTERNATIONAL ENVIRONMENT EXPECTS TRANSPARENCY IN THE DEFENSE SECTOR

All postsocialist countries are exposed to extensive defense reforms due to their international cooperation and negotiations for membership in security and political alliances. In the process of approaching NATO and the EU, countries take on many new security obligations, especially regarding standardization of their systems according to NATO standards, and active participation in international peace support operations under the UN or other organizations. Participation in international missions, exercises, training, and multilateral military settings is bringing about international control over the armed forces.

ENDNOTES

1. C. Bennett, *Yugoslavia's Bloody Collapse: Causes, Course and Consequences*, London: Hurst & Company, 1995.

2. The terms, "social and functional imperative," describe society's expectations regarding the tasks of the armed forces, where the social imperative concerns the social, traditional, and historical tasks of the military within society, and the functional imperative describes expectations relating to the military security of a country. The terms were introduced by S. P. Huntington (*The Soldier and the State. The Theory and Practice of Civil-Military Relations*, Cambridge: Belknap Press, 1957, cit. 1995).

3. K. W. Haltiner, "The Definite End of the Mass Army in Western Europe?" *Armed Forces and Society*, 25 (1998): 7–36.

4. C. C. Moskos and F. R. Wood, *The Military More than Just a Job?* Pergamon-Brassey, 1988.

5. G. Caforio, *The European Officer: A Comparative View on Selection and Education*, Pisa: Edizioni ETS, 2000.

6. Ibid.

7. Moskos and Wood, op cit.

CHAPTER EIGHT

Defense Reform in Turkey

Ali L. Karaosmanoğlu and Mustafa Kibaroğlu

Turkey has been a member of the North Atlantic Treaty Organization (NATO) since 1952. During the Cold War, its armed forces were geared to play a significant role in defense of the Western alliance according to NATO's military doctrine and strategy. As a long-standing NATO ally, Turkey is not facing any serious problems today regarding standardization, interoperability, or military infrastructure. Apart from its NATO obligations, Ankara has maintained its regional perspective on security problems.

In the post-Cold War era, NATO assumed new responsibilities such as peace support operations in addition to its original collective defense function. The strategic environment around Turkey has changed completely: The Soviet threat has faded away, and new security challenges such as separatism, irredentism, terrorism, threats to energy security, and proliferation of weapons of mass destruction have emerged. While its firm commitment to collective defense continues, Turkey has had to adapt its security and defense policy and its armed forces to the changing regional strategic setting as well as to the Atlantic Alliance's new functions. Because of its regional geopolitics, Turkey has somewhat a distinctive position within the Alliance. The Turkish Armed Forces (TAF), therefore, planned and carried out reforms with a view to maintaining the capability to operate either in tandem with the allied countries or alone.

The TAF's reform and modernization program has been successful to a considerable extent, despite economic difficulties, poor research and development (R&D), and continuation of the conscription system. One intractable problem, however, has been the military's paradoxical role in politics. This issue has come to the forefront recently as a result of

Turkey's European Union (EU) candidacy. Turkey also needs more transparency in its defense budgeting. The unsatisfactory level of democratic control over the military, however, is a result, not only of the assertiveness of the military, but also, and probably more important, from the general circumstances of Turkish politics. Nevertheless, some progress has been recorded recently in this field, too.

Changing Security Environment

During the Cold War, NATO doctrine focused on the central front as the main area of the Soviet-Warsaw Pact threat. The contingency of a massive attack through Germany into Western Europe was the fundamental assumption. Turkey's potential contribution in the event of such a contingency was important. The Turkish army, the largest in NATO after that of the United States, tied down approximately thirty Warsaw Pact divisions. Without Turkish alignment, the Soviets would have been able to concentrate more massively against the central front. Second, Turkish membership in NATO exposed vast areas in the Soviet Union to Western monitoring. Third, Turkey and the Alliance controlled the Straits and the Aegean passages. Turkey's neutralization (followed by that of Greece) would shift NATO's defensive line in the Mediterranean back to Italy and to the line from Sicily to Cape Bon, further complicating the Western defense posture in Europe.

In time of war, Turkey would have to engage the Soviet-Warsaw Pact forces in two theaters, the Thrace-Straits area and eastern Turkey, where it shared a 610-kilometer common border with the Soviet Union. Only in the Finnmark area of northern Norway did another NATO ally share a frontier with the Soviet Union. Turkey was the only NATO member facing the Warsaw Pact threat from two opposing directions. In return for these risks and its contribution to the European balance of military forces, Ankara enjoyed NATO's collective defense commitment and received military and economic assistance, primarily from the United States and, to a much lesser extent, Germany. Moreover, NATO greatly contributed to modernization of Turkey's military infrastructure.[1]

After the Cold War, this strategic arrangement ceased to satisfy the requirements of the new era. As a result of the disappearance of the Soviet Union, the center of gravity of security challenges shifted from the central front to NATO's southern region. The collapse of the communist system reopened the Pandora's box of old and relatively new conflicts.

The proliferation of weapons of mass destruction (WMD), terrorist activities, and proliferation of substate entities and paramilitary groups within states added to the feeling of insecurity and uncertainty in the region. Regional instabilities and opportunities led to a new perspective in Ankara's foreign and security policy, encouraging it to assume a relatively active role in the Balkans, the Black Sea basin, the Caucasus, Central Asia, and the Middle East.

The most drastic change, however, has been the demise of the Soviet threat. The most striking outcome of this development was that, for the first time in the four-century-old history of Turco-Russian rivalry, the two nations were geographically separated by the emergence of new independent states. Dissolution of common borders with the Russian power contributed greatly to Turkish security. Moreover, conventional force reductions that were achieved with the Conventional Forces in Europe (CFE) Treaty improved the disproportionate situation between the two states in the area. The radical change in the strategic environment encouraged both states to exploit the vast opportunities that exist for mutual economic relations. The most recent development in Turkish-Russian rapprochement is the "Action Plan" on cooperation in Eurasian affairs that was signed by the two states on 16 November 2001 in New York. The document, entitled "From Bilateral Cooperation to Multidimensional Partnership," stresses that the two countries are determined to move their existing relations into an enhanced partnership in every area from the Balkans to the Middle East.

Similarly, Ankara also has developed close cooperative relationships with Bulgaria, Romania, Moldova, Ukraine, Georgia, and Azerbaijan. Turkey, in pursuance of NATO's Partnership for Peace (PfP) objectives, has carried out special military training and educational programs and contributed to the improvement of military infrastructure in Azerbaijan and Georgia. Through initiation of the Black Sea Economic Cooperation scheme in 1992, Turkey added a regional multilateral dimension to its efforts at bilateral cooperation. However, while the Karabagh dispute remains unsettled, and 20 percent of Azerbaijan's territory is under Armenia's occupation, a Turkish-Armenian rapprochement does not seem possible in the near future.

Despite the recent dissipation of tension between Greece and Turkey, the Aegean and Cyprus disputes continue to spoil relations between these two NATO allies. Nevertheless, thanks to their NATO membership and the crisis-management skills they have developed over their years of rivalry, tensions and occasional crises in the Aegean and Cyprus have been prevented from escalating to war. Under the present conditions, a war between Turkey and Greece seems unlikely.

Turkey's joining the coalition against Saddam Hussein's regime has underlined its importance in maintaining regional security and stability. In the aftermath of the Gulf War, however, the demise of the Iraqi central authority north of the thirty-sixth parallel complicated Turkey's security considerations. The region became a sanctuary for the *Partiya Karkaren Kurdistan* (Kurdistan Workers Party [PKK]) terrorists, who began to operate from northern Iraq against military and civilian targets inside Turkey. On the other hand, during the first days of the Gulf War, Turkey was confronted with the threat of mass migration of more than five hundred thousand Iraqi Kurds, who crossed the Turkish border to escape from Saddam Hussein's regime. Ankara averted this major problem with the help of the allied humanitarian operation, "Provide Comfort," which ensured the fleeing Kurdish population's safe return to their homes in northern Iraq. Furthermore, Syria's active support of the PKK also constituted a serious security challenge for Turkey until 1998, when Syria gave up its support under Turkish military pressure.

As a consequence of these developments and the PKK terrorism in the region, military planners in Ankara shifted their attention from Turkey's northern borders to the southern and eastern borders with Syria, Iraq, and Iran, and redeployed the military units accordingly. In less than a decade, Turkey's troop deployments in the region increased almost five-fold, from about sixty thousand infantry and *gendarmerie* troops in the early 1990s. In addition to the numerical increase, the quality of the troops, including special forces, also improved. Moreover, new equipment, such as light and heavy artillery, armored vehicles, and attack helicopters, was sent to the region, enabling the military to wage cross-border operations in northern Iraq. These deployments have been possible due to the fact that the CFE Treaty does not cover southeastern Turkey, an exceptional arrangement that has increased Ankara's freedom of action in the area (see Figure 1 and Table 1).

Defense Policy and Strategy

Currently, Turkey's defense policy objectives can be summarized as (1) protection of political independence and territorial integrity of the country, including the secular regime of the Republic, and (2) contribut-

Figure 1

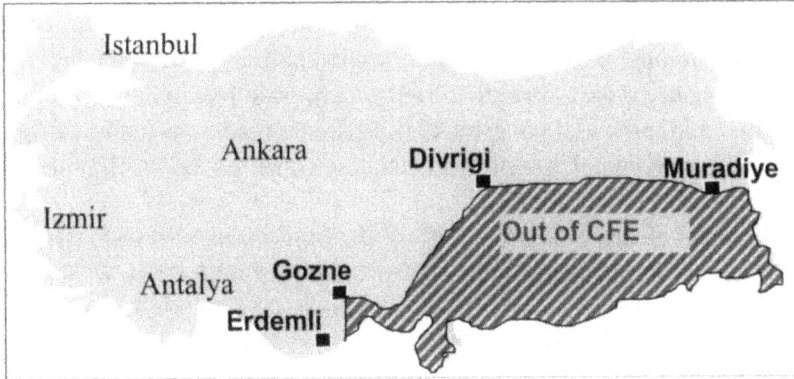

TABLE 1
Turkey's Conventional Weapons Arsenal in Five Categories
as Limited by the CFE Treaty

	Main Battle Tank	Armored Personnel Carrier	Artillery	Attack Hellcopter	Combat Aircraft	Personnel
1993	3,234	1,862	3,210	11	355	575,045
1996	2,608	2,450	3,102	20	383	525,000
1999	2,690	2,552	3,101	26	354	525,000
2001	2,478	2,996	2,953	28	352	515,380
CFE Ceiling	2,795	3,120	3,523	150	750	530,000
Total[1]	4,591[2]	4,558[3]	10,257[4]	37	470[5]	551,000[6]

[1] The total number of weapons categories includes those weapons deployed abroad, mainly in the Turkish Republic of Northern Cyprus (TRNC). See *The Military Balance: 2001–2002*, The International Institute for Strategic Studies, London: Oxford University Press, , 2001, pp. 73–75.

[2] Out of this total number of main battle tanks, including 386 of Mustafa Kemal-48A5 type deployed in the TRNC, thirteen hundred of Mustafa Kemal-48 A5T1/T2 types reportedly are stored; *The Military Balance: 2001–2002*, p. 73.

[3] Including 265 armored personnel carriers of Mustafa Kemal-113, 211 types that are deployed in the TRNC; *The Military Balance: 2001–2002*, p. 75.

[4] Including 612 artillery of different types (plus eighty-one mm) deployed in the TRNC; *The Military Balance: 2001–2002*, p. 75.

[5] Including 4 F-16 C type aircraft that are in Yugoslavia; *The Military Balance: 2001–2002*, p. 75.

[6] Including thirty-six thousand troops deployed in the TRNC; *The Military Balance: 2001–2002*, p. 75.

ing to the creation of a favorable international and regional milieu of security and stability. It should be stressed that these two objectives comprise not only international tasks, but also a fairly broad internal mission that is examined briefly in a separate section of this paper. Moreover, the defense policy does not confine itself to a narrow mission of protecting frontier and territorial integrity. It also assumes the responsibility of contributing to regional security and stability, which became a clear policy objective after the Cold War.

In terms of the *White Book 2000* of the Ministry of National Defense, defense policy objectives are pursued through a military strategy that consists of deterrence, forward defense, military contribution to crisis management and intervention in crises, and collective security/defense.

DETERRENCE AND FORWARD DEFENSE

The *White Book 2000* states, "maintaining a military force that will provide a deterrent influence on the centers of risk and threat in the environment of instability and uncertainty surrounding Turkey constitutes the foundation of the national military strategy."[2] For deterrence, Turkey relies not only on NATO, but also on its own capabilities to balance other powers in the region.

Turkey's defense strategy no longer is confined to mere deterrence, however; it also consists of eliminating imminent threats stemming from the region in general. This forward defense strategy requires preparation to preempt threats before they cross into Turkish territory. The modernization program and reform are geared to provide the Turkish Armed Forces with such capability. For this purpose, the recent procurement of seven KC-135 tanker aircraft has extended the range of the 223 F-16 fighters considerably, enabling the air force to carry out missions abroad. The air force also has increased its lift capability by establishing five transport squadrons with C-130, C-160, CN-235, and CN 235 aircraft. Current plans for the purchase of airborne early warning and control (AEW-C) aircraft will enhance the effectiveness of Turkish air power further.[3]

The Turkish navy also is being modernized in conformity with its new missions, necessitated by the changing circumstances of the post-Cold War era. Modernization efforts are transforming the Turkish navy from a coastal one to a blue water navy that can operate effectively in the Mediterranean and Black Seas with comparatively enhanced capabilities of mobility and power projection. Apart from its wartime missions, such as strategic deterrence, sea control, and participation in allied or coalition operations, the navy's peacetime missions can be summarized as follows: maintaining deterrence through its presence and exercises in the adjacent seas; control and protection of the sea lanes of communication (SLOCs) refugee control; humanitarian aid; search and rescue; environmental protection; and operations against terrorism and organized crime.

Due to its high degree of maneuverability and advanced communication and other electronic capabilities, the navy is regarded as a very useful instrument of crisis management, in that it allows sufficient time and flexibility to political and military decision makers. The Turkish and, indeed the Greek, navy's crisis-management capabilities were conspicuously observable during the Kardak/Imia crisis in the Aegean Sea in 1996. Both governments wisely kept their respective air forces standing by, and relied on their navies instead. This provided them with a high degree of flexibility and the possibility of communication facilitating de-escalation of the crisis.

The blue water component of the Turkish navy has become more and more visible through the gradual procurement of modern frigates, patrol craft, submarines, auxiliaries, and naval air assets. This process has gained momentum during the last decade.

The navy, which initially had defensive littoral warfare capabilities, acquired, after 1950, some antisubmarine warfare (ASW) capabilities and submarines. After 1970, it added guided missile patrol boats and more submarines to its inventory. During the same period, the navy's strength increased by procuring naval aviation, landing craft, and ships. The aim of the ongoing modernization program is to renew existing forces, strike a balance between forces and force multipliers, and improve integrated surveillance and reconnaissance capability with modern command, control, communication, and intelligence (C3I) links.[4]

In the words of the commander of the Turkish Land Forces, "The land forces have emerged as the highest priority power."[5] Although a number of changes are being made in the force structure of the land forces, the main organizational structure that depends on numerous combat brigades and corps is being maintained. However, the Land Forces Command is taking steps to decrease operating and maintenance costs without reducing the effectiveness of the military power. To use resources more efficiently and, at the same time, to keep the effectiveness of the military force, it is deemed necessary to increase intratheater mobility by having "centrally deployed troops which will be used in every region" and "equipped with high-tech weapons and systems." Another change considered indispensable for reducing the size of the forces is improving command and control, reconnaissance, surveillance, and communications through introduction of more information-age technologies.[6]

These reforms, however, would require a new personnel policy aimed at creating a more professional army. Although, at present, the Turkish armed forces have a mixed system, with professional officers, noncommissioned officers (NCOs), and civilian employees combined with a conscription system applied to reserve officers and enlisted soldiers, the General Staff (TGS) is conducting studies for a transition to a more professional army. The personnel reform will begin with professionalization of all the officer cadres by filling them completely with professional contract personnel and abolishing the reserve officer system based on conscription.[7]

The Land Forces Personnel Directorate recently established a Human Resources Selection and Evaluation Center Command to recruit high-quality personnel by using modern scientific testing and evaluation methods. Another step taken by the Land Forces to improve the skills of young officers has been to send them to civilian universities for graduate studies in such fields as management, engineering, international relations, and finance. This has been considered to be an additional method useful to meet the requirements not easily met through a military school education. This practice is an initial step taken to reduce the military's monopoly on military education.

Nevertheless, the Land Forces Command is in favor of a phased and slow transition to a fully professional army. They argue that the economic and demographic conditions of the country, as well as the multiplicity of threats and the country's strategic location, do not allow a rapid abolition of the conscription system (see Figure 1). They also emphasize that the country's manpower sources provide the armed forces with a great advantage by enabling them to recruit sufficient numbers of soldiers in line with changing military circumstances. These views seem to be approved by the TGS.[8]

COUNTERING THE THREAT OF WEAPONS OF MASS DESTRUCTION

Whereas the end of the Cold War created a sense of relief from the danger of nuclear catastrophe, the threat of worldwide proliferation of nuclear, biological, and chemical (NBC) weapons, and ballistic missiles as their delivery vehicles, soon eradicated hope for a more stable and peaceful world order. Unlike the bipolar international system, where the threat of nuclear annihilation was menacing, but stability could be maintained thanks to nuclear deterrence, the post-Cold War era is characterized by highly destabilizing factors, such as the emergence of state and nonstate actors (that is, terrorist and militia groups, cults, etc.) with strong ambitions to acquire weapons of mass destruction (WMD).

Turkey neighbors a number of such states (and other entities), namely Iran, Iraq, and Syria, that are believed to have chemical and biological weapons stockpiles and are doing serious work on nuclear weapons. Turkey is also within range of delivery vehicles (ballistic missiles) deployed in these neighboring countries. One might expect that, in the face of such a threat, Turkey would embark on a crash program to develop its own WMD capability. Nevertheless, relying on NBC weapons development as an effective deterrent or countermeasure is, as has always been the case, out of the question for Turkey. Rather, Turkey has pursued a policy of becoming a state party to international nonproliferation agreements seeking to curb the spread of mass destruction weapons and their delivery vehicles.[9] Turkey fulfills with great care its liabilities stemming from such international documents as the Nuclear Non-Proliferation Treaty (NPT), the Chemical Weapons Convention (CWC), the Biological and Toxin Weapons Convention (BTWC), and the Comprehensive Test Ban Treaty (CTBT).[10] One particular reason for Turkey to give its utmost support to international efforts to strengthen existing international nonproliferation regimes is the widespread belief among the Turkish security elite that effective verification mechanisms of NBC nonproliferation treaties might create serious impediments to aspiring states in their engagements with WMD development and, thus, might provide strong assurances to Turkey in its relations with its neighbors. This expectation has not been fulfilled, however.

Thus, to counter the threat posed by its Middle Eastern neighbors, Turkey believes it has a number of advantages. First, it has long relied on the positive security assurances provided by the Atlantic Alliance. NATO's deterrent is still considered by Turkey to be effective with respect to the threat posed by neighboring NBC-capable states. Second, Turkey relies on a forward defense strategy (the land-air doctrine) that is believed to provide enough credibility to deter even unconventional armed attacks from its neighbors.

As such, during the second half of 1990s, the Turkish military became capable of launching overnight a comprehensive land operation with the involvement of around fifty thousand fully equipped troops. Added to this, its air power capability can provide troops on the ground with close air support. Early warning and refueling aircraft that are being added to the Turkish air force increase both the range and operational capability of combat aircraft involved in operations. Hence, the overall operational capability of ground forces, combined with the air units, is considered to give Turkey the capability to invade parts of the territory of the enemy, if need be, in a very short time. What needs to be done at this stage is quantitative and qualitative improvement of the technical passive defense equipment and protective gear needed to counter a possible chemical and biological attack. Necessary measures are being taken in this respect. Thus, the invasion capability of Turkey in retaliation is believed to constitute a credible deterrent against any of its southern neighbors that may contemplate attacking it with WMD.

Furthermore, its comprehensive cooperation in the field of military relations with Israel and the United States provides Turkey with the opportunity to create a missile shield in its territory. Relations between Turkey and Israel are improving, especially since the upgrading of diplomatic relations on both sides that followed Israel's peace initiatives with the Palestinian Liberation Organization (PLO) and Jordan in late 1995 and beyond.[11] Furthermore, Turkish-Israeli relations entered a new phase with the military cooperation agreement signed in 1996 and have improved much since then. The text of the agreement apparently includes clauses for improving bilateral military cooperation. For instance, Israeli military aircraft are allowed to overfly Turkish territory for training. And Israel, on the other hand, agreed to upgrade fifty-four Turkish F-4 class military aircraft and to provide the Turkish air force with electronic warfare equipment. The significance of the military cooperation agreement between Turkey and Israel goes beyond these usual transactions and reflects a new element of power politics in the Middle East.

The U.S. proposal to establish a "missile shield" in the eastern districts of Turkey at the bilateral level or in the NATO framework, or at trilateral level with the inclusion of Israel, may be seen as an indicator of an emerging defense bloc among the three countries. Although too early to identify their arrangement as a formal pact, Turkey, Israel, and the United States may join forces to counter the threat of ballistic missiles that may be tipped with WMD warheads. The military exercise, "Anatolian Eagle," that took place in central Anatolia in early July 2001 with the participation of air force units of Turkey, Israel, and the United States and the air defense systems of these countries, simulated defense and combat operations against a comprehensive attack from the air.[12] Furthermore, the Council of Ministers recently decided to purchase Israeli cruise missiles (Popeye II) with a range of two hundred kilometers.[13]

This advanced military cooperation among Turkey, the United States, and Israel seems to be contrary to what Turkey pursued during the Cold War: not to get involved in U.S. plans designed specifically to back up Israel. However, the threat of WMD and ballistic missiles is becoming an issue of common concern, and it is quite normal for the Turkish security elite to seek a reliable defense posture and a credible deterrent beyond merely the NATO context.[14]

The U.S. National Missile Defense (NMD) and NATO's Theater Missile Defense (TMD) projects could offer another option for a joint missile defense. Deploying ground-, sea-, and air-based boost phase intercept systems in the country could develop a missile defense architecture for Turkey. Turkey's participation in such a defensive system would satisfy, to a great extent, Ankara's security needs stemming from the proliferation of WMDs and missiles. The boost phase systems should be less threatening to Russia, because their range would not be sufficient to intercept Russian missile launches in their boost phase.[15] Although neither Washington nor Ankara has made a decision about this issue, Turkish defense experts have begun to consider this option seriously, which would be practicable if the U.S. (and NATO's) conception of ballistic missile defense and Turkey's missile defense architecture should complement each other.[16]

PEACE SUPPORT OPERATIONS

After the Cold War, Turkish Armed Forces began to pay particular attention to regional cooperative security and peace support operations, including diverse missions, ranging from peacekeeping to peace enforcement, depending on the consent of the parties concerned. Turkey actively participated in peace support operations in Somalia and the Balkans and has contributed to various peace observation missions. The Turkish Land Forces (TLF) were assigned to the United Nations Protection Force (UNPROFOR) in Bosnia at the brigade level. In December 1995, the TLF were assigned to Stabilization Force (SFOR). The navy participated in "Operation Sharp Guard" in the Adriatic, whose mission was to monitor and impose an arms embargo on the former Yugoslavia. In April 1993, the air force joined NATO's "Operation Deny Flight" with an F-16squadron operating from Italy's Ghedi air base to enforce the no-flight zone over Bosnia and protect "safe areas." During the Kosovo crisis, Ankara contributed a mechanized infantry battalion as well as headquarters personnel to Kosovo Force (KFOR). Moreover, three Special Operations teams were sent to Kosovo to join the Hostage Rescue Force. An F-16 squadron also was assigned to NATO's "Operation Allied Force" in Kosovo.[17]

Although Turkey, as a non-EU NATO ally, cannot participate fully in the decision-making process of the European Security and Defense Policy (ESDP), it has informed the EU of its readiness to contribute to the Headline Goal, a unit at the level of a brigade supported by a sufficient number of air force and navy units.

Turkey's interest in cooperative security extends from participation in peace support operations to initiation of regional security arrangements. It assumed a leading role in the formation of the Southeastern Europe Multinational Peace Force (SEEBRIG) and the Black Sea Naval Cooperation Task Group (BLACKSEAFOR). Turkey also contributes to NATO's PfP programs enthusiastically, participates in PfP's military and naval exercises in the region, and has established a PfP Training Center in Ankara.

Peace support operations are usually manpower-intensive and require diverse skills and special military training for units and individual soldiers. Since TAF are composed primarily of conscripts who serve for only eighteen months, troops assigned to peace support operations are trained specifically for that purpose. Training programs aim to improve not only their combat skills but also their abilities in public relations and to contribute to public order and security.[18] Peace operation troops are selected mainly from among the candidates who can speak foreign languages.

For the purpose of facilitating its adaptation and contribution to peace support operations, the TAF created new institutions in its own organization. Peace missions were assigned to the Third Corps and the Twenty-Eighth Mechanized Brigade, and the TGS and each of the three services (land, navy, and air) established "Peacekeeping Departments."

CIVIL-MILITARY RELATIONS

Civil-military relations have been one of the most intractable issues in Turkey's process of democratization. Turkey's candidacy for the EU has focused European attention on the political role of the military. Another contradiction arises from NATO's new orientation and mission in the post-Cold War era. There is a widely accepted view among NATO members that the function of the PfP is to orient its participants toward the core democratic values of the Atlantic Alliance. Turkey is active in PfP programs and opened a PfP Training Center in Ankara. Moreover, Turkey's membership in NATO and other Western alliances, together with its intercultural characteristics, put it in a unique position to project Western values to the newly independent states. Its democratic deficits, however, complicate its role and ambitions. Therefore, the issue of civil-military relations deserves attention while the limits of military interference with politics require elucidation.

Since the eighteenth century, the military has been the prime Westernizer. Today, it considers itself to be the guardian of the state, established and maintained according to Atatürk's republican and secularist principles. In other words, the task of the TAF is to protect the political and territorial integrity of the state as well as its secular character, not only against external threats but also against its internal enemies. In the military's eyes, there are two main internal enemies: the militant Islamic movements that threaten the secular character of the state and the separatist movement, represented by the PKK, which constitutes a threat to the territorial integrity. The military, however, carefully distinguishes the majority of Turkey's Kurdish citizens from the PKK, which is regarded as a terrorist organization.[19]

Since the 1980s, when the separatist PKK launched its terrorist attacks primarily in the southeastern districts of Turkey, which soon coupled with deeply rooted militant Islamic movements, the military assigned top priority to these threats from within. Motivated by a determination to protect territorial integrity and the republican regime, the military launched a campaign that also incorporated elements of psychological warfare aimed to secure as much popular support as possible. These included the indoctrination of the public, using in particular, the elements of media communication. This has resulted in the involvement of the military in almost all aspects of life in Turkey. During this period, which lasted about a decade until the mid-1990s, there was not much room to discuss, let alone to criticize, the role of the "saviors" of the country. Nor was there a pressing demand for such criticism from large segments of society who have displayed an equal sensitivity to protecting the territorial integrity and the regime.

Toward the late 1980s, and especially the early 1990s, when the PKK benefited from the geopolitical developments in northern Iraq, which turned out to be a sanctuary for them and, thus, enabled them to intensify their attacks, morale was considerably low among most Turkish citizens because the military was not perceived as being adequately prepared to fight guerilla warfare with its classical force deployment, war tactics, and classical weapons arsenal. In the mid-1990s, the military made a radical decision to reorganize its force structure and procure adequate weaponry with higher mobility and greater firepower, such as attack helicopters, light artillery, and armored personnel carriers, as well as high-tech equipment of all sorts, from thermal cameras to global surveillance and intelligence systems, all of which have proved to be highly effective in tracking down and destroying terrorist groups. The struggle against the PKK has provided the TAF with valuable training in low-intensity conflicts. These events, together with the successful military pressure that forced the Syrian regime in 1998 to expel PKK leader Öcalan from Syria, underlined, in the eyes of the Turkish public, the utility of military power in fighting against terrorism. This perception must have been strengthened even further by the recent war in Afghanistan.

Winning the war against the separatists, in the second half of the 1990s, permitted the military to shift its focus to religious extremists on all fronts, from small cells of Hizbullah militants in the countryside to politicians who were claimed to be their masterminds. Only after eliminating the danger of widespread terrorism, external threats, such as proliferation of weapons of mass destruction and ballistic missiles capabilities in neighboring countries, entered the agenda of the National Security Council as high-priority items of immediate concern. More serious consideration of such threats started to pull the military, albeit slowly, toward its principal role of defending the regime and territorial integrity against outside threats.

Having put its house in order, and having acquired such state-of-the-art military assets as Airborne Warning and Control System (AWACS) and refueling aircraft, which empowered the already agile air force, the military showed an unprecedented interest in developments on its periphery, namely the Balkans, the Caucasus, and the Middle East, and contributed significantly to peace-making and peacekeeping operations in these and other regions. Hence, undergoing a modernization process in its weaponry and reorganizing its command and control structure and force deployment to meet challenges from inside and outside the country made the Turkish military less dependent on old-fashioned psychological warfare against the "internal enemy," which in the past had augmented its role and thus its weight in domestic politics.

The Turkish military, contrary to most of the armed forces in the Third World, has a "refined concept of autonomy," by which it controls politicians through constitutional mechanisms.[20] This reflects a certain intention not to undermine the democratic regime by usurping civilian authority. The military also has considerable public prestige; it enjoys the support of the vast majority of the population, including the media, particularly in its struggle against terrorism, separatism, and Islamic extremism.

The Turkish legal system specifically charged the armed forces with responsibility for defending not only the country but also the political regime as defined in the Constitution. The first three articles of Turkey's Constitution define the characteristics of the Turkish state. They are irrevocable, and amendments to them cannot even be proposed. Article 1 stipulates that the Turkish state is a "republic." Article 2 provides that "The Republic of Turkey is a democratic, secular and social state governed by the rule of law. . . ." Article 3 declares that the Turkish state, with its territory and nation, is an indivisible entity. Its language is Turkish. The Turkish Armed Forces Internal Service Law requires the military to assume the duty of protecting and preserving . . . the Turkish republic as defined in the constitution. The Turkish Armed Forces Internal Service Directive, more explicitly, refers to the protection of "the republic, by arms when necessary, against internal and external threats."[21] Another constitutional mechanism through which the military exercises its influence on political decisions is the National Security Council.

In terms of the Constitution, the Turkish General Staff (TGS) is subordinated unequivocally to the Grand National Assembly (Parliament), the President, and the Prime Minister. The Constitution stipulates that "The Chief of the General Staff shall be appointed by the President of the Republic on the proposal of the Council of Ministers; his duties and powers shall be regulated by law. The Chief of the General Staff shall be responsible to the Prime Minister in the exercise of his duties and powers." The Ministry of National Defense, however, has equal status with the TGS. The Minister of National Defense is usually a civilian, a political figure from the political party in power. Both are subordinated to the Prime Minister; they only coordinate and divide labor between them, without any hierarchical order. The Ministry of National Defense is responsible for carrying out the legal, social, financial, and budget services of the national defense functions as well as the conscription system. This arrangement diverges from the practice of the allied countries, where the chiefs of the general staff usually are subordinate to the ministers of defense.

Although the military usually is encouraged by the public and existing constitutional and other legal arrangements to maintain its guardianship over the republican order, there is a widespread desire for further democratization on the part of the public. Turkey is facing considerable pressure from its Western allies for greater democratization as well. In this context, European leverage has increased since Turkey's acceptance as a candidate for EU membership at the Helsinki Summit of December 1999. Traditionally the leading promoter of Turkey's Western admiration, the armed forces cannot remain insensitive to Western democratization views.

Important developments have taken place recently in this regard. A prominent improvement was constituted by the exclusion of military judges and prosecutors from the State Security Courts. Former President Süleyman Demirel approved the revision by declaring that Parliament had rid the country of one of its greatest burdens.[22] Another improvement had to do with the composition and powers of the National Security Council (NSC). In September 2001, the Parliament modified thirty-four articles of the Constitution to adapt them to the Copenhagen Criteria of the EU. Under these amendments, Parliament changed the composition of the NSC by increasing the number of civilian members and reduced the NSC's recommendation powers. At present, the NSC has eight civilian and five military members. As for its powers, the word, "decision," in the old text was replaced with "recommendation," and the sentence, "The Council of Ministers shall give priority consideration to the decisions of the NSC . . .," in the previous text was replaced with "the Council of Ministers shall evaluate the recommendations of the NSC. . . ."

Although the military still plays a significant role in political decisions concerning maintenance of territorial integrity and the secular character of the republican regime, its influence on politics has certain boundaries. Furthermore, limitations imposed on the military's political role tend to be gradually more effective. The present trend reflects the military's slow withdrawal from the political scene. As a student of the Turkish military pertinently points out, "the role of the military in Turkey is the result of a combination of context and circumstance, a symptom rather than a cause of the failure of parliamentary democracy in Turkey to provide stability, prosperity or good governance."[23] It would not be wrong to argue that, under strong and stable single-party governments, the military's political influence will be curtailed considerably.

It is worthy to note that there are deeper reasons for the military's ongoing gradual disengagement from politics. First, in the contemporary era, democratization cannot be disintegrated from Westernization. As the prime agent of Westernization, the military has been increasingly mindful of this historical development since the end of World War II. Second, the military knows, from experience, that its involvement in politics leads to an erosion of its officer core's professionalism as well as a loss of their prestige, particularly among their colleagues abroad. Third, there is growing pressure for further democratization from public opinion and the liberal media, despite the fact that, according to public opinion surveys, the TAF are viewed by an overwhelming majority of the population (more than 80 percent) as the most reliable institution in the country. Finally, Turkey's institutional integration with the West, which began after World War II, has gained a new dimension as a result of the country's EU candidacy. EU membership is promoting further democratization, which is expected to reduce the role of the military in politics gradually.[24]

BUDGET AND DEFENSE EXPENDITURE

Defense expenditures and resources are determined within the framework of the planning, programming, and budgeting system, which generally functions quite effectively. The government assumes responsibility not only for preparing the military budget, but also for controlling payments and contracts by means of the Ministry of Finance. In addition to government control, the auditors of the Court of Public Accounts audit on behalf of Parliament the proper use of all of the items of the central government's consolidated budget to ensure that they are used in accordance with the Budget Law. This political and bureaucratic supervision over preparation and implementation of the military budget, however, does not necessarily mean that parliamentary oversight functions adequately.

The resources of defense expenses are composed of the following items (see Table 2):

- allocated resources of the National Defense Budget;
- resources from the Defense Industry Support Fund (DISF);
- resources from the Turkish Armed Forces Strengthening Foundation (TAFSF);
- budgets of the *Gendarmerie* General Command and the Coast Guard Command;
- foreign state and company loans repaid from the budget of the Undersecretariat of the Treasury (U.S. Foreign Military Sales [FMS] credits were reduced gradually in the 1990s and finally halted in 1999; NATO infrastructure funding continues); and
- revenues based on the special laws of the Ministry of National Defense.

The budget of the Ministry of National Defense (MND) constitutes the most important portion of the resources allocated to defense. The MND budget is distributed to the forces and organizations as follows:[25]

Land Forces	49.3 percent
Air Forces	21.9 percent
Naval Forces	14.4 percent
MND (organization)	7.2 percent
TGS (organization)	7.1 percent

TABLE 2

Resources Allocated to the Turkish Armed Forces (US$ million)

	National Resources					Other Resources			
Years	MND Budget	TAF DF Budget	DIS Fund	Special Allocations	Total (TL)	FMS Loans	NATO ENF Fund	State Company Loans	Total
1995	3,341.8	10.7	826.8	76.5	4,225.7	328.5	184.3	186.0	698.8
1996	3,997.9	9.5	887.3	101.7	4,996.4	320.0	161.2	498.4	979.6
1997	4,407.4	11.8	772.4	111.9	5,303.5	175.0	140.3	400.0	715.3
1998	5,327.2	11.4	1,056.9	107.7	6,503.3	150.0	100.0	400.0	650.0
1999	5,968.2	11.2	1,008.7	53.6	7,041.7	—	165.0	400.0	565.0
2000	7,218.0	11.0	1,466.9	65.0	8,760.9	—	180.0	300.0	480.0

Average foreign currency exchange rates of the Turkish Central Bank for the related years were used.

According to *White Paper 2000*, an average of 30 percent of the MND budget is allocated for personnel expenses, 68.9 percent for other current expenses, and the balance for investment and transfer expenses (see Table 3).

According to *White Paper 2000*, the share of the MND budget in the gross national product (GNP) is an average of 2.5 percent and around 9.7 percent of the consolidated budget (see Table 4).

Defense expenditures in Turkey present a number of measurement problems. Within the context of Turkey's highly inflationary financial environment and ongoing revisions introduced into the government's budgetary accounts, measurement of the relative as well as the absolute size of national defense expenditures (and their sources of financing) pose a number of difficult statistical issues, some of which are discussed below.

Overall national defense spending is financed by three major sources : (a) the Central Government Consolidated Budget; (b) various off-budget funds, the most significant of which is the Defense Industry Support Fund; and (c) foreign official and nonofficial resource inflows. In particular, the resource balances of the relevant off-budget funds are not sufficiently transparent.

The initial and end-year budget appropriations may exhibit large differences, because supplementary budgets are introduced in the course of a given year's budget implementation. To the extent possible, actual expenditures should be used for intertemporal assessments.

TABLE 3
Distribution of the Ministry of National Defense 2000 Budget (billion TL)

Main Service Groups	Share of the 2000 Budget	Percentage (percent) Share of the 2000 Budget
Personnel Expenses	1,270,000	30.70
Other Currrent Expenses	2,850,000	68.90
Special Defense Investments	1,523,011	36.82
Consumption Expenses	1,099,046	26.57
Others	227,941	5.51
Investments	3,050	0.07
Transfers	13,450	0.33
Total	4,136,500	100.00

White Paper 2000, p. 109.

TABLE 4
Comparison of the Budget of the Ministry of National Defense with the Gross National Product and the Consolidated Budget (percent million)

Years	Gross National Product	Consolidated Budget	MND Budget	Share of MND Budget in GNP (percent)	Share of Consolidated Budget in GNP (percent)	Share of MND Budget in Consolidated Budget (percent)
1994	130,519.1	27,742.6	2,607.4	2.0	21.3	9.4
1995	171,736.6	29,340.5	3,341.8	1.9	17.1	11.4
1996	184,037.4	43,846.7	3,997.9	2.2	23.8	9.1
1997	190,836.4	41,785.0	4,407.4	2.3	21.9	10.5
1998	188,060.1	56,683.8	5,327.2	2.8	30.1	9.4
1999	186,264.2	64,910.9	5,968.2	3.2	34.8	9.2
2000	205,273.4	81,719.0	7,218.0	3.5	39.8	8.8

The average foreign currency exchange rate of the Turkish Central bank for the related year was taken as the basis.
White Paper 2000, p. 108. In the general budget of 2001, due to the economic crisis, the Ministry of National Defense's share was reduced to US$5.4 billion.

The real and nominal dollar exchange rates do not behave systematically over time. Thus, dollar-based expenditure estimates are not
always meaningful for annual comparisons.

In recent years, the share of interest payments in total budget expenditures has been very high, increasing from 28 percent in 1997 to 43
percent in 2001. In this context, it should be noted that the bulk of
nominal interest payments accounts for the inflationary erosion of
the domestic debt stock, given the very high rates of domestic
inflation. Hence, it might be more meaningful to measure and evaluate the fiscal burden of defense expenditure in relation to the non-
interest budget expenditure and/or tax revenue collected in the
budget implementation.

In the context of the stabilization program supported by the International Monetary Fund (IMF), coverage of the Consolidated Budget
broadened significantly from 1999 on, by incorporating highly frag-
mented off-budget funds that traditionally have operated outside
the budget. This process is likely to continue in the coming years
to ensure a more realistic consolidation of government accounts for
improved financial management and enhanced parliamentary scrutiny. Thus, one may expect a somewhat declining share of defense

in the Central Government's budget in the medium term, barring unexpected international events that may trigger much higher spending for national security.

Finally, one should note that for proper cross-country comparisons, defense expenditures should include budgetary spending by *Gendarmerie*, coast guard, and the Ministry of National Defense. In fact, this is taken into account in the administrative classification of data given in the official budget documents.

Tables 5 and 6 represent an effort to get over measurement difficulties and to reach more reliable indicators.[26]

The Grand National Assembly, without any opposition, or even any serious debate, in the parliamentary committees usually approves defense budgets. The reason for this stems more from a lack of politician interest than the assertiveness of the military. As a rule, Turkish politicians have

TABLE 5
Relative Size of Defense Expenditure, Turkey: 1997–2002

	1997	1998	1999	2000	2002
Central Government Budget Defense Expenditures (percent)					
1. Percent of GNP	3.0	3.0	3.6	3.5	3.5
2. Percent of Total Budget Expenditures	10.9	10.4	10.1	9.5	10.0
3. Percent of Total Budget Noninterest Expenditures	15.2	17.2	16.3	16.9	17.7
4. Percent of Total Budget Revenue	15.1	13.7	16.0	13.2	13.7
5. Percent of Total Budget Tax Revenue	18.5	17.5	19.2	16.7	16.8
Memo items (percent of GNP)					
Additional nonbudget	0.7	0.8	0.8	na	na
Foreign resources (for national defense)	0.5	0.6	0.6	na	na

Note: The estimates are derived from data given in the 2002 Central Government Consolidated Budget document (*Bütçe Gerekçesi*) submitted to Parliament by the Ministry of Finance. The source for the underlying GNP data is the *2002 Annual Program, State Planning Organization* (p. 16). The estimates for additional nonbudget resources are based on *White Book 2000*, Ministry of National Defense (MND). Defense expenditures are the sum of budgetary spending by the MND, *Gendarmerie*, and coast guard. Figures for 2002 are calculated from 2002 program and budget documents.

TABLE 6
GNP, Budget, and Defense Expenditure, Turkey, 1999–2002

	1999	2000	2002[a]
	US$ billion[b]		
Gross National Product (GNP)	187.5	202.1	155.8
Central Government Budget	67.3	75.4	54.5
Total expenditure	41.6	42.6	31.0
Noninterest expenditure	6.8	7.2	5.5
Defense expenditure	n.a.	n.a.	4.6
Central Government Budget	45.0	53.4	40.0
Total revenue	35.4	42.4	32.5
Tax revenue			
Memo item:			
Real GNP Index, 1998 = 100	94	100	95

[a] Official program estimates.
[b] All data are converted to US$ units at the annual average exchange rates.

not professed great interest in involvement in the technicalities of defense policy. They usually take office with no knowledge of military strategy and weapon procurement issues. Thus, in most cases, the advice provided by TGS members plays a determining role. A growth in the role of civilian politicians in defense policy and budgeting then would depend to a great extent on increasing their interest in and knowledge about defense matters and on creating civilian research institutes of defense policy.

DEFENSE INDUSTRY AND PROCUREMENT

In the mid-1980s, the defense industry underwent reform. Until then, cooperation between the private and public sectors remained limited. Most of the plants were owned by the state and run either by the armed forces or by the Machinery and Chemicals Industries Institution, another state enterprise. Factories belonging to the Institution produced a range of relatively low-cost and low-technology weapons and ammunition, including machine guns, mortars, howitzers, and rockets. In addition, the armed forces had naval shipyards and maintenance and overhaul capabilities.

In 1985, the government began to take steps to use the country's industrial base and technical skills more rationally to promote development of the defense industry. The government established the Defense Industry Development and Support Administration (DIDA), whose aim was to promote cooperation between the private and public sectors and to encourage transfer of technology and capital to Turkey. DIDA also administered a Defense Industry Support Fund that generated income through indirect taxes levied on luxury imports, alcohol, and cigarettes. To a considerable extent, financing of the defense industry and joint projects was realized through this fund. This system continues to operate, with a slight modification. The DIDA, which was reorganized in 1989 as the Undersecretariat of the Defense Industry (SSM) and subordinated to the Ministry of Defense, has a separate legal personality and a separate budget of its own, which does not pass through the Parliament and is not audited by the Court of Public Accounts.

The Defense Industry Support Fund, administered by SSM, is a highly flexible mechanism that guarantees a constant flow of financial resources, free from bureaucratic formalities. Since 1986, the Fund has had revenues amounting to US$11 billion. Eighty percent of this amount was spent for domestic production purposes, 16 percent on direct purchases, and 4 percent on advanced technology projects.[27]

Turkey's defense industry policy envisages that defense industrial activities should be open to foreign enterprises as well as domestic firms. It does suggest, however that defense industrial cooperation with foreign countries should not be sensitive to changing political conditions. It also provides that priority be given to the domestic defense industry to provide any equipment and systems that are procured. If procurement from abroad is deemed necessary, priority then should be given to proposals that allow for offset applications that will contribute to domestic industry. The defense industry aims to develop its international market capability and export potential. Moreover, the policy envisages that the defense industry should not limit itself to defense production; it also should acquire the capability to produce for civilian purposes.[28]

Turkey spent a total of US$27.8 billion on defense procurement over the 1988–97 period. In other words, it annually invested approximately US$3 billion in acquisition of equipment and materiel for the armed forces. According to a current plan, it expects to invest more than US$100 billion for the continuing modernization of its armed forces between now and 2030.[29] On the other hand, efforts are underway for collaborative projects with American and European firms. The Turkish-German frigate program is a good example of such bilateral cooperation.

Turkey actively participates in the Independent European Program Group (IEPG), where it has been involved in collaborative projects such as the manufacture of *Stinger* and *Maverick* missiles. Some other joint ventures include those undertaken by Turkish Aerospace Industries (TAI), such as production of *Cougar* helicopters and CASA CN-235 transport aircraft. TAI also will have a 5.5 percent production share in the Airbus Military Company's A400M transport aircraft program. At the invitation of the United States, Turkey began to negotiate for participation in the engineering and manufacturing development stage of the Joint Strike Fighter (JSF) program at a cost of US$800 million. TAF plans to include the new generation JSF to its inventory, replacing its F-16 fleet by 2015.[30]

The most important step taken in developing the defense industry through joint ventures, however, has been the F-16 project with the United States and the creation of TAI in 1984 for that purpose. TAI has produced 278 F-16 jet fighters, forty-six of which have been exported to Egypt, and the rest have joined the Turkish air force. Turkish partners hold 51 percent of the shares in TAI; General Dynamics and General Electric have 49 percent of the shares. Thanks to this project, Turkey's new domestic aircraft industry has made considerable progress in the 1990s, and Turkey has acquired new technology. In addition, it has contributed greatly to improving managerial capabilities that can carry over to the next generation of aircraft production projects.

Defense industry policy has not attained its objectives fully, however; it continues to suffer from serious deficiencies despite the increasing number of collaborative projects. It is particularly weak in R&D work because of the high cost of such activities. The low level of cooperation between Turkish public and private sectors is another important hindrance to "cross-fertilization" of the economy. The Undersecretary of Defense Industries, Prof. Ali Ercan, points to the poor state of R&D as one of the major obstacles preventing further development of defense industries. He underlines the reluctance of advanced countries to transfer the technology of some critical systems. Although this is not an easy problem to overcome, the Undersecretary argues, Turkey could balance this insufficiency by concentrating on areas that require very little equipment transfer, such as developing indigenous software source codes that rely on human resource capacity. An example of such a project is the "mission computer," composed of hardware and software source codes, which is the most crucial part of the attack helicopter (145 AH-IZ King

Cobra) co-production deal with the United States. When the U.S. administration refused to transfer the most critical parts of the mission computer, the SSM concluded an agreement with the Turkish Scientific Research Board to produce it locally. The SSM expects the project to be successful because it depends primarily on human resource capacity.[31]

Nevertheless, Turkey still depends on foreign companies for nearly 60 percent of its main systems requirements. In the electronics industry, local contribution is about 20 percent; in other projects, the proportion increases to 80 percent. In other words, the average local contribution to defense products is around 40 percent. In addition to weak R&D, other obstacles are the insufficiency of raw materials and the general state of the economy, which has been hit by consecutive crises since 1990. Some legal restrictions worsen the economic problem as well. Defense industry funds cannot be converted into U.S. dollars automatically. The revenues are kept at the Central Bank in Turkish liras, whereas SSM spending usually is transacted in foreign currency. Consequently, the Undersecretariat of Defense Industry suffers from considerable losses because of the high inflation rate.[32]

The defense industry has difficulty increasing its exports. Turkey exports approximately 10 percent of its defense industry products, while 90 percent of them go domestically to the TAF and the civilian sector. The SSM finds it difficult to get the offset agreements implemented by foreign companies. So far, the Undersecretariat has signed forty-one offset agreements with joint venture firms; however, only five of those firms have fulfilled their offset pledges. The total amount of offset pledges is US$3.4 billion, but only US$1.64 of that amount has been realized.[33] Nevertheless, offset agreements have paved the way for many Turkish firms to international markets and promoted their business connections with foreign companies. Taking into consideration the benefits of offset agreements, the SSM recently adopted new offset regulations providing more flexibility to the parties to the agreement.

From time to time, some NATO allies have imposed restrictions on their exports to Turkey on the grounds of human rights violations. For that reason, Turkey has made efforts to diversify its suppliers. An example of this policy of diversification is Ankara's signing an agreement with Korea to procure self-propelled howitzer components. Rapidly increasing trade with Russia may include a significant element of defense procurement in the future. Cooperation with Israel also has provided Turkey with a new and valuable source of weapons procurement.

Restrictions have never been a formidable obstacle to the sustainability of modernization efforts; despite efforts to diversify resources; the United States, Germany, and France have remained Turkey's major suppliers.

EXECUTIVE SUMMARY: LESSONS LEARNED

Defense reform has been successful to a great extent because of the absence of civilian opposition to the demands of the military and the sustained political consensus about threats the country has had to counter. Civilian governments also have a share in the reform, not only because of their passive acquiescence, but also because they had the vision to plan and initiate certain radical reforms. The liberalization of the economy in the 1980s by the Özal government had a very positive impact on the defense industry, and it encouraged the public sector to cooperate with private firms. The technological, financial, and managerial resources of the private sector, combined with foreign partnership, facilitated development of the defense industry. The Defense Industry Undersecretariat and the Defense Industry Support Fund were established through the initiative of the same government. More important, as a result of these changes, the growing role of civilian government in exploring joint venture possibilities has rendered the military establishment increasingly dependent on civilian politicians and managers. By the same token, internationalization of the economy and the increasing role of private foreign business in the defense industry have moderated the military's State-focused concept of internal and international politics.

Turkey's somewhat peculiar geostrategic conditions, its excessively unstable regional environment, and its internal conflicts differ radically from those of Central Eastern European countries, with the possible exception of southeastern Europe. While some of Turkey's experiences may be relevant, others do not seem to be applicable to the new members of NATO and the candidate states whose perceptions of threat are far less pressing, and whose primary foreign and security policy objective is to join NATO and the EU.

Turkey's military reform policy has been influenced by two conflicting trends that characterize the present international system. While its NATO membership, EU candidacy, and participation in peace operations are inspiring internationalization, multilateralism, cooperative security, and democratic control of the armed forces, its regional environment is suggesting security through power politics. As a result, Turkey's reform policy has pursued two broad objectives: (1) to improve deterrence capacity against threats emanating from the region by developing a forward defense capability, and (2) to prepare TAF for the new missions of NATO, EU, and other international organizations, namely peace support, peacekeeping, peacemaking, and crisis-management tasks.

These two different currents in the contemporary international system have had a somewhat positive impact on TAF, which has been able to pursue a sustained reform and modernization policy. The process has been carried out in the form of modernization, further professionalization of the officer and NCO cadres, and a very slow reduction in the land forces conscription system; and in the form of modernization only in the naval and air forces that are already highly professionalized by their nature. The reform and modernization process has not required a thorough overhaul of the defense organization. Nevertheless, creation of a number of new institutions within the existing organization has become necessary for sustainable, effective, and flexible implementation of reform policy. One prominent example of such institutions is the SSM. Others examples are the peacekeeping departments that have been established in the TGS and in each of the three armed forces.

Preparation for peace operations requires establishing contacts with international organizations and NGOs and developing the skills to operate in multinational formations. This implies a certain denationalization of defense policy and introduction of a more pluralistic approach to defense planning.

Transparency of military activities, especially concerning budgeting and spending, cannot be improved without parliamentary oversight and nongovernmental examination by the media, academia, and research centers. Parliament and political parties can hardly offer critical views and alternative strategies in an esoteric field such as defense planning if they are not intellectually equipped to do so. The same is equally valid for media and universities. If the political parties wish to contribute to the security and defense policy and increase transparency and civilian control over the military, they should create research institutes and/or encourage existing civilian institutions by funding them to carry out research projects on defense policy. It is also important to include strategic studies programs in university curricula, especially at the graduate level. This would create a resource of defense experts who might offer their services to political parties, parliamentary committees, the media, and research centers. Such a development, however, would require civilian funding. It cannot be initiated unless the civilian sector seriously believes in the necessity of civilian control of the military.

A long-term modernization program should be considered simultaneously with the development of defense industry. It is impossible to consider the defense industry of a country independent of the general state of the economy of that country, however. An unstable economy would constitute the major obstacle for R&D and the growth of defense industry, even if the country in question has adequate human resources. Another retarding factor is undoubtedly the lack of cooperation between the private and public sectors.

No country would transfer state-of-the-art technologies that cost billions of dollars to develop. A country would transfer a technology to another country relatively easily, however, when it has developed a new system to replace the old one. This problem could be eased in two ways. First, R&D should be oriented to systems that do not require raw material or equipment but human resource capacity, provided the country has that capacity. Second, joint ventures with technologically advanced countries would facilitate the transfer of know-how in factory management and production of technologically sophisticated weapon systems.

Financial problems may be overcome to some extent through cooperative projects and offset agreements that promote exports. It may be useful as well to create a defense industry fund separate from the general budget of the government. Such a solution would provide the government with an additional resource and greater flexibility. On the other hand, however, it would decrease transparency and avoid parliamentary oversight.

ENDNOTES

1. Ali L. Karaosmanoğlu, "Europe's Geopolitical Parameters," in S. Togan and V.N. Balasubramanyam (eds.), *Turkey and Eastern European Countries in Transition: Towards Membership of the EU*, London: Palgrave, 2001, pp. 278–79.

2. *White Book 2000*, Ministry of National Defense, p. 36.

3. H. Sönmez Ateşoğlu, "Turkish National Security Strategy and Military Modernization," *Strategic Review* (Winter 2001): 29.

4. Temel Ersoy, "Changing Role and Structure of the Turkish Navy after the End of the Cold War," unpublished paper, 2001; *Naval Forces* (special issue, 2001).

5. Interview with General Atilla Ateş, Commander of the TLF, *Military Technology*, 24, no. 6 (2000): 78.

6. Ibid., p. 80.

7. Ibid., pp. 80–81.

8. Ibid., pp. 81–82.

9. For a detailed account of Turkey's attitude towards nuclear disarmament, see Mustafa Kibaroğlu, "Turkey," in Harald Muller (ed.), *Europe and Nuclear Disarmament: Debates and Political Attitudes in 16 European Countries*, Peace Research Institute Frankfurt, Brussels: European Interuniversity Press, 1998, pp. 161–93; also see Duygu B. Sezer, "Turkey's New Security Environment, Nuclear Weapons and Proliferation," *Comparative Strategy*, 14, no. 2 (1995): 149–73.

10. There were no harsh debates in the Grand National Assembly during the process of ratifying the BTWC in November 1974, the NPT in April 1980, the CWC in May 1997, or the CTBT in November 1999.

11. See, in this respect, Mustafa Kibaroğlu, "Turkey and Israel Strategize," *Middle East Quarterly*, 9, no. 1 (Winter 2002): 61–65.

12. See Ed Blanche, "Israel and Turkey Look to Extend their Influence into Central Asia," *Janes Intelligence Review* (August 2001): 34.

13. See *Hürriyet* (daily newspaper), 15 December 2001, p. 10.

14. Ibid.

15. Richard Sokolsky, "Imagining European Missile Defense," *Survival*, 43, no. 3 (Autumn 2001): 177.

16. General (Ret.) Çevik Bir "Whom Will the US Missile Shield Protect?" (in Turkish), *Ulusal Strateji-National Strategy*, 3, no. 19 (September–October 2001): 50–51.

17. See an interview with General Hüseyin Kıvrikoğlu, Chief of the General Staff, "Peace in the Nation, Peace in the World," *Military Technology*, 23, no. 9 (1999): 9–20.

18. Interview with General Atilla Ateş, Commander of the Turiksh Land Forces, *Military Technology*, 24, no. 6 (2000): 78–79.

19. Ali L. Karaosmanoğlu, "The Evolution of the National Security Culture and the Military in Turkey," *Journal of International Affairs*, 54, no. 1 (Fall 2000): 213.

20. Ümit Cizre Sakallıoğlu, "The Anatomy of the Turkish Military's Political Autonomy," *Comparative Politics*, 29, no. 2 (January 1997): 153.

21. Gareth Jenkins, "Context and Circumstances: The Turkish Military and Politics," *Adelphi Paper* No. 337, IISS, 2001, pp. 41–45.

22. Karaosmanoğlu, op cit., p. 215.

23. Jenkins, op cit., p. 83.

24. Karaosmanoğlu, op cit., p. 216.

25. *White Paper 2000*, p. 109.

26. The authors are grateful to Professor Merih Celasun for his valuable comments on measurement issues as well as for Tables 5 and 6.

27. "Recently Completed and Ongoing Turkish Defense Procurement Programs," *Military Technology*, 25, no. 9 (2001): 12.

28. *White Book 2000*, p. 115–16.

29. "The TuAF Modernisation Programme: A Status Report," *Military Technology*, 23, no. 9 (1999): 20.

30. Lale Sarýibrahimoğlu, "Turkish Defense Industry in Retrospective," *National Strategy*, 3, no. 19 (September–October 2001): 92, 95. For the current defense industry and procurement projects, see "Recently Completed and Ongoing Turkish Defense Procurement Programmes under SSM," *Military Technology*, 25, no. 9 (2001): 19–30.

31. Sarıibrahimoğlu, op cit., p. 92–93.

32. Ibid., p. 94.

33. Ibid.

Defense Reform in Poland, 1989–2000

Andrzej Karkoszka

The term, "defense reform," may encompass a number of different measures. Many actions undertaken by countries in their military domain are often called reforms, while they amount merely to adaptations, to steps enforced by external pressures or a necessity. They could thus be called measures of rationalization. Such was the case with the first changes implemented in the Polish defense system in late 1980s, now often described as the beginning of transformation, which led to the present state of affairs. While in substance they might be quite similar to measures adopted later as part of a reform process, like reductions in strength, and while there is a continuity of changes of such character, these early steps cannot be taken as real "reforms," that is, actions undertaken with a clear purpose of improving the defense system. Their objective was not to reform the defense system but to adapt it, first, to drastically worsened economic conditions of the state and, second, to the external political conditions of the thaw in East-West relations, exemplified by Gorbachev's *perestroika* and *glasnost* and by a forthcoming breakthrough in the Vienna negotiations on conventional forces in Europe following the Stockholm agreement on CSBMs, and the U.S.-Soviet INF and Strategic Arms Reduction Talks (START) treaties. Since the rapid decline of the Polish economy in 1988, the national defense budget has been cut substantially for the first time in decades, prompting sizeable reductions in some categories of forces, partial restructuring of the land forces, and their redeployment.

In sum, by 1989—that is, before the change of political system in Poland—some sixty-eight military units were disbanded, reducing the strength by about thirty-three thousand soldiers, and some four hundred old tanks and seven hundred artillery pieces were decommissioned. Four divisions were transformed into materiel depots. Four-fifths of the Polish forces were concentrated in the northwestern corner of the country, with only one cadre division left in its eastern part, adjacent to the Soviet Union. The Polish territorial forces, the only ones of this type in the entire Warsaw Pact, virtually ceased to exist. Still, the remaining force totaled some 412,000 soldiers and more than twenty-eight hundred tanks, twenty-four hundred armed troop carriers, twenty-three hundred guns, and five hundred aircraft. Poland could put up an entire "front" of three land armies, second only to the Soviet army among Warsaw Pact countries. With this potential, organized into eleven divisions, three flotillas of warships, and four air corps, Poland entered the period of democratic revolution.

GEOPOLITICAL CONDITIONS OF EARLY REFORMS

Entering the years of democratic transition after the quasi-free parliamentary elections of 4 June 1989, and establishing the first noncommunist government in Eastern Europe, Poland was still a member of the Warsaw Pact and had within its borders some sixty-five thousand soldiers of the Soviet Central Group of Forces, with strategic command headquarters in Legnica. When the first democratic prime minister, Tadeusz Mazowiecki, received permission to form the government, Romanian president Nicolae Ceausescu suggested to other members of the Pact that they undertake "brotherly" intervention in Poland to defend socialism. The quick pace of political transformation in Poland and the other Eastern European countries, all members of the Warsaw Pact, fortified the democratic bent of the changes.

On 27 January 1990, the Polish United Workers Party of Poland, which had ruled the country for forty-two years, was disbanded. Leader of the "Solidarity" movement Lech Walesa became president of Poland, and on 27 October 1991, the country's first free parliamentary elections were held. The fall of the German Democratic Republic and the subsequent rapid reunification of Germany, followed by the dissolution of the Warsaw Pact on 1 July 1991, and then the Soviet Union, created an entirely new strategic situation. The four-decade-old security guarantees, associated with the complete dominance of a foreign power, ceased to function. The whole eastern part of the European continent was in a state of flux, which threatened to destabilize this vast area.

All three of Poland's neighbors transformed into six and, later, seven new states, with uncertain attitudes about the region's security problems. Reunified Germany, while unequivocally democratic and friendly to Poland, did not make clear during its first year of independence what its policy would be with regard to the Polish-German border. The border issue was agreed on and confirmed on 14 November 1990, and by a treaty signed on 17 May 1991.

For the first time in many decades, Poland was left alone to manage its security, notwithstanding its membership in the United Nations (UN) and the Organization for Security and Cooperation in Europe (OSCE). The Western nations welcomed the new democratic Poland and other states of the region, but their primary interest was in preventing an implosion of the Soviet Union and, later, destabilization of post-Soviet territories. They urged caution in dealings with the crumbling Warsaw Pact, later with the dissolving Soviet Union, and, subsequently, with an unstable and uncertain Russia. The emphasis of that period was on institutionalization of the OSCE and implementation of unprecedented reductions in conventional potential through the Conventional Forces in Europe (CFE) Treaty. The North Atlantic Treaty Organization's (NATO's) friendly "hand extended to the former enemies" treated all the states of Eastern Europe, post-Warsaw Pact and the post-Soviet ones, alike in the formal and political sense. Establishment of the NATO Cooperation Council (NACC) on 20 November 1991, which recognized that all 35 states had the same status and same possibilities to build links with the West, exemplified this. None of these states would be considered for NATO membership, however.

By 1991, the old treaty recognizing relations between Poland and the Soviet Union ceased to be operational. Difficult talks on the new agreement began, with the Soviet side basing its position on the Kvicinski-Fallin doctrine, declaring the whole of Eastern Europe to be a traditional sphere of Russian interests and domination. Accordingly, new relations between the Soviet Union and Poland were to be based on renouncing any alliance by either side with a third party and prohibiting the presence of any foreign—that is, non-Russian—military force on Polish territory, while allowing Russian forces free transit through Poland. These formulations, once accepted, would preserve the status of Poland as a state with limited sovereignty and would preclude any positive security binding with the West.

Only Romania signed an agreement, similar to this one; very soon, however, it withdrew its consent to the text. The countries of the region mutually supporting each other—Czechoslovakia, Hungary, and Poland—successfully rejected the "offer." Moreover, similar actions aimed at preserving the old domination were evident in the economic domain. When Poland proposed a gradual shift in its financial accounting with the Soviet Union, from the "transferable ruble" to a convertible currency, the latter decided to institute the change at once, beginning on 1 January 1991, an obvious attempt to drive home to Poles the extent of their economic and trade dependency on the Soviets.

And in reality, the entire Polish exchange with the Soviet Union crumbled in days, from more than 50 percent down to a only a few percent, thus playing havoc with the national economy, which was undergoing drastic reforms already. However, after nearly two years of difficult transformation Poland obtained full economic independence from the Soviet Union, except for oil and gas; Poland remained dependent on the Soviet Union for about 80 percent and 60 percent of these products, respectively. Despite all of these fluctuations, the two states signed a declaration of friendship and cooperation on 22 May 1992, the first agreement of the Russian Federation with a foreign state. The declaration also contained stipulations regarding the withdrawal of the remaining Soviet/Russian armed forces from Poland, a matter of special psychological and political importance for the entire region. The seventeen rounds of negotiations on withdrawal of these forces from Poland was compounded by the similar, though much more massive, process taking place in Germany. The last Russian army unit finally left Poland on 17 August 1993.

FIRST STAGE OF DEFENSE REFORM IN POLAND—1989–93

The deep uncertainties about the course of events outside the country and very fluid internal political and economic situation were not conducive to establishing a well-developed long-range program of defense reforms. Only the most general security framework existed, mandated by Poland's desire for full independence, democratization, and market reforms, all of which opened the possibility of closer relations with the West.

The general tendency towards democratization made some required reforms fairly obvious: the armed forces were to be freed from the tutelage of the communist party, fully renationalized in form and substance, and brought under control of the democratic authorities of the state. These steps were executed swiftly. After communist authorities finally left Poland in January 1991, party cells were banned in the armed forces, with political officers either leaving altogether or, in some cases, being demoted to lower rank within the force. The Military Political Academy was liquidated. The first two civilian vice-ministers, representing new democratic political groups, entered military administration in the mid-1990. Army uniforms, basic regulations, and schooling returned to traditional national patterns, and Catholic and other churches begun to function freely in the armed forces.

While the external characteristics of the armed forces were changed quickly, their substance was still rooted in the past. On 21 February 1990, with a noncommunist government already in power, a new defense doctrine was adopted in Poland. It was agreed that the Warsaw Pact was still a guarantor of nation's security, and Polish armed forces' tasks were still embedded within an allied doctrine of defense. However, wording on the possibility of Poland entering a conflict against its will indicated already growing differentiation among the Pact and Poland's strategic interests. A risk of conflict in Central Europe, stemming from widespread instability around the country, was posited, while NATO was no longer considered to be an enemy.

Although a step forward, the doctrine was obviously nothing more than a passing formulation, in line with similar changes taking place in all of the other Warsaw Pact states and appropriate for the transitional period, but completely outdated just a few months later. In mid-1991, a team of military and security experts was established at the newly created Bureau of National Security, headed by a civilian, to work out a new defense doctrine.

On 2 November 1992, the highest state agency responsible for these matters, the Committee of Defense of the Country, itself reminiscent of the old political system, adopted two doctrinal documents: "The basic premises of the Polish security policy" and "The security policy and defense strategy of the Polish Republic." These documents took note of the positive strategic changes around the country, particularly relations with Germany and other NATO states, and identified the basic values and interests of the Western, democratic countries that were aspired to in Poland, and stating future acceptance into the European Union (EU) as a strategic objective. Eventually, even NATO membership was foreseen, though not as an immediate goal. Until future integration with the West, the Poland's defense would have to be based on national military capabilities only, with no other direct threat but the general instability in the area and possible social and economic internal breakdown. In short, it was a doctrine of a newly independent state, alone in securing its existence and anxious not to remain a buffer zone between the affluent and secure West and the crisis-ridden and unstable East.

The two 1992 documents did not specify any direction for strategic military planning. The only quasi-official guidelines, interpreted by the military from the documents, were assumptions about a "defense on all the azimuths" and, hence, more equitable distribution of forces throughout the national territory, rather than concentrating them in western Poland. Redeployment of units was hampered by a lack of funds, however, so that by 1993, only three brigades were transferred to the eastern part of the country, with a few additional units moving part of their strengths in the same direction, to form the fourth military district in Krakow.

Dissolution of the Warsaw Pact made Poland fully independent in its security policy but, at the same time, raised the issue of "defense sufficiency" in an uncertain, dynamic, and potentially threatening international environment. Poland's armed forces were confronted with an increasingly shrinking defense budget, by 35 percent in years 1989–91 and down to 50 percent during the next two years. The national economy was shrinking steadily, and ongoing market reforms mandated investment in the civilian, rather than the military, sector. As a result, the condition of the armed forces, measured by quality of service and life, level of maintenance of infrastructure and weapon systems, level of training and exercises, and overall readiness, were declining rapidly. Implementation of the CFE agreement caused a tangible reduction of some weapon stocks, but on a short-term basis, it increased spending rather than diminishing it. Manpower was reduced to 234,000 soldiers, in accordance with the CFE agreement, but basic structures of military command—central, district, and divisional ones—were preserved, apparently justified by potential major mobilizations in time of a highly probable crisis but, more likely, because of Poland's unwillingness to execute a major reduction of these structures. The composition of the armed forces, in terms of the proportion of officers to enlisted men, traditionally top-heavy in Warsaw Pact armies, was becoming more and more skewed.

The political authorities of the state sensed quite early on the need for "democratization" of the military bureaucracy and the national command structures. With this purpose in mind, an interdepartmental commission created—the Zabinski Commission—in November 1990, which, during its first year, produced a blueprint for structural change in relevant institutions. The Commission's considerations and the findings were hampered by ongoing political and military alterations, lack of a new constitution, which could give a direction and basis for its work, and the prevailing concept of "depoliticization" of armed forces. The main conceptual recommendation adopted was to separate the civilian-administrative and military parts of the central defense administrations. In theory, this solution would prevent the defense sector from repeating the old party-based meddling in purely military, professional activities. In practice, the civilian component, composed of predominantly military personnel with a few civilians on top, was created without diminishing any of the functions and responsibilities of the military institutions. To a large degree, duplication of functions and responsibilities, controversies about who would lead whom, and wasted resources by an overblown bureaucracy were the result. Worse still, the civilian managers of the military structures, all of them representing new political forces, did not win the support of much of the "old" officer corps, because they made unpopular often mistaken decisions. Confronted with unprofessional civilian leadership, the military, particularly the General Staff and the Military Districts' commands, concentrated on fending for themselves and began to isolate themselves from civilian authorities' influence.

The tendency to fortifying the position of the General Staff was strengthened further by the peculiar behavior of Poland's political elite. The interim "small constitution," in effect by 8 December 1992, defined the major ministries dealing with the state's security—defense, and internal affairs—as "presidential ministries." Maintaining the close link between the president and these ministries allowed the president to take charge of the state's security. As a result, the president, his entourage, and the rest of the body politic, on the one side, began to compete for influence in the military and security sectors, promising financial support and drawing the top brass of the military into their political controversies. On the other side, military commanders eagerly lent their support to various political groups hoping to use these connections for personal and professional benefit. Before and during the parliamentary campaign of 1993, media reported on several cases of military commanders involved in political life.

The most important political fact of the first period of reforms in Polish defense posture was the crystallizing of the pro-Western direction of national security policy. First, an agreement on association with the EU came into being on 1 February 1994. Second, from 1992 on, the issue of NATO membership, a paramount security objective for Poland, has been determined, with an increasing number of visits and joint initiatives among Poland, NATO member states, and the alliance itself.

In sum, the first period of defense reforms in Poland can be summarized as a successful period of predominantly political and general security transformations. The armed forces were renationalized, national security policy was freed from external domination, and the first openly presented strategic doctrine was prepared. According to its wording, the state had no allies or enemies. The military potential of Poland was reduced by half, as was its readiness and quality. Few of these changes were well planned in advance. They were, rather, an outgrowth of external and internal political and economic circumstances. The military structures grew increasingly top-heavy, with the role of the General Staff expanded in response to establishment of rudimentary civilian authority in the military.

SECOND STAGE OF DEFENSE REFORM IN POLAND—1994–96

The subsequent period of reform in the Polish defense system was characterized by a number of conspicuous tendencies:

- first and foremost, strong, popular pressure to realize the strategic objective of the state: NATO membership;
- visible autonomy and political activism of the General Staff in shaping defense policy;
- efforts to increase defense budgets, to avert further deterioration of the armed forces.

Only the first and the last of these tendencies were connected to a sort of plan of action, adopted by the highest state authorities. It can be said that, while implementation of the first has been successful, the last one failed altogether.

The experiences of NACC showed to all observers that it is impossible to maintain forever a policy of nondifferentiation among participating states. Central East European states' desire for ever closer ties grew steadily, and their involvement in NATO policy became a matter of fact. In October 1993, the idea of the Partnership for Peace (PfP) emerged as the United States' solution to the dilemma of bringing willing East European partners closer without losing positive interaction with Russia. PfP was adopted as official NATO policy in January 1994, and, after some early equivocation, Poland embraced fully the opportunities created by the program. On 2 February 1994, Poland signed the PfP Framework Document; on 8 April, a formal request for NATO membership was issued, and on 25 April, the first PfP individual partnership program was officially presented at NATO. In June 1994, the first PfP exercises, with thirteen nations participating, were carried out successfully at the Biedrusko polygon in Poland.

Implementation of PfP programs with NATO, as well as rapidly growing military interactions with virtually all NATO members, had a decisive effect on the Polish armed forces. The notion of interoperability with NATO armies became the order of the day, encouraging several adaptation, reorganization, and education programs in the Polish military. Several Polish officers were sent to Western military academies, thirteen centers to teach foreign languages were established, a growing stream of NATO technical and organizational standards and norms (STANAGs) were integrated into the Polish system of standardization and normalization, a number of various professional courses were organized, and several units took part in PfP exercises and joint events.

In 1995, the PfP programs, encompassing hundreds of initiatives, grew into NATO Planning and Review (PARP) programs, permitting Poland and a few other more active states to enter a more mature stage of military cooperation. The tasks posed by the PARP program often demanded special effort by the officer corps and sometimes drained scarce resources, so they were not always supported fully by the top commanders. However, once the PfP program, designed at first as a palliative for those pressing to open NATO's doors, turned out to be an effective path to NATO membership, the Polish military became strong proponents. It is worth mentioning here that the Polish units, already experienced in a number of UN peacekeeping operations, took part in the UNPROFOR and Stabilization Force (SFOR) (later Implementation Force [IFOR]) operations in Croatia and Bosnia and Herzegovina, respectively, the latter one as a part of the Nordic-Polish Brigade, acting in the operational framework of the First U.S. Division. Building on historic links with the Western allies, dating from World War II, and developing further through involvement of the Polish military in the "Operation Desert Storm" in 1991 and in Haiti in 1995, Poland's links with Western armies became truly close.

In the NATO "Study on Enlargement" (published 28 September 1994), fundamental requirement to be fulfilled by prospective new members was civilian, democratic control over the armed forces. At first, the Polish government thought this policy had been implemented fully, with a civilian minister of defense, president of the country as a supreme commander, and a growing number of civilian employees within the defense ministry. However, symptoms of the General Staff's growing independence, already visible for some time, became a disturbing daily occurrence. Not only were the top commanders of the Polish armed forces masters of the personnel and promotion policy, they also had a decisive voice in procurement and arms production policy and major influence on the shape, though not on the size, of military outlays. They also were increasingly vocal about the country's defense and security policy.

Their attitude and activism could be explained in part by their concern over constantly diminishing defense budgets and the continued deterioration of the armed forces. However, the only remedy they could propose for this situation was to increase the financial resources at their disposal, without regard for the abilities and needs of the civilian economy, and in contravention to prevailing international tendencies. The military had a particular distaste for the proposals to reduce numerical strength and eliminate various commands, leaving only empty shells with many officers but few soldiers. One ill-considered recommendation of that period concerned the Twenty-Fifth Air Cavalry Brigade (later Division), which was to be fielded without the financial resources to buy required helicopters and maintain such an expensive unit.

The internal political situation in Poland became complicated after the 1993 parliamentary elections, which brought a leftist coalition into power. The first cohabitation, with the president coming from the old democratic opposition, and the government having a postcommunist background, begun to function. The ensuing controversies, pitting the president against the government on many issues, created fertile ground for maturation of the young Polish democracy but, regrettably, extended to relations between civilian and military authorities. The infamous "Drawsko affair" of 30 September 1994 (referring to a meeting in Drawsko Pomorskie), during which the president proposed a vote of confidence for the minister of defense by the top military commanders, caused the government effectively to lose control and oversight of the military. Later on, during the 1995 presidential campaign, the same generals organized a number of officer meetings, trying to influence the political attitudes of their subordinates. When the independent press discovered them, the perpetrators tried to cover their actions by keeping the meetings secret and lying to the investigating commission. In this way, an aversion to democratic oversight and an aptitude for political involvement led some of the top Polish military commanders to flout military discipline and fundamental norms of military behavior. It is not a surprise, therefore, that the most serious anxiety, frequently expressed officially and in private by NATO and Western partners and presented as the most serious obstacle to Polish membership in NATO, was linked to the lack of effective democratic control over the military.

The deterioration of the Polish armed forces caused by the scarcity of financial resources was a major concern of both the military and Polish political circles. Frequent calls to reverse the course of military development went unheeded, however, and the need to modernize the national economy and, thus, to create the proper conditions for eventual improvement in defense constantly prevailed over temporary solutions. Efforts to ameliorate the situation in the armed forces concentrated on two proposals: first, reducing the forces even further, to about 160,000 and introducing new methods of planning and implementing budgets, and, second, gathering public support for a future budget expansion, thus committing state political authorities to a long term program of modernization and integration with NATO. The first proposal did not lead to concrete results; the appropriate commission, established by the minister of defense, could not prevail over the military, to whom the proposed level of military strength seemed to be utterly inadequate.

The second track seemed to hold more promise; after several months of preparation, a parliamentary debate on defense matters was organized on 16 February 1995, eliciting a widely publicized solemn declaration obliging the government to increase the defense budget by as much as 3 percent by the end of 1997. Additionally, the declaration called for establishment of appropriate civilian, democratic control over the armed forces, the preparation of a multiyear development plan for the armed forces, reorganization of the state's defense system, elimination of the excessive defense infrastructure—considered a drain on defense resources, creation of several legal measures to modernize defense laws, and, finally, intensification of efforts to integrate Poland with Euro-Atlantic security structures. The declaration was not legally binding, however, so its financial aspects were never implemented. Subsequent improvement in the national economy and the requirements of NATO membership allowed defense outlays to increase over the next few years to approximately 2 percent of the state budget. Even though efforts to enact the two proposals were unsuccessful discussion of financing military developments in Poland prepared the defense administration and the military structure for more ambitious steps in the coming years.

THIRD STAGE OF DEFENSE REFORM IN POLAND—1996–98

The next period of defense reform in Poland had been set up by the previous one. First, the state of civil-military relations, with the growing politicization of the military leadership, became unbearable to the political system of a country on its way to mature democracy. The situation called for immediate and far-reaching reform. Second, growing cooperation with NATO and intensified dialogue on future integration made transformation of the whole defense system and defense policy indispensable to make them more compatible with those of the future allies. Third, continued deterioration of armed forces could not go unaddressed; the forces badly needed a clear vision and a development program that corresponded more precisely to the restrictive budget conditions. It can be said that, for the first time, the country's political leadership, both the ruling coalition and the opposition, had accepted common goals in defense policy, and a wide political consensus on necessary changes emerged.

The decisive moment of reform arrived with the adoption by the Parliament of a bill on the office of the minister of national defense on 14 December 1995. The bill described the minister's office as a supreme organ of state administration in defense, which would execute its tasks with the assistance of the ministry of defense, with the General Staff as an organic part of the ministry. In his portfolio, according to the bill's stipulation in Article 2, belong, among other tasks:

- management in time of peace of all aspects of functioning of the armed forces;
- preparation of premises for defense of the country, including proposals on the development and structures of the armed forces;
- implementation of general guidelines and decisions of the Council of Ministers, dealing with defense issues, and coordination of implementation of these decisions;
- controlling all administrative and economic institutions of state in Defense tasks;

- management of defense personnel reserves;
- management of armed forces personnel;
- controlling the execution of military service;
- securing the material technical and financial needs of the armed forces; and
- management of finances of the whole realm of defense.

According to Article 3, the minister of defense executes his mandate directly and with the assistance of his deputies and the Chief of the General Staff. His decisions concerning the structures, organization, and functioning of the armed forces are to be consulted or carried out on the motion of the Chief of the General Staff. The bill also defined the tasks and responsibilities of the Chief of the General Staff, making him, according to Article 7, unequivocally "directly subordinate to the Minister of National Defense."

Enacting the bill created a good basis for reorganization of the whole ministry of defense and the other central organs of Poland's defense system. A special commission was established to prepare implementation documents concerning the statute of the ministry (to be adopted by the Council of Ministers) and organizational regulations (to be signed by the minister of national defense). The statute concerning the integrated ministry was prepared after more than six months of heated and controversial debates, resulting in the creation of five sectors: defense policy, General Staff, procurement, economic/financial matters, and social/parliamentary matters, each with its own detailed competencies and functions. All duplication of functions among them was eliminated by cutting out as many as twenty-six different departments (civilian part) and directorates (in the General Staff) and 880 individual posts, resulting in streamlined structures. The General Staff lost its influence over military financial matters, procurement, education, promotion of higher ranks (from colonel on), strategic intelligence (now directly under the minister), and supervision and control of the armed forces. All of these tasks—with exception of intelligence—were taken over by the other civilian-led sectors of the ministry.

The next stage of the reform process proved to be even more difficult, as it dealt with minute regulation of relations between different structural elements of the ministry and specified the flow of documents and decision-making processes for various matters. After nearly a year, on 20 November 1996, the minister of defense signed the regulations. Formal subordination of the General Staff to civilian management had been accomplished. What remained, however, was to put all the new relationships into practice and enforce a change of mind-set and behavior among the top commanders. This often required personnel changes at the highest levels, always a politically haphazard process.

During the commission's deliberations on restructuring the defense ministry, it became apparent that the crux of the problem with reshaping the General Staff was its combining the command and planning functions. This feature was reminiscent of the old Soviet solutions, in which the peacetime General Staff was responsible for combat readiness and schooling; during times of war, it was a ready-to-deploy supreme command headquarters. Elimination of this dual function, the main concern of the reform commission, has proven to be difficult because it has had to confront arguments about the decreased ability of central command to perform wartime tasks. Moreover, in view of Poland's forthcoming entry into NATO, the Polish armed forces were visibly lacking a compatible level of command at the operational level. All levels of NATO command structures had to connect with the Polish command structures through the General Staff level, which supervised simultaneously national, district, and divisional levels of command. To address these two concerns, the concept of creating a Land Forces Command was forwarded. After a few rounds of wrangling with the military leadership, which tried to foil the initiative, it was agreed on at the end of 1996 and implemented at the beginning of 1997. Each category of the Polish armed forces now had an operational command, with the General Staff responsible for overall planning, joint operational training, readiness, reconnaissance, mobilization, and basic personnel and logistical management.

As a result of all the changes described above, civil-military relations and state institutions' democratic oversight of the defense system improved markedly. The main political hurdle on the way to NATO membership had been removed. Moreover, the process of preparing the armed forces and military administration for membership—a complex political and organizational endeavor—could be carried out much more smoothly and more effectively in an environment of close and mutually reinforcing relations between civilian leadership and the military. The relationship was improved as well due to the election of Aleksander Kwasniewski in 1995, ending the first cohabitation period in Poland.

Efforts to intensify the process of integrating with NATO took more concrete shape when, in March 1996, Poland began a series of consultations with the alliance, determined by the North Atlantic Council (NAC), and requiring a number of planning documents related to Poland's future obligations within NATO and future development of the Polish armed forces. The exchanges between the two sides intensified: Several bilateral, trilateral, and multilateral exercises were organized within and outside the PfP framework. Special bureaucratic structures were created within the ministry of defense to handle the standardization processes and the growing traffic of communications and documents between NATO and Polish military authorities.

On 10 December 1996, the NAC stated that NATO would invite "one or more" new members at the Summit of July 1997. The armed forces received a clear signal to expand their transformations, oriented to improving interoperability with NATO forces, increasing availability of units for joint activities, and training personnel for future cooperation with the Western partners. Because of budgetary constraints, these tasks proved to be very difficult. In 1996, a number of units were declared available for common activities, within the PfP framework, in addition to the units already working hand-in-hand with NATO forces in IFOR, Yugoslavia. One airborne battalion reached operational readiness according to the NATO standards in December 1995, and a field hospital was prepared with appropriate personnel and equipment. The staff and command of the Eleventh Armored Cavalry Division, with its subordinate brigades as well as the Sixth Air Assault brigade, achieved readiness for common training and exercises in 1996. An Air Cavalry regiment, two rescue warships, and an air search and rescue (SAR) group (two planes and four helicopters) were readied, despite serious difficulties in upgrading their technical standards. The entire armed forces received radio communication equipment compatible with NATO requirements, and the ground forces introduced fuel requirements, including receipt and delivery of liquid fuels, as demanded by NATO norms. Similarly, the Polish Navy prepared to replenish allied warships in harbor and at sea. The military airfields were equipped with interoperable air navigation aids, such as radio beacons, angle-distance systems, instrument landing gear, and appropriate radio indicators. NATO terminology and relevant procedures were put into practice in the units, and ability to mark hazardous areas, such as minefields and unexploded ordnance, was developed according to NATO practices.

In addition, blood group markings, donor requirements, and blood handling were incorporated by the Polish medical services. Various numeric maps, using NATO grid reference and projections, were produced on a massive scale. The aircraft identification of friend-or-foe was introduced slowly. Several measures to establish logistical support for various units, including classification of equipment and supply materiel, were put in practice. In 1996, a national system of airspace management that integrated civilian and military networks, was able to collect and disseminate information on airspace situation, and was linked to civilian traffic control and air defense systems in Poland (and, later, in the allied states), began to take shape. This program required procurement of appropriate transponders on the air platforms, new radio stations, and radar able to operate with digital technology. This effort allowed establishment of the Air Sovereignty Operations Center, enabling an operational link with NATO air defenses soon after Poland entered the alliance. Last but not least, several thousand officers went through intensive courses to learn English and other languages of the NATO partners. When the NATO Summit meeting in Madrid decided on 8 July 1997 to invite Poland, together with Czech Republic and Hungary, to begin accession negotiations, Poland had prepared well for the challenge.

The accession talks ended in November 1997, with the Atlantic Council recommending the three candidates; then, on 16 December of that year, all three countries signed the accession protocols. All NATO members ratified the protocols during 1998, and, on 19 January 1999, NATO formally invited the three states to become parties to the Washington Treaty. After ratifying accession to the Treaty—which Poland did on 17 February 1999—the acts of accession were handed to the U.S. government, the depository of the Treaty. Poland's security policy strategic goal had been achieved.

Having achieved two of its main objectives—establishing democratic control of the military and joining NATO, Polish leadership did not neglect the third one—crafting a cohesive, long-term plan to restructure, modernize, and develop the nation's armed forces. The armed forces continued to deteriorate. Not only did the social and material conditions of military personnel not improve, but, compared with civilian employees, they worsened. The pull of the civilian marketplace exacerbated problems in the structure of the officer corps: The youngest, those best prepared to handle modern weapons technology and foreign languages, and those educated in professions—such as medicine, aircraft flying, computers, or law—were leaving the force instead of the older and less advanced colleagues who were crowding the ranks of colonels and the like.

Because of low pay and a lack of financial resources, the program to enlarge the NCO corps and the number of contracted soldiers—one of the objectives linked to the NATO adaptation programs—was unable to continue its early success. Progress in professionalization of the armed forces stalled, and the backlog of equipment in need of repair, depletion of spare parts stocks, and devastation of infrastructure increased steadily. Cannibalizing older weapons systems was often the only way to keep the rest of them going. The level of training of an individual soldier, be it frequency of live shooting, missile firing, or flight hours, decreased constantly. There were fewer and fewer joint forces exercises, in reverse proportion to the number of PfP (small units) exercises. The need to restructure the forces to improve their quality by saving on their quantity, to reduce further the strength and the number of garrisons, and to eliminate more nonoperational units and nonmilitary services within the armed forces became obvious.

In 1996, general financial outlays for the armed forces improved, due to a growing national economy. For the first time since 1989, the defense budget increased in real terms, reaching about 2.3 percent of gross domestic product (GDP) and staying at this level for the next few years. However, the increase was hardly perceptible to military personnel because there were too many demands for financial resources from all segments of the military. The only unquestioned, politically motivated budget item was integration with NATO. All other needs had to be prioritized systematically, a task not helped by the fact that existing military doctrine, based on security and strategic policy documents dating from 1992, were obsolete and could not serve as a guideline.

The first attempt to work out a long-range plan was undertaken in preparation for the parliamentary debate leading to the declaration of 16 February 1995. Three proposals were discussed, all of which depended on the country's economic development assumptions, with a few principles guiding them: lowering the ceiling of peacetime strength to 160,000, gradually increasing materiel outlays to permit tangible modernization of forces, changing the proportions in defense budgets, reducing personnel costs (then accounting for more than 65 percent of the military budget), and eliminating superfluous infrastructure. Two military districts, the recently established Krakow MD and the old Warsaw MD, were to be disbanded. Though some of these objectives were fulfilled, because of the political upheaval in the country and constant underfunding of the armed forces this plan did not materialize. However, its basic guidelines were adopted in the 1996 by new leadership in the defense ministry as part of a fifteen-year plan to modernize the armed forces between 1998 and 2012.

The new plan was based on an assumption that the average yearly growth of Poland's GDP during that period would be no less than 4.2 percent, and that the part of defense budget devoted to acquisition and modernization would grow by 3 percent over the real growth of the state budget. It was agreed that the peacetime armed forces would not exceed 180,000 troops, with 60 percent in the land forces, 21 percent in the air force, and 8 percent in the navy. (Other types of forces were to account for 11 percent.) The fifteen-year horizon was designed to permit enough resources to facilitate a gradual, socially acceptable pace of personnel reductions and was dictated by the scope of the projected investments in relation to projected budget allowances.

Assuming the budget grew as expected, an increase in the index of expenditure per soldier of US$45,000 dollars was permitted, as was allowing the share of modern weapons to reach some 25 percent to 30 percent of the total inventory. In the latter stages of the program, expenditures for acquisition and modernization would reach 30 percent—from less than 10 percent in previous years. In general, the modernization envisaged improved command, communication, and control systems at each organizational level; a substantial increase in the mobility of forces; professionalizing up to 50 percent of forces; shortening conscript service from eighteen to twelve months; assuring modern training standards; and establishing a modern logistic support system.

Additionally, in view of the coming integration with NATO, the Polish defense system was to have the capability to receive allied reinforcements and substantial amounts of materiel and equipment by land, air, and sea. Poland was to maintain selected units' readiness so they would be able to participate in NATO Rapid Reaction Forces (RRFs), to prepare selected units to participate in multinational corps and divisions, and to integrate fully the command structures of national air defense with the unified allied air defense. Polish RRFs were to be composed of one airborne assault, air cavalry, and two mechanized brigades; two squadrons of multiple aviation and one squadron of combat helicopters; and one ship squadron, one maritime aviation squadron, and an air-marine SAR unit. The only program outside the defense budget but included in the plan concerned the purchase of new combat aircraft. The cost of this procurement item far exceeded what was allowed for in the defense budget. Instead, the government had to finance this purchase from the central state budget.

The plan was deemed a credible, though belated, effort by international and domestic public opinion to improve the Polish armed forces. However, the programs stipulated by "Plan 2012" shared the fate of the previous ones, and, with the exception of the elements linked to integration with NATO, were not put into practice as planned. Its authors sensed the reasons for its failure soon after it was announced in September 1997.

First, the assumptions about the country's economic growth and, hence, about the availability of financial resources, were uncertain from the beginning and soon were proven to be overly optimistic.

Second, the Madrid Summit was only a few months off, and forthcoming membership in NATO meant that the Polish defense system would be incorporated into the defense planning cycle of the alliance, with specific Force Goals and other obligations, which were expected to support modifications in the plan.

Third, none of the structural transformations in the armed forces was based on an updated strategic defense doctrine and, additionally, soon would have to be adapted according to then-specified NATO doctrine. Several projections of force structures thus might have been inadequate or unnecessary. As unfolding events showed, the plan was seriously modified soon after its inception. But the decisive reason for its reshuffle, which was more difficult to predict, was the change in the governing coalition, resulting from the parliamentary elections on 21 September 1997.

Fourth Stage of the Polish Defense Reform—1998–2001

The new government, created by the center-right coalition, adopted a very hands-on attitude toward defense, which did not surprise the public or Poland's Western partners because the nation was a new NATO member. In its first six months in office, the new administration prepared a modified plan of integration and modernization. Its time horizon was six years, and the primary quantitative indicators of the armed forces were preserved from the old program. This meant a more ambitious restructuring pace for the officer corps, a very expensive and socially painful process. To lessen the social burdens of intensified reductions in personnel, a special program was adopted for conversion and readaptation of released personnel.

According to its authors, the new program was to be better balanced in terms of tasks and the finances allocated to fulfill them, a common deficiency of all previous endeavors. The primary official reason for modification was the first sixty-five NATO Force Goals, elaborated jointly and efficiently, thanks to the timely Defense Planning Questionnaire presented to NATO on 29 September 1997. Full integration with the alliance made it necessary to reshuffle and streamline the structures of the General Staff once again so that its functional breakdown would be more compatible with Western-style "joint" staffs. As a result, a new ministry of defense statute was enacted in 1999, though its implementation has been rather slow and erratic.

As implementation of the new reform program began, the economy turned downward; the influence of Russia's financial crisis and the general economic slowdown of Poland's main trading partners was being felt. The gap between the needs of the military and the abilities of the national budget increased again. Earlier hopes of a steady relative growth in the defense budget had to be abandoned, though its 2.1 percent value meant, in real terms, substantially more money than in any previous year during the 1990s. The army had to reduce further the number of garrisons—by more than one hundred—and units: Its overall ceiling was to be 180,000 by 2001, 165,000 by the end of 2002, and 150,000 by the end of 2003. The plan, "Army 2006," envisaged development of the territorial defense units by six to eight low-readiness brigades. Less reorganization and reduction was planned for the air force and the navy, and professionalization of the armed forces was planned differently for various type of forces: 60 percent for elimination of excessive, old equipment—for example, some eight hundred T-55 tanks—and military infrastructure was to be intensified to realize badly needed savings and, sometimes, additional funds. Several modernization and procurement programs much desired by the military had to be postponed or limited. Priority was given to modernizing air defense command systems, combat helicopters, and tanks, and to procuring naval and antitank missiles and new warships and armored personnel carriers. Various modern communication and command systems, fully compatible with NATO standards, were to be introduced in all of the forces by 2002, and, by 2006, investments in military infrastructure, designed to fulfill the requirements of Host Nation

Support, were to be finalized. Several measures were proposed to modernize the logistical system and the military medical, topographic, and hydrographic services.

After several years of debate and failed attempts to adapt a strategic concept of Poland to new international and internal circumstances, NATO accession negotiations in 1997 gave new impetus to these efforts. However, the actual strategy document had been completed as late as more than two years after Poland's entry into the alliance. The early procedural arrangements envisaged one document, comprising both security and defense strategies, to be elaborated by the government on the one hand and the presidential office on the other, and finally approved by the parliament. However, the realities of the second Polish cohabitation, this time between President Aleksander Kwasniewski (who was reelected on 8 October 2000), representing the left side of the political spectrum, and the government, composed of the center-right coalition, did not permit this approach. The security strategy was tabled by the government on 4 January 2000, and the strategic defense concept on 23 May 2000. Both documents were finalized and approved without formally consulting the President, parliament, or public opinion. Formalization of the basic regulations concerning Poland's defense policy were finalized on 24 January 2001, when the government adopted and the President signed a confidential "political-strategic defense directive," a defense strategy implementation. The directive enumerated the tasks and obligations of state organs in defense, regulations concerning crisis management, various threat scenarios, and, finally, of strategic defense planning tasks compatible with NATO's defense planning cycle.

Unlike the strategic defense concept of 1992, the new document took into account all of the changes in Poland's geostrategic situation and reflected appropriately the sense of security obtained by Poland after entering the Western alliance. The new doctrine defined an international, especially local, crisis, as the primary threat to national security, thus deemphasizing the possibility of major military aggression. In addition, for the first time since 1989, Poland's strategic concept defined nuclear policy within its overall defense strategy, wording it to make it fully consonant with NATO's strategic concept.

Since adoption of basic strategic documents on Poland's security and defense policy and formulation of a detailed, long-term modernization and restructuring program for the Polish armed forces, national defense system reform seems to be on the right track. It does not mean, however, that discussion about reform is over. Some basic and important issues are still unresolved, particularly with regard to constitutional regulations and other legal norms, which do not allow for assessment of Polish defense reforms when they are completed. The relationship between the presidential and administrative—government—branches of the executive are not clear: The responsibilities and composition of primary state organs in time of crisis and war has not been settled. Laws concerning citizens' and private enterprises' obligations in national defense, during peace and war, date back to 1967. In addition, the post of supreme commander for wartime has not been defined. In sum, a few bricks are still missing in Poland's defense system structure.

LESSONS FROM THE POLISH DEFENSE REFORMS

1. It is not an exaggeration to say that most of the goals set up before defense reform in Poland were fulfilled. As planned, Poland joined NATO; demilitarized its economy; renationalized its armed forces and reduced them by nearly 65 percent; defined its new security and defense strategy; redeployed military units more evenly over its territory and restructured them according to new political and military requirements; modernized its national defense system; began to modernize its technical and weapons systems in accordance with its restricted financial resources; and introduced effective democratic control over the military and a modern military resources management system compatible with the market economy. The reforms did not undermine the country's defense potential or the strong link between the military and society.

2. Although successful in the end, defense reforms in Poland have never been carried out according to one generic plan. Each stage of reform had its specific circumstances and causes and often was in reaction to the outside environment or an outright necessity. However, throughout 1990s, there was always widespread public consensus on the direction of the transformations: democratization, modernization, and integration with Western democracies. From the very beginning of the reform process, a vast majority of Polish society supported the strategic goals set up by the new democratic political elite and was ready to pay the price: personal and national uncertainty, constant changes, material depravations, and intellectual and physical strains. Over the twelve years of continuous changes, beginning in 1989, more

than a thousand military units were disbanded, nearly 270 were transformed, over 360 new ones were organized. At least five different
reform plans were formulated and, to a greater or lesser degree,
implemented. Eleven ministers of defense and twice that number of
civilian vice-ministers passed through the corridors of the defense
ministry, creating a serious lack of continuation of the process. Without wide public support, based on a desire to "catch up" with history
and with general international technological, cultural, and economic
progress, and with the clear expectation of "reward" from being
among the most progressive, democratic, and affluent group of states,
Poland could not implement massive and deep transformation of its
defense system. Far-reaching defense reforms cannot be sustained if
the state and society do not reform in the same direction.
3. Interaction with Euro-Atlantic institutions created a constant positive
influence, steadily pulling the reform process along when it stagnated
and giving it a clear frame of reference. Bilateral and multilateral
cooperation and assistance from NATO states played an important
facilitating function, not so much in terms of direct material help as
in political and intellectual support of the indigenous institutions,
political groups, and individuals planning and managing the reform
process.
4. The introduction and effective implementation of civilian, democratic
oversight over the armed forces proved to be the most difficult aspect
of reform. Once incorporated into the system, however, it had a decisive effect on the course of events, especially their political and strategic aspects. It has to be said here that the reform process has been
disrupted as much by disobedience, inertia, and distrust on part of the
military as it has been by the ineptitude, lack of professionalism, and
political infighting around defense issues by the civilian political class,
represented by civilian authorities in the defense administration. Lack
of professional civilian cadres was, predictably, one of the reasons for
many failures and difficulties in the reform process.
5. The reforms and transformations of the magnitude of those undertaken in Poland over the last decade cannot help but incur enormous
social costs in terms of material well-being, disrupted family life, and
derailed personal careers of the officer corps, which had to undergo
many reductions and relocations. If the process drags on for too long,
as in case of the Polish reforms, officer corps support for the changes
may disappear. Only in the later stages of the process was more atten-

tion paid to conversion, social adaptation, and, simply, good advance planning.

6. There is no way to execute all-encompassing defense reforms without a serious effort to establish first a comprehensive legal framework for the changes. However, many good laws may remain only pieces of paper if they are not followed by regulations permitting effective implementation of those laws.

7. One of the most difficult aspects of defense planning, especially in the face of the tight financial conditions that characterized the Polish situation, is to match future resources with the costs of desired changes. Any reform that promises tangible savings over time must be paid for first.

8. The sequence of steps leading to execution of the reform process should always have its logic: from doctrinal and legal framework to substantive planning based on sound financial analysis. In the case of Poland, this sequence was interrupted often, to the detriment of the process's efficiency. Of particular importance is the first of these steps: clarifying what the armed forces are supposed to do, for what reasons, and by what means. Moreover, proper implementation of the reform process depends on the existence of bureaucratic and wide public support. Otherwise, one cannot expect the young to be eager to perform military service and pay for national defense in today's benign international circumstances, with no immediate and direct threat to most of the European states.

CHAPTER TEN

Defense Reform and NATO

George Katsirdakis*

INTRODUCTION

NATO's Secretary General has identified defense reform as one of the top-priority objectives for both NATO members and Partner countries in the Euro-Atlantic Partnership Council/Partnership for Peace (EAPC/PfP) community. In the context of NATO countries, defense reform is an ongoing process that has been intensified substantially after the Washington Summit of 1999, when the Defense Capabilities Initiative (DCI) was launched. The process of defense reform was put under further scrutiny after the 11 September 2001 terrorist attacks on the United States. In the case of Partners, and more so in the case of Membership Action Plan (MAP) Partners, defense reform is considered to be a top-priority issue that is being pursued by Partners and monitored closely by the Atlantic Alliance. This paper presents NATO's perceptions on defense reform, focusing in particular on pursuing defense reform in the context of PfP; provides some examples of defense reform; and draws some conclusions and present lessons learned.

THE PERCEPTION OF DEFENSE REFORM IN NATO

WHAT IS DEFENSE REFORM?
There is no NATO-accepted definition of defense reform since its meaning is perceived differently by the various circles of the Alliance.

*This article expresses strictly personal views of the author and does not commit NATO in any way; neither does it profess to express the official position of the Alliance, which is only expressed by statements agreed to by the North Atlantic Council.

However, NATO members usually refer to three "baskets" of ideas, or three areas of consideration, of defense reform:

- defense restructuring and reform of defense management practices and institutions;
- development of defense capabilities required to meet both new and traditional defense-related challenges; and
- actions that will increase countries' ability to contribute to NATO-led crisis response operations.

The general perception, however, is that these areas and, possibly, others may well be considered as contributing to defense reform, which implies a change in the ways of doing business, of mentality on defense-related issues, of objectives, of resource allocations, and of priorities. Because of the complexity of the nature of defense reform, this paper does not define the term, defense reform; what has been said already is enough to convey the necessary basic conceptual understanding of defense reform.

THE ACTORS IN DEFENSE REFORM

Nations The most important actors in defense reform are the nations themselves. Because the defense effort is first and foremost a national effort, national authorities will have to take the lead in addressing it. Areas requiring national action include:

Development of a conceptual orientation of the defense effort: Nations will need to define in their strategic and defense-related documents (security policy, defense policy, military doctrine, etc.) their security and defense objectives. Such definition will have to take into account threat perceptions, national interests, international relations, resource constraints, and other relevant factors. Development of appropriate legislation is part of this effort, including adaptation of existing legislation to meet new understandings.

Development of an appropriate defense planning system: Conceptual perceptions for defense reform need to be implemented based on careful short-, medium-, and long-term planning efforts, taking into account all of the factors that may influence the system positively or negatively. This requires a defense planning system adapted to each country's requirements that is simple, efficient, and rigorous enough to consider the required factors in the context of the country's special circumstances. A defense planning system that may be good for one country may not fit the specific requirements of another. At a minimum, each defense planning system should include a process for strategic guidance; translating strategic objectives into concrete goals for action with clearly defined objectives, time lines, and resources; regular information collection and feedback and reporting procedures; analytical tools and self-adjustment mechanisms; and monitoring and oversight arrangements.

Adequate resource allocations to support the goals developed by the defense planning system: In an era of tight resources, even for more affluent countries, it is of utmost importance to ensure that the resource requirements identified by the defense planning system to support the agreed goals are met by the national authorities. This is obviously one of the most difficult elements, since there is strong competition for the limited resources by many other sectors.

Develop appropriate information strategy in support of defense reform efforts: A very important factor for the success of defense reform is to keep government officials, legislators, the country's political forces, the media, and the public well informed and supportive. Information that is disseminated should explain why defense reform is needed, why there is an urgency to implement it, its main objectives, its expected benefits for the country, the steps planned and how they are phased, and, finally, resources needed and why the required sacrifices are so important. Obviously, a high degree of national consensus is needed for the defense reform effort to be successful.

Developing appropriate social programs to deal with the potential adverse effects of defense reform: Like any important reform, defense reform does have its negative and unpopular aspects, which will need to be addressed. One of the most sensitive issues is downsizing of defense structures, which often results in decommissioning considerable numbers of officers, noncommissioned officers (NCOs), and civilians employed in the defense sector and, in many cases, base closures with their concomitant negative effect on local economies. These issues will need to be thought out carefully and addressed at a very early stage in planning for defense reform. A society that is facing an ailing economy and high unemployment rates, and a government with limited public support for its major initiatives outside the economic and social sectors may find it very difficult to accept sacrifices for defense reform. A priority issue is retraining redundant personnel and rehabilitation plans for bases that will close down eventually, so they can continue making positive contributions to local economies by developing other forms of economic activity.

NATO NATO also can make an important contribution to defense reform efforts, both at the Alliance level—for member countries, and at the national level, by developing guidelines and programs that can help nations to design their national defense reform efforts. Some contributions the Alliance is making toward the progress of defense reform in member countries follow.

THE DEFENSE PLANNING SYSTEM OF THE ALLIANCE The Alliance has a defense planning system that addresses collective defense as well as crisis-response operations and other forms of defense challenges deemed appropriate for Alliance-level consideration. The system used includes strategic guidance, planning objectives in the form of Force Goals, an information and feedback process through the Defense Planning Questionnaire and other forms of reports, a review of implementation and adjustment process through the various steps of the Defense Review process, and Alliance-level guidance and coordination of defense reform efforts undertaken by member nations. Force, armaments, logistics, and civil emergency planning are important components of the system.

THE DEFENSE CAPABILITIES INITIATIVE (DCI) Launched during the Washington Summit in 1999, the DCI aims to reinvigorate the Alliance's defense capabilities by identifying a series of fifty-nine measures that, if implemented by Alliance forces, would result in significant improvement of the defense potential of the Alliance. Improvements are needed to enable the Alliance to adapt to new security challenges and become more effective. These measures address issues such as deployability; sustainability; effective engagement; survivability; and advanced, interoperable, and deployable command and control and information systems. Probably one of the most far-reaching Alliance defense reform initiatives, these measures aim to improve the defense capabilities of Alliance forces. Progress to date is quite encouraging, but defense reform is a long and resource intensive process. However, a considerable amount of work will be required before the DCI's objectives are fully met.

Bilateral and Multilateral Arrangements Another important contribution to defense reform is made through an intricate network of bilateral and multilateral arrangements among NATO member countries for sharing expertise, joint projects, and providing various forms of assistance to countries requiring such assistance, including in the form of common funding.

REFORM IN THE CONTEXT OF NATO'S OUTREACH PROGRAMS
The Programs: Defense reform is one of the priority issues in NATO's outreach programs in the context of the EAPC/PfP, but also in the context of NATO-Russia relations through the PJC, NATO-Ukraine relations through the NUC, and NATO's relations with its MAP and Planning and Review Process (PARP) Partners. Each one of these programs is a vehicle to promote essentially the same vision of defense reform, depending on each Partner's specific case.

Description of Defense Reform in the Context of Outreach Programs
VISION AND OBJECTIVES   The work being done by NATO and Partners in defense reform has its own vision and objectives, which have been pursued consistently since the inception of NATO's outreach process.

The vision of defense reform, as promoted by NATO to its outreach Partners, is to see reformed and democratically controlled defense sectors that can make an important contribution to the development of truly democratic societies, totally divorced from their totalitarian past. Partners that have implemented defense reform successfully then could develop strong and stable relations with the democratic states of the Alliance and other European non-NATO democratic states and ensure stability, security, good-neighbor relations, and prosperity in a Europe without confrontations and dividing lines.

Many of the objectives of defense reform in the context of this outreach are the same for all Partners, while there are several country-specific objectives for addressing local circumstances in the countries concerned.

DEFENSE RESTRUCTURING   The Armed Forces of the Central and Eastern European Partner countries as well as those of the Partners in South Eastern Europe and in the Caucasus and Central Asia are in urgent need of defense restructuring. This restructuring can take many different forms, such as:

• building armed forces where none exist (for example, in the Baltic nations);

- downsizing forces where their size is disproportionate to current security and resource realities (for example, Russia, Ukraine);
- rebalancing forces where the ratio of regular officers to NCOs and soldiers is highly skewed and unrealistic, the constitution of forces does not reflect the ethnic or other makeup of the population (for example, in Central Asian countries, almost 90 percent of the officers are Russian, although Russians represent only a small percentage of the population), or the existing structures represent odd formations put together for specific reasons that should be corrected eventually (for example, the forces in Bosnia-Herzegovina);
- tailoring defense structures to new defense perceptions and priorities in cases of countries where the role of defense forces is perceived differently from in the past, and where new structures are created and former structures are dropped (for example, Romania, Bulgaria);
- making forces more affordable where current economic realities no longer can support the structures of the past (for example, Albania); and
- some Partner countries may have to undergo more than one form of defense restructuring, depending on their circumstances.

DEFENSE MANAGEMENT   Management of the defense effort may require a series of reforms that, again, may be applicable to most Partners, but there are also several country-specific variations. Objectives of defense management include:

- Resource management is a priority issue with most Partners that have had little or no experience in this respect—that is, where, in the case of countries that emerged from the former Soviet Union or the former Yugoslavia, economies were planned centrally from Moscow or Belgrade with little or no involvement of the regional components of those former states.
- Credible, dependable, and efficient defense planning systems need to be developed in many Partner countries, most of which have no experience in real defense planning.
- Democratic control of the armed forces does not characterize several of the Partner countries, while in others, despite visible progress, a lot still needs to be done.
- Equitable personnel policy in defense management—some Partner defense establishments have no discernible personnel policy. For

example, they may have a disproportionately high number of senior and general officers, essentially as a social measure to increase the financial intake of officers without reference to the actual force structure requirements. In other Partner countries, military and NCO academies started operating only recently, and with questionable selection criteria and training objectives.

- Transparency of the defense sector is particularly important in defense planning and budgeting and in personnel-related issues. Transparency is required toward other government sectors, political parties, parliament, the media, and the broader public, with the realization that certain select and sensitive elements of the defense effort may need to be kept nontransparent because of the nature of the issues concerned. However, these latter cases should be only a very small part of the spectrum of defense-related activity and should be the exception rather than the rule.
- Interagency coordination, another objective of defense reform, appears to be difficult to achieve in many Partner countries. The objective in this respect is to coordinate activities of the entire defense sector, not just the ministry of defense (MOD). In many Partner countries, the most difficult coordination and the fiercest turf fighting is between the MOD and the General Staff.
- Managing socioeconomic issues of defense reform is also very important. Downsizing and defense restructuring frequently result in military and defense sector civilian personnel losing their jobs and military bases and other services being closed. Many Partners face such problems, but very few have developed the necessary measures to deal with them effectively.

DEFENSE CAPABILITIES   Current and future security challenges as understood today probably will include small-scale regional or ethnic conflicts as well as humanitarian crises and peace support operations. In such a security landscape, Partners' forces may be required to participate in operations to manage these crises, most likely alongside forces from Allied and third countries. For Partners have to develop certain capabilities to participate in such operations. This represents another set of defense reform objectives that include developing sustainability (including rotation of forces and adequate logistics support); deployability (including capability for short-notice deployments); mobility (for both land and air mobility, including strategic airlift); survivability (including air defense and nuclear, biological, and chemical weapons [NBC] defense); combat effectiveness; engineering capabilities; and medical capabilities.

Most of these capabilities are borrowed from similar objectives of the Alliance's DCI and are required by Partners as well in view of their possible codeployments with Allies in combined operations. Another set of objectives in this respect aims to create capabilities for Partner forces to participate in multinational headquarters that may be deployed for NATO-led operations, such as Combined Joint Task Force (CJTF) headquarters, Multinational Joint Logistic Center (MJLC) staff, disaster relief, and Civil-Military Cooperation (CIMIC).

All the above capabilities are pursued for PARP and MAP countries through Partnership Goals (PGs), developed by the Alliance and accepted by Partners as objectives for capability development. These PGs also aim to create maximum possible interoperability between allies and Partners through modernization of communications equipment, information systems, and logistic support capabilities, among others. In the case of aspirants, in particular, the PGs also aim to create capabilities for Partners that will enable them to deal with the additional requirements related to NATO membership because some of them may become NATO members in the near future.

Ability to contribute to NATO-led crisis-response operations is another area that addresses a number of objectives for defense reform. Partner participation in such operations requires the defense capabilities already referred to in this section. Furthermore, defense reform objectives include achievement by Partners of the necessary legal and security arrangements for participation of Partners' forces in such operations. For some Partners, constitutional and/or legal constraints exist on participation of their forces in peace support operations. An important objective then should be to encourage Partners to lift such constraints.

In the same vein, other related objectives are to encourage Partners' to allocate the necessary resources to allow their forces to participate in NATO-led crisis response operations. Finally, another objective in the context of defense reform is to protect classified information related to such operations.

DEVELOPMENT OF DEFENSE REFORM PROGRAMS   In the context of the Outreach programs NATO has launched, NATO's Partners have developed defense reform programs through several related but different processes.

Among these, the MAP Partners' work on defense reform with the nine MAP countries is probably the most intensive, and the process leading to defense reform is much more sophisticated than for other Partners.

In the case of MAP Partners, the main requirement is to develop Annual National Plans (ANPs), which look in detail at the entire defense sector and identify measures to be taken to implement reforms.

The ANP's first chapter discusses political and economic issues relating to the security policy of the country, good-neighbor relations, public acceptability of potential future NATO membership, participation of the country in various multilateral forums, and describes the economy of the country, including basic economic indicators, and the measures taken or planned to improve identified shortcomings. In this and other ANP chapters, the measures identified not only should be described, but also assigned a time line within which they need to be implemented; the resources required for implementation, with an indication of the degree of their availability; and the expected impact of implementing each measure on the defense or other sectors.

The second chapter is at the core of the defense reform effort and deals with a host of issues, such as defense and military policy, military doctrine, forces and command structure, planning for force restructuring, interdepartmental coordination, PfP activity, bilateral cooperation, and measures having to do with reforms and improvements in the defense sector.

The third chapter focuses on affordability and resource allocation to the defense effort, defense expenditures, and measures to improve resource allocation to implement the defense reform effort.

The fourth chapter, which deals with personnel, information, and document security issues, normally includes information on existing security arrangements and the measures required to improve them.

The fifth chapter normally refers to constitutional and legal arrangements concerning use of the country's facilities and infrastructure for cooperative activities with NATO and other Partners, including requirements for NATO-led crisis response operations where the country may participate. It also refers to potential constitutional or legal restrictions concerning stationing foreign troops in the country or deployment of the Partner's troops outside the country.

In addition to the ANP, which is reviewed every year to ensure that it stays current, the Partner prepares annually a survey response that draws from the ANP and other national sources to report on the latest status and developments in each of the five chapter areas mentioned earlier. This report responds to a very precise, thorough, and extensive questionnaire—the MAP Survey—sent every year by NATO to gather information from MAP aspirants.

NATO's main tool to effect defense reform in MAP countries, the Planning and Review Process (PARP), is modeled after the Alliance's defense planning procedure and is based on Ministerial Guidance for its strategic guidance. NATO force planners generate a series of itemized defense reform objectives, called PGs, which refer to a specific defense reform objective, either of a general nature or for reform of each individual service of the armed forces, including a definition, time line, and other relevant information. Each MAP country receives a set of proposed such PGs, depending on the specific country circumstances, that are considered to be the most appropriate to promote defense reform. After a negotiating process, each MAP country accepts a number of such PGs that must be implemented within the agreed time lines. After accepting the PGs, countries' progress in implementing them is monitored annually through the responses to the MAP Survey (mentioned above), and through NATO Team visits to the capitals of the MAP countries to discuss further details of PG implementation and other aspects of the defense reform effort.

Drawing information from Survey responses and discussions of the NATO Team in each MAP capital, NATO prepares an annual progress report on implementation of defense reform and on overall progress in the various fields of the country's defense effort. The progress report, organized into five chapters mirroring the five chapters of the ANP, is discussed in appropriate NATO committees (PMSC, SPC[R] and, finally, at the North Atlantic Council, with the Partner country present to provide Alliance feedback to the Partner's progress in defense reform.

Non-MAP PARP Partners: In the case of the Partners who are members of the PARP process but who are not MAP aspirants (ten Partners), a process similar to the one described for MAP countries is followed. One difference is that the Partner does not need to prepare an ANP, although some Partners may do so for their own internal use (for example, Croatia, which is not a MAP country but is under the regime of the Intensified Dialogue within PARP). All PARP Partners are offered a series of PGs, specially tailored to their individual case, addressing improvements they need to make interoperability. However, if they wish, they may adopt the far more rigorous and demanding PGs normally addressed to the MAP countries. Implementation and the development progress in the defense sector and in PfP cooperation are monitored through annual Partner responses of to a PARP Survey (Questionnaire), which is identical in content to the MAP Survey, but non-MAP Partners are expected to respond only to some of the questions (only those not specifically addressed to MAP countries). Eventually, a report is prepared for those countries as well, called a PARP Assessment, which is a status report on and assessment of the progress of PfP cooperation and the defense reform effort.

In the specific case of Ukraine, which is a PARP country, but which also has a "distinctive" relationship with NATO through the NATO-Ukraine Charter, the focus of cooperation is on defense reform. In addition to the PARP process, NATO experts have helped Ukraine to develop a series of specially tailored National Defense Reform Objectives (NDROs), which take the place of the country's objectives on defense reform. These NDROs cover a large spectrum of defense reform objectives, and Ukraine has agreed to adopt them as a matter of urgency.

Other non-PARP Partners: For the remaining seven PfP countries that do not participate in PARP, defense reform is not considered to be a priority issue, and the only process for encouraging and monitoring progress is through Individual Partnership Programs (IPPs) and IPP assessments and through ad hoc visits of expert teams. Progress is slow, and there is no other mutually accepted process for this purpose.

Bosnia-Herzegovina (BiH): In the case of BiH, defense reform focuses on more affordable defense structures for the Federation and for *Republica Srpska* (RS) and, eventually, on creating state-level defense structures. The process used is brokerage of talks leading to defense reform led by the Stabilization Force (SFOR) on behalf of the international community.

Implementing Defense Reform CHALLENGES, PROBLEMS, SUCCESSES
Implementing defense reform has not been easy for most countries. Many problems recur, including some that are more country specific. The following paragraphs look at the challenges of and problems in implementing defense reform.

CONVINCING NATIONS OF THE NEED FOR DEFENSE REFORM This is an important challenge, especially for countries in transition, as most Partners are, since many very important social and economic issues require urgent attention. For these countries, the need for defense reform is not immediately evident because, in most cases, they perceive no external threat and are not convinced they need to dedicate scarce resources, in great demand by other sectors, and effort to defense reform.

MAINTAINING THE MOMENTUM FOR DEFENSE REFORM   Even if countries, such as the MAP countries, have accepted the need to proceed with defense reform, another challenge is to convince them to continue these efforts with the same momentum and implement the objectives. MAP countries are faced with the dilemma of what will happen if they have allocated scarce resources to defense reform and, in the end, are not invited to join NATO. In non-MAP countries, the pace of defense reform cannot be maintained easily either because of changing governments or changing priorities.

REACTION OF THE ESTABLISHMENT   One important challenge is the reaction of the defense establishment, which resists any change that may affect the positions, functions, and jobs of those already serving in the sector. This important challenge, which exists in many countries, either will not allow any serious reforms to take place or will try to derail them if they manage to start. Some countries, for example, have many general officers who are totally unjustified by the force and command structure. If a defense reform effort is launched, because of government pressure, these generals, who are afraid of losing their jobs, naturally will be bitterly opposed to the required changes.

REALIZING THAT DEFENSE REFORM IS AN URGENT REQUIREMENT BUT ALSO A LONG PROCESS   The urgency is related to the fact that, on the one hand, defense structures need to be adapted to current security requirements and, on the other, if reforms are not implemented quickly, scarce resources will continue to be squandered on obsolete, heavy, inefficient, and expensive structures, making resource management even more difficult. At the same time, defense reforms need a long time to be implemented fully since all changes require thorough study; establishing a legal foundation for the changes; and long periods to train personnel, procure equipment, and build infrastructure, and all these changes require time to be accepted as well.

DEALING WITH THE SOCIOECONOMIC PROBLEMS OF DEFENSE REFORM Laying off large numbers of military personnel is a usual result of downsizing defense structures. Although several Partner countries have developed quite attractive financial packages, known as "golden handshakes," for those being retired, longer-term measures are needed, such as retraining retired officers so they can find jobs elsewhere. There are programs to address this issue, but more work is required.

PROVISION OF CLASSIFIED INFORMATION In some cases, a major problem has been provision of classified information by the military authorities of the Partner concerned. There have been cases where the required information, which represents a standardized request for all Partners, simply could not be provided because it was classified. Eventually, through Presidential Decree, the information was provided to NATO, and, only later, and after a lot of negotiations, the information was declassified and the relevant documents could be circulated to NATO members for their consideration.

Despite all of these challenges and problems, defense reform has advanced to a considerable degree in many Partner countries, with the MAP countries in the forefront of this effort, as might be expected. Some of these success stories are described below.

BULGARIA Maybe one of the most impressive cases of downsizing of armed forces, considering it was a relatively late starter, is Bulgaria. Of a total force of 112,000 in 1999, planned reforms foresee a ceiling of forty-five thousand for 2004 (Plan 2004). This implies large numbers of personnel retiring and laying off around twenty-three thousand civilians. One important element in this defense reform effort is that demographic trends will reduce the number of conscripts dramatically (from forty-two thousand to twenty-five thousand in 2004), Bulgaria needs to compensate with reductions and partial professionalization of the forces. One important plus has been popular support for the reforms as a result of a successful public information campaign. However, the recent change of government, on the one hand, and base closures, which are disputed by a part of the political forces, on the other hand, threaten to have a negative effect on the momentum for change. The program to retrain retired officers by the Stability Pact and the World Bank will offer a substantial boost to Bulgaria's defense reform effort.

ROMANIA Romania also has a very impressive record of downsizing—from 225,000 in the early 1990s to around 50 percent of that number in 2004, if planned resources are indeed available. If not, the total force could fall as low as eighty-seven thousand. Also, the reduction accommodates annual requirements for conscript intake, which is more than adequate for the planned force. Romania's armed forces also were characterized by a disproportionately large number of officers and, even more, in the senior ranks. By 2003, the officer corps will be reduced to half of what it used to be. The number of colonels, for example, will be reduced from twenty-three hundred to 630. These reductions have not been easy, however. Early cuts were made without any considerable compensation, which created serious discontent. Lately, however, retirement compensation packages have improved substantially, and an option has been added to retrain retired officers, financed by the Stability Pact and the World Bank, which mitigates the negative impact of massive retirements.

OTHER POSITIVE DEVELOPMENTS   In the case of Ukraine, after a lot of effort and difficulties, there has been some important progress in defense reform through acceptance of a number of National Defense Reform Objectives that will cover the entire spectrum of the armed forces.

In all the MAP countries, the net percentage of gross domestic product (GDP) allocated to defense—essentially to finance defense reform—has been increased. The drawback, however, has been that, since planning rarely extends beyond one year, it is not at all certain that the projected resources actually will be available when required.

Another important positive development, essentially in the MAP countries, has been the marked increase of the public support for defense reform, despite its impact on resources. In most cases, this has been the result of a well-thought and coordinated public information campaign.

Defense reform has seen considerable progress in Slovakia and Slovenia as well, where the aim is not downsizing but building adequate, effective, and well-balanced and -trained forces.

FAILURES OF DEFENSE REFORM EFFORTS   Although there has been some defense reform progress in *Ukraine*, it is less than expected mainly because of the country's very centralized system, which requires essentially all important issues to be decided at the presidential level. An additional complicating factor has been the very limited support for defense reform effort among the senior leadership of the armed forces, who are not enthusiastic about the required changes.

Defense reform in *Albania* has not gone very far. Although the crises in the Balkans have had an important negative impact on defense reform efforts, perhaps more important negative factors have been frequent changes of defense, a lack of any realistic resource management system, and a tendency to develop plans for force structures that try to save the jobs of the existing officer corps rather than build on the basis of real requirements as perceived in the security and defense policy of the country.

In the case of the *former Yugoslav Republic of Macedonia*, progress has been checked severely because of serious internal crisis. Defense reform here, obviously, has not gone very far, and it will take some time before such efforts are resumed.

Slow defense reform progress in previous years in *Romania* was due to a plan that was not well thought out: retired officers were given inadequate compensation packages, so, to assuage their discontent, many were rehired as civilians in the defense sector, thus resulting in minimal net changes. This approach has changed, but there was a significant delay in doing so.

LESSONS LEARNED

The defense reform efforts described in this paper have been major undertakings for countries in transition and for NATO countries. Although there is no generally accepted definition of defense reform, the experience accumulated from the efforts of so many countries points to a number of lessons learned that may be particularly useful for countries embarking on this effort. Most of these lessons have been mentioned earlier, but they are included here for reference:

Urgent Need to Adapt the Conceptual Basis for the Defense Sector: As a matter of priority, countries in transition must review their security and defense policy, military doctrines, and basic legislation for the defense sector, to adapt all of them to the new realities.

Defense Reform Is an Urgent Process: The defense sector uses many resources, so it must be adapted quickly to current perceptions in the security and defense policy of the country, and spending badly needed resources on obsolete, inefficient, and expensive defense structures must stop.

Defense Reform Is a Long Process: Before embarking on any serious defense reform efforts, governments should keep in mind that it is a long process and should not grow impatient and abandon their efforts. Defense reform efforts normally last longer than the usual term of office of governments, so broad political consensus is required before embarking on such reform.

Public Support: Defense reform requires resources, major changes, and, often, difficult and unpopular decisions. To have any chance of success, therefore, openness; wide-scale political consensus; and parliamentary, media, and public opinion support are needed. To achieve all these, governments need to study their steps, build consensus, and launch a well-thought-out public information campaign that will need to be maintained for as long as the defense reform effort continues.

Need for an Effective Defense Planning System: No credible defense reform effort can be launched without first developing an effective defense planning system tailored to the specific circumstances of the country. Advice from other countries normally is very useful.

Resources: defense reform is an expensive process, although in the longer term, it usually results in significant economies. In view of these considerations, and the fact that resources in countries in transition are very limited and in great demand, defense reform efforts must have adequate resources. Resources should not be allocated theoretically; there must be long-term resource planning to guarantee resources for the defense reform efforts.

Socioeconomic Issues: Defense reform often results in laying off large numbers of military personnel. This creates serious social problems, which will need to be addressed by the government. In addition to developing satisfactory retirement compensation packages, governments need to arrange and finance (in several cases, with foreign assistance) courses to retrain retired officers.

CHAPTER ELEVEN

Reforms in Finnish Defense

Mika Kerttunen

GENERAL

Talking about reform in Finnish defense might give one perhaps a bit too exaggerated picture as not much has changed, nor has it needed to, since the end of the Cold War. The cornerstones of the Finnish security and defense policy—military nonalignment, national defense based on conscription and mobilization, and the doctrine of territorial defense— remained intact, and will continue to do so under prevailing conditions. Finnish defense is marked by continuity, a fundamental difference from a number of countries in both the east and west.

However, when one ignores these generalizations, the most noticeable abstractions, and enters the realm of defense, one faces complexity. Since the White Paper issued in 1997, some new ideas and emphasis have gained ground within the Finnish Defense Forces. These trends—for example, focusing on high technology, cutting down the number of war-time troops, and giving more weight to international cooperation and interoperability—are common to many European countries, so the various Finnish defense reforms are of greater interest to others as well.

This chapter focuses on two reports submitted by the Council of State to Parliament in 1997 and in 2001. The emphasis is on the 1997 paper because it launched the described development; the 2001 report was meant to be a review of progress only, so the actual and comprehensive report will not be released until 2004. This chapter discusses some general ideas, visions, and objectives and introduces how they were actually executed. In this context, it is important to keep in mind that, in Finland, these reports or previous Parliamentary Comity papers have not been binding on the political authorities as much as the White Papers of some other countries have been. Finland is seeking to increase government's role and possibilities for long-term defense planning following parliamentary tradition and underlining the need for wide understanding of defense related issues. Therefore, these latest reports serve to guide and legitimize as well as inform.

This chapter ends with more theoretical remarks and general lessons learned that, one hopes, are valuable and interesting. As Finnish defense itself is much more than Defense Forces effort and represents a wider perspective on security, these more civilian and societal aspects are evaluated as well. The facts presented here reflect official Finnish positions, but the observations and interpretations are the views of a more or less independent research officer.

Reforms Undertaken since 1997

The Council of State submitted a report, titled "The European Security Development and Finnish Defense,"[1] to the Parliament in March 1997. The purpose of this paper was to set forth guidelines that were to be followed in defense policy and the development of Defense Forces. The paper, which was originally prepared for the then existing Defense Council, described for the first time some overall development within the Finnish security environment and Europe. The changing face of Central and Eastern Europe at the time, and the wars, disputes, or conflicts in the former Soviet Union and Yugoslavia—as well as other post-Cold War symptoms—were causing instability in Europe. New security problems, such as terrorism, organized crime, drugs, and the proliferation of weapons of mass destruction were common challenges. Institutional efforts were important, but state actors and national actions had to play a primary role in meeting these challenges.

The White Paper concluded that, although European Union (EU) membership had strengthened Finland's international position, "no significant changes have occurred in Finland's military situation," so there was no need to revise the Finnish defense stance. Finnish airspace and the northernmost part of the country had retained their significance, and the importance of the Åland Islands and the (southern) coastal areas had increased as well. The disappearance of Cold War confrontation in Central Europe had not pacified the northern frontiers, but there seemed to be no change in the strategic significance of northern Europe. Although a number of positive developments had taken place in Central and Eastern Europe, the remaining, and increased, presence of major military actors in the north affected Finnish thinking.

The report mentioned, for the first time, that, in accordance with the United Nations (UN) Charter, Finland should seek the assistance of other countries in repelling an attack. It should be mentioned that, as a militarily nonaligned country, Finland does not consider any particular country to be an enemy, potential or otherwise. Defense is intended to deter military threats and to protect a nation's independence and security by force if necessary. The fluctuations of international relations and politics today naturally affect Finnish defense, but do not undermine or change these paramount values and objectives.

The second the report listed the following crisis and threat models, which might be considered when planning for Finland's defense:

1. *Political and military pressure*, which is associated with a threat of military force.
2. *A surprise strategic strike*, aimed at paralyzing and seizing vital targets and subjugating the national leadership.
3. *A large-scale offensive* to seize strategically important areas or use Finnish territory as a base for action against a third party.

These models reflect both the overall military reality within Finnish surroundings as well as the changing nature of war, the development of modern operative thinking, and the pursuit of greater readiness and technological efficiency. Capability to prevent and repel a strategic strike became the paramount goal in developing Finnish defense. In this threat model, the potential offender likely would have standing peacetime troops and use high-tech weaponry, effective firepower, and special forces operations. Surprise, speed, and intelligence are of the utmost importance if an attacker is to gain its goals with a limited number of troops.

Thus, the Finnish Defense Forces preparedness and reactive capacity gained more weight. Here, the emphasis was on ground forces when forming readiness brigades. The standard of both materiel and training was raised, thus enabling a substantial numerical reduction of ground forces.

Another major objective was to improve the Defense Forces' ability to cooperate with armed forces of other countries, with two goals in mind: to enhance Finland's capability to participate in international crisis management operations, and to create the capacity to receive outside military assistance in the event of an attack on Finland.

Major actions started or implemented since the 1997 report include:

1. *Establishment of three readiness brigades.* This includes introducing a new brigade organization (Brigade 2005), purchasing modern materiel, and developing doctrine and tactics.
2. *Reducing the number of wartime troops,* from 540,000 to 430,000, and brigades, from twenty-seven to twenty-two. Wartime troops were divided into Operational and Regional forces, to be considered the linchpin of Finland's defense, and include the most capable brigades—Brigade 2005 (three), Jaeger Brigades (six), and Armoured Brigades (two)—and the bulk of the mobile units of the Navy and the Air Force. The Regional Forces are limited in scale and scope, and they focus on defending key areas.
3. *More focus on international crisis management operations.* This in done in accordance with the Partnership for Peace (PfP) program and its goals, and covers a limited number of troops. These troops are earmarked and dedicated to the UN, the North Atlantic Treaty Organization (NATO) or, nowadays, EU crisis-management operations, and include three battalions, a few companies, and two naval vessels. In addition, the government decided later to participate in international exercises with eight fighter planes. This might lead to the Air Force's participation in actual operations, as well.
4. *A new system of training for conscripts.* The shortest time for national service was cut from eight months to six, but more emphasis was placed on training the specialists and leaders, who serve either nine or twelve months. This system focuses not only on cost savings, but also on increasing the internal cohesion of wartime forces because the leaders and the rank and file will conduct their national service at the same time and in the same unit.
5. *Procurement of modern materiel.* The most important factors here are intelligence, operational mobility, and effective firepower. Purchases have been concentrated on the readiness brigades, and practically no money is left to develop the Jaeger brigades. At the same time, acquisition of the F-18 C fighters has been completed.

One should keep in mind that the abovementioned developments are in line with the concept of territorial defense, which has continued to be the guiding principle of Finnish defense. The above steps have been taken to adapt territorial defense to meet the challenges of the developing political, doctrinal, and technological reality than to change it.

The report issued in June 2001, "The Finnish Security and Defense

Policy 2001,"[2] continued the ideas of the 1997 White Paper, emphasizing the importance of international cooperation in facing various threats and risks. The EU was of central importance to Europe's stability and security. As it considered the years 2001 to 2008, the report reiterated that territorial defense and general conscription should remain key defense principles.

Major differences in defense policy between the two papers include:

1. *Funding should be longer-term.* The government seeks to anchor defense funding because "the maintenance of the defense capability cannot follow the fluctuations of economic cycles." It was agreed that funding will average, at maximum, 10.8 billion FIM per year for the period 2001–2008. The current level is about 10.2 billion FIM per year, and, the 1997 report estimated that the level for 2005–2008 would be at the 9.2 billion level.

2. *The threat scenarios of 1997 have been revised.* Primarily this means paying more attention to regional crises, which may require varying degrees of enhanced readiness or may have only an indirect effect on or repercussions for Finland. Otherwise the scenarios presented already form the basis for defense planning.

3. *The question of the main weapon system for the Army* has been raised. Here, the debate fluctuated between opposing views supporting combat helicopters, new battle tanks, antitank missiles, or artillery systems.

4. *Wartime strength should be reduced* to maximum of 350,000 by the end of 2008. At the same time, the firepower and mobility of operational forces should be increased, but how that will be achieved remains to be evaluated in the next few years. Reductions will lead to organizing training and depot systems—that is, to close down some garrisons and depots. Maintaining fewer than 300,000 troops was mentioned unofficially. This would mean a force structure where a number of brigades would be reduced drastically while their performance would be raised to match any standard, and where the Navy and Air Force would retain their high-scale technological and operational capability. It is much too premature even to guess when, if ever, these ideas are put forward because current domestic and territorial demands favor large ground forces.

5. *Mobile maritime defense and improved interceptor capacity* are vital. Implementing greater capacity could include procurement of a

hovercraft squadron and taking advantage of the F-18's application properties and close combat capacity.

6. *Civilian crisis management* within the international forum should be emphasized. This suggestion is due mainly to the work on EU's civilian crisis management that was started at the Helsinki European Council and continued at Feira and Göteborg. Additional input has come from ongoing operations where the needs in this field are obvious and visible. In civilian crisis management, the priority should be on policing, the rule of law, civil administration, and civil protection.

7. *Importance and vulnerability of information systems* merit more attention. In safeguarding the operation of various technical systems in society, the focus has been on telecommunications, public media, information systems, payment systems, and money supply, as well as information technology repair, support, and maintenance functions. In addition, the energy sector is of utmost importance to a country as northern and well developed as Finland.

The focal areas in developing the defense system as stated in the 2001 report are:

1. *Command and control systems.* The objective here is to develop intelligence, surveillance, and command and control systems to enhance the capacity to produce the strategic and operational situation picture needed for decision making. The number of command echelons will be reduced, but no hints were given about the future of the three current defense commands or other regional (provincial) commands vis-à-vis a briefly mentioned "secure joint system."

2. *Army readiness formations.* Three Jaeger brigades should be upgraded to readiness brigades, already suggested in 1997. This requires acquisition of infantry fighting vehicles, armored personnel carriers, armored self-propelled mortars, and antitank missiles, which has been going on since 1997, but which has been intensified as initial research and development is completed.

3. *Interoperability for military crisis management.* In this area, goals set as part of development of the Common European Security and Defense Policy (CESDP), and agreed on within the PfP, program play a major role. The number of PfP/Planning and Review Process interoperability areas or partnership goals rose from thirteen to sixty-four during 1994–2001.

4. *War economy arrangement in an information society.* The dilemma here is the Defense Force's dependence on society's security supply at the same time as societal and technical development is decreasing the very same security. The aim is to establish a logistics framework linked to existing trade and industry systems. In addition, a proper balance among domestic production, national stockpiling, and external delivering is needed.

The views and concerns expressed in the 2001 report are more general in nature than those in 1997. Belief in both the EU's and NATO's capabilities to solve crisis seems to have increased, this naturally at the less threatening end of conflict spectrum. Financial, technical, and international development issues are better taken into consideration when developing Finnish defense and the country's Defense Forces. The concept of total defense has gotten more impetus, and national and international cooperation, collaboration, and interaction are considered vital now.

A rough summary of the factors, assessments, and conclusions in developing Finnish defense are presented in Table 1. One must keep in mind that, although the basic factors are more or less the same in each country, it is very easy to end up with totally different assessments and conclusions.

PROBLEMS AND CHALLENGES

Security perceptions, and the defense policy based on those perceptions, is more complex for Finland than for the most of her partners. For the outset, remaining militarily nonaligned does not provide the benefits of collective defense; rather, it requires national resources and independent capabilities. The end of the Cold War did not change Finland's geostrategic location; any instability on the other side of the thirteen-hundred-kilometer-long Finnish-Russian border will be felt immediately. And finally, unlike most other European countries, the issue of defending territory has remained on the Finnish agenda.[3]

Due to the complex of Finland's defense position, answering some of the more obvious questions was postponed until the next and comprehensive report, in 2004. The following issues have however been debated, and some of them will reappear in the near future. On the political level, the debates have tackled NATO membership and a more national question—the political preparation and drafting procedures of Finland's defense policy. One issue discussed is the balance between territorial

TABLE 1

A Summary of the Most Important Factors, Assessments, and Conclusions in Developing Finnish Defense

Factors	Assessment Drawn	Conclusions Made	Remarks
Strategic	Changes in Central Europe—continuity in the North with qualitative improvement within the surrounding armed forces; no immediate threat seen	Military nonalignment and national defense while continuously assessing ongoing development. Readiness for surprise and sudden attacks and threats must be increased.	Quantitative improvements made in the early 1990s
Political	Commitment to EU's Foreign and Security Policy and Western values	International participation and capability vital; defense is not just defending one's territory.	Participation within CESDP and Partnership for Peace/PARP
Economic	Scarce economic resources (1.2 percent of GPD); no intention to increase or decrease level of defense spending	Stable budget of 10.8 billion FIM for the next few years; no resources to professional/regular defense forces	
Geographic	Relatively large country with population density in the south. Lapland still in between NATO and Russia. Dependence on the Baltic Sea routes for foreign trade.	Territorial defense with large ground forces needed; small but high-quality naval and air forces to safeguard and defend values and assets	

Military	Well-functioning system based on territorial defense and large reserve. High-quality naval and air forces and some ground forces. Large number of still effective weaponry	Existing systems function well for the next few years. Technical and strategic developments make it possible, or even mandatory, to cut down number of the wartime troops to maintain adequate quality. Reaction and readiness forces needed	From 540,000 to 350,000 troops; from 27 to 22 brigades; 64 F-18 C fighters. Mines and missiles the backbone of maritime defense
Societal	High readiness to defend country; well-educated population concentrated in the south and in the cities; high-tech society	Conscription and mobilization form basis for wartime defense forces; information technology and high-tech systems offer new possibilities but are also vulnerable within military and society	

defense and the emphasis given to strategic strike and international crisis management. A question closer to home involves allocation of resources within the Defense Forces, mostly the balancing act between operating and materiel costs. These intertwined and interrelated issues increase the complexity, so a comprehensive vision of and approach to developing defense is vital.

The probable NATO membership of some, if not all, of the Baltic countries, and the Russian reaction, have cast a pall over decisions about some of the defense issues Finland is facing. As to the question of NATO membership, Finland follows a certain wait-and-see policy, while stressing that no dividing lines should be drawn in Europe. At the same time, Finland is waiting for a way into NATO. This options-open policy builds on two assumptions: Under prevailing conditions, NATO membership would not increase Finland's security (because there is no imminent threat), and under changed conditions, it is possible, even probable, that Finland's application would be accepted. No government or other officials have elaborated on what changing conditions or factors would cause Finland to reconsider NATO membership. Perhaps the most likely path is the European one. If integration within European security and defense policy and the EU cooperation with NATO intensifies, Finland naturally would want to be included. Similarily, Finnish nonalignment could turn out be obsolete if Sweden decides to apply for the membership; each country is observing the other closely in terms of this issue. An external threat that would force Finland to seek security from the Atlantic Alliance is not likely in the foreseeable future.

In general, the arguments against NATO membership have been political—Finland being dragged into conflicts that are not in her interest, an isolated Russia tempted to react in a way that would jeopardize Finland's security; economic—Finland would have to increase defense spending; and military—no reinforcements the allies could muster would be enough to defend Finland. On the other hand, there is some fear that Finland would be left alone and outside of her natural Western framework. In addition, defense is arguably more cost-effective within the Alliance. At any rate, Finnish public opinion is not in favor of membership—some 20 percent to 25 percent support it—but the majority of Finns still support an options-open policy.

With regard to the EU's Common European Security and Defense Policy (CESDP), as in Finland's policy on the EU in general, Finland is eagerly participating in development of the Union's capability to manage crises. This is not seen to contradict nonalignment as crisis management is not developed as part of a common or collective defense. The same deep commitment goes with the Partnership for Peace and other cooperation with the NATO. The institutional and operative developments within both organizations[4] are in Finland's interest and, at least indirectly, increasing her security. These developments contribute to the vitality of the transatlantic link,[5] a vital factor for Finland that is important in the EU context, too.

The second political debate focused on domestic procedures. Both the 1997 and 2001 papers were drafted and prepared within the government, by the ministries and Defense Forces, respectively, and submitted to Parliament, along with the opinions of the standing foreign and defense policy committees. This differs from procedure in the 1970s and early 1980s, when Parliamentary Defense Comities prepared the reports. This enabled all political parties to be involved in the process, and the reports were based on consensus, although they did include some opposing remarks. During the years of the Cold War and the Friendship, Cooperation and Mutual Assistance Treaty with the Soviet Union, defense was an issue that was above day-to-day politics, and parliamentary consensus on it was one way to guarantee trust and peaceful coexistence with the Soviet Union.

The current, government-centered approach is one of the steps taken to increase government's role and emphasize parliamentary procedures. As in other political arenas, especially in regard to EU issues, government has more constitutional powers, so it is also natural that defense should as well. Another example of this development is abolition of the Defense Council, whose duties were reassigned to the Government Committee on Foreign and Security Policy and the Ministry of Defense. A new Security and Defense Committee, consisting of the permanent undersecretaries of respective ministries, was set up to assist these authorities.

These developments have shunted opposition out of the preparation process. These opponents doubt the government's commitment to maintain military nonalignment and question the rationality of certain cuts, shutdowns and weapon acquisitions, all of which are interpreted as undermining territorial defense, an issue of utmost partisan importance to the current main opposition party.

A more practical problem relating to the preparation process has been the unclear status of the submitted reports. The previous reports issued by Parliamentary Defense Comities were not binding on either Parliament or government, although the Ministry of Defense and the Defense Forces referred to them as the resources given were not at the level seen necessary by the Comities.

During debate concerning the 1997 report and its implementation, this very issue arose again. According to the report, "A central procurement . . . will commence in the beginning of the next decade when helicopters are purchased to transport forces and provide fire support." The defense establishment interpreted this to mean that approving report gave Parliament a mandate to actually purchase both transport and combat helicopters. Parliament saw the case differently. This was the first time since World War II that Parliament had intervened so decisively in acquisitions.[6] Without entering this debate, one can observe that perhaps members of Parliament refused this kind of wider interpretation because some of them felt they had been misled with the purchase, in the 1990s, of the F-18 C interceptors. This acquisition was approved at a cost that did not include major weapon systems, so it required more resources later. The final decision on helicopters authorized procurement of the transport but not the combat helicopters.

The 2001 report handled the case of combat helicopters more carefully expressed and made no promises to anyone: "Weapon systems to be examined will include at least combat helicopters." NH-90 transport helicopters finally were ordered in September 2001. The actual status and importance of these reports was increased indirectly by this very concrete and occasionally hectic debate.

Examples mentioned earlier show the sensitive nature of defense policy domestically, too. Although this issue rarely wins elections, it does affect employment regionally and locally. It is said that all politics is local, especially when reform is interpreted as cutbacks and shutdowns. One cannot expect to get any so-called peace dividends from these "savings." Rationalizing the organization and closing down garrisons does, in fact, increase costs: new barracks, garrisons, and training facilities have to built elsewhere, and newly unemployed people must be reeducated, relocated, or otherwise supported. Some barracks and buildings can be sold, but the demand for them has not been as great as expected, and to whom would one want to sell old but still lethal weapons systems?

Financing has been, and always will be, a challenge. Funding is a question itself, but for the purposes of this paper, it is enough just to say that resources should meet the tasks of the defense. Although defense spending in Finland is only about 1.2 percent of gross domestic product (GDP), this kind of imbalance has not been seen to exist, at least not in the official statements given or actions taken. One could argue, however, that it just has not been fully discerned yet. This leads to the question of whether the current tasks of national defense, in the form of territorial defense, and increasing international commitments are too much to expect, considering the accepted level of defense spending. The answer is not, at least not in the Western world,[7] to increase spending, but to decrease it or maintain it at the same level.

In the case of Finland, a limited defense budget, too few units to develop, and downsizing from wartime strength are problematic. There is an imbalance between the desire to defend the whole territory (337,000 square kilometers) and the limited number of operationally capable troops. Politically, the government could not be perceived as favoring any particular part of the country over any other. The essence of the territorial defense, and the reasoning behind it, has been to take advantage of Finland's large size and use guerrilla warfare and local units to slow and wear down the enemy, and to protect the most important areas while at the same time preparing and concentrating operative units for counterattacks. The scenario, the most threatening one for a nation's independence, is not very probable at the moment.

The mobilization strength of seven hundred thousand of the Cold War era has been reduced to 350,000 troops, which, though better equipped than before, are increasingly divided into those who have and those who have not. And although the focus is now on the three readiness brigades and, as before, the Jaeger brigades, there just has not been enough money to procure all the needed and planned materiel. The bulk of the wartime army, Jaeger, and the infantry brigades have to settle for older equipment and leftovers from the better-equipped units.

Finland's overall material status was improved considerably by two major arms deals in the 1990s. A great deal of secondhand equipment was purchased from Germany, which was a cheap and fast way to increase the army's firepower and mobility, but even this situation was not without its problems. The existing maintenance and storage system could not handle all the material, particularly the T-72 main battle tanks, which had not been modernized and had no proper shelter. Replacing J-35 and Mig-21 interceptors with modern F-18 Hornets had been pre-planned, but took longer than expected and did not increase the overall number of interceptors. At least the acquisition was completed without any major setbacks and ahead of schedule. Training, command and control, maintenance, and logistic systems were restructured adequately or adapted to receive a totally new-generation fighter. Collateral costs, such as education and training systems, repair and maintenance, and other logistical needs must be considered when calculating the cost materiel, and should cover the lifetime of the equipment.

Another financial imbalance was apparent between material and operative expenditures. Material expenditure currently accounts for 35 percent of the defense budget. During the Hornet acquisition, however, this proportion exceeded 45 percent, so there literally was very little room to maneuver. Operations—exercises, educating conscripts, and refresher training—account for 18 percent of the Finnish defense budget. This covers training some twenty-eight thousand conscripts annually, and calling some thirty thousand men and women to refresher training. The goal is to call thirty-five thousand, which would maintain the "performance of forces required to repel a strategic strike," as stated in the 2001 report. This is an illuminating example of how scarce resources have to be allotted, this time in response to a single threat scenario and involving a limited number of troops. Ever increasing rising technological costs—which are generally assessed at around 5 percent to 7 percent—should not compromise operative demands and competence. Chief of Defense Staff Lieutenant General Ilkka Hollo has elaborated on this issue by stating that one of the vital challenges for the 2001 revision is to bring materiel, personnel, and operating costs in line with the responsibilities of the Defense Forces. The current level of resources should afford the following:

1. forces based on general conscription for defending all of Finland and her citizens;
2. skillful (and professional) troops to repel a strategic strike; and
3. well-trained and equipped forces for international missions.[8]

Not having enough proper equipment to not having enough trained troops leads one to question the rationality of financial allocation or the defense system itself, or both. It is not the purpose here to solve this problem but, rather, to raise it, and point out that it will worsen if it is not solved. Finland's neighbors, Norway and Sweden, have resolved very similar financial problems—with 1.5 and 2.5 times larger budgets, respectively—by more comprehensive cuts and sharper focusing. This has been possible for them because they are relying either on allied support and reinforcements or on domestic capability to adapt flexibly to threatening situations. From a Finnish viewpoint, they are taking a calculated risk by downsizing their existing capabilities. Due to her nonalignment, geographic location, and scarce financial and technological resources, Finland can follow neither path. The Finnish paradox is understanding the need and the willingness to defend one's country while being reluctant to grant the financial resources to do it.

Another bifurcation that has concerned Finns is between national security issues and demands for international participation. Once again, this is perceived to be a question of money: Should international operations and cooperation take resources away from national defense? This is not the case if we look at the whole defense budget. The amount of money spent for international responsibilities is a relatively small percentage of Finland's defense budget. The problem is the resulting division of resources and, thus, of capabilities as a result of these financial restrains. Exercises focus on either crisis management or repelling strategic strikes. International participation hampers the more national needs, but the experience, both personal and material, gained from such participation benefits national tasks as well. Doubt also has been expressed about the impact of international participation on Finland's nonalignment—on how increasing and intensifying cooperation within and between the EU and NATO eventually will lead to military alliance and, thus, drag Finland into conflicts that are not in her interest. In a country where the will to defend is a value itself and a force-multiplier in the reserve-based field army, extensive and expensive international commitments could become an undermining factor. Even the domestic actions taken can be interpreted to represent some hidden agendas, especially when the need for change and reform is not stated explicitly.

Major cuts in the size of the field army lead to questions about the need to train 80 percent of the male population. To have a reserve of 350,000 troops requires 17,500 trained reservists annually who commit twenty years, so the reservists range in age from twenty to forty. This means the current volume of conscription exceeds military needs by about 30 percent. Once again, political and societal reasons and the doctrine of territorial defense favor both conscription and its volume.

Given the certain changes in Russian attitudes toward NATO, and the events of 11 September incidents, political and public opinion is asking for another evaluation of defense policy. The government has remained calm, however, and sees no need to review current policy or any actions taken or implemented. These developments are to be assessed and submitted in the 2004 report. The challenge, of course, is to balance between long-term and often status quo-based planning and the demands of a rapidly changing world environment.

LESSONS LEARNED

POLITICAL PROCESS AND DECISIVENESS

In a democratic country and society, it is of utmost value to engage not just the politicians and the military—that is, the decision makers and strategic community—but the media and people as well to engage in thinking about defense. This cannot be done with simple advertising campaigns but by long-term commitment and confidence. The Finnish experience is based on the country's history of an open relationship between the military and the rest of society, exemplified by conscription, and continuous dialogue shows the importance of this practice. This engagement has helped to make the Defense Forces one of the most reliable and trusted institutions (together with the police) in Finland! In times of crisis, both the Defense Forces and the people know they will get the support and help they need. This forms the true platform for any reform that is supposed to have any significance to one's country.

Keeping in mind this need to commit to existing democratic and parliamentary procedures, one has to strike a balance, perhaps even choose, between bureaucratic/governmental or political/partisan planning and drafting procedures. That is, should defense policy planning be conducted within the executive body, government, ministry of defense, and defense forces, or should it be handled within the political realm, Parliament, and the parties? Both have their pros and cons. Through the political process, one can count on wider support at the start. However, if the domestic climate is turbulent or divided, the results can be either contradictory or diluted. Government procedure emphasizes the parliamentary responsibility of the government and executing authorities, so it does not undermine Parliament's role or democratic principles. If a nation is divided politically as to hinder multipartisan participation or coalition governments, a government-centered procedure might leave the opposition bitter and angry. Even in times of lesser crisis, these dividing lines can cause the loss of parliamentary support. More generally, the questions are: What is Parliament's role in defense planning, can it be the same as in other fields of politics, and could it be different without undermining democracy itself?

COMPREHENSIVENESS

Defense is a subsystem, part of national apparatus, so no reform can be complete or successful if it does not take a top-down approach. This does not mean that progress focuses entirely on the top echelons of the nation or the defense forces, but it has to start there. Defense has to have its defined place in a nation's security policy or national strategy, and it must be based on legislation. Defense itself consists of subsystems; therefore, it has to build on a comprehensive concept, a doctrine that legitimizes, guides, and informs actions taken and plans executed. Finland has followed the doctrine of territorial defense since the mid-1960s; all of the organizational, technological, and material changes and revisions that have taken place should have served this overall vision or doctrine. All new ideas, concepts, and gadgets ought to fit in; they should solve new problems within the existing framework, not cause more problems by destroying it. And once a certain major change—a revolutionary reform—takes place constant development, constant reform, and continuous revising begin. Reforming one's defense policy is never finished business.

ASSESSMENT OF FACTORS

Change and Continuity   Defense policy in general, and defense reform in particular, is guided and affected by a broader agenda and by different and sometimes opposing trends within the military domain. These gradual but sometimes surprising developments can be described as follows:

A broader agenda for defense policy

- from military to wider security
- from threats to risks and uncertainties
- from national tasks to international commitments
- from national to regional/global focus
- from state to nonstate actors

Trends within the military

- from territorial defense to crisis management
- from standing to mobile forces and operations
- from conventional to nonconventional
- from force-oriented to effect-oriented
- from conscripts to professionals
- from antagonistic to cooperative

These agendas, trends, and factors guide and enable the process, but limit it as well. Although analysis of this international, technical, and conceptual environment is difficult, it should form the first pillar of any reform process. This forms the demand side of the defense; what should be considered in terms of threat and risks, tasks and objectives, and national and international commitments. The second pillar consists of an analysis of the domestic sphere and available national resources—political, financial, human, educational, technical, or geographical in nature. This gives the effort organizational and doctrinal structure, and shows what is acceptable and obtainable. Here lie the Scylla of lucrative quick fixes promised by turnovers in international politics or achievements in technological performance and the Charybdis of conservatism, dug into the established trenches, where no change is the only option and no progress is possible.

Time and Friction   Time, perhaps the most crucial limiting factor, consists of intermediate periods between steps in the planning cycle. These are identification and definition of the need to reform, followed by actual decision making, and, then, by the action itself. Add all of these together, and one can estimate that getting even a single weapon system into operative use takes years. (In wartime, one can acquire a weapon system and deliver it to the front in just weeks or days, as the cases of bazookas and Stingers prove.) Defense reform with adequate education, logistic, operative, and decision-making systems and facilities, easily could take one to three decades. There is evidence for this in the case of newly independent countries after each World War and after the Cold War ended. Defense can be torn down quickly, but building it up takes a considerable effort. Given this slow process, one has difficulty to balancing today's agenda and more permanent demands, and between the occasionally clashing and differing rationales of political life and the military. What is militarily reasonable in terms of tasks and priorities can be politically unacceptable in terms of money and employment. Reforms take a lot of time, and the friction of human life remains as important a limiting factor as Clausewitz wrote about the friction of war.

Defense budget allocation is a careful balancing act between defense's differing needs. If one puts too much weight on technological and material development, one narrows possibilities to train and operate and vice versa. Even secondhand material that is either purchased cheaply or donated by sponsors can become a burden if its operative and maintenance requirements and costs exceed the capacities of the receiving nation. If defense becomes a collection of incompatible subsystems, for example, fighters without a command and control system, rocket systems without fire observers, tanks without maintenance, it will turn out to be ineffective and, in the long run, more expensive than it already is. Finally, the resources allocated must fit the big picture: What are the tasks of the defense forces and what are not, what is priority and what can be left with lesser resources, and what is the system, the concept of defense?

ENDNOTES

1. *The European Security Development and Finnish Defense*, Helsinki: Edita, 1997.
2. *The Finnish Security and Defense Policy 2001*, Helsinki: Edita, 2001.
3. Pauli Järvenpää, "Security Perceptions and Defense Policy: Finland," in Tomas

Ries and Axel Hagelstam (eds.), *Sweden and Finland: Security Perceptions and Defense Policy*, Series 2, no. 13, Department of Strategic and Defense Studies, Helsinki, 2001.

4. The EU's Common European Security and Defense Policy should achieve its first goals by 2003 as well as development of NATO's Combined Joint Task Force concept.

5. Jan-Erik Enestam, "Finland and the Common European Security and Defense Policy," in Ries and Hagelstam, op cit.

6. Lea Ahoniemi, *Taistelu helikoptereista* (The Battle over the Helicopters), Series 1, no. 16, Department of Strategic and Defense Studies, Helsinki, 2000.

7. The United States is an exception to the rule, especially after 11 September.

8. Ilkka Hollo, "Finnish Defense Forces—The Present and the Future," in Mika Kerttunen (ed.), *Security in the North—Change and Continuity*, Series 2, no. 9, Department of Strategic and Defense Studies, Helsinki, 2000.

CHAPTER TWELVE

The *Bundeswehr* on Its Way into the Twenty-First Century

Policy Planning and Advisory Staff of the
German Ministry of Defense

INTRODUCTION

Since the end of East-West antagonism, the task spectrum of the *Bundeswehr* has become more diverse and differentiated. In the last few years, in particular, it has undergone fundamental changes. Together with allied and partner nations, Germany now participates, through the *Bundeswehr*, in international conflict prevention and crisis management missions beyond collective defense. This emphasises the significance of the Bundeswehr as a proactive political instrument.

For foreign and security policy, however, military forces will remain a convincing instrument only if their design, equipment, and organization are up-to-date. Changes for and within the forces are caused by political framework conditions, so the reorganization of forces and their structures is not an end in itself; politics becomes a pacemaker for reforms—it and nothing else determines the beat and the speed.

The present *Bundeswehr* reform started in autumn 1998 with a review at the Federal Ministry of Defense. Following the conclusion of the planning phase in early 2001, implementation of the reform projects started a process that will result in significant goals being achieved when the restructuring of the forces and the Federal Defense Administration has been completed, by the end of 2006.

This chapter begins with a description of the security context, which is decisive for the Federal Republic of Germany, and the structural, organizational state of the *Bundeswehr* at the end of the 1990s. This is followed by an explanation of the necessity of *Bundeswehr* reform that derives from this and a presentation of the benchmarks of the new *Bundeswehr*.

Since progress thus far in implementing reform does not allow it to be appreciated fully in a final review, and evaluation of only certain sectors would distort the overall picture, we consider progress made with respect to the challenges reform poses.

FRAMEWORK CONDITIONS

CONSTITUTIONAL FOUNDATIONS

The German Basic Law commits Germany to serve world peace as an equal partner in a united Europe. Being a member of the North Atlantic Treaty Organization (NATO) and the European Union (EU), Germany contributes—on the basis of an assured defense capability—to security, especially within the Euro-Atlantic area, on a scale that corresponds to its economic and political weight. This includes a commitment to participate in conflict prevention and crisis management measures within the framework of the alliances and the United Nations.

Under Article 87a of the Basic Law, the Federation provides defense forces. In 1994, initiated by political changes, the jurisdiction of the Federal Constitutional Court extended the possibilities for deployment of the *Bundeswehr* considerably; it is now fully available for the complete spectrum of tasks earmarked for armed forces.

THE *BUNDESWEHR* IN THE INTERNATIONAL ENVIRONMENT

Germany's foreign and security policy is a policy for peace and freedom. Germany pursues its interests, according to this aim, in joint cooperation with its allies and partners of NATO, the EU, the Organization for Security and Cooperation in Europe (OSCE), and the United Nations (UN). The commitment to provide military forces is applicable to NATO, the EU, and the UN. Multinationality is an important principle of modern armed forces that are integrated in alliances and coalitions.

NATO and the European Union   NATO will remain the backbone of the peace order in Europe and a foundation for Germany's security. NATO prepared itself for the challenges of the twenty-first century at its fiftieth anniversary, which it celebrated at the Washington Summit in April 1999. NATO's tasks have been reassessed and its political and military structures brought into line with the changed circumstances. The Defense Capabilities Initiative (DCI), unanimously adopted on this occasion, is aimed at altogether improving the military capabilities of NATO forces and, especially, at considerably enhancing interoperability in multinational formations.

It is good for European stability as a whole if the EU has the capacity to act in the field of security. When it comes to assessing current military capabilities and future requirements for successful crisis management, the EU comes to basically the same conclusions as NATO's DCI.

It is only logical that the European Headline Goal, a common European goal concerning establishment of a rapid-reaction force, was adopted in Helsinki in 1999. The German contribution to EU-led operations consists of a maximum of eighteen thousand soldiers and related means from the services.

The United Nations   To enable the UN Security Council to react to crises and conflicts more rapidly and efficiently, Germany has stated that it will contribute high-quality military capabilities to the UN within the scope of the "Standby Arrangements System."

Current Missions   The *Bundeswehr* will continue to contribute substantially to the Stabilization Force (SFOR), deploying some two thousand soldiers. At present, approximately fifty-two hundred soldiers are deployed in the Kosovo Force (KFOR); here, the German brigade is the key formation of the "South" sector and is playing a key role. In the Former Yugoslavian republic of Macedonia, the *Bundeswehr* is in charge of Operation FOX, deploying about five hundred of its own soldiers.

Germany is contributing up to thirty-nine hundred soldiers to Operation "Enduring Freedom," which was initiated in response to the terrorist attacks of 11 September.

In addition, the *Bundeswehr* will continue to participate in the UN Observer Mission in Georgia (UNOMIG) to control and monitor the armistice and separation of forces agreement between Georgia and Abkhazia (eleven soldiers at present).

With approximately 11,600 soldiers, Germany is currently one of the major troop providers for international peace missions. Until the end of 2001, control of the missions was the responsibility of the respective lead service command; since then it has been the responsibility of the new Joint Operations Command.

The Necessity for and Aims of Reform

THE *BUNDESWEHR* IN THE 1990S

The last adaptation of the concept and planning targets for the *Bundeswehr* took place after the reunification of Germany in the first half of the last decade. The organization and structure were geared primarily to national and Atlantic Alliance defense.

Before the reform was started, the *Bundeswehr* had a peacetime strength of 335,000 active soldiers, fifty thousand of whom were available for deployment at short notice in the Reaction Forces (RF) component. Another 185,000 soldiers could be fully ready in the Main Defense Forces (MDF) within six months. In peacetime, the RF and MDF were backed by approximately a hundred thousand soldiers in the Basic Military Organization, whose job it was to ensure that military training and needed support was provided.

Approximately 135,000 of the soldiers in the *Bundeswehr* were basic service conscripts/draftees. In a state of defense, the forces could build up to an overall strength of 680,000 soldiers.

In peacetime, the services were organized as follows:

Army (approximately 231,000 personnel)

Army Forces Command with
- Three corps, two of them binational, with
  - seven divisions (doubling up as Military District Commands) with a total of
    - twenty-six brigades, twelve of these semi- or nonactive

Army Support Command
Army Office

Air Force (seventy-seven thousand personnel)

Air Force Command with Air Force Communications and Information Systems Command and Air Transport Command
- Two Air Force Commands with
  - four divisions with a total of
    - four fighter wings
    - six reconnaissance and airstrike wings
    - six surface-to-air missile wings
    - two tactical air control regiments

Air Force Support Command
Air Force Office

Navy (approximately twenty-seven thousand personnel)

Fleet Command with
- Six flotillas
  - Communications and electronics services

- Naval Aviation
- Mine warfare forces
- Corvettes/fast patrol boats
- Submarines
- Destroyers/frigates
- Naval Support Command
- Naval Office

Central Military Agencies of the Bundeswehr   The organizational area of the Central Military Agencies of the *Bundeswehr* comprised a total of 180 agencies in Germany and abroad, employing some seven thousand military and about five thousand civil personnel. Characterized by a host of different tasks performed on a largely separate basis, this area was a service provider for the forces. On the whole, these tasks can be categorized into contributions to the estimate of the situation, training and research, binational and multinational relations, and international cooperation.

Medical Service   The members of the Medical Service were organized into central medical agencies (for example, *Bundeswehr* station hospitals), the Army Medical Service (for example, medical battalions), and the Organizational Medical Service. However, the medical service was not an independent military service; a total of twenty-six thousand soldiers were integrated into the Army, Air Force, and Navy. Two transportable RF hospitals with a capacity of two hundred beds each have been established to ensure the Reaction Forces get high-quality clinical care.

The Federal Defense Administration   According to Article 87b of the German Basic Law, a Federal Defense Administration (with, at present, approximately 135,000 employees) has been established as a component independent of the armed forces. It includes:

- the Territorial Defense Administration, which satisfies the manpower and materiel requirements of the forces, and is also responsible for environmental protection and industrial safety, and
- the Armaments Organization, which is responsible for providing the armed forces all the equipment they need.

FOUNDATIONS OF DECISION MAKING

The *Bundeswehr* reform is a project whose implications will be felt well into the future. To be able to meet the goals set, an extensive assessment of the situation must be made and an analysis of the weak points conducted. The internal results of a ministerial work group were summarized in the review of the state of the "Bundeswehr on the Threshold to of the 21st Century." This document, issued on 3 May 1999, formed the basis for all further steps.

- Under the chairmanship of former Federal President Richard von Weizsäcker, the members of the independent Commission on the Common Security and Future of the Bundeswehr, set up by the Federal Government, held their consultations. Simply from its composition, this independent expert commission had broad-based expertise, and it was supported by numerous studies and professional work done in a range of different areas. The commission's report, containing recommendations on the form of military service to be adopted for the *Bundeswehr*, its personnel, command structure, organization, equipment, training, and finances, was presented to the Federal Chancellor by former Federal President von Weizsäcker on 23 May 2000.
- At the same time, the Chief of Staff of the *Bundeswehr* presented the Federal Minister of Defense his "Benchmark Figures for Concepts and Plans for the Further Development of the Armed Forces" prepared at the FMoD.
- To complement the analyses and assessments by his own personal impressions, the Federal Minister of Defense held a total of twenty-five meetings with military and civilian personnel from all ranks and levels of command (February 1999 to March 2000).

RESULTS AND THE NEED FOR ACTION

The conclusion reached in all of the studies on how the *Bundeswehr* should develop in the future is that current problems cannot be solved by isolated steps. On the threshold of the twenty-first century, changes in the demands and the absence of reforms had caused a need for action to build up that could only be relieved by a fundamental transformation of the *Bundeswehr*.

The change in the security situation over the past decade and Germany's increased international commitments called for the *Bundeswehr* to undergo a profound transformation.

The lessons learned in international missions have sharpened the requirements profile for modern forces in peace missions further. However, they also revealed the existence of deficits in many areas. The conceptually balanced transformation of the *Bundeswehr* into a force capable of participating in multinational operations has not yet been completed. As the Defense Capabilities Initiative of NATO and the European Headline Goals of the EU show, this is not just a problem facing the *Bundeswehr*. These lessons set requirements for the capability profile of the allied and European forces of the future.

The following examples indicate the need for action in the personnel sector:

- To be able to accomplish the missions abroad, considerable personnel restrictions have to be accepted at home.
- Sustainability, particularly in logistics and medical support, is insufficient. Both fields are still oriented toward the former situation, in which national defense tasks were performed in a stationary manner. This has resulted in an unacceptable, continuous burden on certain specialists and units as well as on reservists, only a limited number of whom are available.
- The high burden on key personnel, whose pay does not always match their achievements, will have negative effects on the motivation of the active military personnel in the long term, and on recruitment, unless suitable measures are taken.

Examples of the considerable deficits in materiel held by the *Bundeswehr* are:

- insufficient dedicated strategic reconnaissance resources for acquiring timely and detailed information in crises;
- insufficient quality and quantity of strategic air and sea transport resources;
- deficits in powerful means of communication at the strategic and tactical levels;
- a lack of modern precision and stand-off weapons;
- insufficient electronic warfare means;
- a lack of powerful systems for armed air rescue operations;
- increasing susceptibility to breakdown of partially obsolete weapon systems and limited availability of spare parts; and
- high operating costs, preventing investment in modern materiel; the result of this is that only some capabilities available can be improved. It has not been possible to establish every new capability needed.

To sum up, the following can be said:

- Lessons learned in operations have shown that the *Bundeswehr* only has the personnel, materiel, organization, and financial resources to conduct one major protracted mission abroad at a time.
- An inappropriate distribution of powers, obsolete C^2, administration, and procurement procedures, as well as inadequate and incompatible information and communication technology, have led to an inefficient commitment of resources and have impeded development of creativity in the search for innovative solutions.
- In addition, the *Bundeswehr* was underfinanced for years. Between 1989 and 1997, investment funds were reduced by more than 40 percent and did not increase again until 1998; today, however, they are still far below the desired rate of 30 percent of the defense budget.
- In 1998, the defense budget totaled almost 47 billion DEM (approximately 10 percent of the federal budget), and the rate of capital defense expenditure was 23.7 percent.

DEMANDS ON THE *BUNDESWEHR*

When drawing up its plans, the *Bundeswehr* assumes it will have to provide forces for several operations simultaneously. Regardless of this demand, performance of routine military tasks must be ensured. This includes such tasks as maintaining the national command and control capability, ensuring logistic and medical support, guaranteeing the conduct of central military training, and subsuming the build-up capability to wartime strength for the purpose of national defense.

The *Bundeswehr*'s deployment forces must be capable of conducting

- one large-scale operation with up to fifty thousand military personnel for up to one year after a one- to six-month period of preparation, or
- two medium-scale operations with up to ten thousand military personnel each over several years, also after a one- to six-month period of preparation.

In parallel to each of these, the capability to conduct several small-scale operations with up to a thousand military personnel must be ensured.

- Forces earmarked for estimating the situation, ensuring unrestricted national command and control capability, and performing routine military duties as well as sovereign and national territorial tasks must be available constantly. These include integrated air defense assets, nuclear operations forces, and NATO standing naval forces.

- Forces earmarked for rescue and evacuation operations, as well as advance forces for crisis management operations, must be immediately available and operational (within a few hours up to five days).
- Forces earmarked for deployment first in crisis management operations have to be ready at short notice (between six and thirty days).

The remaining force components earmarked for conflict prevention and crisis management missions and for collective defense must be capable of being available and operational after a medium-length preparation period (thirty to 180 days). Their augmentation and relief elements also must be available after a medium-length preparation period.

A longer preparation period (more than 180 days) can be granted to the bulk of the forces earmarked to relieve or augment the forces employed in conflict prevention, crisis management, or collective defense operations. Full operational readiness has to be established in the course of preparations for deployment.

All other standing forces, as well as the elements of the armed forces earmarked to be mobilized for national defense in an Alliance context, will only have to be available after a very long preparation period. In national defense operations in an Alliance context, the *Bundeswehr* will have ample time to build up to wartime strength and complete the training of reservists.

Operations are categorized by their duration as very short, short (less than six months), medium (six to twelve months), long (one to two years), and very long (over two years). The deployment cycle is determined by specific conditions in military organizational areas. The Army generally adheres to a six-month period of deployment in the theater, followed by a two-year deployment-free period, so the deployment cycle is thirty months. Limited availability of specialists may warrant exceptions.

DEMANDS ON THE FEDERAL DEFENSE ADMINISTRATION

The Federal Defense Administration has to be reoriented toward future demands on the *Bundeswehr* and undergo further modernization. Efficiency, cost-effectiveness, and process-oriented acting are the key factors determining the shape of the defense administration, alongside social security for the staff and a reliable basis on which they can make their plans. For this purpose, the organization has to be streamlined, internal routines have to be optimized, and the agencies have to be provided with functional and modern equipment, especially modern information technology. In addition, modern management strategies and instruments have to be used consistently to create a competitive personnel structure and incentives for the staff.

Through intensified cooperation with industry and trade, the Federal Defense Administration will be able to promote the transfer of new and more economical methods of satisfying the forces' materiel requirements.

BENCHMARKS OF THE REFORM—THE *BUNDESWEHR* OF THE TWENTY-FIRST CENTURY

THE POLITICAL DECISIONS

The foundation for long-term reform of the *Bundeswehr* is provided by a document known as the "Cornerstones for the Concepts and Plans for the Reorientation of the Bundeswehr," adopted by the Cabinet on 14 June 2000. These cornerstones are decisive for reforms in personnel, equipment and materiel, strengths and compositions, form of military service, and cooperation with trade and industry.

Further planning of the structures was concluded up to the level of the units and comparable agencies. This formed the basis for the "Departmental Concept on Stationing," concluded on 16 February 2001. With the approval of the "Materiel and Equipment Concept for the Armed Forces of the Future" on 16 March 2001, the FMoD set the course for materiel equipment planning of the forces. The interministerial agreement reached on 3 July 2001 between the Federal Minister of Finance and the Federal Minister of Defense concerning the 2002 budget, which included medium-term financial planning until 2005, created the necessary secure basis for elaborating financial plans. The "Bundeswehr Reorientation Act," which came into effect on 1 January 2002, and the "Sixth Payment Amendment Act" will finally define the legal framework for implementation of *Bundeswehr* reform.

THE NEW CAPABILITY PROFILE

To be able to conduct missions in an international framework, the *Bundeswehr* needs a continuum of military capabilities covering the complete spectrum of tasks, ranging from minor operations, like evacuation and assistance operations, through low-intensity peacekeeping missions up to high-intensity combat operations.

To be able to fulfill all of these tasks, the forces need a new capability profile. In this context, advantage must be taken of the opportunities to perform tasks on an integrated joint and multinational basis. The aim of this is to avoid overcapacity and to make joint use of resources that do not have to be held by all the services. The new capability profile of the *Bundeswehr* is determined by all six interlocked capability categories, namely command and control capability, intelligence, mobility, effective engagement, support and sustainability, and survivability. These categories also serve as a central classification system for the concepts and plans for reorientation of the *Bundeswehr*. They are mutually dependent and must always be considered to be of equal importance.

Command and Control Capability   The command and control capability, a decisive prerequisite for deploying *Bundeswehr* forces in a manner that fits the scenario, is based on a strict command and control organization, clear-cut command and control procedures, and efficient command support. Effective and interoperable command, control, information, and communications systems are of paramount importance. The diverse spectrum of potential missions and rapidly changing mission demands call for flexible modular structures.

Intelligence   Intelligence establishes the prerequisites for identifying a crisis early and successfully exercising command and control over the deployed forces. Due to the increased importance of preventive measures in preserving stability and peace, worldwide satellite and long-range airborne reconnaissance capability is of particular significance.

Mobility   Mobility is based on the availability of powerful tactical, operational, and strategic means of transportation. Since German soldiers have to be able to be deployed in a timely manner and be appropriately equipped for distant theaters, fast access to adequate strategic sea- and airlift capacities is required.

Effective Engagement   Effective engagement means the capability to engage ground, air, and sea targets directly or indirectly, and to exert an influence on the attitudes and actions of others. Specific capabilities for the conduct of information operations come under effective engagement. They are supported considerably by the capability to project combat power and deliver long-range and deep precision fire.

Support and Sustainability   Support comprises providing personnel support, medical care, logistical support, and other support, for example, administrative or infrastructure support. Sustainability is ensured when this support can be provided over long periods of time, which requires personnel and materiel resources adequate in both quantity and quality as well as facilities for training and repair capacities.

Survivability   Survivability, the indispensable prerequisite for accomplishing missions, comprises the protection of personnel, platforms, facilities, areas, and infrastructure. The capabilities of countermining, mine protection, search and rescue (SAR), combat search and rescue (CSAR), and the ability to identify friendly and enemy forces reliably, are of special importance.

Other Capabilities   The *Bundeswehr* assists in protecting and restoring the social order and infrastructure in crisis zones. Besides purely military tasks, crisis management operations increasingly involve humanitarian assistance and postcrisis rehabilitation tasks as well. The planning and coordination of such support measures, conducted in cooperation with the authorities and the population in the theater and with the civilian reconstruction assets of the international community, requires a certain number of specialists to be trained and provisioned. The *Bundeswehr* can build up to full wartime strength as the situation demands. This requires the potential to mobilize trained reservists sufficient in number and quality and the build-up of appropriate structures.

ORGANIZATION AND STRUCTURE

Strengths and Form of Military Service   Altogether, around 150,000 military personnel—available at different times—will be needed to make up the Deployment Forces, which will be supplemented by approximately 110,000 military personnel in the basic military organization.

In addition, twenty-two thousand posts will be established for training, in particular, for enabling service personnel to acquire qualifications that will enhance their chances of finding civilian employment when they leave the *Bundeswehr*. This will result in a higher proportion of leaders, instructors, and specialists in the forces, because training-related vacancies will be able to be filled immediately. Germany's future peacetime strength will thus total 282,400 soldiers.

This strength can be built up to a wartime force of approximately five hundred thousand military personnel to adequately accomplish the core mission of national defense. For this reason, Germany will maintain universal conscription. The security environment allows compulsory military service to be reduced to nine months beginning in 2002, thus rendering this service more flexible.

Since the beginning of 2001, the armed forces have been open to female volunteers. Military personnel are enlisted and assigned on the basis of aptitude, qualification, and merit alone.

Structures The essential factor determining the way the *Bundeswehr* is organized is the concentration of the armed forces on their operational tasks, which results in streamlined structures and increased efficiency in how the armed forces and the defense administration perform their tasks. This enables the organization to be streamlined, the command and control responsibility to be concentrated wherever possible, and administrative tasks to be separated from operational ones. In the future, common services will be provided jointly for all users and performed either by one service as an interservice function or by one of the two central organizational areas, that is, the Joint Support Service (JSS) and the Central Medical Service of the Bundeswehr.

CENTRAL ORGANIZATIONAL AREAS

JSS The JSS is the central military organizational area for support of the armed forces. It will absorb the central military agencies of the *Bundeswehr* and will be assigned forces and responsibilities from the single services and the Central Medical Service to perform joint tasks. The Joint Support Service will be responsible for providing all the *Bundeswehr* military organizational areas with the materiel, supplies, and services they need.

Concentrating the appropriate tasks in separate organizational areas will enhance economic efficiency and effectiveness of the armed forces. This will apply, in particular, to planning and control of operations, command support, military intelligence, and logistics. Transferring responsibility for providing a host of support services to the JSS as a central military service provider will allow the *Bundeswehr* to adopt a mission-oriented, modular, and flexible structure that will be more able to meet the demands posed by both the Alliance and the EU.

The primary joint tasks of the Joint Support Service are:

- command support in Germany and in theaters;
- military intelligence, including strategic intelligence;
- logistical support of the armed forces in the performance of routine

military tasks and during operations, including all central logistical support not associated with specific weapon systems; and
• organization of the National Territorial Tasks, including civil-military relations in Germany and abroad as well as military police functions.

In addition, the Joint Support Service will perform tasks that will also remain a national responsibility in an Alliance defense environment. It is headed by the Chief of Staff of the Joint Support Service at the Federal Ministry of Defense.

The target structure is as follows:

Joint Support Service (approximately fifty-one thousand personnel)
■ Joint Support Command in command of
  • Four Military District Commands (WBK) with
    • Berlin Garrison Headquarters
    • twenty-seven Military Region Commands (VBK)
    • command support and military police forces
    • basic motor vehicle training and major training area organization
  • *Bundeswehr* Logistics Center
  • *Bundeswehr* Logistics Office
  • Psychological Operations Center
  • Strategic Intelligence Command
■ Armed Forces Office
■ Joint Operations Command

Central Medical Service of the Bundeswehr   The benchmark for reorganization of the Medical Service is the medical care provided to *Bundeswehr* military personnel on deployment. Military medical services must be held to the same standard as the civilian health service in Germany.

The organizational area represented by the Central Medical Service will be under the administrative and technical control of the Chief of Staff of the Central Medical Service of the *Bundeswehr*.

The target structure is as follows:

Central Medical Service of the *Bundeswehr* (approximately 26,300 personnel, plus a small number of medical personnel in the JSS and the single services)
■ Medical Forces Command in command of
  • four Regional Medical Commands in turn in command of
    • *Bundeswehr* station hospitals
    • outpatient treatment centers

- tactical medical units
- reserve hospital organization
■ Medical Office

THE INDIVIDUAL SERVICES

Army The Army is adapting its structures to conflict prevention and crisis management, which have gained in importance. To this end, it is enhancing its capability for rapid reaction and protracted operations outside Germany. Command and control and effective engagement capabilities have top priority in the revamping process. The proportion of standing deployment forces suitable for operations across the task spectrum will be increased markedly. The ratio of mechanized to light forces will be changed in favor of the latter. The German Army's participation in several multinational corps and other large units below the corps level is a visible expression of its growing international involvement. By developing new capabilities, especially with the Special Operations and the Airmobile divisions, by rigorously applying the principle of modularity, by providing additional planning capacities at division and corps level, and by making available the II (GE/US) Korps as Force Headquarters for EU operations, the Army is highly instrumental in implementing the mission-oriented reorientation of the armed forces within NATO and the EU.

The—peacetime—target structure of the Army is as follows:

Army (approx. 133,000 personnel, seventy-five thousand of whom are in the deployment forces)
- ■ Army Forces Command in command of
  - German elements in multinational corps headquarters
  - Seven divisions (five mechanized divisions plus Special Operations Division and Airmobile Division) with a total of
    - nineteen brigades (nine active mechanized brigades, two airborne brigades, a mountain infantry brigade, an air-mechanized brigade, an army aviation brigade, and three nonactive mechanized brigades, the Special Forces Command, and the German element of the Franco-German Brigade)
  - Army Support Forces Command with two logistics brigades, an artillery brigade, an engineer brigade, an army air

defense brigade, and a nuclear, biological, and chemical weapons (NBC) defense brigade
- Army Office

Air Force   The outcome of the additional goal-directed development of Air Force capabilities to cover the complete task spectrum will be a marked improvement in the service's effective engagement capability and considerable enhancement of its command and control capability. In this connection, the new Air Force Operational Command constitutes a significant German contribution to operational planning and the command and control of multinational air forces during deployment.

Modernization of equipment—especially procurement of the EUROFIGHTER 2000 and development of strategic air transport and air refueling capabilities—will close major capability gaps. The Air Force must also prepare for future challenges by further developing its capabilities, however. This includes ballistic missile defense.

The future capability profile of the Air Force, with a markedly enhanced level of performance in all key capability categories and more flexible structures, will make it easier to integrate Air Force contingents into NATO and the EU for multinational tasks.

The—peacetime—target structure of the Air Force is as follows:

Air Force (approximately fifty-one thousand troops)
- Air Force Command in command of
  - German elements in the multinational headquarters
  - Air Force Operational Command
  - Air Transport Command with three air transport wings (plus the Special Air Mission Wing of the FMoD)
  - Four Air Divisions in command of
    - one reconnaissance wing
    - three fighter wings
    - four fighter bomber wings
    - four surface-to-air missile (SAM) wings
    - four tactical air control units
- Air Force Office

Navy   The German Navy operates in close cooperation with allied and partner navies. Its participation in the four NATO standing naval forces, its intensive participation in combined exercises within the Partnership for Peace program, its close cooperation with the countries bordering on the Baltic Sea, and its active involvement in the Mediterranean dialogue of the EU and NATO intensify the multinational orientation of the German Army. It will perform its share of joint tasks in the future by providing direct sea-based support. The Navy is geared to the new requirements of joint action in the broadened military task spectrum and is continuing to develop as a Navy integrated in NATO and the EU.

The—peacetime—target structure of the Navy is as follows:

Navy (approximately twenty thousand personnel)
- Fleet Command in control of
  - Five flotillas
    - Naval aviation
    - Mine warfare forces
    - Fast patrol boats/corvettes
    - Submarines
    - Destroyers
- Naval Office

THE FEDERAL DEFENSE ADMINISTRATION

The Federal Defense Administration is being reorganized into four military district offices to turn it into a modern service enterprise that will provide maximum support to the armed forces and the general public in cooperation with trade and industry. This, and the reduced strength of the armed forces, will enable the *Bundeswehr* to reduce the number of civilian posts by about a third, to approximately ninety thousand.

The Armaments Organization will be geared to project management and will focus on specialist technical tasks. New and more economical procedures for the development, testing, and procurement of defense products will be introduced.

MODERN MANAGEMENT FOR THE NEW *BUNDESWEHR*

The Federal Minister of Defense laid the foundation for further essential innovation in the *Bundeswehr* in 1999 when he issued the guideline paper entitled "Modern Management in the Armed Forces and Defense Administration." The entire way in which the *Bundeswehr* is run will undergo fundamental reform. The armed forces and administration agencies will confine themselves to performing core and sovereign tasks. Analogous to optimization programs in trade and industry, the *Bundeswehr* will apply new methods and instruments to improve the use of resources and exhaust the organizational and technical potential for making its operating procedures more cost-effective. The rationalization process is a medium- to long-term matter. Economic thinking and action will become a binding maxim at all levels in all areas and will become measurable and transparent by means of a universal controlling system to support the executive level.

The Framework Contract   The Framework Contract on "Innovation, Investment and Economic Efficiency in the *Bundeswehr*" concluded by the Federal Government with representatives from trade and industry in Berlin at the end of 1999 provides the groundwork for a strategic partnership and close cooperation between the *Bundeswehr* and trade and industry, the purpose of which is to use trade and industry's capacity for innovation, boost investments, and put operating and procurement procedures in the *Bundeswehr* on a wholly new and viable footing. Lasting improvements in economic efficiency in running the *Bundeswehr* and in procurement, both of which will be influenced more strongly by entrepreneurial thinking and action, will free up the funds urgently needed to modernize military equipment.

The new operating management system is characterized by

- opening up and testing new methods for satisfying the materiel and service requirements outside the core tasks of the *Bundeswehr*, including efficient private cooperation partners with a capacity for innovation, and
- internal instruments for opening up further potential for optimization.

THE DEVELOPMENT, PROCUREMENT, AND MANAGEMENT GROUP
The Executive Group of the FMoD will be assisted by the newly founded Development, Procurement, and Management Group (*Gesellschaft für Entwicklung, Beschaffung und Betrieb mbH* [GEBB]), which started work on 1 September 2000. This organization's aim is to maximize economic efficiency systematically and institutionally in how the *Bundeswehr* is run and how its requirements are satisfied in close cooperation with trade and industry. At present, its operational activities are focused on information technology, vehicle fleet management, real property management, and clothing supplies.

Information Technology (IT)   In the future, the *Bundeswehr* will make extensive use of IT services provided by a private-law IT company that will be founded with an industrial partner. Sales to third-party customers and industrial operational sequences and processes will enable the *Bundeswehr* to fill its needs more economically than if the *Bundeswehr* were to provide them itself.

Vehicle Fleet Management   The *Bundeswehr* now uses approximately 108,000 soft-skinned (commercial, semimilitarized, and military) wheeled vehicles in addition to combat vehicles or weapon system carriers. A company will take over management of the (wheeled) vehicle fleet with the essential aim of drastically reducing both the vehicle inventory and the average age of commercial and semimilitarized vehicles within a few years. Procurement, use, maintenance, repair, and disposal will be controlled efficiently.

Real Property Management   Several companies will coordinate management of the real property owned by the *Bundeswehr*. For this purpose, external investors will contribute know-how and capital, with the aim, for example, of using the real property more efficiently or promoting its development, lease, or sale. This way, military building space and land will be reduced considerably within a reasonably short time.

Clothing Supplies and Logistics   A clothing company will introduce innovative, industry-based procurement and distribution methods to supply the armed forces with uniforms and other personal military equipment. This will help to reduce stockpiles and cut down on unneeded storage capacity.

Armaments and Procurement   Responsibility for planning, determining requirements, and procuring military equipment for the *Bundeswehr* has been reassigned and the procedures revised to make them more efficient. Each requirement for new military equipment submitted by an area, and the manner in which it is to be met, will be agreed upon in the Armaments Council under the chairmanship of the Chief of Staff of the *Bundeswehr*. Using modern management methods (Customer, Product, Management 2001 [CPM 2001]), the Armaments Organization will plan the implementation process, specify the services to be provided by trade and industry, conclude the necessary contracts, and ensure they are duly fulfilled.

The market will be screened closely to identify appropriate materiel. Whenever commercial equipment satisfies military requirements and can be acquired at customary market terms, no special military equipment will be developed and procured. Whenever special military equipment does have to be developed, functional purchase descriptions will leave latitude so that marketable components can be used and innovative technological solutions found. Armed forces requirements must be geared to ensuring the necessary military capabilities. Streamlining the requirement procedure and combining certain phases will slash the amount of time it takes from submission of a requirement order to the item of equipment being delivered to the user.

Government management will be reduced to controlling performance, time, and cost and verifying quality during an acceptance test. Since the beginning of 2001, all new procurement projects have been managed to CPM 2001 specifications. Eliminating the administrative obstacles posed by the old procedures and enabling the armaments organization to concentrate on its core task of closing the forces' capability gaps within reasonable performance, financial, and time limits will boost efficiency considerably.

DEVELOPMENT OF THE DEFENSE BUDGET

In the medium term, the *Bundeswehr* will have an annual defense budget of 46.2 billion DM at its disposal. Additional funds, which will always be available from the federal government program to strengthen internal and external security, a policy adopted as a consequence of the events of 11 September 2001, will thus increase defense budget funds to 47.7 billion DM. Alternative financing arrangements resulting from the use of new management procedures will make additional funds available. The aim remains to reduce operating costs and increase the capital expenditure share.

THE REFORM—AN INTERIM REVIEW

The reform of the *Bundeswehr* started in late 1998 and will take around a decade to complete. Because implementation of the reform projects is still at an early stage, a final assessment in terms of a planned/actual comparison is not possible. To achieve the objectives, however, the process must be followed carefully and evaluated continuously.

As mentioned before, the *Bundeswehr* comprised approximately five hundred thousand military and civilian personnel in 1999, making it one of the largest employers in the Federal Republic of Germany. The reform does not affect only *Bundeswehr* personnel, however; their families and friends also are affected by it considerably, with the interests of society resulting from the universal draft acting as an additional reinforcing factor. Moreover, the ongoing and upcoming operations of the *Bundeswehr*, and the reform, have been the subject of much media attention.

There are a wide variety of challenges connected with the reform. Two key areas of activity that have to be coped with are discussed here.

- The diverse interests of the people concerned delay the reform, and
- Topical issues push the main concern aside—the reform is becoming a matter of secondary importance.

THE FIRST THESIS

Following a painstaking assessment of the situation and careful planning, the primary initial accomplishment was to ensure that the reform process quickly gathered speed.

We know from experience that large organizations need a start-up phase before they embark on a new predetermined course and simultaneously reach the required speed, not the least because of the inertia inherent in the system. Since the *Bundeswehr* is made up not only of soldiers, but also of many civilian personnel, including established civil servants, salaried public employees, and wage-grade employees, a host of interests have to be identified and noted. A wide range of legitimate concerns has to be taken into account, for example:

- a staff reduction program that complies with the ideals of a constitutional state based on a system of social welfare;
- the consequences of disbanding long-standing units often deeply rooted in the civilian environment that have proven their worth in both peacetime duties and operations;
- the reassignment of personnel, which also affects their families; and
- the resulting unavoidable closure of garrisons whose elected representatives fear the loss of jobs just as much as they do the loss of purchasing power.

In addition to these recognized challenges, however, new challenges are appearing that did not matter during previous reforms, but are characteristic of the present reform because of the sweeping cuts involved. They are the consequences of implementing new management procedures derived from trade and industry and the ensuing partial privatization. The *Bundeswehr* is becoming more efficient—in fact, it recently started generating profits by itself.

The cooperation between the *Bundeswehr* and trade and industry is resulting in both parties becoming partners in the sense of equal beneficiaries. However, now and then it is impossible to ignore the objection that the *Bundeswehr* might become a profit-oriented competitor for a share of the market, for example, by offering transportation services, thereby damaging the hauling trade. No attention is paid, however, to the fact that the profit generated goes back into the defense budget, easing the strain on the treasury considerably. The winner in the end is the taxpayer.

THE SECOND THESIS
The second field of activity is just as important as the first: The reform itself must be understood and accomplished not only as a primary task, the same effort must be made to counteract tendencies that divert attention from the primary task.

What is important in this context are the conditions—the macrocosm—under which the reform is implemented. These fields of activity may explain these tendencies, but do not provide any reason for their justification:

- Even while the reform is being implemented, the *Bundeswehr* is contributing a considerable number of personnel to the contingents the international community provides for stabilizing peace and combating international terrorism, and
- by implementing the reform, the *Bundeswehr* is facing up to a tremendous task at a time when the economy is stagnating and the recovery of the federal budget is imperative.

These framework conditions sometimes result in the reform and its significance being perceived by the public as a matter of secondary importance, since the debate is reduced to subjects such as the financial situation of the armed forces with all its facets, the closure of garrisons, and the debate on the increasing (and—a development that receives less notice—decreasing) number of conscientious objectors that recurs at irregular intervals anyway.

The Federal Minister of Defense, therefore, took the initiative in this area from the beginning and promoted reform on the ground during his numerous visits to units and his many meetings with soldiers and civilian personnel from different levels and areas of the *Bundeswehr*. In the course of the series of presentations, entitled "The *Bundeswehr* and Trade and Industry," held throughout the Federal Republic, the Minister recently discussed with the representatives of the chambers of industry and commerce and of crafts and trades the objectives and progress of the *Bundeswehr* reform. He also took the opportunity to review relations with trade and industry and the partners that had agreed to cooperate with the *Bundeswehr* under the Framework Contract on "Innovation, Investment and Economic Efficiency in the *Bundeswehr*" thereby lending impetus to further development of the partnership.

These reform efforts are supplemented by extensive supporting measures that satisfy the need to inform people by employing expert teams and using high-tech media, such as the satellite television station, "Bundeswehr–TV," or the Internet to generate understanding and acceptance.

SUMMARY

The reform of the armed forces and defense administration is well under way and, considering the events of 11 September 2001, on the right track—what matters now is to expedite implementation of individual selected subprojects.

The reform is an investment in the future. Above all, it will ensure that the *Bundeswehr* remains an attractive employer because it is oriented toward the future. Adherence to the universal draft will keep the *Bundeswehr* mentally young and highly transparent for society. The reform will restore the balance among the mission, strength, equipment, and resources of the *Bundeswehr*, which is indispensable for ensuring that the armed forces also remain an effective instrument of German foreign and security policy in the future.

CHAPTER THIRTEEN

U.S. Defense Reform in a Decade of Change

Eric V. Larson

The United States' post-Cold War efforts at defense reform had four distinct objectives: (1) *downsizing* (or, as some had it, "rightsizing") the force to create a smaller force capable of protecting and promoting the nation's interests with an acceptable level of risk; (2) *modernizing* the force to ensure that it retained near-term qualitative advantages through routine replacement of systems reaching the end of their service lives; (3) *reshaping and transforming* the force to achieve a revolution in military affairs (RMA), and ensuring that the "military after next" would be without peer; and (4) *reforming defense business practices*, including infrastructure reduction, and acquisition, management, financial, and other reforms, to realize efficiencies that could provide additional resources, and increase "tooth to tail" ratios.[1]

The engine for these reforms was largely—although not exclusively—four major force structure reviews—the (George H. W.) Bush administration's 1989–90 Base Force, the Clinton administration's 1993 Bottom-Up Review (BUR) and 1997 Quadrennial Defense Review (QDR), and the (George W.) Bush administration's 2001 Quadrennial Defense Review.[2] Each defined needed changes to the United States' military strategy, force structure, manpower, and infrastructure; addressed modernization needs; and provided guidance regarding management reforms that were needed to realize greater efficiencies in the defense program.

This chapter begins with an overview of the United States' defense reform efforts since the end of the Cold War. It then turns to a discussion of the problems and challenges encountered in the course of their development and implementation. The chapter then concludes with some broader lessons for new and emerging democracies.

AN OVERVIEW OF POST-COLD WAR DEFENSE REFORM EFFORTS IN THE UNITED STATES

Each of the defense reviews was a comprehensive administration effort to review strategy, forces, and budgets. In each, senior civilian leaders in the Office of the Secretary of Defense (OSD)—and, to a lesser extent, the White House—worked with senior military leaders in the Joint Chiefs of Staff (JCS) and the services. Civilian leaders were responsible for defining key assumptions, such as national interests and objectives and the core elements of the administration's national security strategy, and providing overall policy leadership for each review. Military leaders were responsible for developing the core elements of a compatible military strategy, posture and force structure alternatives, and assessing risk.[3] Programmatic and budgetary issues were considered by OSD, JCS, and the services.

THE BASE FORCE (1989–90)

The Base Force was developed by Chairman of the Joint Chiefs of Staff (CJCS) Colin Powell in 1989–90 in parallel with a larger administration review of national security and defense strategy.[4] It aimed to establish a new military strategy and force structure for the post-Cold War era while setting a floor for force reductions, both to hedge against the unexpected and to avoid "breaking" the force by executing reductions too rapidly.[5] In this latter regard, the Base Force effort aimed to provide a reasoned alternative to some of the more drastic reductions that were being discussed by congressional and other observers.

The strategy that emerged from the Base Force study replaced the former Cold War strategy of global containment of the Soviet Union and forward defense with a new strategy focused on regional threats and forward presence.[6] A capabilities-based approach (as opposed to a threat-based one) was used to size future forces;[7] the two-major-theater war (MTW) construct that would come to dominate defense planning later in the decade was an afterthought, not an intrinsic capability of the Base Force. Needed forces were estimated on the basis of their ability to protect and promote the United States' interests in key regions with an acceptable level of risk. Military forces were needed to provide continued strategic deterrence and defense, but also for regional forward presence, crisis response, and reconstitution in the event that a major threat arose in the future. U.S. forces were conceived in terms of four national force packages, including strategic (offensive and defensive) forces and three conventional force packages: Atlantic Forces and Pacific Forces (each of which included both forward presence and crisis-response capabilities) and Contingency Forces. The last were to provide a more substantial crisis response and mobilization capability, and were to be based primarily in the continental United States.

The Base Force called for substantial reductions in military forces, including a 25 percent reduction in force structure by fiscal year (FY) 1997, and an approximately 20 percent reduction in manpower. These force structure cuts fell somewhat unevenly on the services. The Army, and to a lesser extent, the Air Force, saw the deepest reductions (in the 33 percent–40 percent range), largely the result of reductions in forward-deployed forces in the European theater. The Army was to be reduced from twenty-eight to twenty divisions, and the Air Force was to be reduced from thirty-six to 26½ tactical fighter wing equivalents (TFWEs).[8] Navy aircraft carriers—the principal basis for organizing battle fleet forces—were to be reduced from fifteen to twelve, with the total number of battle force ships falling from 546 to 451. The Marine Corps, specified by law at three active and one reserve division, saw reductions in personnel-end strength. Overall active-end strength was to fall from nearly 2.1 million to 1.6 million personnel.

Finally, notwithstanding congressional calls for much deeper defense budget cuts, planning for the Base Force was predicated on a 10 percent reduction in defense budget authority from FY 1990.[9] The growing budget deficit strengthened the hand of congressional critics, however, who were able to impose in the October 1990 Budget Enforcement Act the deeper cuts they sought (25 percent as opposed to 10 percent). These deeper-than-expected defense budget cuts led in turn to accelerated reductions in active-end strength, the cancellation or reduction of a number of defense modernization programs, and creation of a "bow wave" of delayed procurement that would raise the costs of the defense program in its out-years;[10] the Base Force also planned for a high level of research and development to ensure that new capabilities would continue to become available in the future.

Defense policy makers hoped that infrastructure reductions and defense management reform would eliminate some of the more costly inefficiencies in the defense establishment and free up additional resources for the defense program. In fact, although savings did not begin to accumulate until well after the first Bush administration left office, two rounds of the Base Realignment and Closure (BRAC) Commission—the commission charged with making the politically sensitive decision of which military bases should be closed—were conducted before or during that administration.[11] The administration also undertook a broader set of management reforms under the Defense Management Review (DMR).

THE BOTTOM-UP REVIEW (1993)

The 1993 *Report on the Bottom-Up Review* (BUR)[12] was the second major force structure review of the decade that aimed to define a defense strategy, forces, and resources appropriate to the post-Cold War era, and the first conducted by the Clinton administration.[13] The aim of the BUR was to provide "a comprehensive review of the nation's defense strategy, force structure, modernization, infrastructure, and foundations." More fundamentally, it aimed to reduce forces and defense budgets below the levels established in the Base Force, and closer to the levels sought by many congressional detractors of the Base Force, including former chairman of the House Armed Services Committee—and then-Secretary of Defense—Les Aspin.

In fact, planned budget cuts well beyond those envisioned in the Base Force preceded decisions on strategy and force structure. In carrying them out, Clinton administration policy makers hoped to reduce defense spending without raising questions about their commitment to the nation's defenses. The result was that a strategy—really a force-sizing criterion—providing the capability to fight two nearly simultaneous major theater wars was overlaid on a force structure justified primarily in warfighting terms, but that soon would become preoccupied instead with peace operations in support of the still-crystallizing strategy of "engagement and enlargement." The BUR reported that the new program would yield $104 billion in savings beyond the earlier Bush baseline budget, roughly the savings that had been estimated in the FY 1994 budget submitted in the spring of 1993. Privately, however, some OSD policy makers were said to have expected only about $17 billion in savings, yielding a program that was substantially underfunded.

While embracing the Base Force's regionally focused strategy and emphasis on strategic deterrence, forward presence, and crisis response, the BUR redefined the meaning of engagement. It gave increased rhetorical and policy importance to participation in multilateral peace and humanitarian operations and set the stage for an increased operational tempo and rate of deployment, even as force and budgetary reductions continued or were accelerated.

Whereas the Base Force had envisioned force reductions of approximately 25 percent below FY 1990 levels, the BUR's threat-based approach yielded somewhat deeper reductions, about 33 percent. Force-level targets were lowered from twenty to eighteen Army divisions and 26½ to twenty Air Force tactical fighter wings; the number of Navy aircraft carriers was maintained at twelve, one of which was a reserve/training carrier. Further cuts in personnel end strength also were planned. The BUR aimed at "selective modernization," which meant additional cuts in many acquisition programs so that key modernization programs could be sustained. In particular, the BUR sought to eliminate the "bow wave" in the theater air modernization program that had emerged as a result of the procurement cuts following deeper-than-expected budget cuts that were imposed on the Base Force in late 1990. A number of "new initiatives" also were planned to improve the military's capability for "nontraditional" missions such as peacekeeping. The BUR also promoted environmental security and defense reinvestment and economic growth initiatives that would alleviate some of the economic impacts of defense downsizing.

Like the Base Force, the BUR anticipated that infrastructure reductions and management reforms would yield savings that could be plowed back into the defense program, assist in the goal of achieving the administration's lower defense spending targets.[14] For the Department of Defense (DoD), recommendations included measures to improve acquisition reform, including purchasing the best-value common supplies and services, and outsourcing noncore department functions.[15]

THE QUADRENNIAL DEFENSE REVIEW OF 1997

The 1997 *Report of the Quadrennial Review* (QDR)[16] considered the potential threats, strategy, force structure, readiness posture, military modernization programs, defense infrastructure, and other elements of the defense program needed for the 1997–2015 time frame and beyond. Unlike the Base Force and BUR, the 1997 QDR was congressionally mandated, and statutorily required.[17]

The QDR was intended to provide a blueprint for a strategy-based, balanced, and affordable defense program. Lingering concerns about the federal deficit resulted in continued spending caps being imposed on defense discretionary spending. These led to the QDR's assumption of flat US$250 billion a year defense budgets for the foreseeable future. Equally important, the QDR aimed to rebalance the defense program— within a flat budget and with only modest adjustments to force structure—to address some of the key problems that had developed during the BUR years, including the adverse effect of smaller-scale contingencies (SSCs) and the "migration" of funds from modernization (and especially procurement) accounts to operations accounts.

The QDR generally accepted the normative and other underpinnings of the BUR's strategy, reaffirmed the BUR's emphasis on two nearly simultaneous MTWs as the principal basis for force sizing, and posited that the United States might have to fight one or two MTWs over the 1997–2015 period. It also anticipated continued involvement over the same period in the kinds of SSCs that had been described in the BUR, including peace and humanitarian operations. The QDR gave only rhetorical recognition to the demands of SSCs and the need to respond to multiple concurrent SSCs, while articulating a somewhat more cautious and nuanced employment doctrine than had the BUR.

The QDR rejected a 10 percent cut in force structure because it would result in unacceptable risk, and sought to achieve savings largely through manpower cuts of 150,000 active duty personnel by FY 2003, which were expected to provide US$4 billion–US$6 billion in recurring savings thereafter. Given the modest changes to force structure advocated by the QDR, it was little surprise that, with only a few exceptions, force structure changes for major force elements were already in place by the time of the FY 2001 President's Budget and defense program.

The QDR concluded that DoD could not achieve its modernization and readiness goals without a concerted effort to reduce infrastructure costs and, accordingly, proposed continued reductions in civilian and military personnel associated with infrastructure; two additional rounds of base realignments and closures (BRACs); major initiatives to reengineer and reinvent DoD support functions; and greater emphasis on using the private sector to perform nonwarfighting support functions.[18] To achieve the QDR's goal of achieving US$60 billion a year in procurement spending, another round of cuts to acquisition programs and additional infrastructure reductions and defense management reforms were authorized under the rubric of the Defense Reform Initiative (DRI).

THE QUADRENNIAL REVIEW OF 2001

The defense reviews conducted in 2001 by the new Bush administration culminated, on September 30, 2001, in the release of another Quadrennial Defense Review.[19] The aim of this review was to "establish a new strategy for America's defense . . . premised on the idea that to be effective abroad, America must be safe at home. It sought to set the conditions to extend America's influence and preserve America's security."[20]

The QDR seems to have diagnosed correctly most of the problems and challenges facing the defense establishment. It argued that the DoD must reverse the readiness decline of many second-echelon operational units, selectively recapitalize the force, arrest the decay of aging defense infrastructure while simultaneously reducing and streamlining that infrastructure, and redress personnel accession and retention problems and pervasive management problems.[21]

The new strategy was built around four defense policy goals: assuring allies and friends; dissuading future military competition; deterring threats and coercion against U.S. interests; and if deterrence fails, decisively defeating any adversary.[22] These goals were supported in turn by seven "strategic tenets": managing risks in a more balanced way; shifting defense planning from a threat-based approach back to a capabilities-based one; defending the United States and projecting U.S. military power; strengthening alliances and partnerships; maintaining favorable regional balances; developing a broad portfolio of military capabilities; and transforming defense.

Force sizing was to be based on a new construct—described by the QDR as "a paradigm shift"—that aimed to shape forces to accomplish four distinct ends: defend the United States; deter aggression and coercion forward in critical regions; swiftly defeat aggression in overlapping major conflicts while preserving for the President the option to call for a decisive victory in one of those conflicts, including the possibility of regime change or occupation; and conduct a limited number of smaller-scale contingency operations.[23]

The QDR assessed the capabilities of the current force and judged it as presenting moderate operational risk, although certain combinations of warfighting and smaller-scale contingency scenarios presented high risk.[24] The QDR did not advocate further changes or substantial changes to the "above-the-line" composition of force structure.[25] Rather, it aimed to produce "significantly higher output of military value from each element of the force" through transformation of this force structure. Put another way, while force structure size essentially would be fixed, it was essential that it be transformed to reduce the risks associated with the strategy.

The transformation effort was to be focused on developing new operational concepts and capabilities to meet six operational goals: protecting critical bases of operation and defeating chemical, biological, radiological, nuclear, and high-explosive (CBRNE) weapons and their means of delivery; assuring information systems in the face of attack and conducting effective information operations; projecting and sustaining U.S. forces in distant anti-access or area-denial environments and defeating anti-access and area-denial threats; denying enemies sanctuary; enhancing the capability and survivability of space systems and supporting infrastructure; and leveraging information technology and innovative concepts to develop an interoperable, joint C4ISR architecture and capability that includes a tailorable joint operational picture.[26]

Transformation was to rest on four pillars: strengthening joint operations and joint and combined command and control; new concepts, capabilities, and constructs such as standing joint task forces; exploiting U.S. intelligence advantages; and developing transformational capabilities through increased and wide-ranging science and technology, selective increases in procurement, and innovations in DoD processes.[27]

The DoD establishment also was to be transformed through management reform directed at streamlining infrastructure further, improving the visibility provided by financial systems, and reengineering processes that discouraged action and acceptance of reasonable risk. This was to be accomplished largely by encouraging talent to enter and stay in the military and civilian service, and modernizing DoD business processes and infrastructure.[28]

Finally, the QDR introduced a new risk framework that would provide a more balanced basis than the two-MTW construct for assessing the health of the defense establishment. This framework consisted of four dimensions of risk: force management (the ability to recruit, retain, train, and equip personnel and sustain readiness); operational (the ability to achieve military objectives in a near-term conflict or contingency); future challenges (the ability to invest in new capabilities and develop new operational concepts to dissuade or defeat mid- to long-term military challenges); and institutional (the ability to develop management practices and controls that use resources efficiently and promote the effective operation of the defense establishment).[29] As much of a strength as a weakness, as described above, the QDR lacked much of the programmatic specificity that had accompanied earlier reviews.

PROBLEMS AND CHALLENGES ENCOUNTERED

The Base Force   Due to the change in administration as a result of the 1992 elections, the Base Force was implemented over two years only (FY 1992–93). While reductions in the major elements of force structure generally occurred as planned, active personnel reductions occurred more quickly, and reserve personnel reductions more slowly, than had been planned originally.

The Base Force was almost immediately—if somewhat unfairly—criticized as a strategy and force structure that was still driven by Cold War-era threats, and providing force reductions that many deemed inadequate in light of the greatly reduced threat environment.[30] The country's poor macroeconomic circumstances, moreover, including recession and a ballooning deficit, increased the calls for a "peace dividend" that would be realized only through additional defense cuts.

Base Force policy makers recognized the challenges of attempting to balance strategy and forces in the face of additional budget cuts.[31] In fact, they appear to have anticipated a number of important program execution risks in the out years, including the need to increase spending substantially later in the decade to carry out needed modernization. Among the principal challenges the Base Force faced were continued congressional pressure to reduce defense budgets further, and the possibility that these cuts would bring defense resources below the levels that were necessary to sustain the force as planned.[32] By December 1992, the list of challenges facing DoD planners had grown—a "significant mismatch" between the $1.4 trillion FY 1993–97 defense spending plan and budget realities had emerged, possibly necessitating additional program reductions of more than $150 billion.[33] Although infrastructure reductions had not yet started to yield savings, the management reforms undertaken under the Defense Management Review were estimated to have yielded an estimated $50 billion of the $70 billion that had been anticipated initially.[34]

The Bottom-Up Review   U.S. policy makers generally achieved their force structure and manpower reduction goals. Reductions were accelerated and quickly surpassed those planned in the Base Force, most of which had been achieved by the end of FY 1993. While the BUR addressed the highly acrimonious (but salient) issue of roles and missions,[35] it made no more progress on the issue than CJCS Powell had,[36] and also failed to accomplish much reshaping of the force as reductions were being implemented. This failure was due for the most part simply to the fact that achieving consensus support from the service chiefs for further reductions of forces and budgets posed a significant challenge in its own right. It also was complicated by the new administration's plans to promote the military more actively as a tool in peace operations, and several other initiatives that caused discomfort in the military.[37]

The force structure chosen by the BUR seems to have been inadequate for the high levels of peacetime engagement in contingency operations that actually occurred in subsequent years. Moreover, although this would not become clear until the fall of 1998, a mismatch between an engagement strategy more ambitious than the one envisioned in the Base Force, coupled with forces and resources declining at different rates, made it impossible to support the dual priorities of readiness and modernization during the years in which the BUR was implemented.

By FY 1998, the final year in which the defense program would be guided by the BUR, DoD had achieved only about $15 billion of the planned $104 billion in savings. The shortfalls had two principal results. First, despite the high priority and high levels of spending on operations and support (O&S) accounts, readiness problems emerged, many of them resource-related, while the risks associated with executing the national military strategy also grew. Second, over the 1995–97 period, spending on modernization fell well below the levels planned in the FY 1994 (transition) and 1995 (BUR) budgets; instead, funds routinely "migrated" from investment accounts to O&S accounts, resulting in program stretch-outs and delays of planned modernization efforts. Support for transformation of the force to achieve the goals set by *Joint Vision 2010* was funded even less adequately. In the end, the BUR seems to have required a Base Force-sized budget.

While the 1993 and 1995 BRAC rounds had not yet begun to yield savings by 1998, net savings began accumulating over the FY 1993–98 period for the earlier rounds. Management reforms appear to have yielded substantially less than the savings that resulted from the earlier Defense Management Review, which were in the low billions.

The Quadrennial Defense Review of 1997   The QDR, together with its claim to have balanced the defense program successfully, was met with some skepticism by both Congress and many other observers. Nevertheless, rather than adjusting discretionary defense spending caps to ensure the defense program was balanced, the administration and Congress continued their previous pattern of addressing shortfalls through emergency supplemental funding and modest year-to-year increases.

By the end of the decade, numerous short-, mid-, and long-term problems had emerged as a result of the growing imbalance among strategy, forces, and resources.

Evidence of readiness problems continued to accumulate in the wake of the QDR until the fall of 1998, when the Joint Chiefs testified before Congress that these problems were both more prevalent and more serious than had been reported earlier. The risks associated with executing the two-conflict strategy also had increased over this period, a result of lower readiness levels for forces earmarked for the second MTW and shortfalls in strategic mobility. The result of these developments, which played out in late 1998, was a FY 2000 budget request that entailed the first real increase in defense resources (approximately US$112 billion) in more than a decade.

The QDR's modest modernization goals appear to have been met, although the US$60 billion target fell well below the estimated US$80 billion–$US90 billion a year (or more) that was believed to be needed for recapitalization of the then-aging force. Despite the QDR's principal goal of balancing the defense program to achieve the desired levels of modernization, these efforts continued to be plagued by the "migration" of funds to operating and support accounts. Efforts to achieve the so-called transformation of the force also stalled, in large part due to underfunding, which was well below the US$5 billion–US$10 billion a year recommended by the National Defense Panel, a congressionally created commission that critiqued the QDR.[38]

Although few disagreed that additional infrastructure reductions were needed, the Congress declined to approve additional BRAC rounds after the 1995 round.[39] Nevertheless, by 2001, although infrastructure reductions through BRAC rounds had cost an estimated US$22.2 billion, they had yielded savings of US$37.7 billion, for a net savings of US$15.5 billion; annual savings after 2001, when the last of the rounds was to be completed, were estimated at US$6.1 billion annually.[40] Thus, savings from defense reform efforts, while not insubstantial, were somewhat disappointing.

In 2001, a wide range of fundamental management activities in DoD that were addressed by various reform efforts of the decade were still judged to be high-risk activities for the DoD. These included systems modernization; weapon systems acquisition; and financial, infrastructure, inventory, and contract management.[41]

THE QUADRENNIAL DEFENSE REVIEW OF 2001

At the time this chapter was being written, few of the programmatic, budgetary, or implementation details of the new strategy were available. In his statement on the QDR, CJCS Hugh Shelton indicated his expectation that force structure, budget, and infrastructure impacts would become clearer with the FY 2003 budgets and Program Objective Memoranda (POMs), and that transformation efforts would become clearer once the services had completed their transformation road maps.[42]

We return now to the question of how successful policy makers over the last decade were at achieving their four principal reform objectives.

Downsizing. As described, while defense policy makers generally were quite successful at reducing force structure and manpower, only limited reshaping of the force was achieved. Although there were deeper cuts to Army heavy divisions and Air Force tactical fighter wings than to Navy carrier battle groups and Marine divisions, these "above-the-line" units remain the principal elements of force structure.

Modernization. Nor did policy makers achieve their near-term modernization objectives. Modernization plans were scaled down repeatedly or slipped in response both to the budget constraints imposed on the defense program, and as a result of the "migration" of funds to pay higher-than-expected operating and support costs.

Reshaping and Transformation. Efforts to transform the force by designing, testing, and fielding new, truly joint operational concepts that could realize a revolution in military affairs (RMA) were even more disappointing than near-term modernization efforts. Despite CJCS John Shalikashvili's *Joint Vision 2010*, which provided a vision of the future force, and despite rhetorical attention to the issue of transformation in the QDR, efforts to transform the force have been limited by available funding.

Business Reform. Defense business reforms yielded diminishing returns over the decade. Whereas the Defense Management Review was estimated to have achieved US$50 billion of the US$70 billion in savings it had identified initially, savings from the Defense Reform Initiative associated with the QDR appear to have been in the low billions. Although the estimated US$6.1 billion in recurring annual net savings from infrastructure reduction that is expected after FY 2001 is not insubstantial, it represents less than 2 percent of the overall defense budget. Moreover, as infrastructure reductions lagged force structure reductions, defense infrastructure is estimated currently to be about 20 percent–25 percent more than what is needed.

As described above, most of the difficulties associated with the United States' defense reform efforts in some way point back to the inadequacy of defense budgets to support strategy and forces. On the one hand, there seems to have been a chronic reluctance to acknowledge what reasonable-risk versions of a strategy and force structure actually might cost, and, on the other, there was undue optimism regarding the savings that might be expected from infrastructure reductions and defense business reform.

As suggested above, while there appear to be some reasons for optimism, it will not be until the FY 2003 President's Budget submission that we will understand the critical details of how the new administration hopes to balance strategy, forces, and resources, and not until final congressional action will we know how much of the administration's plan will, in fact, survive.

LESSONS FOR NEW AND EMERGING DEMOCRACIES

The United States' status as a mature, Western democracy characterized by a somewhat idiosyncratic configuration of separate political institutions and mass political parties urges caution in drawing lessons for others, in particular for new and emerging democracies. Nevertheless, we now turn to this subject.

As Huntington has argued, the foundations for civil-military relations in the United States that were established in the U.S. Constitution in 1789 reflected a historically unique set of concerns. The United States' military character at that time was one of citizen-soldiers affiliated with state militias, rather than a large, standing army. Thus, the emergence of a military class that might threaten nascent U.S. democracy was viewed by most as highly improbable.[43] The specific arrangement agreed to in the Constitution addressed the constitutional authors' most pressing concern—that the greatest danger would arise from placing the military under a single political institution, because it forever would be tempted to use the military to advance its political interests. The prescription that flowed from this line of reasoning was to ensure sufficient checks and balances on civilian political control of the military by creating a framework in which the president and congress *shared* control of the military.[44]

The resulting institutional setting—in which the U.S. military has sought effectively to serve two masters who frequently (some might say, more often than not) fail to agree—continues to shape the nature of this *pas de trois* of presidency, Congress, and the military on defense matters.

With this background in mind, a key lesson from the United States' post-Cold War defense reform experience is that democratic control of defense policy can be made much more difficult when those who share political control of the military fail to agree on critical issues of strategy, the purposes of the military, and budgets. In the United States' case, stable political support for key defense policies remained an elusive goal for most of the decade, and the failure of elected leaders to debate these issues arguably retarded recognition and remediation of the growing problems.

In the United States, the President and Congress have natural political advantages over the military, and retain unquestioned authority and unparalleled influence in ensuring military compliance with their policies. Congress continued to cut defense budgets well beyond the levels preferred by the JCS (and the first Bush administration), and there was little either could do about it. And until the fall of 1998, the Clinton administration managed to keep the chiefs from exercising their prerogative to go to Capitol Hill and dissent collectively about the impact of budget shortfalls on military readiness and strategic risk. In spite of reservations regarding the administration's force structure and budget cuts, force employment doctrine, and other decisions, the professional ethos of the chiefs prevented them from questioning their legitimacy.

Nevertheless, the absence of institutional consensus frequently presents fleeting opportunities that can be exploited by the military. Some observers have argued that in cases where mass democracy has emerged, intervention of the military in domestic politics has become limited, its influence felt mainly in the conduct of foreign affairs and defense policies.[45] The military's influence on foreign and defense policies in the United States arises in part from its professionalization, in part from its ability to enhance its bargaining power by forging consensus among the service chiefs,[46] and in part from its responsibilities to two masters—the President and Congress.

The appearance of military professionalization—the perception of a monopoly of military expertise—is enhanced when the Joint Chiefs express unanimous support for (or opposition to) a policy; in such cases, their bargaining position also is enhanced vis-à-vis their civilian masters.

A divided JCS, on the other hand, "permits (or obliges) the administration to intervene to arrive at decisions when its military advisors cannot."[47] It should be little surprise that the JCS has been a consensus-seeking organization,[48] and, at times, has been able to use consensus to its advantage.

For example, while the Base Force did result in a modest amount of reshaping, the chiefs managed to scuttle the threat of a more penetrating reexamination of roles and missions. Neither Powell's nor Aspin's efforts in 1993, nor the Commission on Roles and Missions in 1994, nor Secretary of Defense William Cohen's 1997 QDR was able to make headway on this issue. In a similar vein, the chiefs' fall 1998 decision to appeal to the Congress for budgetary relief by laying claim to a part of the emerging budget surpluses, and thereby redress emerging readiness and modernization problems, left the White House with few options other than to accede to their request. As noted above, however, such opportunities are somewhat rare, and limited in their scope.

There seems to be broad agreement that, for new and emerging democracies, the simplest way of minimizing military power is maximizing the power of civilian groups in relation to the military.[49] This is accomplished largely by fostering pluralism and the political participation of mass parties, and establishing political and legal rules that channel political activity away from undesirable activities (for example, coup and rebellion), and toward more desirable ones (voting, letter writing, lobbying, etc.). This may offer cold comfort to the leaders of many emerging democracies, however, as the ultimate success of such prescriptions rests on what often will appear to be a glacial pace of change in the tectonics of the political landscape. Fortunately, the United States' experience does suggest some tools that may be of immediate and lasting value to civilian leaders in new democracies.

It suggests, for example, the use of promotion systems to favor advancement of senior officers who are most sympathetic to civilians' policy goals.

- In the interests of reducing interservice competition and producing officers better prepared to work with—and for—civilian leaders, the Goldwater-Nichols Act of 1986 strengthened the requirement for professional military education and joint service. Since that time, and in spite of some concern about a widening "civil-military gap," civilian leaders in fact have increasingly been the beneficiaries of the changes undertaken in compliance with this Act.[50]

- Recognizing that they frequently lack the means to force compliance from subordinates, presidents also have tended to promote to those chairmanship (or service chief) officers who appear predisposed to promote the president's own goals. For example, in 1989, President George H. W. Bush appointed to the chairmanship General Colin L. Powell, a Reagan administration insider who previously had served as National Security Advisor. Similarly, President Clinton promoted to CJCS Army Generals John Shalikashvili and Hugh Shelton, two officers who supported use of the military in the sorts of peace operations favored by the administration. And in 2001, President George W. Bush promoted Air Force General Richard Myers, an officer with a strong record of joint service from the service that arguably is the most technologically bullish, and who was expected to be a strong proponent of the administration's transformation efforts.[51]

Civilian leaders also can use budget and other processes to establish incentives that can influence the structure and activities of the military.

- Both the Bush and Clinton administrations successfully used their defense reviews to promote force reductions and, in a much more limited way, to reshape the force.
- The early Clinton administration hoped to use the Joint Requirements Oversight Council/Joint Warfare Capabilities Analysis (JROC/JWCA) process as the forge for creating future capabilities through competition of alternative operational concepts. This failure probably has less to do with any inherent flaws in the JROC/JWCA process than the under-resourcing of modernization and transformation activities.[52]

Finally, forging executive-legislative agreement on defense matters also can enhance civilian control by minimizing "daylight" between the White House and Congress that might be exploited.

- When, during the first Bush administration—and to an even greater extent in the early Clinton administration, when Democrats controlled both the executive and legislative branches—there was agreement that force reductions were necessary, the military had little choice but to comply with civilian masters.
- When the Republicans reclaimed Capitol Hill, and divided government returned in 1995, however, military leaders who were disen-

chanted with the new directions in defense usually could find a sympathetic hearing from congressional critics of the Clinton administration who might place countervailing pressures on civilian defense leaders.

- Nevertheless, in spite of the growing gaps between budgets and defense needs, it was not until the fall of 1998—more than 5½ years after the Clinton administration took office, and more than a year after the second of its defense reviews—that the chiefs publicly confirmed in testimony to Congress what many critics had suspected for a number of years: the shortfalls were having an impact on the long-term readiness of the force and its ability to execute the strategy with an acceptable level of risk. Put another way, until the problems had become undeniable—and the emerging budget surpluses irresistible—the chiefs did not challenge the administration publicly on the question of the adequacy of the defense budgets it was willing to provide.

While the above examples are anecdotal and somewhat impressionistic, in the final analysis, whether a society is a mature Western democracy or an emerging one, the best way to ensure that delegation of authority leads to desired actions is to ensure that organizational actors appreciate the rules for their advancement and face strong incentives—both positive and negative—to comply with civilian leaders' own preferences.

ENDNOTES

1. The "tooth-to-tail" ratio is the ratio of combat forces to their support.

2. For a detailed critique of each of these reviews and their implementation, see Eric V. Larson, David T. Orletsky, and Kristin Leuschner, *Defense Planning in a Decade of Change: Lessons from the Base Force, Bottom-Up Review, and Quadrennial Defense Review*, Santa Monica, CA, MR-1387-AF, 2001. Programmatic and budgetary detail were not available at the time of writing, so implementation of the September 2001 Quadrennial Defense Review is not discussed in this paper.

3. The defense reviews generally preceded the formal release of the administration's national security strategy and the military's national military strategy. In the case of the 1997 Quadrennial Defense Review, the national security strategy also was released in May 1997, the same month in which the QDR was released.

4. This review was National Security Review 12 (NSR 12).

5. The Base Force is described at various levels of detail in Colin L. Powell, "Building the Base Force: National Security for the 1990s and Beyond," annotated

briefing, September 1990; Joint Chiefs of Staff, *Joint Military Net Assessment*, Washington, DC, 1991; Joint Chiefs of Staff, *1992 National Military Strategy*, Washington, DC, 1992; Joint Chiefs of Staff, *Joint Military Net Assessment*, Washington, DC, 1992.

6. President Bush would announce the new regionally based strategy at the Aspen Institute on 2 August 1990, the day Iraq invaded Kuwait.

7. For a fuller discussion of capabilities-based and threat-based planning, see James A. Winnefeld, *The Post-Cold War Force-Sizing Debate: Paradigms, Metaphors, and Disconnects*, Santa Monica, CA: Rand, R-4243-JS, 1992, pp. v, 1–9. Winnefeld provides an excellent discussion of the debate between the Bush administration (notably, then Secretary of Defense Cheney) and its congressional critics, especially then chairman of the House Armed Services Committee Les Aspin and Chairman of the Senate Armed Services Committee Sam Nunn. The "two-MTW" construct posited that U.S. forces needed to be capable of conducting two nearly simultaneous major theater wars.

8. The initial plan, to reduce the Air Force to twenty-four TFWEs, was modified in response to Air Force plans to field composite wings that included support aircraft as well, resulting in 26½ TFWEs.

9. The U.S. government's fiscal year runs from October 1 to September 30.

10. U.S. Department of Defense planning is centered on a Future Years Defense Program (FYDP, formerly Five Years Defense Program), which entails a six-year projection of force structure, manpower, programs, and budgets.

11. Base Realignment and Closure (BRAC) rounds took place both before and after the disestablishment of the Soviet Union, with the closures implemented over a six-year period following the commission. In the 1988 BRAC round, there were sixteen major closures; in 1991, twenty-six major closures; in 1993, twenty-eight major closures; and in 1995, twenty-seven major closures. Each of the rounds required six years for full implementation.

12. Les Aspin, *Report on the Bottom-Up Review*, Washington, DC, October 1993.

13. The Clinton administration entered office in January 1993.

14. The principal mechanism was Vice President Gore's "National Performance Review," which Secretary Perry described in his "mandate for change." See White House, Office of the Vice President, "From Red Tape to Results: Creating a Government that Works Better & Costs Less," Report of the National Performance Review, White House press release, 7 September 1993; William Perry, "Mandate for Change," plan provided by Secretary of Defense Perry to the House Armed Services Committee and the Government Affairs Committee, February 1994, at http://www.acq.osd.mil/ar/doc/mand24.pdf

15. By 2000, the U.S. General Accounting Office would report that one of these recommendations had been implemented, and the other partially implemented.

DoD estimated that implementation of the outsourcing recommendation yielded an estimated US$528 million in savings; GAO, *Reinventing Government: Status of NPR Recommendations at 10 Federal Agencies*, Washington, DC, GAO/GGD-00-145, September 2000.

16. Department of Defense, Report of the Quadrennial Defense Review, Washington, DC, May 1997.

17. The seeds of a requirement for a quadrennial defense review are to be found in the 1995 Commission on Roles and Missions' (CORM) recommendation that a quadrennial defense review be undertaken at the beginning of each newly elected presidential administration; Secretary of Defense William Perry endorsed the recommendation. The statutory requirement was established in the Military Force Structure Review Act of 1996, Subtitle B of Public Law 104-201, the National Defense Authorization Act of 1996. A permanent requirement for a quadrennial defense review was established in 1999, in Public Law 106-65, the National Defense Authorization Act for Fiscal Year 2000.

18. GAO, *Defense Reform Initiative: Organization, Status, and Challenges*, Washington, DC, GAO/NSIAD-99-87, April 1999, p. 15.

19. In preparation for the Quadrennial Defense Review, Secretary of Defense Donald Rumsfeld created nearly twenty panels and charged them with responsibility for making recommendations on various issues. Perhaps the most notable of these were the strategy panel, led by Director of Net Assessment Andrew Marshall; the conventional forces panel, led by RAND vice president David Gompert; the transformation panel, led by Air Force General, ret. James McCarthy, and a panel on morale and quality of life led by retired admiral David Jeremiah.

20. Department of Defense, *Quadrennial Defense Review Report*, Washington, DC, September 30, 2001.

21. Ibid., pp. 7–10, 49–56.

22. Ibid., pp. 11–13.

23. Ibid., pp. 17–21.

24. Ibid., pp. 67–70; CJCS Shelton indicated that the QDR reduces the strategy-to-structure imbalance and results in moderate near-term risk for the current force executing the revised strategy, an apparent reduction in risk. He also indicated, however, that the strategy would address the current and emerging challenges of the strategic environment adequately only if it was matched with resources over time, and that transformation efforts will be able to be assessed accurately only when the services have completed their transformation roadmaps.

25. "Above-the-line" force structure consists of the number of divisions, carrier battle groups, tactical fighter wings, and other major force elements in the force structure.

26. Department of Defense, op cit., 2001, p. 30. Another desirable capability was making forward forces capable of swiftly defeating an adversary's military and political objectives with only modest reinforcement; ibid., p. 26.

27. Ibid., p. 32.

28. Ibid., pp. 49–56.

29. Ibid., pp. 57–58.

30. Perhaps the most prominent critics were then chairman of the House Armed Services Committee (and later Secretary of Defense) Les Aspin and chairman of the Senate Armed Services Committee Sam Nunn. Then Presidential candidate Bill Clinton also criticized the Base Force, describing it as a "Cold War-minus" force, that is, a force that was little more than a slightly scaled-down version of the Cold War force, rather than one reshaped to meet the needs of the post-Cold War world.

31. As the Joint Chiefs of Staff's 1991 Joint Military Net Assessment put it: "Our assessment of the emerging world order suggests that meeting the demands of our global military objectives with fiscally constrained forces based largely within CONUS will continue to be an enormous challenge." See Joint Chiefs of Staff, op cit., 1991, pp. 2–3.

32. See GAO, op cit., 1991, p. 1.

33. See GAO, op cit., 1992, pp. 5–6.

34. Defense Science Board, *Task Force on the Fiscal Years 1994–99 Future Years Defense Program (FYDP)*, reports of 3 May 1993 and 29 June 1993.

35. Aspin, op cit., pp. 85–89.

36. CJCS Powell had sought to address seriously the issue of unnecessary duplication in service roles and missions in a congressionally mandated report that was released in January 1993. However, the recommendations in his draft report reportedly were watered down to achieve a least-common-denominator consensus from the service chiefs, and the final report was met with some disappointment. This disappointment led to hopes (and Secretary Aspin's stated intention) that the BUR would address the issue and, when it, too, failed, resulted in the creation by Congress of a Commission on Roles and Missions (CORM); see Barton Gellman, "Aspin Gently Criticizes Powell Report; Overlap of Military Functions Needs Another Look, Secretary Says," *Washington Post*, 30 March 1993.

37. One indication of these tensions was CJCS Powell's argument with then UN ambassador Madeleine Albright regarding the use of U.S. forces for peace operations in Bosnia. Powell reportedly argued that the United States should not commit military forces to Bosnia until there was a clear political objective, at which point Albright responded: "What's the point of having this superb military that you're always talking about if we can't use it?" "I thought I would have an aneurysm," Powell later wrote, "American GIs were not toy soldiers to be moved around on

some sort of global game board"; Colin L. Powell, with Joseph E. Persico, *My American Journey*, New York: Random House, 1995, p. 576. There were other reasons for service discomfort as well. The new administration created additional sources of friction with the uniformed military, for example, as a result of pressing the issue of gays in the military as soon as it entered office, and by proposing a pay freeze to free up additional savings, while at the same time trumpeting the issue of "fairness to personnel" as one of its "defense foundations"; see Aspin, op cit., pp. 81–84.

38. For example, GAO found that only about three-quarters of a billion dollars a year was being spent on Joint Vision 2010-related Defense Technology Objectives (DTOs), less than .3 percent of the defense budget; GAO, *Military Operations: Status of DOD's Efforts to Develop Future Warfighting Capability*, Washington, DC, NSIAD—99-64, March 1999. Funding for advanced concept technology demonstrations (ACTDs) also declined by about 90 percent (from about US$1 billion to US$100 million) in the second half of the decade, and annual funding for the Defense Advanced Research Projects Agency (DARPA) stalled at about US$2 billion a year.

39. The Congress refused to authorize additional rounds as a result of alleged administration interference in the BRAC decision on McClellan Air Force Base near Sacramento, California.

40. GAO, *Military Base Closures: DoD's Updated Net Savings Estimate Remains Substantial*, Washington, DC, GAO-01-971, July 2001, p. 2.

41. GAO, *High-Risk Update*, Washington, DC, GAO-01-263, January 2001, p. 10.

42. DoD, op cit., 2001, pp. 67–70.

43. According to Huntington: "The Framers' concept of civilian control was to control the uses to which civilians might put military force rather than to control the military themselves. They were more afraid of military power in the hands of political officials than of political power in the hands of military officers. Unable to visualise a distinct military class, they could not fear such a class. But there was need to fear the concentration of authority over the military in any single governmental institution. As conservatives, they wanted to divide power, including power over the armed forces"; Samuel P. Huntington, *The Soldier and the State*, Cambridge: Harvard University Press, 1957, p. 168. Also see C. Kenneth Allard, *Command, Control, and the Common Defense*, New Haven: Yale University Press, 1990, pp. 21–22.

44. The political control of the military is, in Richard Neustadt's words, a classic case of "separated institutions sharing powers"; Richard E. Neustadt, *Presidential Power: The Politics of Leadership*, New York: Wiley, 1960, p. 33.

45. Morris Janowitz, *Political Conflict: Essays in Political Sociology*, Chicago: Quadrangle Books, 1970, p. 136.

46. This is true even when consensus means embracing inferior, least-common-denominator solutions.

47. As Kanter puts it: "The Chiefs' behavior in this regard is consistent with *their* acceptance of the hypothesis that the extent of civilian participation (and control) is positively related to the intensity of interservice rivalries [emphasis in the original]"; Arnold Kanter, *Defense Politics: A Budgetary Perspective*, Chicago: University of Chicago Press, 1979, p. 28.

48. The record of official JCS recommendations between 1953 and 1968 shows that the percentage of "split" (nonconsensus) recommendations rarely exceeded 1 percent annually. Kanter, op cit., pp. 25–26.

49. Huntington, op cit., pp. 80–81.

50. The Triangle Institute for Security Studies conducted a study on the subject a couple of years ago; see Peter Feaver and Richard Kohn, *Soldiers and Civilians: The Civil-Military Gap and American National Security*, Cambridge, MA: MIT Press, 2001.

51. See Carl Builder, *The Masks of War: American Military Styles in Strategy and Analysis*, Baltimore: Johns Hopkins Press, 1989. Before being promoted to CJCS, General Myers was Vice Chairman of the JCS.

52. Kanter advises "taking a politically instrumental view of issues relating to formal organizational arrangements and for trying to exploit, rather than overcome, the characteristics of the national security bureaucracy. In particular, it has directed attention to the resource allocation process as a way to increase the leverage which politically accountable officials can have on the shape of national security decisions and actions"; Kanter, op cit., p. 123.

CHAPTER FOURTEEN

Defense Reform in Hungary: A Decade of Strenuous Efforts and Missed Opportunities

Zoltán Martinusz

"In Hungary defense reform is 80 percent in concept but only 20 percent in implementation."

—A U.S. Army colonel after six months in Hungary as head of the
Mil-to-Mil Cooperation Team

INTRODUCTION

The life of the Hungarian military in the 1990s was characterized by permanent reform and restructuring efforts. It was also characteristic that none of these efforts was implemented fully or carried to its originally planned conclusion. In fact, the first restructuring was initiated back in 1985. Still, the Hungarian military belongs to those large social systems—together with health care and pensions—where a true system change has not occurred yet. Thus, Hungary marches into the twenty-first century with a basically Soviet-type, heritage military.

This statement obviously does not intend to mean that nothing positive has taken place in the defense sector in the last ten years. Hungary's accession to the North Atlantic Treaty Organization (NATO) provides most convincing proof of all the progress that has certainly not left the military untouched. Hungary made military contributions of crucial importance to NATO's missions in the Balkans. It established a firm institutional and legal background for civilian control of the military, actively participated in and contributed to the Partnership for Peace (PfP) program, played a major stabilizing role in an otherwise rather unstable region, and clearly met the accession criteria outlined in NATO's Enlargement Study of 1995, in both the political and military fields.

Nevertheless, the basic structural and functioning problems of the

Hungarian military have not found a satisfactory solution in the course of the last fifteen years. In fact, the size of the military has shrunk to one-third of what it was fifteen years ago, but the most important problems are just the same:

- lack of funding for daily functioning and O&M;
- lack of sustainability;
- obsolescent equipment and lack of modernization funds;
- outdated management and decision-making procedures;
- distorted human resources structures; and
- lack of capabilities for the most likely mission requirements.

In addition, continuous restructuring, downsizing, and instability have led to a moral decline.

This chapter does not wish to deny positive results, but, rather, concentrates on problems and hindering factors. Its aim is to contribute to a better understanding of why defense reform efforts in Hungary—a relatively better-off country that proved to be successful in most areas of social and economic transformation—were stranded on a regular basis. Through the Hungarian example, it seeks to understand whether defense restructuring in Central and Eastern Europe is necessarily a painfully slow process characterized by setbacks and failures, or if there are some identifiable pitfalls that other countries should and could avoid.

Hungary's Security Environment in the 1990s

With the end of the Cold War and the political changes in Eastern Europe, Hungary's security environment has undergone basic changes. The Warsaw Pact and the COMECON have disappeared, Soviet troops were withdrawn, and the high-risk-high-stability environment of a potential global confrontation was replaced by a low-risk-low-stability environment. Instead of its previous five neighbors, all of a sudden Hungary bordered on seven countries, five of them new state entities burdened with completely new internal and external tensions; ethnic problems; and the instability caused by political, economic, and social changes. The sharply contrasting results—or lack thereof—of individual countries in managing these changes have contributed further to instability and already have foreshadowed a split in the region into haves and have-nots, in terms of both internal stability and prosperity and the success of their Euro-Atlantic integration efforts.

For the first time in nearly a century, Hungary has witnessed an increase in its geostrategic significance, as a result of its location on the communication lines between the geographic and strategic center of gravity of NATO and the potential crisis areas on the periphery of Western Europe. The scare of the 1991 Soviet coup, the painful dissolution of the former Yugoslavia, the war(s) between Serbia and Croatian, and the international trade embargo and ensuing economic losses quickly revealed that the increased strategic significance carried a negative side as well. Thus, defense reform had to be implemented in an unstable international environment, which proved to be a limiting rather than an inspiring factor, in terms of both visionary thinking and disciplined implementation.

REFORM PROGRAMS IN THE 1990S

Before analyzing the difficulties that arose throughout different reform programs, it is worth a brief look at the main features of such programs in the past decade.

The first reorganization efforts may be traced back to 1986, when the military leadership had to face functional bankruptcy for the first time. Project RUBIN tried to reorganize the military in the face of financial and resource constraints. Due to a lack of concept and conditions, the only significant result of the hastily arranged program was the start of a moral decline and an exodus of well-trained officers from the military to the civilian sphere.

A major reorganization of the higher levels of leadership took place in 1989, just before the change in the political system. The reform communists—expecting to win the presidency—basically separated the line of command from the elected government of the country and put the commander of the Hungarian armed forces under authority of the president. This step was disguised as a move to protect the military from the day-to-day political influence of political parties. The plan did not work; the reform communists could not win the presidency, but the uncertainty in the line of command laid the seeds for a decade of bitter debates and rivalry among the presidency and the chief executive, the Defense Staff, and the Ministry of Defense (MOD). It took twelve years, Constitutional Court decisions, several changes in different laws—and destruction of a number of careers—to overcome this problem, clarify the line of command, and reintegrate the Defense Staff into the MOD.

In the years between 1990 and 2001, restructuring of the Hungarian military may be divided to three phases, according to the major objectives of force development.

The main objective of the first phase, between 1990 and 1994, was creation of a sovereign country's national force. The most important substantive elements of the process were creation of the institutional and legal background pf civilian control, dismantling of the legacy offensive structures, and creation of an armed forces that better reflects the country's needs and capabilities in both size and structure. The second phase started in 1995 with the main—declared—objective of creating a transparent and effective system for defense and resource planning, and preparation of the military for Hungary's NATO accession. The third phase started with the 1999 strategic review, aiming at radical structural changes and a dramatic increase in the peacetime operational capabilities of the Hungarian Defense Forces (HDF). Each of the three phases—even though their main objectives clearly were different—contained some common elements, such as adapting the size of the military to the economic capabilities of the country, efforts to repair the military's structural imbalances, and moderate technical modernization.

At the time of political change in 1989–1990 the Hungarian People's Army was a slightly below-average Warsaw Pact armed force in terms of doctrine, equipment, structure, and combat readiness. The first major task of the period beginning in 1990 was to define the defense requirements of a country just leaving the Warsaw Pact and to restructure its military forces accordingly, creating a sustainable national force that could still meet its primary function of credible deterrence. This reorganization was accompanied by a significant downsizing. Overall, the military did not become more modern, its combat readiness did not improve, the living and training conditions of soldiers deteriorated further, and each reorganization effort was terminated prematurely and replaced by another plan that was doomed to end prematurely and without reaching its original objectives, just as the earlier ones had. Still, the overriding objective of creating an independent national force on the ruins of the Warsaw Pact legacy was achieved, and that constituted an undeniable success.

In the actual implementation of reorganization tasks, the political and military leadership took an extremely cautious and, to some extent, conservative approach, basically leaving the forces' internal structures untouched. (Due to a number of changes in capabilities, however, the forces were not considered capable of offensive operations any longer.) By 1994, the peacetime size of the HDF shrank to ninety thousand; its SCUD missiles were decommissioned and destroyed; the number of main battle tanks decreased by 45 percent and the number of combat aircraft decreased by 40 percent; and the wartime structure of the land forces decreased by seven brigades, twenty-two tank battalions, and ten artillery battalions. The dislocation of the units was changed to create a relative geographical balance within the country, conscript service was reduced to twelve months, the concept of contract soldiers started to take shape, and a new mobilization system was introduced. A significant amount of equipment and numerous spare parts were acquired from the former German Democratic Republic (GDR) armed forces and, as an offset to outstanding Soviet debts but parallel with that acquisition, modernization and development funds were cut back below 10 percent.

By 1994–95 it became clear that the first phase of the reorganization was not addressing the basic functional problems of the military, the target of sustainability has not been reached, and further restructuring— that is, major downsizing—was necessary. In addition to a functional and financial crisis, in the wake of the rapidly worsening living and working conditions, evidence of a moral crisis started to emerge.

Thus, in 1994–95 MOD leadership faced a triple challenge of—yet another—short-term crisis management, the development of—yet another—mid-term plan, and preparation for NATO membership. It is not surprising that the main theme of the reform was harmonization of the country's defense capabilities with its economic capabilities. (Also not surprising, the effort failed again.) Armed forces size was reduced further, to sixty thousand—with an aim to retain professional personnel, particularly officers; the command structure was reorganized several times to eliminate a number of headquarters (HQs) and introduce a NATO-compatible internal structure; the number of conscripts was reduced further; the duration of conscript service was cut back to nine months; and a significant number of units were either disbanded or relegated to a lower level of readiness—with fewer personnel and reduced requirements for materiel, supplies, and mobilization time lines. The original plans had to be changed several times for a number of reasons, including lack of funding, the Implementation Force (IFOR) mission, etc.

In addition to reorganization, preparations for NATO accession took immense energy, time, and effort from just about every individual and organizational structure of the MOD. While the process was obviously not free from mistakes and difficulties—none is—the priorities were defined correctly, implementation in general exceeded standards, some enterprises—for example, IFOR—even belonged to the category of spectacular success, and the invitation in Madrid provided the Hungarian armed forces with their single largest collective experience of success and redemption in the 1990s.

Still, the success of invitation to the Atlantic Alliance could not hide the fact that the new mid-term plan did not provide adequate remedy for the military's deep structural, financial, and functional problems. Combat readiness and training standards continued to decline, living conditions deteriorated further, technical obsolescence became even more obvious, and the military used up most of its wartime reserves to support peacetime functioning. While some combat units maintained acceptable standards, logistics and combat service support units came close to losing functioning capability.

This situation, together with the fact of NATO accession, the Defense Capabilities Initiative (DCI), and the lessons of the Kosovo war forced Hungary's political and military leadership in 1999 to initiate a strategic review and try to take a radically new approach to the nagging problem of defense restructuring.

The strategic review outlined the following general tasks and objectives:

TABLE 1
Changes in CFE Limited Equipment and Personnel Holdings in the 1990s

	Tanks	ACVs	Artillery	Attack helicopters	Combat aircraft	Personnel
1990	1,345	1,720	1,047	39	110	—
1992	1,345	1,731	1,047	39	143	82,728
1994	1,191	1,645	991	39	171	75,294
1996	835	1,540	840	59	144	66,051
1998	835	1,316	840	59	138	43,816
2000	806	1,439	839	51	107	43,790
2001	753	1,479	839	51	107	33,885
CFE ceiling	835	1,700	840	100	160	100,000

(Note that the actual number of operational combat aircraft in 2001 was only twenty-seven, and the personnel figures do not include civilians.)

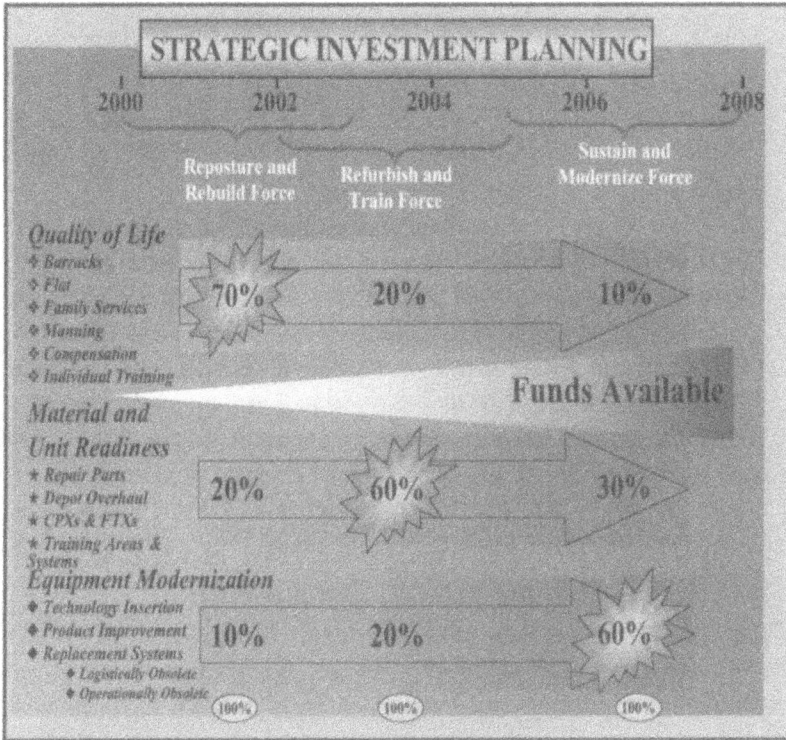

STRATEGIC INVESTMENT PLANNING

• Restructure and reposture the Ministry of Defense and the HDF to achieve increased military capability and retain only the essential command and control, support and services, and background organizations.

• Reduce total Ministry of Defense active "trained manpower" authorizations to approximately forty-five thousand personnel, both military and civilian, including the Ministry and HDF elements, and limit the mobilization manpower requirements.

• Eliminate nonessential units and obsolete capabilities, move to an increasingly professional but smaller force, and recommend trends for conscript manpower.

• Where practical, convert essential support and services to "self-supporting" configurations of either a commercially or government-owned foundation.

• Reduce background organizations and strengthen tactical units. Retain only units in the force structure that will be essential in the future and are a major active duty component.

- Dispose of all excess equipment and facilities not required by the restructured force.
- Refocus manpower into combat type units and modernize organization of essential and retained forces. Design the units to accommodate future materiel and training modernization and achieve tactical and operational compatibility with allied nations.
- Restructure and realign combat forces and close numerous nonessential garrisons to generate fiscal and manpower savings to establish, modernize, and train an effective and resilient combat force consistent with national needs and international commitments, especially NATO. Restructuring and garrison closures also should be implemented in the logistics units and background organizations.
- Establish combat forces in a limited set of major garrisons that focus on strategic situations, manpower requirements, economies of scale, and support of infrastructure and family support. Resiliency and readiness of combat units is of special interest to, and the first military priority of, the government.

To achieve the goals outlined, a strategic investment concept was established, aimed at the most effective use of generated savings (from garrison closures, functional reductions, force reductions, for-profit conversions, etc.) and additional budget authority. The restructuring was to be implemented in three phases that would focus resources according to the following priorities:

- Phase 1: Reposture and rebuild the force—establish a sufficient quality of life for service members and their families.
- Phase 2: Refurbish and train the force—develop equipment readiness and unit training readiness for combat operations.
- Phase 3: Sustain and modernize the force—introduce new technologies and modern systems that will expand the units' combat power.

Implementation of such a conceptually innovative approach entailed some management requirements that, at least at the very beginning of the process, were quite new to the Hungarian military and contradicted some traditions and well-entrenched bureaucratic positions and procedures. There was an absolute need to develop and sustain a Force Modernization Master Plan that is updated annually and records and tracks all of the various and integrated initiatives required for the planned total force modernization. Savings generated by the various initiatives needs

TABLE 2
Projected Changes in Manning Levels

Unit Type	Manning Levels in 1999 (fact)	Manning Levels in 2010 (plan)
Army	22%	63%
Army combat	30%	77%
Air Force	47%	91%
HDF total	30%	52%

to be documented carefully to ensure precise reapplication of all available resources to essential and time-phased priorities of force modernization. Also, there was a strong need to accelerate the maturity of a Defense Planning System to ensure detailed visibility of all resource requirements and resource applications and account for derived results.

SPECIAL CHARACTERISTICS OF THE PRESENT "STRATEGIC REVIEW"

The government's 1999 resolution initiating the strategic review was of a special nature in that it represented the first step "out of the box" and gave up the decade-long habit and shackle of mutual lies between the political and military leadership about the real capabilities of the Hungarian armed forces. It intended to implement philosophical changes in the military's functioning, resulting in long-term qualitative improvements. The main target of the strategic review was radical improvement of peacetime rapid-reaction capabilities.

Nevertheless, this new reform effort was burdened as well by a number of internal contradictions—some of which simply were unavoidable—from the very beginning. First, in addition to an increased defense budget, it relies heavily on further internal resources becoming available through downsizing and base closings. However, the Hungarian military lacks the financial resource management system necessary to identify such savings, and the reform effort has not even included creation of such a system among its primary objectives. Second, postponement of equipment modernization to the third phase of the reform—though logical from a resource management-oriented approach—created a strange paradox in capabilities. Instead of a "small but modern," mostly professional military, Hungary will have to live with the contradictory reality of a "small and obsolete" force that still carries most of the characteristics but not the size of a mass army.

The 1999 reform was special as well in the sense that Hungary's financial condition was better than when any previous effort was undertaken—or so it seemed at the time. The MOD has convinced the government to lift the obligation to generate income by itself. This obligation was increased regularly in earlier years and, by 1999, it reached such levels—about 15 percent to 20 percent of the total defense budget—that clearly were way beyond the realm of the possible. This measure, the steady and guaranteed share of gross domestic product (GDP) (1.61 percent), and a projected annual GDP growth of 4 percent to 5 percent meant a significant increase in the real value of the defense budget. Improved funding, together with the planned freeing-up and reallocation of internal resources, was supposed to bring about a significant increase in the purchasing power of the defense portfolio as soon as the second year of restructuring. (In a period of mostly decreasing defense spending within the Alliance, the above measures could and should have brought significant political dividends for Hungary, somewhat balancing the criticism about its stepping back from some of its earlier military commitments. But, also characteristic, the Hungarian government tried to oversell its case, provided contradictory figures about the increase in defense spending, and, instead of being rewarded for an otherwise positive and brave step, was rather challenged for not delivering on its budgetary promises.)

The positive start was hampered quickly by the efforts of the Ministry of Finance, a clear sign that the highest political leadership was starting to lose confidence in the reform effort soon after its initiation. The Ministry of Finance burdened the defense budget with the social security costs of the conscripts—about HUF 10bn, roughly 4 percent of the defense budget—and ordered any and all income generated within the defense portfolio transferred to the Treasury. To alleviate the negative consequences of this last step the MOD intended to restructure quickly all sectors that generated a significant income—for example, health care, place them outside the MOD structure, have them function as public benefit not-for-profit companies, and acquire their services in an outsourcing arrangement. Internal lobbying interests, however, managed to slow down and then completely reverse this process, practically negating most of the financial and budgetary advantages the MOD could secure in initial phases of reform planning. The slowness of other processes, particularly personnel downsizing, further narrowed the financial playing field, because the costs associated with release of personnel have been pushed back some twelve to eighteen months, by definition delaying availability of any additional funds generated by downsizing. As expected, base closures also proved to be a tough nut to crack: A number of bases and garrisons originally planned for closure—but, curiously enough, located in the electoral districts of key government politicians—had to be kept open and, occasionally, even enlarged. Further problems arose in the relationship between the MOD and the State Holding and Privatization Company (APV). With the radical decrease in the military's wartime structures, a gigantic amount of surplus equipment and supplies had to be got rid of, most of it useless junk that had no market value whatsoever. Even though the government ordered the APV to take over all the surplus materiel and equipment from the military, the APV's delaying tactics and sometimes blunt refusal to implement the government's decision forced the military to continue to store and guard the unwanted surplus, tying down resources badly needed elsewhere. Considering that a relatively expeditious availability of additional resources as a result of downsizing and base closures has been one of the conceptual and financial cornerstones of the strategic review, the above situation certainly contributed to the reform's apparent stall.

In addition to most unfortunate budgetary infighting, Hungary was probably the only NATO member that had to fund its contribution to the Kosovo mission from its normal operating defense budget, without any additional resources made available by the government or the legislation. As mentioned earlier, the Hungarian military has managed to make a decent contribution to the IFOR/Stabilization Force (SFOR) mission, but only at the cost of considerable cutbacks in other programs and strains in human resources. This has been true at a significantly increased rate in the case of the Kosovo Force (KFOR), and the mission could be funded only at the expense of already depleted development and modernization funds, primarily those planned for implementation of NATO Force Goals.

The 1999 strategic review was also special in that it built heavily on outside advice. The MOD originally contracted the U.S. company, CUBIC Applications Inc., to conduct a review of human resources, but CUBIC's activities gradually grew into a full review of the functioning and capabilities of the Hungarian military and development of a comprehensive concept of defense reform. CUBIC has reviewed the very same situation, facts, and data as the authors of previous reform efforts, but it still came to radically new conclusions and offered alternatives that proved to be understandable and manageable not only—and maybe not even primarily—for the military leadership, but political leaders as well. Many believed the main reason for the new approaches was not the different professional background, intellectual system of reference, or vision of the foreign advisors, but primarily the fact that they had no professional or institutional interest in or attachment to maintaining obsolete structures and procedures. As CUBIC—at least at the beginning—enjoyed strong support from the upper levels of military and civilian leadership, openly criticizing CUBIC's—sometimes truly radical, but mostly correct and commonsense—concepts and proposals was not "politically correct." Thus, opponents of radical and meaningful change developed the argument that the American ideas—while excellent conceptually—simply could not be implemented under very special Hungarian legal, social, and military conditions, and tried to water them down to such an extent that they no longer had any impact. In fact, the reality was just the opposite, because the proposals themselves were aimed primarily at exactly these special conditions that proved to be the biggest hurdle in the way of a meaningful defense restructuring.

A further characteristic of the 1999 strategic review of grave consequence was the inefficiency of internal communications. The already disappointed, pessimistic, and skeptical officer corps, particularly at the lower levels of the command structure, did not identify with the reform concept or objectives. The MOD and military leadership also failed to sell the reform to different interest groups and unions and convince them to voice strong public support.

Challenges of NATO Accession and Membership

Before going on some general features and pitfalls that have been characteristic of Hungarian defense reform efforts throughout the 1990s, it is worth taking a look at the special role NATO accession played in furthering and sometimes hindering defense restructuring and modernization.

Hungarian desire for NATO accession was by far the strongest motivator of the country's political leadership toward defense reform, much stronger than any of the internal motivations rooted in the armed forces' perceived or real crisis situation. The undeniable and sometimes spectacular successes of the military—PfP participation, exercises, performance of selected "cornerstone" units—were all grouped around the overriding political objective of NATO accession. Without doubt, the decisive factor was Hungary's contribution to and participation in NATO's mission in Bosnia (IFOR/SFOR). NATO's largest-ever land forces deployment traveling primarily through Hungary provided ample opportunity for the country to prove its political commitment, showed its readiness and capabilities for host-nation support and reinforcement, and shattered the myth that Hungary would not be accessible in case of an Article 5 emergency. The Hungarian contribution of an engineer battalion was also a critical success, providing capabilities in an area where NATO was limited and contributing from the very beginning to military tasks and to creation of a civil-military relationship and trust between NATO and the local population in Bosnia.

In a way, Hungary was fortunate. In the case of the 1997 round of NATO enlargement, the military requirements of an invitation to join NATO were strictly separate from the military requirements of actual membership. Invitation in 1997 depended primarily on political factors, with military requirements focusing on the existence of a legal and institutional background of civilian control, active participation in PfP, contribution to NATO's mission in Bosnia, and a strong and visible political commitment to embark on a road of defense reform. These were exactly the areas where Hungary and its military performed well.

Nevertheless, the warning signs were apparent already in 1997. Preparation, training, and equipping the contingents performing in an absolutely convincing and first-class way in international peace support missions—particularly IFOR/SFOR—cost eight to ten times more than for any other unit. Yet, again, this preparation was done at the expense of planned modernization and development projects. Recruiting and maintaining the contingents' personnel stretched the capabilities of the sixty thousand-strong Hungarian military to the very limit, even though the overall size of the contingents was fewer than five hundred. This situation foreshadowed the conclusion that the Hungarian military lacks the necessary capabilities for the kind of mission that seems to be most likely in NATO's foreseeable future.

Still, the political—and to some extent the military—leadership was content with the situation and developed a tendency to "lean back." NATO membership in Hungary's pocket, the main focus of political efforts shifted back to requirements for European Union (EU) accession.

The wake-up call came with brutal bluntness only two weeks after formal accession to the Alliance, during the Kosovo crisis. No one was really surprised by the complete lack of interoperability of the Hungarian Air Force with NATO. This was to be expected, but it caused considerable anxiety on the part of the political leadership that the Hungarian military had significant difficulties in balancing the military situation and movements on the other side of the Hungarian-Yugoslav border. The fact that the contribution of a three hundred-strong guard and security contingent had almost surpassed the capabilities of the armed forces was the final blow, because the government already was convinced of the need for radical defense reform.

Oddly enough, desire for and requirements of NATO accession often proved to be a more complicating factor for defense reform efforts. For most of the decisive structural and philosophical issues, there simply is no "NATO solution"; in the Alliance's history, these issues traditionally have belonged to national competence. With some effort, one could find within the armed forces of one Alliance member or another a potential solution for any given structural and functional issue—and for its total opposite as well. Thus, internal debates on structural and functional issues often revolved around trying to find one national example as the only and exclusively "NATO-compatible" solution. Instead of concentrating on and trying to adopt a coherent system, each interest group within the military tried to select a specific national example that served its own interests best and sell it to the others. No wonder a balanced, well-structured, and effectively functioning model within the military proved to be as elusive as the Holy Grail.

In addition, against the background of its painful resource constraints, Hungary simply could not afford to tackle every problem at the same time; it needed to establish priorities, even among the most critical needs of NATO interoperability and defense reform. The problem is that the Hungarian military is in desperate need of an overall consolidation, but the requirements of such a consolidation do not always coincide with the requirements of NATO interoperability and the DCI. In fact, sometimes it is hard to find any common ground between them.

The primary need of defense consolidation is to reformulate defense philosophy. Without such consolidation, in a matter of only a few years, Hungary would find itself in a situation where its military functionally disintegrated. Simply stated, the mass army structures designed to fight World War III need to be transformed into capability-based, flexible, combat-ready, and reaction-capable entities. Such a change requires transformation of the whole intellectual and conceptual basis of a highly hierarchical organizational culture, so it is obviously more painful and difficult than any of the previous downsizing and reform efforts. After all, the question is not simply about changing, but about practically building a new military. These structural issues run deeper than most of the NATO commitments that primarily address operational capabilities of units assigned to common tasks. Turning a Soviet-type military to a NATO-type military involves the complete overhauling of staff practices and decision-making procedures; fundamental changes in the relationships and functions of different rank categories, such as officers and non-commissioned officers (NCOs); complete overhaul of the logistics support system; radically new approaches and methodologies in personnel and financial management; and, more widely, it also should include a thorough reevaluation of the military's role in society.

In terms of practical implementation, such a process has to start with radical restructuring, including base closings and unit relocations, to release the funds necessary for modernization. The first stage also has to devote significant attention and resources to improving the military's recruitment and retention capabilities, because Hungary faces serious manpower shortfalls, and conscription seems to be a less than adequate solution for them. (Hungary has reduced the tenure of conscript service to six months, a step that brought some political dividends to the government but practically eliminated the rapid-reaction capability and short-term combat readiness of any units manned by conscripts.) Just to break even with the costs and benefits of the first stage requires a lot of political will and financial prudence, skills that have been practically nonexistent during the past ten years of defense reform efforts. The second stage of defense consolidation should concentrate on stabilizing the new structures, training the units in new doctrines, strengthening their readiness, and firmly establishing new procedures. This also could and should be the time when savings from base closings and personnel structure realignments start to appear and offer a bit more breathing room for decision makers concerned with harmonizing defense reform with NATO commitments. Sadly, even with projected strong economic growth and highly disciplined implementation of defense philosophy transformation, it is only in the third stage where significant technical modernization realistically may appear on the agenda.

It is perhaps a most stunning and surprising phenomenon that meeting

NATO commitments and embarking on the road to truly meaningful defense reform more often than not form a set of competitive requirements instead of integrating naturally into a mutually reinforcing framework. The overall direction of NATO force planning and requirements aims at interoperability of designated units, commands, and other structures. This, by definition, includes modernization efforts, particularly in command and control, airspace management, simulations, communications, and logistics support. Meeting NATO criteria and delivering on the commitments made at the accession talks has always been the number one stated political priority of new members. At the point of practical implementation, however, they often find themselves in a situation where funds available for any technical developments have not covered even half of the estimated costs of NATO requirements. (In Hungary, for example, HUF 190bn over six years was allocated to meet NATO Force Goals and DCI requirements—a significant amount compared to the country's defense budget, but insufficient to complete most of the tasks within the defined time frame.) While it was only proper that NATO's planning system did not make any exceptions for new members, the system was unable to overcome its conceptual limitations and address the new members' structural and philosophical problems that carry with them the true opportunities of progress. Furthermore, being a relatively quantifiable measurement tool, the implementation statistics of NATO's force planning system have gathered political weight they were never meant to carry. (It is worth noting in this context that, although critics like to analyze them in isolation, implementation statistics of the new members tend to be at the top of the bottom third, meaning they perform better than some of the Alliance's "traditional" members.)

At the beginning of the 1999 strategic review, it was already clear to the Hungarian MOD's leadership that a reduction in the number and capabilities of units offered to NATO's reaction forces would be unavoidable. Hungary declared this to the Alliance with full openness and in complete conformity with NATO's established procedures. Smooth management of the process took the rough edges of the ensuing criticism off, but the allies committed themselves to scrutinizing Hungary's further performance more carefully than usual.

THE MOST IMPORTANT PITFALLS OF DEFENSE REFORM

Following is a list of elements and considerations that proved to be more or less significant hindering factors in reform efforts. Although their intensity varied throughout the 1990s, most of them appeared in one form or the other in the second half of the decade. In addition, while the actual examples are Hungarian, most of these factors played a role in the region as a whole and may be considered characteristic of Central and Eastern Europe.

LACK OF POLITICAL INTEREST AND SUPPORT

In Hungary, the intensive force development of the 1960s was followed by a stagnation in the 1970s and a clear decline in the 1980s. Quite understandably, the political focus of the 1990s concentrated on more urgent social and economic restructuring issues than defense reform. In addition, defense reform that continues through more than one government cycle is subject to hardships at the beginning, with political dividends coming only later, if at all. Therefore, the political elite has not been particularly interested in taking the associated political risks. Thus, for almost three decades, the defense sphere has enjoyed the benefits and burdens of political neglect. In addition, the last decade was characterized by development of political and military doublespeak, where statements and declarations on both sides were in sharp contrast with actual intentions, deeds, developments, and capabilities.

The most obvious evidence of a lack of political interest may be found in the budgetary situation of the defense sphere. Peace dividends, of course, were a logical and justified expectation of Hungarian society, and successive governments met with little opposition when they had to reduce defense spending to promote other social and economic restructuring priorities. Funding and sustainability thus became the central issues of successive reform initiatives. But the military leadership has always argued for an armed forces that proved to be financially unsustainable, and the political leadership has never committed itself to grant the one-time larger funding that would have been absolutely necessary to break through the old barriers and restructure the military. For more than ten years, the MOD leadership had been declaring a crisis and retaining basic functioning capabilities simultaneously. The contradiction that it seemed to be impossible to maintain basic functioning capability through ten years of deep crisis has never been challenged.

It should not come as a surprise then, that the Hungarian political elite is not willing yet to consider the military as a reliable instrument of national power that can and should be used actively to promote and achieve appropriate objectives in the country's security strategy. Lack of recognition of the military's potential role here is even more striking in view of the fact that whenever the military actually was used to support national security objectives, it brought long-term, enduring, and spectacular success. (The long list of examples stretches from the hyperactive Hungarian-Romanian military cooperation and confidence-building projects of the mid-1990s, through the sometimes seemingly overburdening activity in PfP exercises, to the performance of Hungarian units in peace support operations.) Paradoxically, it seems that whenever the military is pushed out of its daily peacetime mode, it is up to the challenge and elicits international recognition. But when its main function becomes its own restructuring, it regularly fails and draws criticism not only from Hungary but from abroad as well.

Another sign of the lack of political interest was that ten years proved to be insufficient to create an effectively functioning interagency coordination system in security and defense. The socialist-liberal government established a relatively smooth coordination mechanism to prepare for NATO accession, but it has never been meant to be a kind of a national security council and quickly faded away after Hungary joined NATO. At present, the government has a national security cabinet, but it functions irregularly, it lacks correct decision preparation and coordination functions, and its decisions more often than not are influenced by informal and peculiar agency interests.

All in all, the political elite has not fully recognized yet that defense restructuring and, in particular, military performance in NATO, has a direct bearing on the country's international credibility. The allies' perception of Hungary's military performance in and contribution to NATO will create an impression about Hungary that will not be forgotten when Hungary's EU accession talks reach to their final stage. Thus, there is a strong, if indirect, relationship between the two issues, regardless of how much politicians wish to separate the two.

CIVIL-MILITARY RELATIONS

The basic legal and institutional framework of civilian control over the military was established quickly in Hungary after the political changes in 1990, and led to one of the strictest regimes in terms of both parliamentary oversight and regulation of military activities. In 1995, Hungary even invited a UK review team to assess civilian control procedures, and although the team did make some recommendations, its overall impressions were quite satisfactory.

Still, civil-military relations in Hungary in the 1990s often turned sour, within the defense sphere and between the military and the political elite. In the latter case, the most significant and potentially the most serious issue was that the country's overall defense concept—large-scale mobilization in case of an outside attack—has been built on assumptions and conditions that were completely impossible to fulfill. According to independent assessments, it would have taken about eighteen months and roughly three years of defense spending for the Hungarian military to reach its wartime capabilities in terms of trained personnel, technically available equipment, and sufficient material supplies. None of the governments before 1999 was brave enough to break out of this cycle of mutual lies, and implementation of the strategic review initiated in 1999 will bring only limited progress in this regard.

Civil-military relations within the defense sphere could be described mostly as a roller coaster, but the general tendency in the relationship of the civilian policy side and the military leadership has been competitive rather than cooperative. The number of professionally capable civilians within the MOD has always been limited, and there has been no conscious effort to increase their numbers and influence. (The previous social-liberal, and the present conservative, government showed remarkable similarity in filling the highest executive positions of the MOD with active-duty or retired general officers. The number of officers in senior executive positions of the MOD during 1994–2001 was double the number of civilians. If lower-level executive positions also are taken into account, the picture becomes even worse.) With a few exceptions, the MOD remained basically a military ministry, where MOD officers and officers of the defense staff—wearing the very same uniform—fought bitter turf wars with each other over such issues as budgetary controls, direction of the restructuring process, and integration of the two organizations. This last issue regularly gained political dimensions as well, as politicians expected that integration of the two entities would increase their direct influence automatically over military matters and resolve the lack of coordination and harmony between the administrative and the military arms of the house. Not many people realized that a simple structural integration, as the current example shows, would not resolve any of the above problems without functional integration, clear delineation of roles and responsibilities, clear definition of coordination obligations, decision preparation and decision-making procedures, and elimination of duplicate structures.

Keeping the number of civilians in the MOD low may have eased the politicians' and the generals' headaches in their daily lives—civilians tended to ask uncomfortable questions and pushed for a coherent strategic vision—but this strategy was completely counterproductive and probably contributed greatly to the MOD's woes in the interagency processes. The MOD simply spoke a different language from the civilian ministries and was at a significant disadvantage when competing for political attention and scarce budget resources. With mostly military officers in charge, the MOD was unable to adapt to the radically changed outside environment of government bureaucracy.

LACK OF A STRATEGIC VISION AND A
NATIONAL MILITARY STRATEGY

Almost eleven years after the political changes, Hungary still has not produced a coherent national military strategy. The reasons for this are manifold—sometimes even understandable and acceptable—but the consequences are grave.

The lack of a long-term strategic vision led to a concentration on the present instead of the future. The successive leaders of the MOD obviously cannot escape responsibility for this situation, but some of the blame belongs to others as well. The basis of any sound national military should be a long-term national security strategy, but such a document has not been published either. The Parliament of Hungary passed resolutions on the basic principles of the country's security and defense policy, and those were updated following Hungary's NATO membership. Still, they do not provide adequate and detailed strategic guidance for defense planning, force missions and related capabilities, or functioning philosophy.

The security environment of Hungary in the 1990s was heavily burdened with instability, and most of the armed conflicts that took place in the aftermath of the breakup of the former Yugoslavia were within two hundred kilometers of Hungary's borders. (In fact, during the Serb-Croat war, some units and aircraft actually violated Hungarian territory and airspace, respectively.) While instability and armed conflict legitimately concentrated the day-to-day focus of the political and military leadership on short-term issues, it has been clear from the very beginning that the worst-case scenario for Hungary was not a direct attack against the country but, rather, an inadvertent and limited spillover of military activities to Hungarian territory. Still, the situation served as a good excuse to delay radical changes and reforms within the military.

In addition, the lack of a long-term vision also forced the political and military leadership to work on an ad hoc basis when dealing with the successive internal crises of the military. None of the defense reforms started with development of a national military strategy, all claiming that, though it was desirable in principle, there was no time for such a time-consuming effort when short-term crisis management was needed to avoid financial bankruptcy. As a consequence, the need to tackle financial crises and avoid financial bankruptcy increasingly pushed the military toward a capabilities bankruptcy where serious doubts emerged about the real ability of the military to live up either to its primary constitutional function of territorial defense or to the most likely NATO mission out-of-area crisis management.

THE BUDGETARY SITUATION

Budget limitations and restrictions have been the central theme of the 1990s. As mentioned earlier, the so-called peace dividend was exploited heavily in Hungary. While resource management may, should, and will be criticized heavily, the fact of the matter is that today's defense budget is simply not sufficient to cover either the homeland defense function or the international functions—collective defense, crisis management, etc.—of the Hungarian armed forces. Until the GDP proportion of the defense budget is raised, the idea of an effective and small but strong military will remain an elusive dream in Hungary.

Having said that, use of presently available resources is far from being efficient. At a time when the leading militaries of the Western world—in fact, our most important allies—take every effort to introduce and adapt modern management practices and accounting methods, resource management of the Hungarian military still relies on old-style practices. Attempts to copy some of the modern practices, such as outsourcing, tended to backfire and end up costing more than the original solution. Effective controls do not exist; after years of investment in a comprehensive information technology background and database for financial and resource management, these are nowhere near the horizon, and a comprehensive independent due diligence review of financial management practices has been opposed repeatedly on the grounds that the defense sphere is absolutely "special."

In this situation, the top executives of the financial management system

TABLE 3
Trends in Hungarian Defense Expenditures in the 1990s

	Nominal Value (HUF bn)	Real Value (HUF bn)	GDP Proportion (%)
1989	47.8	47.8	2.79
1990	46.2	40.9	2.52
1992	61.2	28.8	2.08
1994	97.9	21.8	1.83
1996	85.9	17.4	1.26
1998	122.5	18.7	1.24
2000	184.0	26.9	1.51
2001	230.0	—	1.61

gained unprecedented power in both the daily life of the armed forces and in longer-term issues. Instead of policy objectives and military requirements playing the lead role, planning is dominated completely by financial resources and by the priorities established in and by the financial management sector. Apart from the slight conceptual flaw of the tail wagging the dog, this situation creates rather grim chances for any defense reform whose success heavily depends on the ability to identify and track internal savings and resources. Furthermore, it complicates the harmonization of national planning and NATO's well-established collective planning processes. The incompatibility of data and time lines is mainly a technical problem that proved to be manageable through a lot of paperwork and some creative accounting. The incompatibility of planning philosophies, however, has not been overcome. As a result, "national" problems tend to enjoy a priority over NATO requirements whenever a financial crisis situation is declared, and the solution usually is found at the expense of already-depleted modernization and development funds. Despite ten years of repeated and mostly honest efforts to develop an indigenous system or adapt a foreign model—there has been a lot of tinkering with the PPBS—the Hungarian defense sphere still is compelled to function without a defense planning system that could even come close to meeting the multiple requirements of:

- being policy driven,
- building on military requirements,
- being resource-sensitive,
- being compatible with NATO,

- being compatible with the changed outside environment in terms of both government practices and the business sphere,
- being transparent enough to tie budget lines to actual missions,
- allowing for a strong and close to real-time controlling function, and
- providing decision-making alternatives to those who carry the political responsibilities for the functioning of the defense sphere.

HUMAN RESOURCES MANAGEMENT

In human resources management, successive defense reforms all have taken aim at the crucial problems of professionalization, a large and rank-heavy officer corps, the military's weak retention capability, and outdated personnel management procedures. Until now, a spectacular breakthrough in any of these areas is yet to happen.

Despite a lot of political statements, the steps aimed at increasing the professional nature of the Hungarian military proved to be rather controversial. The continuous and rather radical decrease in the overall number of conscripts and duration of conscript service was not balanced with a similar increase in the actual number of contract soldiers. While the number of slots for medium-term—three to four years—contract soldiers was increased in the tables of establishment (TOEs) of different units, the lack of a well-functioning recruitment system has led to these slots remaining empty most of the time. (At present, about half of the contract slots are vacant.) Furthermore, low salaries, bad working conditions, and loose regulations allowing for easy termination of the contract have resulted in contract soldiers' average length of service being only nine months, practically equal to that of conscripts. The present government's decision to reduce conscript service further, to six months, without first creating the necessary conditions for a radical increase in the number of contract soldiers has aggravated the situation. With the lack of contract soldiers, even the NATO-assigned rapid-reaction units are forced to use six-month conscripts in certain positions, seriously limiting their own combat readiness. In 2001, the MOD embarked on a spectacular national recruitment campaign that has brought some results already, but it will be years before an effective balance is created within enlisted personnel.

The situation has not been much better within the officer corps. Downsizing has not been accompanied by appropriate retention programs and packages, and whole age groups—particularly younger officers

TABLE 4
Trends in Authorized Manpower Allocations in the Different Rank Categories

	Officers	NCOs	Conscripts
1989	17,800	12,700	91,900
1990	17,300	12,700	81,000
1992	14,400	8,950	51,100
1994	16,320	10,680	47,340
1996	14,360	9,710	37,960
1998	11,450	10,600	26,580
2000	11,350	11,000	20,500
2001	8,400	10,460	13,260

(Note that actual figures usually remained below the authorizations.)

with marketable professional skills—have left the military service, seeking better financial and moral redemption opportunities in civilian life. At the same time, the number of officer slots, particularly lieutenant colonels, within the TOEs remained too high, creating an upward movement in the rank structure. By 1999, the Hungarian armed forces had more lieutenant colonels than lieutenants. The 1999 strategic review made an attempt at least to remedy this problem, but the number of officer slots—currently eighty-four hundred—was still set way too high, and this foreshadows the reemergence of the same old problem.

Retention has been a problem throughout the rank structure. Retention of contract soldiers, lieutenants, and NCOs suffered from the absence of clear responsibility for retention. Contracts were—and still are—poorly written, giving soldiers "easy outs." Laws also allow lieutenants to avoid service, and there are no "pull through" financial incentives

TABLE 5
Authorized and Actual Numbers of Contract Soldiers

	Authorized Slots	Filled Slots	%	Vacant
Army	4,327	2,060	47.6	2,267
Logistics	473	321	67.9	152
Budapest HQ	21	24	114.3	0
Mobilization HQ	265	132	49.8	133
Air Force	1,226	747	60.9	479
Total	6,312	3,284	52.0	3,031

(Note that in Hungarian terminology, a contract soldier is an enlisted soldier with a three- to five-year-long contract.)

to encourage retention. Turbulence remains high, leading to reduced unit readiness and a self-sustaining cycle of loss, recruit, train, loss, recruit, etc.

Personnel management has suffered from the lack of an integrated personnel management system and clear definition of tasks and responsibilities between the MOD and the Defense staff, including coordinating processes between them. The constant restructuring and changes to TOEs made determination of military-civilian requirements by grade, service, and branch almost impossible. Efforts to create a centralized performance evaluation, promotion, and assignment system showed significant progress, but are still far from comprehensive implemention for either officers or NCOs.

FUNCTIONING PHILOSOPHY AND DECISION MAKING
Back in 1995, the first MOD concept paper on the tasks of NATO integration identified—correctly—"intellectual interoperability" as being the first and foremost priority of the preparation process. However, most reorganization efforts approached NATO interoperability from the structural side but failed to pay enough attention to changing functioning and decision-making philosophy and processes. Command and staff functions and procedures, planning, and execution modes were mixed up regularly, resulting mainly in dominance of the command philosophy, even in areas and functions where "battleground commander approach" seemed to be counterproductive. In fact, decision-making procedures—or a lack of them—were the part of the pre-1990 legacy that proved to be the most difficult to get rid of. Hopes were high that officers returning from Western military education institutions would bring in fresh ideas and implement change. However, major disturbances in the selection system and the repositioning of such officers into jobs of real influence has limited significantly any impact they might have had.

Summary and Conclusions

Before reaching general conclusions that may be beneficial for reform efforts in other countries of the region, it must be stressed once again that the main objective of this study has not been to give a balanced and politically correct picture of Hungarian defense reform in the 1990s, but to identify the mistakes, misconceptions, challenges, and pitfalls Hungary has had to face throughout the process. The objective is not to criticize Hungary but to assist other countries by providing a list of warnings and "don'ts." It also should not be forgotten that, despite all of its difficulties, no one raised significant doubts about the Hungarian military meeting NATO invitation criteria to in 1997. Most important, when real performance counted—in Bosnia and Kosovo—the Hungarian armed forces lived up to the challenge and made a significant military contribution to the common effort.

Having said that, following is a list of general conclusions drawn from the Hungarian processes.

In general:

1. For any defense reform to be successful, political consensus not only about the basic principles but also about the more important details is a must. Defense reforms by definition stretch beyond government cycles, and the most certain way to lose any chance for success is to start reform efforts over again whenever a new government assumes responsibility.

2. To meet the above requirement, defense reforms must provide for regular built-in political successes for the actual government. Defense reform by itself is never going to be an election winner, but without careful handling, it could be an election loser. Negative tendencies and bad news related to the process—which, unfortunately, are quite unavoidable—will surface almost automatically. To balance that, and, most important, to preserve and maintain the political leadership's constant focus, defense reform planners must be able to identify political opportunities, plan carefully for good news, and communicate it effectively. Such a situation may occur only if clear and mutually understandable communication between the political and the military spheres is developed and carefully maintained.

3. Only joint efforts of political, policy/administration, and military players can lead to success. Such cooperation, however, is not automatic, because most of the key players have contradictory short-term interests. This problem may be overcome only if individual and institutional responsibilities are defined appropriately, with exacting and obligatory mechanisms and procedures for cooperation, decision preparation, decision making, implementation, and quality control.

4. There is no chance for success without a long-term strategic vision

and a stable national military strategy. Such a vision and strategy must enjoy the strongest possible support of the entire political spectrum and the vast majority of the defense sphere.

5. Quantitative changes in themselves will not result automatically in qualitative changes. On the contrary, they will recreate the very same problems at all levels. The holy trinity of funding, sustainability, and modernization is not exclusively a function of personnel size, but of the materiel, supplies, equipment, and training that are necessary to meet the capability requirements of the military.

6. Any defense reform needs to be modernizing in nature. Preservation of national traditions should not mean an attempt to retain anachronistic attitudes instead of leaning toward adoption of the most modern international trends.

7. While the noble principle of independent and professional military advice sounds convincing, no political leadership may or should expect defense sphere leadership in deep crisis to speak out radically against its very own individual and institutional interests to push through revolutionary changes. Thus, it seems to be beneficial to involve such independent outside groups in preparing the principles, plans, and the implementation of the reform that have neither individual nor institutional attachments to the defense sphere about to be reformed.

On the practical level:

1. Discipline of implementation is the most crucial issue. However, daily pressures and short-term—real or perceived—resource crises work against such a discipline. As a result, there seems to be the following tendency: When the first stage of implementing any reform veers off its original course, this aggravates the general crisis in the military and makes the originally planned further stages of the reform both impossible and irrelevant. Such short-term crisis management actually generates further and deeper crises.

2. Coherent, integrated, prioritized development and budgetary programs must be developed, and resources (time, money, materiel, leadership) should be applied to implement them. Responsibility and authority should be assigned to execute tasks. Fiscal execution should be aggressive to ensure full, timely expenditure for approved programs. Savings and expenditure must be quantified and tracked for each program and the entire program as a whole.

Taking into account that the realistic time frame for a comprehensive defense reform is about ten years, development of an objective controlling mechanism that allows for objective tracking of priorities, timing, and implementation is a key element of success.

3. Programs must be consistent with force requirement priorities. This should be an annual process, which then influences budget planning. Funds should be allocated to the highest priorities, but in the context of integrated programs. Integrated programs have many elements, and each one must be accorded the same resource priority. Budget requirements—and program planning—should meet critical Defense Review Objectives

Greece Ventures onto New Ground: The New Greek Security and Defense Policy, 2000–2015

Margarita Mathiopoulos

BACKGROUND

In January 2000, then Greek Minister of Defense Apostolos-Athanassios Tzohatzopoulos asked Margarita Mathiopoulos, professor of U.S. Foreign Policy and International Security at the Technical University of Braunschweig, to form and chair an International Advisory Committee (IAC) to prepare a study on the requirements for the Greek Armed Forces 2000–2015. Among the members of the IAC were General Harald Kujat, chief of staff of the German Armed Forces; General Klaus Naumann, former chairman of the North Atlantic Treaty Organization (NATO) Defense Committee; Manfred Opel, member of the Defense Committee in the German Bundestag; Carl Bildt, former Prime Minister of Sweden; Robert Cooper, National Security Adviser to Prime Minister Tony Blair; Field Marshal Lord Inge, former chief of staff of the Royal Armed Forces; General Rupert Smith, former NATO deputy commander in chief; Dr. Ronald Asmus, former undersecretary, U.S. Department of State; Dr. William Schneider, Jr., former deputy secretary of defense, U.S. Department of Defense (DoD) and chairman of the Defense Science Board at DoD, or Robert Zoellick, former State Secretary U.S. State Department and currently U.S. trade representative. The Commission presented its results to the Greek Minister of Defense and his staff at the end of 2000. The results and findings furnished by the IAC form an essential part of the official Greek Strategic Defense Review, which was prepared in 2001–2002 and was concluded in the beginning of 2002.

Following British and German models (Weizsäcker Commission), the study focuses on the new geostrategic environment Greece is facing at the beginning of the new century; points out challenges and chances for Greek foreign, security, and defense policy; and draws conclusions for structure, training and equipping the Greek Armed Forces. As in the case of the British Strategic Defense Review, the IAC was not guided primarily by cost issues, but by the challenges and targets of Greek foreign and defense policy in the twenty-first century. The basic question was not: "What might it cost?" but "What foreign and security policy role can and will Greece play in the future?"

ATHENS—A FORCE FOR STABILITY IN SOUTH-EAST EUROPE

Years ago, Greece used to be more of a weak candidate within NATO and the European Union (EU) than a strong partner whose economic, strategic, and military capabilities the allies would have regarded as indispensable to their common policy. Inflation rates exceeding 20 percent, political bickering over recognition of Macedonia, or the permanent conflict with Ankara over territorial waters and air sovereignty in the Aegean Sea and over Cyprus, which tended to escalate time and again, downgraded the strategic importance of Greece to its transatlantic and European partners.

OUT OF THE "TRAP" OF A TURKISH THREAT?

Since the government under Kostas Simitis took office in 1996, Greece's role within NATO and the EU has been upgraded significantly. In January 2001, Athens became member of the European Economic and Monetary Union (EMU)—who would have considered that possible some years ago? This turn is due primarily to strict monetary discipline and a coherent policy of liberalization, privatization, and deregulation under the leadership of former Minister of Finance and Economy Jannos Papantoniou. As the Greek-Turkish policy of détente cautiously initiated by his cabinet colleague, Foreign Minister Georgios Papandreou, it has found recognition beyond Greek borders. As a result, both ministers have earned respect for their policy at home and abroad.

Since taking office, former Defense Minister Apostolos-Athanassios Tzohatzopoulos (and today Minister of Industry and Development) has concentrated on leading Greek security and defense policy out of the "trap" of its one-sided fixation on the Turkish threat. The economic engineer who studied in Munich and speaks—as his head of government—perfect German, is the first Greek Minister of Defense after

World War II to maintain excellent relations with his American and European allies—a fact reflected by a balanced procurement policy for modernization of the Greek Ministry of Defense's Armed Forces.

With the Greek Strategic Defense Review he initiated, Tzohatzopoulos has chosen a revolutionary starting point. His project, to put Greek security doctrine, armed forces structure, and procurement policy to the test against a background of the new foreign and security policy challenges Athens faces as a regional power within NATO and the EU, has earned him the respect and recognition of allies on both sides of the Atlantic.

Under Tzohatzopoulos, Athens has come to realize that Greece can and wants to play a far greater role in the new strategic environment after the Cold War. This applies to the crisis-ridden Balkans as well as to the Caucasus, which the former Minister of Defense visited five times during his six years in office, and which is of increasingly vital importance to the EU due to its rich oil resources. Tzohatzopoulos paid several visits to North African states and established close ties with Israel and Egypt. Greece wants to demonstrate that it has parted from the security doctrine of a passive fixation on the "Turkish threat" it has pursued for decades, and has opened a new era of creative security diplomacy that actively promotes peace, democracy, and stability in Greece's geostrategic environment. Athens's new security policy aims further at a stronger and more active role for Greece within NATO and with regard to the new security-related political ambitions of the Europeans within the framework of the European Security and Defense Policy (ESDP).

As the head of government, Kostas Simitis, and his Foreign Minister, Georgios Papandreou (and Apostolos-Athanassios Tzohatzopoulos as well) did favor better relations between Ankara and Athens. Tzohatzopoulos's support of the Greek-Turkish rapprochement, however, was evidence of a necessarily pragmatic and realistic attitude of a defense minister who measures Ankara's political declarations of intent primarily by whether and to what extent the Turkish military supports this course and draws the corresponding consequenses.

THE NEW STRATEGIC ENVIRONMENT—CHALLENGES AND CHANCES

The end of the Cold War, the impact of globalization on security policy; demographic shifts; the increase of ethnic conflicts; the increasing shift from interstate to intrastate conflicts; new challenges emerging from misuse of modern information technology (information warfare); new forms of terrorism (cyberterrorism); and the "Revolution in Military Affairs" (RMA), with its retroactive effect on the relations among military, industry, and society, pose considerable demands on modern security and defense policy. In particular, at the southern European periphery, new zones of insecurity and instability have emerged. It was for good reason, therefore, that, at its Washington Summit Meeting of April 1999, the Alliance declared the Mediterranean region as key in its fight against terrorism, pointing out the increased danger of the proliferation of weapons of mass destruction, and emphasized the need to develop the capability of power projection into this region to secure regional stability as well as to react faster and more efficiently to humanitarian crises.

These targets provided challenges as well as chances for Greek Security and Defense Policy. In view of the military strategic developments under NATO's Defense Capability Initiative (DCI) aimed at strengthening the Alliance's defense capability, and in the framework of the Headline Force Goals declared at the Helsinki EU Summit meeting calling for creation of a crisis reaction force of sixty thousand soldiers until 2003, there is a clear expectation on the part of the Americans and the Europeans that Greece, too, will prove to be a committed regional partner in restructuring the Euro-Transatlantic Security landscape—an expectation which is in line with the new way Greece sees itself.

ATHENS'S NEW ROLE: GUARANTOR OF STABILITY IN SOUTH-EAST EUROPE

Greece already presents itself as a model of transatlantic integration in the Balkans, as an exporter of democracy, market economy, and stability in a crisis-ridden region. This stabilizing role corresponds to the country's political weight, which has grown markedly through its membership in the EMU. Greece's chances to exert greater influence within NATO, the EU, and a wider global security environment are favorable. Its geostrategic position, Athens's constructive regional commitment, and its preparedness to take on new tasks and roles in a rapidly changing security environment are pillars the future European security policy can rely on. This implies the availability of armed forces with a modern structure and material equipment that can make a substantial contribution to multilateral missions.

Parallel to the new security policy challenges, Greek defense policy is facing traditional challenges. Though the conflict with its Turkish neighbor has been defused in recent years, there are still unresolved political and military-strategic questions. In addition, there are dangers emanating from unpredictable regimes in the immediate neighborhood—the Near East. Those countries' conventional armament, and their ambition to obtain access to weapons of mass destruction, threaten Greece directly and indirectly. The same applies to such interstate security risks as organized crime or international terrorism.

Yet, Greece is not facing these diverse security policy risks all on its own, but as part of a multilateral security framework in the form of NATO and of a developing European security policy and corresponding European defense capabilities that aim to create more balanced burden sharing within the Alliance.

This allows Athens to develop from a mere importer of security to a guarantor of regional stability and, thus, to secure strategic influence as regional player. Such a new political security doctrine will raise Greece's position among its European and American allies. With this new role, Athens will move into the center of a multilateral security framework for the Balkans, which will have a de-escalating impact on Turkish-Greek tensions as well, since any Turkish aggression would appear as an attack on the new regional security architecture.

STANDING THE TEST IN AN ENVIRONMENT OF PENTAGONAL
SECURITY ZONES
Greece's strategic defense planning will be determined, therefore, by a security policy that focuses on five targets:

The *first* priority will be acting to defuse tensions with Turkey by political and diplomatic means, economic cooperation, and confidence-building measures in the military field. Mere reaction to an alleged direct Turkish threat is no longer sufficient as deterrent under the new security conditions Greece is facing. While Athens, on the one hand, remains obliged to maintain core elements of its previous deterrent and defense capability with regard to the Turkish Armed Forces, Greece, on the other hand, has begun to create modern, flexible, mobile, and inter-operable forces able to act under an integrated joint command structure. In view of latent security threats by Russian activities in the Caucasus, unstable developments in the Balkans, and tensions with Syria, Iraq, and Iran, as well as domestic challenges by Islamic fundamentalists and the unresolved Kurdish question, Ankara's sole intent can only be substantial improvement of the Turkish-Greek relationship. Such a development eventually will lead to reduced military potential in and around the Aegean Sea, thus releasing means for other missions and tasks, and, last but not least, accelerating Ankara's accession to the EU.

The *second* priority will be active participation of Greek forces in peacekeeping missions and in crisis management in adjacent regions, particularly the Balkans.

A *third* and decisive target will be Greece's successful participation in NATO and the EU defense planning with regard to modern intervention forces. Athens vowed at the Capability Commitment Conference in November 2000 to put four thousand personnel, forty aircraft (thirty fighter aircraft), six helicopters, six frigates, and one submarine at the disposal of the EU deployment force.

As *fourth* priority, Athens will pursue an active political and diplomatic engagement in North Africa, within the framework of the Barcelona process, especially with Egypt.

Fifth, Greece will pursue intensive defense diplomacy with regard to developments in the Caucasus and Central Asia to be able to react in time to potential security threats from this region, for instance, within the framework of the Organization for Security and Cooperation in Europe (OSCE).

STRATEGIC MISSIONS

For the Greek Armed Forces, *five* strategic missions are imperative from the described security-policy-environment:

- defense of national territory,
- securing stability in the Balkans,
- collective defense within the NATO framework as foreseen by Article V,
- EU interventions, and
- peacekeeping United Nations (UN) and OSCE missions.

The ability to protect its national territory against increasingly unlikely Turkish aggression remains a benchmark of Greek security policy. Given the new security conditions, territorial defense often follows an asymmetric pattern rather than remaining a merely static forward defense of the islands. Medium-range missiles and ABC weapons also can pose a threat to the Greek mainland in the coming decade. The national defense concept also will have to take into account new threats to Greek and European economic structures emanating from information warfare or cyberterrorism. The greater the instability in the Balkans or Caucasus, the more important it is to secure stability in the peripheral regions.

Collective defense missions in a changing transatlantic and European alliance will confront the Greek Armed Forces in the coming decades with the task of learning how national forces can cooperate efficiently with allied forces. In this context, it will be of paramount importance to extend operability internationally and to find solutions to integrate the communication and power projection capability effectively—in particular in the European Mediterranean region. Specifically, the Greek Air Force and Navy will intensify cooperation with American forces in the region; as for the Americans, too, this region will become a strategic priority. In doing so, Greece, as well as other European states, finds itself exposed to the pressure to integrate elements of its defense capability and armed forces into a comprehensive joint European pool.

CONSEQUENSES FOR THE GREEK ARMED FORCES

These tasks will have an impact on the size, structure, organization, and equipment of the Greek Armed Forces. Athens now spends 4.7 percent of its gross domestic product (GDP) on defense, a proportion that exceeds by far the German share of 1.3 percent. Nevertheless, defense planners cannot draw on plentiful resources; they have to face the general trend toward armed forces that are reduced in size, qualitatively better equipped, under a more professional command structure, and have greater mobility. Therefore, Greece will reduce the present armed forces of 159,000 to 140,000 men. In the future, eighty thousand conscripts will join forces with sixty thousand professional soldiers, from the ranks of which fifteen thousand Crisis Reaction Forces (CRF) will be recruited. To support military operations efficiently, the Greek CRF will establish a logistics and organizational structure compatible with those of its allies.

The central defense problem Greece faces is the need to defend an extensive maritime area and maintain extensive air control to protect the coastlines and mainland. As the extent and diversity of threats in the Mediterranean region increase, the Greek Armed Forces are required to develop a capability to coordinate their tasks in such a way that army, navy, and air force are able to reach their aims through joint operations. Thus, modernization of the armed forces will have to concentrate on mobile armored forces with a point-target attack capability on land; on naval forces able to gain sea control in the combat area, to defend Greece's sovereign rights and to keep sea routes open; and on an air force capable of supporting air defense and operations of other armed forces. To prepare for this epochal change of security policy, a joint force structure development system, analogous to the British and German models, will be introduced that will define requirements and standards for doctrine, armed forces structure, equipment, personnel, and training.

The more Greek security policy emphasizes an integrated national defense and a joint crisis intervention ability within NATO and the EU, the greater demand will be for more mobile, flexible, and deployable armed forces. This implies consequences for investment and procurement. Heavy armored vehicles, unguided artillery, and missile systems to fight naval forces will lose their importance eventually. On the other hand, there will be growing demand for investment in strategic sea- and airlift, modern guided weapon systems, and communication logistics. The new Five-Year Procurement and Modernization Plan 2001–2005, adopted by the Greek government in autumn 2000, takes this into account. It represents a dynamic response to DCI and the EU Headline Goals.

Following the era of nuclear stalemate, we are now in a new historic phase in which regional conflicts once again appear as a possible continuation of policy with other means. For Athens, this means reviewing its military activities in the country's political context and against the background of the Alliance: Training, procurement, privatization of Greek defense industries, relations with allies, and regular exchange of higher military staff should become part of a political network strong enough to protect Greece against potential threats and to secure stability in its adjacent regions.

CHAPTER SIXTEEN

Defense Reform in Romania: An Ongoing Process

Liviu Mureşan, Executive President, EURISC Foundation

DEFENSE REFORMS PLANNED AND UNDERTAKEN

Since the historic changes of 1989, the military sector has been one of the most challenged sectors in Romania. From a political perspective, defense was in a very special situation. Romania ceased to have Soviet advisors within its armed forces starting in the late 1950s, stopped sending high-ranking military to the Frunze Military Academy in Moscow starting in the early 1960s, and did not participate in the Prague invasion 1968. In the framework of the Warsaw Pact, Romania's special position recognized in both the East and the West as advocating not for its own interest but unofficially representing the discontent of other Warsaw Pact countries toward "Big Brother."

From a military perspective, due to strengthening relations with Western partners, mainly France, Germany and United Kingdom, the first steps were taken toward an end to dependence on Soviet procurement. Also, a number of bilateral agreements of cooperation were established with other countries in which Yugoslavia and China played a special role. From this point of view, Romanian defense forces seemed better prepared to cooperate with Western partners after 1989 than did other candidate countries for the North Atlantic Treaty Organization (NATO).

From an economic perspective, the defense sector has developed productive capacities far beyond the real domestic necessities. Export of equipment and ammunition played an important role, especially in periods of crisis, such as the Iran-Iraq conflict.

Research and development (R&D) of military equipment was slowed down in the 1980s, due primarily to budgetary cuts resulting from a lack of financial resources, which were directed toward pharaoh-style objectives: the House of the People (the second-largest building in the world), the Danube-Black Sea Channel, the Bucharest-Danube Channel, etc. The whole defense industry was affected by the dictator's authoritarian megalomania, and huge resources were used for purposes other than training and procurement (military units used and misused for agriculture, construction, etc.).

The social perspective has to be considered from a threefold perspective. Typical of a communist system, social problems were solved by assuring low but certain payments, cheap housing facilities, priorities regarding the workplace for spouses, and educational facilities for children of the military personnel. At the same time, social issues were handled according to political criteria and political education programs coordinated by the Political Military Committee of the whole defense structure. From a career planning perspective, military personnel were under complete control of the human resources department, which was closely linked to the Communist Party branch in charge of this.

Despite the fact that one of Nicolae Ceausescu's brothers held a high-ranking position in the defense structure, one can say that the dictator never trusted or enjoyed the full support of the military forces.

The irony is that the real political life of the dictator started in the 1950s, as a boy propaganda leader in the defense structure with the rank of general, and ended tragically, after four decades, by military execution of Targoviste city on 25 December 1989.

It is important to focus on the special role played by the Romanian military in December 1989, which reflected both sides of the coin. On the one side, it played a beneficial role, as a supporter of the Revolution and against the dictatorship, and on the other side, because of the role played by part of the Romanian military leadership and some military units during the first hours of the riots, a confusing role.

From the huge expectations and real support of the civil population and the military in 1968, Ceausescu "succeeded" in establishing one of the most irrational and brutal personal dictatorships that has overshadowed at least the first decade after 1989. His dictatorial system left a tragic legacy throughout society, so that Romania could not avoid painful transformation of its national defense system.

After a short intermezzo of an "old guard" general in the position of minister of defense, general Nicolae Militaru, the next one, Victor Atanasie Stanculescu, tried to take the first steps toward restructuring defense. The real reform of the Romanian defense was promoted by general Nicolae Spiroiu, who made a rather shocking statement during his first press conference after being nominated as minister of defense in April 1991: His main role was as the last military person as minister of defense, preparing for the next minister, who had to be a civilian. The reform was designed to ensure the transition from a politically oriented defense structure, as it had been during communist times, to a politically neutral system under civil democratic control. This had to be done simultaneously with modernization of military structures, education, and training, while maintaining the capacity to defend the country.

PRIMARY OBJECTIVES OF DEFENSE REFORM:

- "depoliticization" and stability of the army after the shock of change in December 1989;
- creation of a framework of laws and norms for democratic management of the defense system;
- education of politicians, parliamentarians, civil servants, and mass media to educate them about the country's new defense problems and implementing this knowledge in their decision-making process and in the information and communication process with the civil society;
- reorganization of strategic and operational command and control (ministry, major staff of the army, air, and navy) to separate political-military decisions from purely professional military ones, a prerequisite for the first civilian minister of defense; and
- reconsideration and reestablishment of the moral norms, symbols, and institutional traditions of the defense forces in full compatibility with genuine Romanian military traditions before World War II and with the democratic values of Western partners from the perspective of NATO membership.

THE REFORM PROCESS
Romanian defense structure reform took place during several successive periods.

December 1989–February 1990   The first period of spontaneous measures started in the days of the December Revolution and lasted about two months (until February 1990, when General Nicolae Militaru was dismissed as minister of defense). During this period, the first democratic measures were established by abolishing the main restraints of dictatorship, but, at the same time, many measures were undertaken on an emotional and subjective basis. Within the span of some weeks, a number of decisions were made, such as promoting more than eight thousand personnel to higher ranks, including nomination of retired generals to key positions—people who had been fired by Ceausescu, but who were still marked by a conservative type of thinking and behavior. The first tensions occurred between the so-called old guards or newcomers and the rest of the military with the December Revolution.

February 1990–Mid-1991 The second period of army stability, which ended in mid-1991, followed a draft plan of reform approved by the newly established Supreme Council for the Defense of the Country. Some decisions made during this period were abolished later, since they were not perceived as reformist enough or were in contradiction to the concept of modern defense reform.

Mid-1991–Mid-1993 The third period of preparatory measures for defense reform lasted about two years, till mid-1993. A main characteristic of this period was the drafting of reform and restructuring plans for different areas of the defense system; of the first group of draft laws (six) and government decisions about national defense, the first draft of the Military Doctrine and National Defense Strategy was sent to competent authorities for approval.

Fall 1993–1995 The fourth period was dedicated to implementing reform. It started in the fall of 1993, benefiting from the new legislative, normative, and structural framework of defense and characterized by vision, dynamism, and efficiency. Minister of Defense Nicolae Spiroiu had the vision and courage to take a number of measures that distinguished military reform. He appointed the first civilian in a command position in the Romanian Ministry of Defense system as deputy director of the National Defense College in 1993 (Dr. Liviu Murean). Three months later, he appointed a civilian as deputy minister of defense (Dr. Ioan Mircea Pascu), now minister of defense and leading the current reform period of and the Romanian Euro-Atlantic integration efforts. The third step in the process of nominating civilians took place in 1994, when the first civilian became full minister of defense (Gheorghe Tinca).

1995–Present The fifth period is the current one, characterized by renewed efforts to reform the Romanian defense system.

The following actions have been accomplished:

- 35 percent of military doctrines (rules, instructions) are compatible with those of NATO;
- 40 percent are in the process of being redesigned and will be compatible in the years to come; and
- 25 percent are foreseen only for the future.

Romanian defense system reform has been assisted by professional advisors and programs, primarily from the United States, Great Britain, France, Germany, etc.

The military authorities in Romania are aware that, for Prague 2002, the most important considerations will be the performance of the candidate countries' armies regarding reform, modernization, and the increased level of interoperability with NATO forces.

SPECIFIC MEASURES TAKEN AND THEIR FORM OF
IMPLEMENTATION

- The communist political structures in the Romanian Ministry of National Defense were abolished. The political instructors in high positions were obliged to retire, while the young ones, with democratic views, were retrained for new positions in social and public relations, etc.
- The communist political structures of the Department of the State Security belonging to the Ministry of Interior were abolished.
- New, clear intelligence structures were set up in the Ministry of Defense.
- The generals and other high officers who completed their studies in the Soviet Union before 1962 were retired.
- A group of dissident officers (*Comitet de Actiune pentru Democratizarea Armatei* [CADA]) who, in the name of army democratization, rejected the fundamental principles and values of the military systems and diluted the command and control functions was dissolved.
- Internal discipline committees were established to assess the role of each military sector in the events of December 1989 with a view to "cleaning" from the defense structure any discipline problems and any possible prejudices resulting from obeying orders.
- The military salute, uniform elements, and institution names have been changed.
- Religious services have been reintroduced into the army, with full respect for all faiths and basic human rights.

- Romanian officers and noncommissioned officers (NCOs) were sent to Western countries for military education and training, with the help of assistance programs (U.S. and IMET and military-to-military programs; France's: Saint Cyr Academy and *Ecole Nationale d'Administration*; and universities, colleges, and centers for military and political military studies in Great Britain, Italy, Germany, Canada).
- Funded in December 1991, the National Defense College in Bucharest was the first postgraduate institution in Central and Eastern Europe for training in national security of the political elite, parliamentarians, government officials, high-ranking military, civil servants, mass media, etc., including Romanian students and students from other countries as well.

PRIORITY OBJECTIVES FOR CURRENT GOVERNMENT REFORM

- implement a solid and transparent career management system,
- develop a reconversion program,
- implement a joint planning system,
- implement the ASOC,
- implement a solid system of budgetary programming and evaluation,
- implement STAR,
- participate in NATO-led Partnership for Peace (PfP) exercises and operations,
- improve English/language skills,
- develop NCO training,
- restructure the armed forces,
- assure compatibility with NATO forces,
- develop a procurement concept, and
- develop a consistent strategy of endowment for defense.

For its NATO integration, Romania will allocate 2 percent of its gross domestic product (GDP)—the equivalent of US$1 billion per year—over the next five years

THE CURRENT REFORM SITUATION

- Identified and launched programs to fulfill the basic requirements for NATO integration. Seven foreign advisors from NATO countries and a team from the U.S. company, CUBIC, are assisting the Ministry for National Defense leadership.

- Improved relations between the army and civil society by instituting transparency, democratic control, trust in the military institution as a whole, and support by the Romanian people for their Army and NATO integration.
- Restructured the General Staff of the Army into six directorates (J1 to J6).
- Substantially reduced personnel and equipment under full control of and in accordance with national and international agreements.
- Reorganized the leadership and command of the Armed Forces.
- Redrafted the structure of forces in peace and wartime—112,000 military for peacetime, down from 280,000 in 1995, and, for wartime, 230,000 from the previous eight hundred thousand in 1995.
- Reorganized military units according to the NATO model.
- Established a national system of defense planning.
- Set up a concept of wartime unit mobilization—location, role, mission, and preparedness.
- Multinational Operations Doctrine was adopted and the rules and instructions for compatibility with NATO norms and standards are being drafted.
- New military training is in accordance with NATO standards for big units and units ready for PSO missions, and it will be in the future for missions under Article 5.
- Starting in August 2001, military personnel are positioned according to their competence, military rank, and function.
- Six Centers for Foreign Languages were set up for studying English in Bucharest, Constanta, Boboc, Brasov, Sibiu, and Ploiesti.
- Each year, fifty Romanian military attend courses in NATO countries and another 120 attend NATO training courses.

CHALLENGES, PROBLEMS, SUCCESS

After December 1989, reactivation of "old guard" generals at the Ministry of Defense level has caused a lot of confusion. A strong reaction of rejection from the whole military body was necessary "to clean the courtyard."

The new political leadership took quite a while to grasp the complexity and the requirements of the military structures to be reformed.

Some discontinuity resulted from the transfer of power between the last military and the first civilian ministers of defense.

There was some initial confusion when new leaders who had little or no military expertise took over the Ministry of Defense.

It took a while to fine-tune civil-military relations, which was accomplished eventually with foreign training and assistance.

Defense reform had to be accomplished in the shadow of crises in surrounding areas—mainly in Yugoslavia, Transnistria.

At the same time, Romania's contribution to peacekeeping missions in the region, and its support of the NATO campaign in Kosovo, were appreciated.

As a result of political decisions to support democratic country embargoes, Romania lost the equivalent of US$3 billion during the Iraq embargo, US$7 billion during the Yugoslavian embargo, and US$1 billion because of the Kosovo embargo. During the last decade, Romania registered suffered losses of US$11 billion, while the country's entire foreign direct investment amounted to about US$7 billion.

The 1990 Convention for reduction of conventional forces of the CSCE in Vienna brought a lot of confusion because the Romanian army was underscored in comparison with Bulgaria and Hungary.

A lack of political will and a poor economic situation challenged the reform efforts already begun by Romania's civil-military leadership. This was exacerbated by Romanian military authorities' unrealistic deadlines in light of budget resources.

The decision not to include Romania in the first round of enlargement at the 1997 Madrid Summit actually helped to speed up Romania's reform of its armed forces.

In the history of defense, Romania's leadership stability often was more evident than that of neighboring countries. Romania's contribution to the stability of the region was also a result of its successful, though slow and painful reform of its armed forces. Another asset in the face of reform difficulties was the political neutrality of the Romanian army.

The sometimes confused political leadership of the Ministry of Defense, and its at times fragile political equilibrium, has not had much effect on the internal reform process. Witness the change in ministers because the ruling coalition departed, or the presence of two MoD ministers from two different parties—Minister of Defense Victor Babiuc, from the Democratic Party, and Deputy Minister Constantin Dudu Ionescu, from the National Peasant Party—as well as changes in the chiefs of General Staff, none of which has had serious impact on the course of reform or the commitment to NATO integration.

One of the problems in attempting to bring about reform is the sometimes inappropriate use of the human resources. For example, out of the sixty graduates of the Monterrey courses (held in the United States) who specialized in the management of military resources, none was involved in integrated defense planning activities or management of resources. There is also a certain transparency deficit in the process of military reform. Progress in transparency of reform measures has been made at international level, while the level of the national and internal reform is still characterized by not enough transparency.

Under these circumstances, officers with major responsibilities do not know what to tell their subordinates about future placement of their units in the organizational structure or the missions these units will have to undertake. Even if much of this information can be found on the Internet, very few military units have Internet access. One of the direct consequences of this situation is that many military personnel are under continuous stress, because they do not know where they will be, or whether or how they will be able to sustain their families; the military has neither the necessary resources or the instruction to provide this information.

LESSONS LEARNED

Defense reform refers to both military and nonmilitary institutions, to military and civilian personnel, structures, and planning staff and to Defense Committees of the Parliament, other civil research institutions, nongovernmental organizations, and the media as part of the country's security community. The success of armed forces reform is also linked to the success of the restructuring and privatization of the domestic defense industry. Among others, military intelligence has to change from the remnants of the Cold War to an important tool for the Euro-Atlantic integration of the country.

Some significant integration possibilities lie with the networks that can function as multipliers of reform efforts, such as the networks of military academies and defense colleges, military press, and alumni of international security courses (for example, George C. Marshall).

In any case, reform has to be started as soon as basic conditions are met. It has to be based on a clear vision, a well-prepared plan, with clear objectives and deadlines. All of the political forces have to support the process, both those in power and the opposition. The political neutrality of the army is crucial for success of the reform. The position of minister of defense of civilians has to be filled by a person with a strong personality, credibility, knowledge of defense matters, and experience in the new international security environment and the requirements of NATO's integration process.

If such a person cannot be at first, it is better to start with an active or recently retired high-ranking military officer who is fully committed to the reform process, and who has international experience and domestic and international credibility. The position of civil deputy minister could prepare this person and the system for future tasks.

In this respect, the experience in Bucharest could be considered a success: General Nicolae Spiroiu was the last military defense minister and his deputy, Ioan Mircea Pascu, is now the civil minister of defense leading the process of reform and Euro-Atlantic integration of Romania.

Any postponement or slowing down of reform will bring supplementary costs and a lot of "collateral damage" to Romania's democratic processes.

CHAPTER SEVENTEEN

The Restructuring of the Swedish Armed Forces after the Cold War

Karlis Neretnieks, Major General,
President of the Swedish National Defense College

This chapter briefly outlines the transformation process the Swedish Armed Forces have gone through during the last decade. The main emphasis is on describing the problems that have been encountered and the solutions adopted to solve some of them.

BACKGROUND

Throughout the Cold War, the Swedish Armed Forces had a clearly defined task. In the event of war in the surrounding world, our Armed Forces, by demonstrating a credible capability to defend Sweden, were to keep the country out of the war. The theory was that a potential aggressor would judge the losses too great in relation to the gains to be made. If, despite this, Sweden were attacked, she would defend herself to the last.

Politically, this concept was supported by a security doctrine based on nonalignment during peace changing to neutrality in the event of war. It is important at this stage to point out that Sweden's policy of neutrality was certainly not unconditional. Rather, it was seen as a political instrument that afforded the important option of being able to threaten to reverse the policy should the country be in danger. A potential aggressor would always run the risk, therefore, that Sweden would join the opposition's camp should the pressure become too great.

In part the neutrality policy was determined in the light of the situation in Finland. Should the Soviet Union threaten Finland, the Russians always had to speculate that Sweden might reconsider her nonalignment.

One of the inherent problems with this neutrality policy was to be able to conduct relations with the North Atlantic Treaty Organization (NATO) in such a way that they appeared credible to the Soviet Union while at the same time not allowing relations with other nations of the Western bloc, in particular the United States, to suffer. Sweden was particularly dependent on the import of U.S. arms. There was also a difficult balancing act to be performed in domestic politics, where political attitudes ranged from "immediate membership in NATO" to antagonism toward the United States. It is quite clear, however, that the majority of Swedes were behind the idea of a policy of neutrality supported by a strong defense capability. It goes without saying that the aggressor against whom all Swedish defense precautions were taken during the Cold War was the Soviet Union.

At the end of the Cold War (1990), the Swedish war establishment comprised twenty-one brigades, four hundred combat aircraft, thirty warships, twelve submarines, and one hundred regional defense battalions. The need for soldiers and sailors was met through general conscription. The annual intake was approximately forty thousand men, who remained on reserve for twenty years. All reservists were required to complete a number of continuous training periods. In total, this meant mobilization strength of 750,000 men who could be put on a war footing within a few days. There were approximately eighty peacetime training establishments and bases at fifty places around the country.

The defense budget was roughly 2.5 percent of gross national product (GNP). In light of the continuing debate on the (current) restructuring process, it is interesting to note that the Armed Forces at that time had approximately seventeen thousand professional and noncommissioned officers.

The Defense Review of 1992 involved certain reductions in the war establishment and the peacetime training organization, for example, less continuous training. However, developments in Russia were so difficult to predict that a "wait and see" policy was adopted that avoided any drastic structural change. The 1993 budget allocation to defense was maintained at approximately 2.5 percent of GNP.

In 1993, a special political standing committee was formed to analyze developments in the security situation continuously and then advise the government on the direction of defense policy. The committee's first report, presented in 1995, resulted in a considerable change of role for the Armed Forces. Admittedly, the main task remained the defense of

Sweden, but international missions and the ability to counteract new threats, such as information operations, were given greatly increased priority.

The committee's recommendations led to a parliamentary resolution in 1996 to reduce the war establishment to approximately thirteen brigades, 250 combat aircraft, twenty-four warships, and nine submarines. The annual intake for National Service was reduced to twenty-nine thousand, the number of officers and noncommissioned officers was cut to fourteen thousand, and the defense budget dropped to 2.1 percent of GNP. In addition, ten peacetime establishments were slated to close. Also in 1996, the decision was made to give priority to international operations and to counter threats other than conventional war.

In 2000, previous resolutions were followed by a new resolution involving dramatic reductions in both the war establishment and the number of peacetime defense locations. Among other things, the number of brigade equivalents was to be reduced to four, the Fleet to twelve warships and five submarines, and the Air Force was to plan on 160 combat aircraft for the long term. The number of conscripts to be trained each year was set at approximately seventeen thousand. The resolution also resulted in the largest percentage reduction of peacetime regiments in modern Swedish history: twenty-six establishments were disbanded, and professional and noncommissioned officers were slated to be reduced to approximately eleven thousand. In addition, the defense budget would be reduced to less than 2 percent of GNP.

Parallel with the political and parliamentary process, the Armed Forces were carrying out their own conceptual analysis with the aim of creating a doctrine and structure for future defense. This led to, among other things, the Armed Forces' "Vision 2000" aimed at creating an organization that made maximum use of modern information technology. Developments were to ensure that the acquisition and rapid handling of information, precision engagement, and close integration of weapon systems were to replace pure physical numbers of men and equipment.

It is important to note that both processes, the political and the military, were closely integrated, and that political departments and military authorities often sat on joint working groups. The opposition of senior service chiefs to cuts in the number of units was limited when the change from "quantity to quality" was recognized as both necessary and desirable. An indication that things were going in the right direction was demonstrated by the fact that 50 percent of the 2001 defense budget was allocated to procuring equipment. During the 1980s, only 30 percent of the budget was set aside for equipment renewal, which resulted in a continuing decline in wartime defense capability.

It should be pointed out that the change of direction has not gone as fast in training as it has to introduction of new weapon systems. There have been considerable problems during 2001 with the financing of training. The main debate, both in civilian and military circles, has centered on the magnitude of cuts within the National Service system and the closing of military establishments. I will return to these topics later in the discussion.

Many Challenges and Some Solutions

the need for a clear vision

The single biggest problem that the Armed Forces faced and will face during the whole restructuring process, and the one considered the least beforehand, is how to convince people that the changes are necessary and the future is positive. It is not easy to convince people who have been brought up to think in terms of air wings, army corps, armored divisional attacks, etc., that this is something of the past (at least at the moment).

In Sweden, with her tradition of neutrality, people also have to accept that international operations and service abroad are a natural part of the job. Even if, at an early stage, politicians in the Department of Defense and members of the higher military command had a relatively clear idea of the direction of future change and the reasons why, they generally failed to make these things clear to the rest of the organization. As a result, higher commands lost the confidence of those lower down in the organization. This also probably contributed to the excessively large number of resignations and the mainly ill-founded media debate that gave the impression that all was gloom and despair.

Clearly, there is reasonable cause to question whether reform has taken the right direction. Is it possible to retain conscription as a means of recruiting if only a few are called up for service? Are we overestimating the capability of the new technology? Will our operational commitments abroad take priority over the defense of our country? All these questions can and should be discussed, but what is crucial is that higher command presents a clear vision that everyone can understand; only then can people work wholeheartedly to put that vision into practice—even if they do not like the course that has been set. In this respect, the process has not been a happy one in Sweden. The impression of the vast majority of those serving in the Armed Forces is that financial circumstances, not the vision (which, in addition, is difficult for many to understand), are steering the process.

Economic reality will always be decisive, of course, but this only serves to emphasize the importance of having a clear vision, understood by all, that will act as a guide for the way into the future. Experience indicates that all too little trouble was taken concerning vision and doctrine and the spread of these ideas throughout the organization, compared to all the energy put into the task of planning how the restructuring would be carried out in practice.

Probably the greatest mistake was that, despite everything, the vision formulated did not answer the question, "What does this mean for me in the long and short term?" Apart from the vision needing to be clear and farsighted it also must be reflected in new regulations, exercise instructions, etc., so that everyone in the organization sees how he or she is part of the process. If this does not occur, what could otherwise be a fruitful debate will change to dissatisfaction and lack of motivation. The importance of speedily converting the vision to reality at unit level cannot be overemphasised. It is better to have experiments and exercises go a little wrong than not take place at all. As long as people feel things are moving forward, they will accept that the intractable block of stone at which they are hacking away at the moment will become (part of) a great cathedral in time—even if a few blocks have to be discarded in the process.

REDUCTION OF THE PROFESSIONAL OFFICER CORPS

As with all reductions in the services, the professional officer corps presents probably the most demanding challenge. This is true for many reasons.

People, who, often for idealistic reasons, have devoted a large part of their lives to working for the Armed Forces deserve to be treated with respect. In addition, reductions should also not result in the loss of skills and abilities that will be needed in the future because the wrong people have been allowed to leave. Personnel cuts must be sufficiently large to allow room for new recruitment, otherwise the organization will fossilize, with serious consequences for both wartime defense capability and the potential for future development.

The matter is complicated further by the fact that the Swedish Armed Forces mostly comprise county regiments spread throughout the country where officers and families are an integral part of the local community. An officer can be posted to another job where his competence is needed, of course, but this often means that a house has to be sold and the wife has to find a new job, etc.

Therefore, the Armed Forces have created processes that contribute to both a smooth transition to civilian life and retention of those needed for the future. Three main schemes have been used by the Armed Forces to encourage people to leave: severance pay amounting to as much as three years' salary, retirement on a full pension of approximately 65 percent of salary from as early as age fifty-five, and support to find a civilian job or start one's own company. All three methods have proved to be very popular, and the reduction targets set for 2004 may be reached in 2003.

In addition, it is clear that former officers are in great demand in the civilian job market, possibly in too great a demand. Many highly qualified officers who are sorely needed in the defense organization receive offers from the civilian market they find very hard to refuse.

The most important measure to retaining competent personnel is to provide various forms of assistance to ease the process of moving to a new location. Today it is possible to commute between home and a new place of work for a period of two years, with related expenses covered by the service. A transition period is thus created to provide the individual and his family every opportunity to settle in the new place. It is also possible to be compensated for any loss that may occur if a house has to be sold in conjunction with a move. Despite these important economic measures, the most influential role is played by commanders at all levels when an individual is considering whether to stay in the service. Commanders who discuss with the individual in an open and honest way the opportunities for career progress—this does not necessarily mean the promise of promotion, rather a look at jobs that may be available in the future—often will convince him to stay. After all, the vast majority of those serving are happy doing so and will be only too pleased to stay on providing they can be assured of interesting and challenging jobs in the future.

Another encouraging tendency today is that officer and noncommissioned officer recruiting is better than it has been for a long time—despite the well-known fact that the Services are undergoing comprehensive change and cuts.

EQUIPMENT SURPLUS

The reduction of a war establishment from more than 750,000 men to roughly 150,000 generates a vast surplus of equipment of many types. By way of example, six hundred tanks, four hundred thousand automatic rifles, a thousand howitzers, thousands of tons of munitions, and a quarter-million jerrycans will no longer be needed. Certain advanced weapon systems can be sold, for example, the three submarines that were sold to Singapore. Other modern equipment can be given to nations that are building up their armed forces. With a few such exceptions, the challenge is to destroy the majority of the surplus equipment and ammunition in a way that is both economically viable and environmentally acceptable. Equipment other than ammunition often can be sold as scrap metal and reused by industry to manufacture other products. The times are gone when old ammunition can be dumped in the sea or blown up in a secluded spot.

The Swedish defense industry has recognized the commercial opportunities in this process and has developed environmentally friendly methods of destroying various types of ammunition. Over the next few years, several hundred million SEK will be spent in this process. Clearly, a reduction in military forces involves not only saving money but also incurring considerable costs, at least in the short term.

However, an interesting problem arises in the case of equipment that can be sold commercially on the civilian market. Such business can generate immense income for the state, but what are the consequences for those who earn their livelihood from dealing in these goods? There is a considerable risk that the market will be ruined. What would happen if the Armed Forces were to release a half-million new or partly used, but therefore inexpensive, jerrycans into the market? The problem is not restricted to jerrycans and similar items but encompasses cross-country vehicles, mechanical diggers, electric generators, water treatment equipment, and other specialized machinery as well.

There are obviously no easy solutions. One method currently being tried is to "water down" the effect by allowing in international buyers, thus broadening the market among several countries.

THE HOLLOWING OUT OF THE NATIONAL SERVICE SYSTEM

The fact that now only 30 percent of the male population is called up for National Service raises a number of issues. Will the Swedish people's positive attitude toward the Armed Forces still hold when fewer and fewer personally experience the military system and its organization? Will those who *are* called up accept that they will lose a year of study or work compared with their friends of the same age? There is no clear answer. For the moment, these problems have not become acute. Surprisingly, there appears to have been no apparent negative reaction among those who have been called up. Instead, being called up for military service is seen in a positive light. Quite understandably one feels that one has been chosen from among the best of the male population. National Service has acquired a certain status. The numbers volunteering for the more demanding types of training, such as that carried out in various ranger units, are also greater than ever before. The attitude appears to be, "If I *am* going to do National Service, then I'm looking for a challenge and really tough training—the added status of qualifying as a ranger can't be bad either."

If this positive trend is to continue, then considerable demands are going to be placed on the Armed Forces. If training does not meet the expectations of our young people, there is a clear risk that attitudes will change, with all its attendant problems, conscripts cheating on entrance tests, low morale during training, a bad reputation for the Armed Forces in society, etc. So intense effort is being made to develop training methods that use the latest simulator equipment, ensuring that training is made as realistic as possible, exercising situations that will be encountered on international operations, etc. Economic benefits are being reviewed as well. The possibility of granting military training a civilian qualification is being considered, for example, academic merit points for the leadership training undergone by many conscripts. Unfortunately in this latter case, considerable opposition has been encountered from certain civilian institutions that, for various reasons, want to slow down this move in what appears a very logical direction.

In Sweden, the idea of changing to fully professional Armed Forces is also being debated. The foremost reason for having professional forces is related to the benefits of being able to take part effectively in international operations. At the same time, there is little doubt that the quality of our soldiers would decline. If we had professional forces, it is unlikely that potential civil engineers would be sitting in our tanks or computer programmers would be guiding our anti-aircraft missiles. It is by no means clear which system would be best in the long run. Indications are that National Service will continue for the foreseeable future. It is likely, however, that with the requirement for specialists and the need for a high state of readiness for certain overseas operations, a number of posts that are today filled by National Servicemen will be manned by professionals in the future.

DISBANDING PEACETIME REGIMENTS

As usual, the disbanding of peacetime regiments has led to an extensive debate in the media, with headlines that often speculate on the number of jobs that will be lost in one place or another. Although it is hardly the job of the Armed Forces to keep unemployment low, it is still a political problem that cannot be ignored. The solution chosen has two main components: as far as possible, avoid disbanding regiments in areas where unemployment is high, but if such disbanding is unavoidable, then try to create new, civilian jobs supported by special subsidies. This policy has been successful in the short term, but in certain cases the consequences can be more serious in the long run.

Large exercise areas are necessary, but that argument will not serve as a reason for keeping a military base open in a sparsely populated area. Modern military units need the support of dynamic civilian surroundings. Apart from the fact that the families of military personnel, quite reasonably, want access to good jobs and good schools, today's military units must have comprehensive interaction with highly professional industrial and training organizations. As has happened already, retaining military units in remote areas to the detriment of those that are based near some of the most dynamic university towns will not contribute to an effective, forward-looking organization.

The need for efficiency aside, the good reputation of the unit in the surrounding area and its support of the local community are also important factors. If the Armed Forces maintain high standards and, therefore, deserve the respect of the people, then they have to be visible. It does not matter how good they are if the Swedish people do not know about them. After all, they are the ones who ultimately must be convinced that there is good cause to spend tax money on defense.

Another important role for the Armed Forces is to provide assistance to the civil community, for example, disaster relief. Regular, close cooperation with the relevant civilian authorities, even before a disaster occurs, will lead to a more effective response when assistance is called for. Both these factors support the idea that military units should be based reasonably close to population centers, providing that is acceptable from an efficiency and environmental point of view.

FINANCIAL CONTROL

As with all major changes to large organizations, it is never possible to foresee the consequences of every decision. It is also clear that no one person, even one with a comprehensive overview, can understand how the various elements interact in reality. In this respect, restructuring the Swedish Armed Forces is no exception. Here are a few examples. It has not been possible to dispose of surplus equipment as quickly as civilian staff have been released. The reduction in numbers of conscript soldiers in some areas—for example, as drivers in various vehicle pools—has meant that civilians have had to be employed to meet duty requirements. Where units and staffs have been disbanded, more officers than expected have left the service resulting is some disorganization in routine. This situation has been exacerbated by the fact that the new command organization has taken considerable amount time to establish effective control. As a result, restructuring has been much more expensive than originally planned.

Two conclusions, among others, can be drawn from the Swedish experience: a clear tendency toward too much optimism when assessing the possibilities of short-term savings, and a lack of understanding of the consequenses of breaking up old, functioning command structures and routines before new ones are up and running.

If there is an acute need to change the organization, for example, to provide more troops for international operations, the old organization will suffer. In addition, large reserves must be set aside to cover the cost of reorganization. The common truth in business, that long-term savings require investment in the short term, is equally applicable to military organizations. Justification also can be found for forming special controlling bodies that continuously follow up in detail what is happening in the organization and can step in when unexpected costs arise. To state afterward what went wrong is always of interest and will help avoid the same mistake being made twice, but it is an expensive way of doing things.

Without belittling the abilities of the officer corps, in fact, quite the reverse, it is important to point out that officers are not and will never be company general managers or experts at adjusting to market changes with all the commercial knowledge and experience that requires. Nor do military organizations have the flexibility of civilian companies that can change from one product to another quickly. To expect the same adaptability from the Armed Forces as from General Motors or Microsoft is a pipe dream. And to believe that the appointment of large numbers of civilian consultants will speed up or improve the process is also a misconception. Consultants often have only a faint grasp of what makes the Armed Forces effective in their primary role—waging war. The attempts that have been made in this vein are frightening. In summary, it is probably best to accept that large changes in military organizations will take considerable time, and that external expertise can be of great help, but it is no shortcut to a better or cheaper solution.

THE INTRODUCTION OF NEW EQUIPMENT IN A SHRINKING ORGANIZATION

In many ways, the Swedish forces are fortunately situated in that, parallel with reductions, a comprehensive introduction of new equipment is taking place. In principle, all remaining units in the Armed Forces will be completely reequipped between 1995 and 2005. As examples one can mention introduction of JAS 39 Gripen aircraft, Visby class coastal corvettes, Gotland class submarines, Leopard 2S tanks, CV90 armored fighting vehicles, and the BAMSE air defense missile system. The last time such a radical replacement of equipment took place was during World War II. This introduction of new equipment, in conjunction with the necessity for new doctrines to reflect a changed role since the end of the Cold War, will involve an enormous allocation of resources to research, development, and training.

As a result, the costs for research and development have been allowed to increase in proportion to other areas of expenditure. This has meant that current war readiness clearly has suffered, but this is deemed acceptable in today's military political situation.

Another measure taken to speed the introduction of new equipment is to allow older, but fully functional equipment to be phased out early. This involves considerable erosion of capital, but it is one way to free up money for new investment and to familiarize personnel with the new weapon systems quickly. Early indication was made of those units that would be receiving the new equipment and, therefore, would be part of the future organization, which fostered optimism and confidence in the future and boosted recruiting.

At the same time as announcing cuts, something had to be offered that would give confidence in the future—in this case, new equipment, cannot be overemphasised. The Armed Forces are not a machine, but a living organism, and people's belief in the organization to which they belong and a desire to do a good job are decisive.

THE INTRODUCTION OF NEW TECHNOLOGY VERSUS
THE ROLE OF PEOPLE IN THE SYSTEM

Restructuring of the Swedish Armed Forces involves, for the most part, a transition from a large number of relatively technically unsophisticated units to an organization equipped almost exclusively with high technology. This situation is especially true of the Army. Use of the latest technology has always been characteristic of the Air Force and large parts of the Navy; however, there is a tendency in this process for the human being, both the soldier and the officer/commander, to be overshadowed. The risk is that too much faith is placed in the capability of technology. The most extreme scenario of modern warfare is one where it is conducted by hitting keyboard buttons in front of a computer screen, and various technical systems gather intelligence, sort the information, transmit the orders, and, ultimately, fight the battle. It is also apparent that the less experience one has in soldiering or other situations involving leadership of people, the more one is dazzled by technology's capabilities. This is hardly surprising; no one is born with experience.

Changing to a defense organization based on high technology also requires that resources be allocated to test the capabilities and limitations of technology. For example, comprehensive exercises involving complete units and staffs will have to be carried out. This is the only way everyone will realize, irrespective of the capability of a technological system, that it is human weaknesses—such as the inability to make decisions, fear, misunderstanding information, bad leadership, or human strengths such as initiative and leading by example—that will decide the outcome of an operation. In other words, those qualities that are difficult or impossible to assess, even in the most advanced games or simulations. The fact that information technology creates both possibilities and problems makes it even more essential to test ideas and technology under the most realistic conditions possible. There is, after all, very little experience to fall back on.

The limited restructuring experience in Sweden does not contradict this—quite the reverse. Planning in Sweden is directed, among other things, toward full-scale annual exercises at brigade level in the Army and at the equivalent levels in the Air Force and Navy. Likewise, command systems are being developed "from the bottom up" to ensure that people at those levels of the organization where the human individual's reaction is crucial are not forced to rely on technical solutions or methods that will not stand up to the realities of the battlefield.

THE DEFENSE INDUSTRY

By tradition, and as a result of experiences from World War II, Sweden always has had a large defense industry of her own. Domestic suppliers have catered to the majority of the Armed Forces' demand for advanced equipment: Fighter aircraft and missiles from Saab, submarines and warships from Kockums, fighting vehicles from Hägglunds, cross-country vehicles from Volvo and Scania, radar and communications equipment from Ericsson, to name but a few. The large orders placed by the Swedish Armed Forces have maintained this comprehensive advanced defense equipment industry. The situation has posed a number of problems for the government, however. How does one retain, for the benefit of industry as a whole, the valuable, technological, leading-edge competence that is inherent in an advanced defense industry? How can one reduce the negative effects on employment in those areas where the defense industry is a big employer? How do we ensure retention of the expertise that is difficult to buy abroad, for example, in electronic warfare? In the event of rearmament, how can we guarantee the supply of military equipment, probably in a situation where many countries are rearming at the same time, so the chances of importing war materiel are limited?

The government and the Armed Forces have decided on various solutions. Mergers have been encouraged between companies with similar products. In certain cases, amalgamation of several companies has been a precondition for placing orders. Cooperation or merging with foreign companies has been encouraged as well. Examples include Saab's cooperation with British Aerospace, the acquisition of Hägglunds by Alvis, and Kockums' amalgamation with the German company, Hohwaldtswerke. In some cases, the government has gone in as a minority shareholder to facilitate financing of cooperation or merger agreements. In some areas, it has been decided that an industry has such economic self-sufficiency that no special support is necessary should defense orders be drastically reduced or even cease altogether. This applies in the case of cross-country vehicles from Scania and Volvo.

The most common method to retain expertise in certain vital areas of technology (apart from cooperating with foreign companies) is to invest in research and development with a commitment to buy demonstration models. In addition to being good for industry, it means that the Armed

Forces continually get new high-tech weapon systems, albeit on a limited scale.

Parallel with these structural measures and to a much greater degree than before, the government has committed itself to promotion of defense equipment export, and with encouraging results. In summary, one can state that the reorganization of the Swedish defense industry after the Cold War has gone surprisingly smoothly. In many areas, the industry is more successful today than ever before. The foremost reasons for this success are most likely not the results of individual initiatives but cooperation among government, the Armed Forces, and industry, and the priorities this cooperation has established.

SOME CONCLUSIONS

It is of course not possible to draw clear-cut conclusions from the Swedish experience that would apply directly to other countries with different traditions and social structures. However, it is likely that peoples' attitudes do not vary greatly among different countries, so these conclusions have been considered in that light.

Most indicators point to the importance of ensuring that everyone involved is made aware of the motives behind a restructuring process. It is not enough just to explain what needs to be done; a clear answer to the question, "Why?" also must be given. In addition, those who are to remain in the organization should become involved at an early stage preparing for the way ahead; they must feel that they are an integral part of the future.

Nor is it enough just to take care of those who are to remain; those who are leaving the organization also must feel that society values their contribution and that everything possible will be done to ensure a secure future for them as well. Apart from this being a social moral obligation, there is also the risk that bitterness might result that not only will make the restructuring process more difficult but also will damage the country's faith in the Armed Forces to such an extent that talented people will no longer look in that direction for a career. At a time when human resources are increasingly more important, this would be a catastrophe.

That the political and military leadership must present the same message should be a foregone conclusion. Nevertheless, it is important to point this out, and sufficient measures must be taken to ensure that this is the case. Compromise will be necessary. The Armed Forces command must support government decisions, even if, from a strictly military point of view, they are not ideal, and, in the same light, government leadership must be prepared to shoulder responsibility for any unpleasant consequences that may affect potential voters, for instance, increased unemployment in a certain region.

Another truth that is probably universal is that restructuring is not achieved without cost. To the contrary, all indications are that successful restructuring will initially cost more than can be saved in the short term. Apart from the sums that need to be spent to effect the release of personnel honorably, it is virtually impossible to predict all the attendant costs that will accrue as the result of various decisions. When reshaping an existing structure, a number of ways to do this, about which nobody knew, will always appear—in other words, practical solutions that have been arrived at peripheral to the formal organization. Many of these are so important that the savings planned in certain areas cannot be carried through. In addition, time and resources seldom (if ever) suffice to plan a restructuring in such detail that even all known factors can be taken care of to achieve an optimal result. Probably the best way to counteract this is to set aside sufficiently large economic reserves so that even relatively big surprises can be managed without having to change the overall intended course. Otherwise, there is a considerable risk that planning has to be changed to such an extent, to save even more money, that the whole process is put in jeopardy. This, in turn, will lead to a loss of prestige and credibility for both politicians and the higher military command, while critics will be given wind for their sails.

Finally it is important to point out that the raison d'être of the Armed Forces is their ability to fight. Modern military equipment of course plays an important role. Ultimately, however, it is the people in an organization who determine the strength of that ability to fight. Irrespective of the structural measures taken or the equipment that has been acquired it will always be true that effective training and good morale are the decisive factors in creating efficient Armed Forces. He who forgets that will be making a big mistake from which it will take decades to recover.

CHAPTER EIGHTEEN

Creating Defense: The Estonian Case Study

Andrus Öövel

INTRODUCTION

In the 1990s, as a result of the end of the bipolar world order, states were born or reborn and others have disappeared, the regions of Europe have been rearticulated or simply reformulated. Some of these transformations have materialized peacefully, others have brought about the resurgence of ethnic problems and resulted in armed conflicts or even all-out wars. Some of these transition processes are not complete; nevertheless, the strategic landscape of the European continent has transformed considerably. Even the definition of Europe has changed.

New "strategies" evolved according to the new strategic landscape. In the last decade, we have experienced an era where the definition of what constitutes security has broadened; "new risks and challenges" have arisen; preventive diplomacy, conflict prevention, and conflict management have gained new importance and even new meaning; the old boundaries of international law are being stretched; the "future of warfare" is argued to be in cyberspace; the European Union (EU) has been working toward the realization of a Common European Security and Defense Policy (CESDP); and the North Atlantic Treaty Organization (NATO) has finally gone out-of-area and declared an Article V situation first time in its history. The concept/doctrine of "collective defense" is increasingly being replaced by that of "collective security," and, as a result, by international cooperation in the security and defense fields. Even these old "new definitions" presumably will be affected by our newly declared war on international terrorism, a new type of war led by liberal democracies. These actions inevitably will necessitate reconsideration of many ideas.

This era of formative transformation has resulted in a significant, or rather historical change, for the Baltic states—Estonia, among others—in their rebirth as independent nation states. The changes resulting in a "new Europe" have made it possible for these countries to join the international vein of cooperation, partly through the Nordic-Baltic collaboration, partly through their work with NATO and other international organizations. However, the prerequisite for this was that they had to establish themselves as states. As defense is arguably the most important task of the state,[1] one of the main factors ensuring its legitimacy, and undoubtedly the main factor guaranteeing its existence, the first and most important task the Baltic countries had to face was that of establishing their defense systems. In doing this—differently from most of the other postcommunist countries, where the main task has been to restructure and modify the existing systems—the Baltic states had to start from the absolute zero, having almost no experience, little knowledge, and very limited resources. Though they have received considerable support from the United States, Western Europe, and the Nordic countries, the task was still incredibly challenging. Establishment of a defense system from the absolute nothing implies that all basic decisions are to be made, all basic questions are to be answered in terms of "what makes an army": what kind of defense system/force it should be: professional, following the new wind of change, or conscript, drawing on an old tradition, and accordingly what kind of tasks and organizational structure should it have?

History has provided us with various security and defense models, only some of which have proved to be sufficient. On the basis of the "lessons learned" from distant and recent history, we can conclude that the most important factors to be taken into consideration when making a decision about what kind of defense model is best for a certain country are "time and space": the historical period—including the stage of nation-state development—when and the geopolitical location where we design such a force. In terms of space, naturally, factors such as size, population, aim, interest, and prospects for defense—self-defense, coalition defense, or integration through cooperation—cannot be neglected. As Alfred Vagts wrote: "each stage of social progress or regress has produced military institutions in conformity with its needs and ideas, its culture as well as its economics."[2] These characteristics determine what kind of defense model and, accordingly, what kind of defense system is the most suitable and beneficial for a country. Furthermore, some key political, military, and functional considerations must be taken into account. The roles/functions the defense forces should serve, on the one hand, depend on the abovementioned factors and, on the other hand, cannot be determined in isolation from how security is defined in the rest of the world and how a particular country sees its position and role in this regard.

The task in transition countries is to build or to rebuild. The aim of this chapter is to present an example of how to build and the lessons learned in the course of this work. The chapter discusses the main factors that were taken into consideration in the course of establishing the Estonian defense system as well as its process.

In the course of researching this chapter, primary as well as secondary sources have been consulted. Furthermore, some of the conclusions have been made on the basis of the experiences of the author, who—between 1990 and 1993, as the commander of the Estonian Border Guard, the first military unit in independent Estonia, and between 1995–1999, as the minister of defense—has participated in the establishment of the Estonian defense system/force and was actively involved in the decision-making process leading to it.

COMPLEXITY OF SECURITY

The broadening definition of security has had an ever increasing impact on how the role and functions of defense forces are seen. Security concerns have changed dramatically and become more complex in the post-Cold War world. Several dimensions refer to the broadening of the security concept from its narrow politico-military basis pre-1989—the so-called hard security-based notion—to a wider concept, covering a number of softer areas. Writing about security, we not only are using the terms of two-block rivalries or national confrontation or arms-race or geopolitical military scenarios, but also other elements of the spectre that are gradually gaining more importance—such as proliferation, terrorism, ethnic hatred, environment, integrated economies, illegal drugs, and the arms trade. In this context, the key words are stability in its broader sense, the indivisibility of security, and unpredictability instead of only military threat as it used to be. In addition, military threat has grown in its complexity; the single and predictable one has been replaced by an increasingly multiple and unpredictable one.

As a guide, the new dimensions of security can be defined as follows:

- "military security concerns—the two-level interplay of the armed offensive and defensive capabilities of states, and states' perceptions of each other's intentions;
- political security concerns—the organizational stability of states, systems of government, and the ideologies that give them legitimacy;
- economic security concerns—access to the resources, finance, and markets necessary to sustain acceptable levels of welfare and state power;
- social security concerns—the sustainability, within acceptable conditions of evolution, of traditional patterns of language, culture, and both religious and national identity and custom; and
- environmental security concerns—the maintenance of planetary biosphere as the essential support system on which all other human enterprises depend."[3]

Thus, when thinking about how today's defense forces are being designed, "we need a substantial widening in terms of issues and actors to encompass economic, cultural, religious and environmental issues addressed by the trans-national and sub-national groups."[4]

FUNCTIONS OF DEFENSE FORCES

The new concept of security also has had a major effect on how we define the functions of defense forces in the new era. Defense forces have grown multifunctional, with a spectrum of functions, including, among others, the old concept of self-defense as well as a new type of peacekeeping and civil-military relations. Consequently, the broadening spectrum of "defense" tasks correlates with the increasingly complex definition of security. Nowadays, defense forces also have to carry out a number of "peacetime tasks." The "additional value" of these is that they contribute to breaking the alienation between the military and society, proving that forces can play an important role in a long-lasting peace as well.

CAPABILITY FOR ARMED RESISTANCE

In spite of the growing importance of nonstate actors, the nation-state is still regarded the primary "survival unit" of the modern era.[5] Thus, national defense forces must possess the following:

- capability to deter threats and ability to prevent third parties from using territory in case it is not stipulated otherwise by international agreements between the parties; and

- combat readiness to resist foreign intervention and defend the sovereignty and independence of the country.

In defense planning and in the development of the defense forces, this means that everything, from political pressure to a large-scale offensive, has to be taken into account.

As stipulated in the Guidelines of the National Defense Policy of Estonia: "When developing an independent defense system, we must take into account the fact that as a small state, any possible enemy force would likely be vastly superior and thus we cannot exclude a defense scenario, involving the partial occupation of our territory. Because the size of our armed forces do not enable us to create a continuous front to stop an attacking force at the border, we must rely on a total defense system, where combat activities are carried out according to the territorial defense doctrine."[6]

The territorial defense strategy and tactics differ significantly from military methods used by big powers. The solutions defined by the founder of the Finnish territorial defense principle, General Ermei Kanninen, have become a role model for Estonia:

- defensive battles should not be fought on the positions or in the assigned defense regions, but in the areas of territorial depth, using the so-called extended combat tactics;
- deficiency of equipment and mobility should be compensated by purposeful organizing and deployment of forces and territorial defense;
- in the near future, we will not be able to improve the mobility of our units, so we have to try to slow the enemy down to our level;
- we are unable to increase our firepower drastically, so we have to hinder the enemy from using concentrated firepower;
- to gain local superiority, the enemy should be engaged in extended battles, thereby avoiding its concentration;
- partisan warfare should be initiated immediately in occupied areas;
- to reduce loss of your own forces, a widespread and immediate use of all simplest protective measures is essential; and
- the effectiveness of territorial defense is multiplied by massive and skillful use of antitanks, land mines, and other kind of hindrances.[7]

According to these principles, the Estonian territorial defense system is based on the following:

- division of armed forces according to their tasks;
- use of tactics, which exploit state characteristics; and
- a flexible system of readiness and a corresponding territorial mobilization system.

The precondition of a territorial defense system's success is conscription, readiness of an extended command structure, a territorial mobilization system, and a high level of a nation's will-to-defend spirit.[8]

A FOREIGN POLICY TOOL

It is remarkable that Clausewitz's perhaps most often quoted and most well-known idea: that "war is the continuation of politics by other means" or, as he puts it, "[w]e maintain . . . that war is simply a continuation of political intercourse with the addition of other means. We deliberately use the phrase 'with the addition of other means' because we also want to make it clear that war in itself does not suspend political intercourse or change it into something entirely different. In essentials that intercourse continues, irrespective of the means employed,"[9] is more relevant in our modern world than ever before. By this statement, Clausewitz completely rejects the idea that when war begins, politics and diplomacy have no place any longer. Today, it is more important than ever before to ensure that armed conflict does not create its own logic, that war is the continuation of politics, not a substitute for it, and that war has its own grammar, but never its own logic.

In parallel, the military is becoming a significant foreign policy tool for "peaceful purposes" as well. International military cooperation is growing, and defense forces are increasingly designed to be capable to take part in international missions. Thus, the issue of integration is highly relevant to the shaping of security policy and defense systems in many countries, as it was in Estonia. On the one hand, cooperation in the military field—like in the Baltic—can be made an integral part of cooperation in other areas; on the other hand, cooperation in general can be an effective means of confidence and security building. As Anders Bjurner claims: "[T]his new subregional cooperation has helped to increase security by promoting confidence and trust between the states and peoples of the region, reinforcing mutual dependence, strengthening democratic structures, reducing economic differences, promoting economic and social development, reducing region-specific risks and threats, and promoting further regional integration."[10] Furthermore, "[S]ubregional contributions to security are not absolute and isolated. They are part of complex processes . . . they are generally all positive contributions to greater security."[11]

Besides self-defense, crisis management is becoming the most important area of operation for defense forces and, at the same time, for international cooperation. At the Cologne European Council Summit in June 1999, the European states finally came to the understanding that a decision is needed to actually develop and enunciate a true common defense policy, and we are in the process of committing forces to back up this policy. Today, we can witness a strong political will to define common interests and, from these common policies, a common ability can grow to cope with twenty-first-century cataclysms.

A MEANS OF PREVENTING INTERNAL INSTABILITY AND A NATION-BUILDING TOOL

This may be one of the key roles of the armed forces, one that has been a key "player" in the success of the establishment of the Estonian defense system. We should come to the understanding that the rationale behind the existence of defense forces is not that they should exist at the expense of society or be a means of force in the hands of governments against their people, but they should be—a "service"—*for* society.

The function of defense forces as a society stabilizing "agent" underpins the significance of their optimal composition. On the one hand, optimal development of the armed forces can contribute to stability and justice. On the other hand, its ill-suited progress or rather, regress, or ill-fitting form that is not in correlation with the development of society as a whole, can even lead to the destruction of an independent state. Based on the Estonian experience, it can be stated that a healthy relationship between society and the military can contribute to the stability of the nation to a large extent.

Citizens' positive attitude toward participation in the defense system, and the actual realization of this attitude, can help to preserve the "mental health" of society in multiple ways, for instance:

• by serving as a unifying factor and increasing the nation's dignity, and
• by promoting the integration process between native citizens and non-native inhabitants or ethnic groups by demanding tolerance.

AN INSTRUMENT OF EDUCATION AND SKILLS TRAINING

To be credible, the force must be capable of performing the military task for which it has been designed. In the current international environment, this also involves readiness for rapid reaction on a global scale—given, of course, that the state it serves defines its role in the international scene in a particular way. Developing flexible, responsive, and effective combat capability calls for extensive and precise training and education, which remains a continuing challenge to the military.[12] In the case of Finland, Norway, and the Baltic countries, where more than two-thirds of the youth is conscripted, one can say that the army, in fact, can be considered a "nation wide university, which practically all the main citizens of the country attend and 'graduate from.'"[13] This high skills level, of course, implies and improves on—as has been stated—a lot of knowledge and skills needed in civilian life as well. Thus, acquiring a high standard qualification in several areas in the course of military service can increase young men's chances of becoming more successful in the job market and serving society better.

CIVIL-MILITARY RELATIONS[14]

The demands of national security preclude the professional military from restricting its peacetime activity to preparing for war. On the other hand, military force must be used in any field in a manner consistent with democratic social values, since in modern democracies legitimacy of means has become a paramount factor. Probably the most challenging task of the military profession is ensuring sensitivity and responsiveness to social change, while retaining values essential to success in combat.[15]

Bearing this in mind, we can state that in building up normal civil-military relations, we must avoid images of a military force as a "caste with caste privileges. Either if the military is seen by the outsider either by an aristocratic image,"[16] "in which mainly nationalism, political conservatism, and authoritarianism dominate; or by a heroic image,"[17] which accepts the nation-state as the highest form of political organization, and which holds that the security of the state depends on the creation and maintenance of a strong military force. This can lead to a situation where the military and the public cannot share "the single whole which belongs to all."[18]

Discussion and cooperation between the military and society are crucial. The alienation of the military—the only organization with "armed force"—can lead to catastrophic results. On the one hand, military must consider itself as a part of society, not "above" it. On the other hand, society must be aware that the military is a tool on hand in case of emergencies that can help and rescue if other resources are not sufficient. Civil-military relations in humanitarian emergencies are essential. Above all, military must not only be on hand but "in hand" as well.

For purposes of this chapter, civilian guidance is discussed under the heading, "civil-military relations" as the author believes a normally functioning guidance of the military and on the other hand, the military's respect toward this guidance, is an integral part, or even the basis of, any good civil-military relations. Civilian guidance of the military—or as it is most often called, "civilian control"—is also an essential element of democracy.

As Peter D. Feaver points out, the problem of civilian control is a paradox: "because we fear others we create an institution of violence to protect us, but then fear the very institution we created for protection."[19] However, this seems to be a slight overstatement of the essence of civilian control, the democratic oversight of the military, and the reason why its existence is essential. But what is this "fear" about? "As recently as ten years ago, military regimes ruled at least seventy of the world's countries."[20] Thus, this fear is, on the one hand, the fear of possible military overthrow of the regime and, on the other hand, of collapse on the battlefield. However, there are other, less dramatic, but nevertheless significant things to be aware of: The military could drag civilian leaders into an unwanted war or, nowadays, just the contrary, oppose a "wanted" war or intervention—both of which can have cost and other implications. Furthermore, the military could extract higher resources from society than necessary.[21] In other words, it should be guaranteed that security is subordinate to the larger purposes of a nation, rather that the other way around, and that the purpose of the military is to defend society, not to define it.

The keyword here is the civil-military relationship, which can be one of either mutual cooperation or conflict. Therefore, politicians and civil servants must understand that, in decisions concerning national defense, the advice of the armed forces must be taken into account, not just considerations of economic rationale or party policy. At the same time, the military should realize that its duty is to obey decisions made by civilians, even if these civilians are not experts in military issues. Decisions should be influenced by discussion, not by public criticism or argument. Getting into debates with politicians inevitably leads to politicizing the army itself, which can result in replacing the idea of defending the state with the idea of defending certain political ideologies.

In a democratic society, civil control must arise from a process of establishing certain obligations and rights, together with the unification of civil and military factors and normalizing relations among politicians, civil servants, and the military. All actors must understand the necessity of the existence and activities of the others. Civil control is more than just the result of some declarative decision; it cannot be established merely with an act of legislation. However, establishment of all the necessary legislation is vital—indeed a precondition—in terms of democratic reform of the armed forces.

THE CREATION OF THE ESTONIAN DEFENSE SYSTEM: THE PROCESS

"Small nations will count as much as large ones and gain their honour by their contribution to the common cause."[22]

—Winston S. Churchill

European security is indivisible. All states—including small ones—are needed and must share the responsibility of building a stable Europe. This is how Estonia has seen its role in the security of Europe: not only as a consumer but also as a provider of security.

The creation of the national defense forces of Estonia has been in accordance with the ideas described at the very beginning of this section in deep correlation with the understanding that the Estonian defense force must be characterized by highly educated officers and well-trained soldiers. "Only the best is good enough," together with the idea: "Help yourself, then God will help you as well!" constituted the driving force. This, some sort of life philosophy, has been turned into reality according to the following principles:

First—capability of self-defense: It has been our understanding that our own defense forces should be first and foremost capable of being a means of prevention via their existence, size, preparedness, and mobility. But, in case of aggression and threat to the vital interest of Estonia (that is, independence, sovereignty, territorial integrity), they have to be able to act for defense independently, or together with allied forces.

Second—cooperation and interoperability: Estonians have considered it most important that their national defense forces are interoperable with NATO forces and capable of international cooperation and participation in peacekeeping and peace enforcement missions and rescue operations. This presupposes respective command structures, technical equipment, logistics, and training. It is through the framework of international cooperation that our individual defense ability could obtain its real dimensions.

Third—polyfunctionality: combat-readiness, ability to fight new types of war as well as capability of assisting civilian structures in catastrophes (environmental, industrial) and rescue and evacuation operations.

Estonian national defense has been implemented as well according to the principles of civil control based on the country's democratic governance. Civil control, as the author wrote five years ago when a minister in charge of creating the Estonian Defense Policy Guidelines, "is a legally regulated system in which bodies of democratically elected legislative power and on behalf of them officially appointed executive power decide on the utilization and financing of defense force and control their command and status, in order to build up civil-military relations which can be managed and maintained within the structures of defense system through the sharing of responsibility between civilian leaders and military officers."[23] This is to be taken into account strictly in building up national defense. The roles of the most important state institutions related to civil control have to be separated.

In Estonia, the *Riigikogu* (Parliament) establishes the legal bases for national defense, ascertains the budget for the Defense Forces, controls the status of national defense, and makes inquiries, regarding the above, to the Government of the Republic and corresponding officials.

The President of the Republic is the supreme commander of national defense. The President will declare a state of war, order mobilization and demobilization and decide on use of the regular armed forces in fulfillment of Estonia's international obligations.

The National Defense Council advises the President of the Republic on issues of national defense. It discusses and provides an opinion on the overall plan of national defense and other fundamental issues concerning national defense.

The Ministry of Defense develops the guidelines of the national defense policy and ensures execution of the developed principles. The Minister of Defense controls and reports on the status of national defense to the *Riigikogu*, the National Defense Committee of the *Riigikogu*, the Prime Minister, and the Government.

Civilian control over the armed forces is enhanced further by the media. Freedom of the press is guaranteed by the Constitution of Estonia.[24] The army is also under the control of individual citizens, including families of conscripts.[25]

Establishing defense forces demands time and resources. Both are at utmost value, yet, without clear visions and determined aims how to use them, both can be easily wasted. Consensus—which has been reached among the different political forces of Estonia—on the essence of national defense in the process of preparing, discussing, and finally passing the "Guidelines of the National Defense Policy of Estonia," has converted the notion of national defense into a process with a clearly defined aim. The substance of this document specifies the principles of the Estonian National Defense model, which serves as the basis for future planning of national defense and national defense programs and concepts of a broader or narrower scope.[26]

We have come to agreement on aims about "good life" and "life" meaning accession to EU and NATO, and Parliamentary approval for implementation of the major programs was achieved. These programs included:

- creation of a training and educational system to prepare soldiers, noncommissioned officers (NCOs), and the officer corps in which civilian and military educational standards were unified;
- investments in infrastructure with an emphasis on improving service conditions in terms of reconstructing or constructing all military establishments as well as increasing the standard of living; and
- establishment of procurement and armament projects, including development of information technology on a large scale, etc.

All of this leads us to the main question about resources: money. With approval of the directions and principles of defense force development programs, we established the cornerstones of the annually increasing defense budget, which will be 2 percent of gross domestic product (GDP) by 2003. This ratio has contributed to the credibility of Estonia's image in the international arena.

Today, ten years after starting from less than zero, Estonia has its own Defense Forces, consisting of active infantry units with sixty-five hundred men;[27] the Defense League,[28] with about 12,500 men; and the best military unit, the Estonian Border Guard,[29] with about three thousand men. The defense structure also has Navy[30] and Air Force[31] components.

The existence, development, and goals of the established system are characterized by openness and the need for self-sustaining development.

Estonia's total defense concept of both armed and nonviolent forms of resistance is based on conscription, constant military training of Regular Forces, preparedness of reserves, and citizens' determination to resist aggression. By developing and maintaining its military strength, Estonia aims to deter any external threats and challenges that might endanger the sovereignty and territorial integrity of the country. We can argue, of course, that continued attachment to territorial defense in Europe is no longer appropriate, given the absence of a major threat and the new strategic landscape. Furthermore, to see security simply in terms of territory is to fail to understand international security after the Cold War,[32] but total defense as the concept and territorial defense as the strategy still constitute main value for Baltic countries due to their geopolitical location.

The precondition to the success of a territorial defense system is conscription, readiness of an extended command structure, a territorial mobilization system, and a high level of a nation's "will-to-defend" spirit.[33] Although the Estonian Constitution sets up the principle of conscription,[34] discussions about creating a professional army have not ceased. The advantages of a professional army can include high professionalism, permanent preparedness, and effective use of weaponry. Arranging national defense on the basis of a professional army frees citizens from the obligation to participate in defending the state, keeps down costs in terms of training reserves, and does not impose defense-related obligations on legal entities.

We can argue that, as a result of the changed threat scenario in Europe, numerically large armed forces have become irrelevant in Europe. The multipolar and global conflict scenario compels modern armed forces to comply with multiple tasks that are independent of a given threat scenario. Smaller, faster, more mobile, functionally and technologically more flexible military organizations that can be integrated into multinational armed forces as well, meet today's requirements much better than armies based on compulsory military service.[35]

However, in the case of Estonia, a professional army would have had many drawbacks in the context of national defense of a small country with a small population. Destroying the army of the state would mean destroying the comprehensive system of national defense as well. In addition, a small professional army and the lack of reserve would not allow compliance with international obligations in partnership—later member-ship—in military alliances. Examples worldwide—as well as examples of countries in the region with similar "particular characteristics"—have shown that a conscript's army is the optimal solution for national defense of small states. The advantages of a conscript army might be outlined briefly as follows:

- using all available resources in national defense is essential to create the preconditions for:
- credible defense capability of the state;
- creating a niche to implement the obligations of international cooperation and interstate programs in the field of defense is a prerequisite for acquiring international aid; and
- unification of people under a "common goal" improves society in general.

Furthermore, it is essential to pay attention to the important sociopolitical attributes of conscript armies, such as the role of the military as a national emergency force, a training institution for citizens, and, more generally, a symbol of the state and an integrating force for all citizens. At the same time, however, it is necessary to recognize that there has been a global tendency toward professionalism, as has been discussed here, and even today, 40 percent of the Estonian defense force is volunteer.

The other side of the coin is money. Both the pro and contra arguments—that conscription is cheaper or that volunteer army is cheaper—can be proved, even though they are quite contradictory. If a country wants to transform its force structure, a proper study should be carried out by that country. In this case, the outcome will not depend, one hopes, on the political will only.

INTERNATIONAL COOPERATION
Although Estonia has set a goal to build up a reliable national defense, she understands that a small state with scarce resources cannot be independent in an interdependent world, as has been stated from the beginning. Therefore, Estonia's national defense doctrine is based on two complementary and interdependent principles: an independent national defense capability and international military cooperation. In this way, Estonia's security is directly linked to European security.

The ultimate aim of international defense cooperation for Estonia is to ensure the country's national defense by means of security guarantees.

Defense cooperation must be based on the principle of equal participation and shared responsibility. Estonian defense policy today foresees the need for international defense cooperation in three areas:

1. Multilateral relations, through international security and defense organizations (mainly NATO). Security guarantees should arise from sharing responsibilities/burdens and participation in decision making; in seeking security guarantees, Estonia's focus is on NATO. NATO, at present, is the only Western collective defense organization vested with the means of guaranteeing security and collective defense on the basis of democratic principles. Contacts between Estonia and NATO have evolved since 1992, when Estonia joined the North Atlantic Cooperation Council (NACC). Our relations with NATO intensified when we joined the Partnership for Peace (PfP) program in February 1994—as only the fourth country to do so. PfP has become the main framework for our relations with the Alliance; however, participation in the PfP program is not a goal in itself, but we view it as part of a process leading to eventual NATO membership.

2. Regional cooperation through bilateral relations—that is, defense cooperation with individual countries as the best way to acquire experiences as well—and multilateral ones. International cooperation based on regional cooperative "cells" is crucial in our interdependent world. Estonia participates in the Baltic cooperation, cooperation among the littoral states around the Baltic Sea. The defense-related cooperation among Estonia, Latvia, and Lithuania has resulted in four long-term military cooperation projects:

   • the Baltic Peacekeeping Battalion (BALTBAT)—infantry battalion for participation in international peace support operations. Currently, the project's main objective is to develop BALTBAT into a standard capability infantry battalion.
   • the Baltic Naval Squadron (BALTRON)—a naval force with mine countermeasures capabilities;
   • the Baltic Air-Surveillance Network (BALTNET)—an air-surveillance information system for the acquisition, coordination, distribution, and display of air-surveillance data; and
   • The Baltic Defense College (BALTDEFCOL)—a joint military educational institution for training senior staff officers and civil servants.[36]

All of the Baltic defense cooperation projects share the dimensions of security policy and development of national defense, just as the projects demonstrate the will of the Baltic states to cooperate in security and defense. In the case of the Baltic states, it has been important that these common projects have been built on real combat readiness capability. They are aimed at developing the national defense capabilities of the Baltic states and preparing them for NATO membership by enhancing their interoperability with NATO forces, thereby contributing to regional security and stability in the Baltic Sea area and to international peace and security.

3. International participation in peace operations as a member of the international community. Estonia does not intend to be merely a consumer of security; she also intends to participate in creating security. To this end, Estonia's active participation in peacekeeping and peace support operations is essential. Estonian peacekeeping units participated with Danish peacekeepers in the United Nations (UN) missions in Croatia (UNPROFOR). Estonian servicemen have had the opportunity to assist in securing peace in the NATO-led Implementation Force (IFOR) and Stabilization Force (SFOR) operations in Bosnia-Herzegovina, as a part or the Nordic-Polish Brigade and serve under UN command in South-Lebanon (UNIFIL).

Thus, it can be seen that even though Estonia's main aim is self-defense, she considers international cooperation essential.

RECOMMENDATIONS

The primary intention of this chapter has been to share some of the experience the author has gained in helping to establish the defense system of his country. Some of these experiences are universal and some of them are more specific and cannot be used for general purposes. One thing is certain, however, when making a choice about what defense system to establish: One has to think about the actual "time and space" as well as the political, military, and functional questions. These include, among others, the purpose and functions of defense forces, the issue of civil guidance—which is vital for any country, especially for one that would like to belong to the family of democracies.

Underpinning the key findings of this chapter, the four main factors regarded as essential in the establishment of a defense system by the author can be summarized as follows:

- "philosophical" foundation of the reform, with new ideas and self-initiative as crucial components in any transformation process;
- definition of the roles/functions of defense forces;
- appropriate process of creation based on open discussion as well as social- and political-wide consensus; and
- a clear and unambiguous command line founded on an adequate legal basis.

PHILOSOPHICAL FOUNDATION

In the Estonian case, the most significant lesson has been that when such a process is being launched, we should, above all, have clearly defined aims laid down in appropriate legal documents. This (these) document(s) should provide for the legal as well as the "philosophical" foundation of the reform. In the case of Estonia, it was the "Estonian Defense Policy Guidelines" adopted by the Parliament on 6 May 1996, six years after launching the creation of the defense system. It probably was too late, but it still had much more significant impact than one could have expected. In this way, a lot of energy and time could be saved for real development efforts instead of having never ending talks about what should be done.

The Estonian Defense Policy Guidelines were drafted by the Ministry of Defense without having a national security strategy. This step was necessitated by time constraints. Undoubtedly, creation of a national strategy should precede defense policy guidelines, but if fundamental principles and aims are relatively consolidated—as they were in the Estonian case—the delay of such a document should not hinder commencement of the creation process. From this aspect, countries in possession of some kind of defense system, and countries starting to establish such a system from absolutely nothing—like Estonia—are in different positions. The latter ones cannot afford the luxury of not having a national defense system at all. If the main directions are laid down, establishment can be launched, leaving room for possible further refinements. National security strategies, defense concepts, and military doctrines usually need constant upgrading in the course of the reform process because these documents—however they reflect fundamental changes in ways of thinking, aims, and interests—are usually not up to real-world challenges in defining force requirements. In the case of Estonia, the targeted aims and functions of the defense forces served as a prerequisite and a basis for further development of the defense system. The aim—the kind of defense we would like to build—naturally must be reflected in the roles/functions of the defense forces. Thus, clear and precise definition of these can contribute to achieving the ultimate aim to a large extent.

In the reform process, the fundamental aim for Estonia was creation of a self-defense capability that, in case of a small country, is based on two equally important foundations: self-defense and international cooperation through which self-defense gains real meaning. Estonia chose total defense as a doctrine and territorial defense as a strategy simply due to our limited recourses and geopolitical location next to Europe's largest land power, which is still wobbling between different identities.

In terms of international cooperation, regional cooperation in the Baltic has been exceptionally crucial. Four Baltic cooperation programs were created: the Baltic Battalion (BALBAT), the Baltic Naval Squadron (BALTRON), the Baltic Air-Surveillance Network (BALTNET), and the Baltic Defense College. These projects had two significant common characteristics: (1) They were unique in a way that had never been achieved before—that sovereign countries entrusted international units with a big part of their defense without establishing a military alliance at the same time. These aroused the interest of foreign countries. (2) They were highly cost-effective; they generated foreign participation and foreign investment, both of which were of utmost value to Estonia. Foreign participation contributed to national knowledge and expertise—because the lack of materiel and "human" resources (that is, qualified personnel) are problems that usually confront countries in transition. On the other hand, through unification of the Baltic countries' resources, each country managed to triple its domestic material means. It is important to underline that, in terms of cooperation with foreign partners, it is also essential to set clear and realistic objectives—especially speaking about programs of assistance with defense reform. A good set of objectives should clarify the requirements and expectations of providers and recipients.

In sum, new ideas that can interest potential partners, investors, and self-initiative are crucial factors in any transformation process. Furthermore, it is desirable to begin the transformation process with setting the aim—the kind of defense we would like to achieve—and including the main principles in a basic document.

FUNCTIONS

As has been stipulated above, defining the right functions for defense forces can contribute much to achieving success in the reform process. The main aim of any defense should be combat readiness, which can be merely a means of prevention, but must be credible based on real capabilities in case it comes to war. Furthermore, one should bear in mind what roles one would like defense forces to play in the wider context of society.

In the case of countries in transition, defense forces can serve as an essential "foreign policy tool"—especially in the case of new democracies whose aim is to join NATO. Of course, countries under transition are mainly concerned about their own security and about how to obtain security guarantees from the Western Military Alliance, namely NATO.

At the same time, they must prepare themselves to participate in the decision-making process of an alliance and share responsibility, and they must guarantee the interoperability of their forces—which necessitates openness and self-development. What could be more desirable for both sides and from the aspect of democratic development?

Furthermore, building or rebuilding a defense system should be beyond everyday political battles between different political parties and, in this way, play a crucial role in nation building. In the case of Estonia, defense forces play a major part in the integration of foreign-language-speaking minorities into society as well as in the unification of society in general. Of course, this is possible only if there is consensus on and an understanding of what role defense forces should serve.

In the case of countries where a considerable part of the youth is being conscripted, one can say that the army, in fact, can be considered a "nationwide university," that practically all the main citizens of the country attend and "graduate from."

And, finally, it enhances civil-military relations to a large extent if defense forces can be seen by the population as a search and rescue force as well—that can lend a hand in case of civil emergencies—whose task is simply to help and defend, not to define society.

APPROPRIATE PROCESS

As for the process itself, no matter whether aims and roles have been defined as a result of solid academic research or simply formulated in people's minds during years of oppression, it is important to enter into a free and open discussion about them. Finally, based on the outcome of this discussion, political decisions should be made at the legislative level.

Based on legally approved, legitimate principles, referring to the first two points, the executive power and civilian experts, in close cooperation with the military, must reach a consensus concerning priorities. They should work out short- and long-term development programs in accordance with these priorities that must be secured with stable financing (we set up an action plan in Estonia to increase appropriations from 1.2 percent of the GDP in 1994 to 2 percent in 2003).

It is important that the political consensus on objectives and priorities in terms of the establishment of a defense system should come as a multi-party agreement among political powers represented in Parliament. Coalition and should take part in this agreement, and it must be legitimate.

Reaching social and political consensus on aims and priorities, in the case of Estonia, consisted of a long series of discussions involving the Ministry of Defense and different authorities; several government bodies, such as the Defense Commission of the Estonian Parliament; academics; and the public. Before entering into such discussions, it can be useful to set up an information strategy—focusing on how to bring the message about the desirable defense system to different players—with a public information strategy as one part of it. The public information strategy should concentrate on the "opinion makers," clearly articulating for them the priorities in the course of the establishment process and explaining how these can benefit society as a whole. In this way, we can gain public support for our aims as well as the military's. On the one hand, this is the best way to prevent political battles; on the other hand, we should not forget that building or reforming a defense system is a costly business, and we need the full support of the public to raise the needed resources.

In Estonia, the priorities were and still are: (1) education and train-ing—which can result in the creation of a "smart force"; (2) investment in infrastructure to raise training and living standards; and (3) invest-ment in information technology and research and development (R&D)—to guarantee combat readiness according to future requirements and pro-curement and armament programs. In these projects, domestic industry must play an important role.

These priorities, especially better living standards and improving the quality of life and service are the best ways to gain public support. It is important—as it is in all matters—to articulate and "sell" intentions in the right way. In terms of political consensus, the opposition in defense issues can be largely reduced if the ultimate aim of defense is defined in the right way and backed up with the right functions. This is because, as in the case of countries in transition, defense forces usually do serve as foreign policy tools. Defense usually constitutes a main part of how a nation defines its place in the international arena. If national-foreign policy interests and the type of defense to be established converge, political consensus is usually not difficult to reach.

A CLEAR AND UNAMBIGUOUS COMMAND LINE

To provide for the success of these programs, we should establish a clear and unambiguous command line over and within the Armed Forces, where all organs involved must have precisely defined responsibilities and the means to act on them. Even though practices are different, in most cases the Constitution should be developed to achieve the set aims. At a minimum, general laws about the Armed Forces—their status, structure, composition, and leadership—as well as about Military Service—including regulation of professional career management and a wide spectrum of social guarantees—must be drafted, enacted, and applied.

In Estonia, this issue was rather complicated and unsuccessful because the chapter in the Constitution concerning defense was taken from the 1937 Constitution. In 1937, Estonia was a presidential republic where, similar to the Polish Marshal Pilsudski and to Mannerheim (in Finland), General Laidoner, as Chief of Defense of Estonia, was vested with power and authority largely exceeding the extent tolerable in a parliamentarian republic—which Estonia is now—that claims to understand the essence of civilian control. This—that the military has too much influence and power—is a matter that inevitably evolves in most countries in transition as the military—naturally—is trying to defend its "bastions" of power with all means, thus hindering the reform process. For this reason, creating sufficient legal basis in which authorities and tasks are defined and divided clearly is a crucial foundation for any reform process. To "put the puzzles into the right place," we should not refrain from thought and hard decisions—even at the price of dismissing people whose mindset cannot be changed. Serious alterations and restructuring in the officer corps can be a prerequisite for creating a clear command line. The actions this can necessitate may vary from country to country. In most former Warsaw Pact countries, such restructuring usually involves reductions in the officer corps and the need to build the (NCO) corps.

Furthermore, as has been referred to above, realization of these tasks requires the establishment of career paths—human resource management is crucial—and rigorous personnel policies.

With this, we have returned to the starting point: One of the foundations of the creation of a defense system is the elimination of constitutional and legal system inadequacies and establishment of a proper legal basis.

While the achievements in terms of the first three factors can be considered a success in Estonia, the fourth can be considered rather a failure.

CONCLUSION

The options and choices in case of Estonia have been demonstrated in this chapter, which describes the actual "project" and provides insight into the thinking process and rationale behind the decisions.

The Estonian case has been regarded as a success story. Today one of Estonia's security pillars, which also serves the country's most comprehensive interests as well—along with the developing economy and the increasing educational and cultural integration with the world—is the reliable defense system. Estonians have reached a consensus on the necessity of substantially increasing resources for national defense as a means of enhancing the stability of both the country and the region.

In addition to developing different branches of the armed forces and solving questions concerning equipment and logistics, training, education, and social guarantees for servicemen, they have understood the significance of increasing the efficiency of the army and civil structures and the establishment of civil control typical of a democratic society. The second pillar of Estonian national defense—beyond an independent defense capacity—is international defense-related cooperation, aimed at reinforcing national defense by means of international security guarantees. However, common defense or international military support is feasible and effective only if the national defense system is built up, "nurtured," trained, and equipped so that it is interoperable with potential allies. Defense structures, technical means, and procedures should be compatible with those of NATO. Therefore, international military cooperation is seen as a means to achieve this goal.

Thus, one of the most vital messages should be that, ideally, defense systems should be established in the future keeping in mind the prospect of international cooperation instead of international confrontation.

Finally, let us illustrate what the Baltic states mean about being successful in establishing their defense system with a quotation from General Michael H. Clemmesen, who wrote: "The three Baltic States have developed a uniquely close and comprehensive cooperation in the Security and Defense field. This has taken place within a very short span of years, and it has been accomplished in spite of heavy handicaps in nearly all fields. The combined result is that in a couple of years' time the armed forces of the Baltic States will have a higher average level of NATO interoperability than any other forces in Central and Eastern Europe. It will actually be higher then the average typical interoperability level of the forces of 'old' NATO members."[37]

Finally, let us sum up the main criteria to be taken into consideration when developing a defense system/force. It is crucial that consensus should be reached by any nation if the aim is to build a cost-effective defense system/force suited to the requirements of the country, the region, the Trans-Atlantic area, democracy, and the new concept of security (this could be defined simply as "modern" defense system/force). The elements of such a consensus can be summarized as follows:

1. The spirit, the "wish and will" of the nation, has to be in place to reach the common aim of building a modern defense system/force.
2. There should be a clearly defined aim that should materialize in a proper legal basis (that is, "security guidelines") as a precondition to building such a system/force.
3. The Parliament and respective authorities should reach agreement on the project. This should include a package consisting of education and the improvement of service and living conditions (conscript and professional as well).
4. There should be a clear command line developed where all authorities are represented and the duties are clearly divided.
5. The process of development should be based on two basic forms of cooperation: international and regional (in the case of Estonia, it has been Baltic) and national cooperation.

Last, but not least, all of these elements must be founded foremost on civil-military cooperation, which means that there is consensus between the two sides, and that it is the duty of politicians to define the aims and provide the necessary financial means while the military should deal with force development.

ENDNOTES

1. Martin van Creveld, *The Transformation of War*, New York: The Free Press, 1991.

2. Alfred Vagts, *History of Militarism*, New York: Free Press, 1967.

3. Barry Buzan, "Is International Security Possible?" in Ken Booth (ed.), *New Thinking about Strategy and International Security*, London: Harper Collins Academic, 1991, pp. 34–35.

4. Robert Mandel, "What Are We Protecting?" *Armed Forces and Society*, 22 (3) (Spring 1996): 335.

5. David Held and Anthony MacGrew, "Globalization and the LIBERAL Democratic State," *Government and Opposition*, XXVIII (Spring 1993): 226.

6. "Guidelines of the National Defense Policy of Estonia," *Riigi Teataja* (May 1996): 877.

7. Ermei Kanninen, "Our Territorial Defense System," Presentation in Art of War Society, Helsinki, 1 March, 1971; Ermei Kanninen, *The War Material Procurement of the Finnish Defense Forces after the Second World War and the Political Decisions Closely Connected with Them*, No. 46, Suomen Sotatietieteelisen Seuran Vuosijulkaisu (Helsinki, 1988); Ermei Kanninen, "The Development of the Finnish Defense System from Front Defense to Territorial Defense," Lecture for Estonian Officers, Tallinn, 19 June 1999.

8. Ants Laaneots, Eesti Kaitsejõud 2000. aastate algul. Helsinki: Soome Riigikaitse Kõrgkool, 2000, p. 24.

9. Carl von Clausewitz, *On War* (p. 605) cited in Robert Carlyle, *Clausewitz's Contemporary Relevance*, Strategic and Combat Studies Institute, 1995, p. 12.

10. Anders Bjurner, "Reflections on Subregionalism and Wider European Security," in *Northern Europe and Central Europe: Hard, Soft and Civic Security*, Stockholm: Olaf Palme International Center and Budapest: European House, 1999, pp. 31–32.

11. Ibid., p. 32.

12. Robert G. Gard, "The Future of the Military Profession" in *Force of Modern Societies: The Military Profession*, Adelphi Papers No. 103, London: International Institute for Strategic Studies, 1973, p. 3.

13. Stanley Kober, "To reduce military tensions in Europe, Ban Conscription," Policy Analysis No. 116, March 1989, p. 5.

14. In the context of this paper, civil-military relations does not mean Civil-Military Cooperation (CIMIC), but is defined in a wider context.

15. Gard, op cit. p. 4.

16. Bengt Abrahamsson, "*Military Professionalization and Political Power*," Beverly Hills, CA: Sage Publications, 1972.

17. Samuel P. Huntington, *The Soldier and the State*, Cambridge, MA: Harvard University Press, 1957.

18. Danah Zohar, "Tolerance Is Not Enough," in Andrei Grachev (ed.), *The Meeting of Civilisations*, Tbilisi, 1998, p. 125.

19. Peter D. Feaver, "Delegation, Monitoring, and Civilian Control of the Military: Agency Theory and American Civil-Military Relations," p. 3. Available at http://www.wcfia.harvard.edu/olin/pubs/no4.htm

20. Richard H. Kohn, "An Essay on Civilian Control of the Military," p. 1. Available at http://www.unc.edu/depts/diplomat/AD_Issuesamdipl_3/kohn.htm

21. Feaver, op cit., p. 9.

22. Speech of Prime Minister Winston Churchill, Geneva, Switzerland, 19 September 1946.

23. "Guidelines of the National Defense Policy of Estonia," *Riigi Teataja* (May 1996): 872.

24. Eesti Vabariigi Põhiseadus, *Riigi Teataja*, 26 (1992): 349.

25. William Rompkey and Jan Hoekema, p. 8.

26. "Estonia on the Threshold of NATO," Ministry of Defense of Estonia, Tallinn, 1999, p. 9.

27. The primary branch of the armed forces is the infantry, the creation and management of which is considerably cheaper than air or naval forces.

28. The Defense League (*Kaitseliit*) is viewed as an evolving and changing national defense organization according to current needs. The Defense League's main task in national defense is to contribute to forming battalions of territorial forces and to conduct training and ensure their fighting effectiveness. During peacetime, professional servicemen, NCOs, officers, and volunteers make up the Defense League, and during times of war, they make up the principal part of established military units.

29. Estonia had no frontier controls whatsoever before 1990; now she is entirely in conformity with Schengen.

30. Estonia's naval forces help to maintain the military balance in the region. The naval forces are suited to the special conditions of the Baltic Sea, and their purpose is to defend territorial waters. In case of war, the Navy, including vessels at the disposal of the coast guard in peacetime, must be capable of defending coastal areas and territorial waters against enemy naval forces and preventing landing operations. Special attention must be paid to the effective use of, and protection against, mines. In peacetime, the Estonian Navy must be ready to participate in international search and rescue operations and to help in the fight against environmental threats. Its peacetime duties also include helping to maintain order at sea and carrying out oceanographic research

31. The role of the air forces is to secure control of the country's airspace and provide air defense of strategic sites. The air forces include air surveillance and air defense units, as well as a unified civil-military air traffic control system. The task of the unified civil-military air traffic control system is monitoring airspace, search and rescue missions, and military transport flights necessary for national security. Estonian air forces must be established in a manner that ensures the maximum degree of integration with other national defense and civil structures. At the same time, they must prepare for cooperation in an international air defense system of the Baltic region and possible integration with NATO air defense systems. Estonians are also seeking to work more closely in the field of air traffic control to be compatible with NATO standards. The United States has put forward a Regional Airspace initiative for the Baltic states to help each country develop a strategy for modernizing its air traffic control system and peacetime elements of its air defense system.

32. Paul Cornish, "NATO at the Millennium: New Missions, New Members . . . New Strategy," *NATO Review* 5 (Sept.–Oct. 1997): 23.

33. Laaneots, op cit., p. 24.

34. Eesti Vaariigi Põhiseadus, *Riigi Teataja* I (1992): 26, 349, §124.

35. Karl W. Haltier, "The Definite End of the Mass Army in Western Europe," *Armed Forces and Society,* 25 (1) (Fall 1998): 8.

36. Annual Exchange of Information on Defense Planning, 2000, pp. 12–13.

37. Michael H. Clemmesen, "The Baltic Defense Cooperation: Getting Ready for NATO," *Estonia Today* (9 May 2000): 5.

CHAPTER NINETEEN

Norwegian Defense Reforms of the 1990s

Jonny M. Otterlei*

INTRODUCTION

During the 1990s, Norwegian defense has been transformed from primarily homeland defense against an invasion to a wider spectrum of defense tasks of which homeland defense remains the most important. At the same time, substantial downsizing has been carried out to adapt to the economic reality of the 1990s, and to free up funding for high-priority areas. During the 1990s, defense budgets were insufficient to implement existing plans, and operating costs have shown an undesired increase, especially since 1995. This has happened in spite of several attempts to reduce and rationalize the peacetime organization. In Norwegian defense planning, these two factors have been referred to as the double imbalance. The new long-term defense plan addresses the double imbalance and prescribes the number of employees to be cut by 20 percent to 25 percent within the next few years.[1] Also, focus has been placed on increasing force readiness to meet challenges stemming from international involvement and new threats.

As of today, the Norwegian defense amounts to about thirty-nine thousand personnel in peacetime, about twenty-seven thousand of whom (including fifteen thousand conscripts) are considered to be on active duty. In addition, about thirteen hundred to fourteen hundred troops are deployed abroad in peacekeeping missions—twelve hundred of those are in the Kosovo Forces. In times of crisis and war, a total of 222,000 personnel could be mobilized; the Army could expand to eighty-nine thousand

*The author is employed at the Norwegian Defense Research Establishment. Opinions expressed in this article are those of the author and not necessarily the views of the Norwegian government.

troops, the Navy to twenty-five thousand, the Air Force to twenty-five thousand, and the Home Guard to eighty-three thousand personnel.

The Army consists of cadre and training units for a division with three tactical brigades (one armored brigade and two infantry brigades), two independent mechanized infantry brigades, and one armored brigade. During the 1990s, both overall structure and readiness have been reduced. In 1990, the Army had a total of thirteen independent brigades organized within three divisional commands. The equipment of these brigades was, however, of variable quality. Toward 2005, the Army is planning to reduce and reshape its forces further, leaving three brigades and a division level marginally intact. The reduction in readiness resulted in decreasing the number of active personnel from nineteen thousand in 1990 to 14,700 in 2000. In addition, the number of conscripts has been reduced significantly. However, the new long-term defense plan stresses the need for increasing force readiness over the next few years and, as a consequence, units have been earmarked to fulfill this requirement.

The Navy consists of four frigates, ten submarines, fifteen missile craft/fast patrol boats, nine mine countermeasures vessels, and some coastal fortresses. In 1990, a substantially larger structure was present in terms of anti-invasion components, especially fast patrol boats and coastal fortress. The substantial downsizing of the stationary anti-invasion structure will continue to 2005, when a large number of fortified positions will be closed. Also, the number of missile craft and submarines will be reduced substantially. Personnel on active duty as well as in the reserve have not been cut similarly, for two reasons: First, a large part of the stationary anti-invasion structure, including personnel, has been preserved at low operational status without training and exercises (mothball status). Second, the Navy has maintained its readiness to fulfill its peacetime tasks during the 1990s—though with some variations in activity level. This has resulted in a steady level of active personnel.

Today, the Air Force has fifty-eight F-16s, six medium- and ten short-range ground-based air defense batteries, six transport aircraft, eighteen tactical helicopters, and six maritime patrol aircraft. During the 1990s, downsizing was targeted toward fighters and ground-based air defense, but support aircraft and helicopters were maintained at the same level. Reduced readiness and base closures have cut active personnel from about nine thousand to five thousand over the last ten years. Toward 2005, the air base structure and ground-based air defense batteries are to be reorganized and reduced further. The number of reserve personnel is constant, to a large extent, to enable mobilization of civilian airfields for allied reinforcements in times of crisis and war.

The Home Guard was maintained at the same level during the 1990s to protect military and civilian key targets and functions in crises and war. The task of protecting the mobilization of defense forces has become less comprehensive. Instead, protection of critical objects (personnel, infrastructure, etc.) from terrorism and Special Forces attack has been given increased weight. Home Guard personnel can be mobilized from their civilian jobs within twenty-four to seventy-two hours.

DEFENSE CONCEPT EVOLUTION

Since 1949, Norwegian security has been founded on four pillars: a nationally balanced defense, allied military and international cooperation, the concept of general conscription, and the total defense concept. The content and strength of these pillars have been subject to substantial changes over the last ten years. Before addressing these changes, a brief overview of the defense task development during the 1990s is in order.

DEFENSE TASKS

Homeland defense, based on the lessons learned from the German invasion of Norway during World War II and the Cold War, has been dimensioning for Norwegian defense until 1990. The major defense task was to deter and defend against an attack or invasion of Norway by the Soviet Union. The basic instruments were a nationally balanced defense, membership in the North Atlantic Treaty Organization (NATO), and strong bilateral ties with the United States and the United Kingdom.

In this context, Norway was regarded as a net importer of security. The nation's unique location with respect to transatlantic sea-lines of communication and Soviet Kola bases exposed Norway to a Soviet attack as part of any major attack on Western Europe. Soviet armed forces represented such an overwhelming capability compared to Norwegian armed forces that an attack could be dealt with only with substantial early allied reinforcements. However, as a confidence-building measure, Norwegian policy was that no allied forces were to be stationed permanently on Norwegian territory in peacetime. Instead, extensive preparations for rapid allied reinforcements were made, such as construction of airfields, quays, stockpiles, and depots. To make this concept work, Norwegian armed forces would have to deter and defend against any pre-emptive strikes and establish a military threshold, enabling rapid and substantial transfer of allied reinforcements to Norway.

After 1990, the security environment became multifaceted. Following the collapse of the Warsaw Pact and, later, the disintegration of the Soviet Union, the direct, visible, and overwhelming Soviet threat vapor-ized and was replaced by an uncertainty about developments in Rus-sia—in the medium term, a political instability and, in the longer term, a potentially military offensive and capable Russia. Norway's proximity to Kola and the Barents Sea implies particular attention to our national security interests in the Northern Region. At the same time, however, any perceived potential military challenge to South Norway was down-graded substantially. Another important implication was that other NATO members altered their view of the Norwegian security situation in such a way that Norway is now required to be a net exporter of secur-ity. Closer ties between NATO and Russia, combined with emerging threats from rogue states and extremist groups and active military involvement in the Balkans, have been important drivers for this shift in Norwegian security priorities.

Defenses against an invasion and more limited attacks have been reduced gradually from including all of Norway to only Northern Nor-way, and now they are more generic in nature because major challenges to Norwegian territory are integrated within a joint allied operational context. Longer warning times have led to reduced readiness and ability to reinforce Norway's own forces. However, the new long-term defense plan put more weight on reaction capability, but from a perspective of the new security challenges to Norway and requirements from primarily international operations. Territorial defense has shifted its primary emphasis from protecting and supporting mobilization of the armed forces to protection of facilities and activities vital to society in case of limited attacks from Special Forces and/or terrorists.

The Defense Commission of 1990 emphasized crisis management.[2] Changes in the security environment made military crises with a very low risk of escalating to war more likely than they were before 1990. Disputes about the use of natural resources and other conflicts of interest were considered possible within a bilateral context between Norway and other nations.

Military presence is an important element in upholding national sov-ereignty and exercising national authority. However, this presence has been reduced gradually from "in all areas" to "in priority areas" to adjust to a significantly smaller defense force.

National ambitions with respect to participating in international military operations have been raised substantially. Until 1993, the primary focus was supporting United Nations (UN) peace support operations. After 1993, more explicit weight was given to potential participation in NATO's reaction forces, including high-intensity operations. In 1999, the Norwegian parliament (the *Storting*) emphasized Norway's commitment to contribute to international military operations and designated about thirty-five hundred personnel, including elements from all services, for such operations.[3]

A NATIONALLY BALANCED DEFENSE

Norwegian defense, since World War II, has been developed as a balanced defense that includes the most critical components of modern defense, while maintaining a balance among the defense components in the armed forces. Behind this principle stands a Cold War national ambition of having a defense capability to fight a major invasion long enough for NATO reinforcements to arrive. A balance in defense components would prevent "holes" that could be exploited for a quick breakthrough by an attacker.

As stated, the principle of balanced defense has been under considerable strain during the 1990s due to funding constraints and cost escalation. The cost of major defense components has continued to escalate more quickly than budgets have increased. Studies of U.S. and UK materiel procurements after World War II reveal an annual cost escalation of 5 percent for main battle tanks, 10.5 percent for frigates, 9 percent for submarines, and 11 percent for fighters.[4]

Substantial initiatives have been undertaken to reduce the impact of cost escalation on defense materiel. On the weapons manufacturers' side, alternative design solutions with extensive use of commercial technology and more effective production methods have been pursued. On the armed forces side, procurement solutions involving lower capabilities and cheaper materiel have been explored.

However, cost escalation is likely to remain a challenge to long-term defense planning and will have the greatest impact on small nations. For Norway, technological level is determined more or less through the principle of balanced defense and the need for interoperability with other NATO forces. Norwegian armed forces are so small in all sectors that there is little room for further downsizing. The NATO Defense Capabilities Initiative (DCI) stresses the need for nations to strengthen priority capabilities and interoperability with other forces; therefore, nations will have to make substantial investments in command and control in nations in the years to come.

Still, the principle of a balanced defense remains a pillar of Norwegian defense planning as confirmed by the *Storting* in its spring 2001 debate of the long-term defense plan. One key argument for this decision is Norway's geopolitical situation. However, a more offensive approach to force pooling and allied cooperation is required to improve weakened defense components.

ALLIED MILITARY AND INTERNATIONAL COOPERATION
During the Cold War, military cooperation was exercised mainly within the NATO framework. The key elements were joint planning for allied reinforcements to Norway, extensive NATO-funded infrastructure development in Norway, and large-scale and frequent allied exercises in Norway. As a separate force production trade, Norway was also a significant troop contributor to the UN's traditional peacekeeping missions.

In the 1990s, a wider perspective on allied and international cooperation has been adopted. Emphasis has been placed on stronger integration and ability to participate in joint allied operations in Norway both and other countries, while, at the same time, keeping attention focused on the national dependency on allied reinforcements to meet any major national security challenge. Political support for contributions to UN peacekeeping operations is still very strong, as is a willingness to contribute to a wider range of international operations, including peace enforcement.

NATO and bilateral agreements are important security policy instruments for Norway. NATO's revised strategic concept highlights transformation of allied forces to encompass a wider spectrum of tasks, including collective defense. This implies increased emphasis on higher readiness forces and a stronger focus on the areas identified in the DCI. The DCI establishes requirements for national defense planning with respect to effective engagement, deployment, and mobility; survivability for forces and infrastructure; and sustainability of forces and logistics. The current defense plan clearly states that Norwegian defense does not fulfill DCI requirements in a number of important areas. On the bilateral side, cooperation with allies and, especially the United States, on reinforcements and predeployment stockpiles is considered important.

Norway participates as well in development of a stronger defense identity within the European Union (EU). But the fact that Norway is not a member of the EU makes an active role difficult. Future involvement will depend on the degree of EU willingness to accept nonmember participation, and on the cooperation established between the EU and NATO. Norway has committed about thirty-five hundred soldiers to the EU headline goal.

The importance of multinational cooperation within the Atlantic Alliance and in Europe is growing. Factors such as new security challenges, reduced defense budgets, cost escalation of defense components, and requirements for interoperability influence nations to increase their cooperation. Specifically, small nations like Norway would not be able, by themselves, to procure and sustain a desired capability spectrum to fulfill DCI and national defense needs.

THE CONCEPT OF GENERAL CONSCRIPTION

In its spring 2001 debate on the new long-term defense plan, the *Storting* confirmed that it wanted to retain compulsory military service as a pillar of the Norwegian defense. Such a system is considered critical to preserve close relations and a "hands-on" feeling between the Norwegian defense system and the nation's citizens. It is also a key instrument for recruitment to the armed forces. However, adjustments to current implementation are required. Both number of males drafted and total service time have to be reduced. The total number of conscripts to be called up is still a difficult political issue, since drafting about 50 percent of the male population does not comply with a concept of general conscription. As for the duration, initial service would be twelve months for most conscripts, with the exception for those drafted for the Home Guard, who would serve four to six months. In addition, Home Guard conscripts have annual one-week exercises until they reach age forty-four.

The number of males drafted has been limited throughout most of the period since 1814, when the concept of general conscription was included in the constitution. Successful implementation of a conscription system rests on two fundamental assumptions: First, the level of advanced military technology in the armed forces has to be relatively low to avoid overly complex system operations requirements for conscripts to be maintained over time. Second, sufficient funding for equipping and training the units has to be available. These assumptions have never been fully met, and, today, about 55 percent of nineteen–year-old males complete their initial service.[5]

Compulsory system was the subject of political and military debate during the 1990s. There has been tension and a lack of convergence between those arguing from a rational military cost-effectiveness perspective and those taking a more overall national view. The debate has gained additional momentum from the shift to a professional system in European nations such as France, Belgium, and the Netherlands. Still, compulsory service is still favored among the politicians and the population, not only for Norwegian defense, but also as a foundation for building and developing a national identity.

From a militarily rational point of view, developments over the last twenty-five to thirty years have made topical the question of whether a more professional force would be more adequate for the future. The level of military technology and operational complexity makes it hard to exploit force capabilities within the limited initial service. Also, substantial downsizing of the Army has lowered the need for conscripts substantially. Force production to handle a rigid general conscription system, where 70 percent to 80 percent of the age group is drafted for initial service, is a significant cost driver.

THE TOTAL DEFENSE CONCEPT

The intended purpose of the total defense concept is to enable Norway to mobilize all national resources and unite military and civilian assets in times of crisis and war. It was developed primarily to support full national mobilization in an all-out war during the Cold War era. This integrated perspective was required to maintain the will and capability for national defense, to protect life and health, to prevent damage, and to uphold society and civil functions. The military component is the Norwegian armed forces, and the civilian component is the civil emergency system, which is responsible for society functioning, protection of citizens, and support of the Norwegian armed forces.

During the 1990s, the concept has been subject to debate concerning both relevance and content. The movement toward extremely cost-effective operations, internationalization of ownership, and privatization makes military requisition from civil society more questionable. The military's move toward more mobile and reaction-oriented forces increased civil support requirements, often seen to be too extensive to fulfill, without substantial government funding. Increased international military involvement also would represent new challenges to civil preparedness. New threats have increased attention to society vulnerability in such areas as transportation, telecommunications, power supply, and top-level management of the civil emergency system.

In the new long-term defense plan, the total defense concept is considered a pillar of our national defense, but major revision is required to achieve a more flexible concept. This process has barely been started in the last few years.

THE NORWEGIAN DEFENSE PLANNING PROCESS

Norwegian defense planning is a continuous, periodic process with a normal cycle of four years, each period of which has three phases. The first is establishment of alternative plans for long-term defense development, assessment of each alternative defense capability to meet defense needs, and an estimate of total costs of carrying out the plans. The second phase comprises high-level military and political choices of the preferred planning alternative to be pursued as a primary long-term plan. In the third phase, more detailed, shorter-term execution plans for the preferred alternative are developed.

The first phase, development of planning alternatives, is particularly important. Due to the fundamental uncertainties related to the basic assumptions that, over time, will influence the development of defense forces, the ability of each planning alternative to meet the desired defense mission must be addressed with respect to these uncertainties. The overall objective is to identify alternative defense development plans that are as robust as possible to meet changes in the most critical and uncertain assumptions.

THE POLITICAL PROCESS

The *Storting* seeks a broad foundation among representatives of the political parties and the armed forces. Normally, the overall vision and development perspectives for Norwegian defense are debated every four years in the *Storting*. This debate might not result in formal defense decisions, but a joint perspective for the next four years is sought among the representatives, which determines the overall context for Ministry of Defense (MOD) preparations of the annual defense budget and bills to be introduced before the *Storting*. Defense budgets and bills constitute formal decisions on which the MOD and the Chief of Defense (CHOD) have to act.

In situations where a fundamental reorientation of defense policy and defense forces is necessary, a parliamentary defense commission has been established. Representation on the defense commission ensures a broad perspective and best possible rethinking of the national defense strategy. The first commission was established in 1946 after World War II, the second commission in 1974, and the third in 1990.

The last commission was established as a direct consequence of political developments in Eastern Europe and East-West relations, including the positive trends in disarmament talks. It comprised fifteen members; nine of whom are appointed by the leading political parties, and six members from the Norwegian armed forces, the civil emergency directorate, and the defense and security policy research institutes. The mandate included an appraisal of the security policy and technological and strategic development, and how these relate to defense policy and structure. The commission also was asked to evaluate funding needs for the period 1994–98 and economic perspectives for the next ten years. The Commission suggested a comprehensive downsizing of defense structure. During the 1980s, the defense budget had an annual real growth of 2 percent to 3 percent, but the Commission foresaw a zero-growth budget. However, the Commission also believed investment could be increased to more than a 30 percent share of annual budget by significantly reducing manning and its concomitant operating costs. The final report was presented to the *Storting* two years later. The report and the parliamentary debate shaped White Paper No. 16 to the *Storting* (1992–93).

The *Storting* has debated and decided on restructuring of Norwegian defense at three different times (1993, 1998, and 2001) over the last ten years. In 1993, the focus was on adjusting to the new security environment after the collapse of the Warsaw Pact, the disintegration of the Soviet Union, and an expected 0 percent growth in defense budgets. As a consequence, the defense structure was downsized substantially—for example, the number of brigades was reduced from thirteen to six. In 1998, the debate did not take off fully, and a "steady state" solution was chosen, keeping the 1993 structural goals with some minor adjustments.

THE CHIEF OF DEFENSE'S PROCESS

In his defense studies, the CHOD expresses his independent longer-term view on the structural development of the armed forces. The defense studies are initiated by the CHOD and carried out independent of the

MOD. However, the conclusions are made available in time to support the MOD in its white paper work. This model fulfils the *Storting*'s request for independent military advice concerning future defense reorganization.

Three defense studies were carried out during the 1990s: in 1991, 1996, and 2000. Defense Study 1991, which provided military input to the 1990 Defense Commission, focused on the minimum defense structure necessary to fulfill the missions of the armed forces.

Defense Study 1996 recommended continuation of the 1990 Defense Commission structure (steady-state) based on the overall security situation. The size of this force structure was considered to be the minimum needed to fulfill the mission. Rather than scaling down, the need for increased funding was stressed because imbalances between needs and actual funding had continued to accumulate after the Commission's work. If this condition could not be met, a new defense study would have to be carried out, focusing on how to reduce the imbalances.

A fundamental shift in planning strategy was chosen for Defense Study 2000. In this study, the CHOD described a substantially smaller defense structure that could be achieved within a funding level comparable to development after the Defense Study 1996/White Paper No. 16. The proposed structure was not a recommendation, but a description of how best to adapt to the funding level of the last few years. The accumulated imbalances between funding requirements and defense budgets and between operating costs and material procurements had become intolerable, and would lead to full collapse of normal planning if not taken care of promptly. A major adjustment was critical to reduce strain on the organization as well as avoid overinvestment in units and weapons. To a large degree, Defense Study 2000 set the context and recommendations for the current defense plan, with some significant adjustments during the political process, however, as outlined above.

THE ANALYTICAL SUPPORT

Over the last thirty years, the Norwegian defense research establishment has played a key role in providing independent analytical support to the MOD and the CHOD in shaping the future armed forces. The establishment's major contributions have been to develop alternative long-term perspectives concretized as defense structures, assess funding needs over a twenty-year period, and assess each structure's defense capability. The ability to perform credible cost calculations over a longer period is crucial to ensure realism between long-term plans and expected budgets to avoid a sneaking, incremental imbalance between defense ambitions and defense means. Insight into defense effectiveness is necessary to ensure that a given structure is cost-effective in relation to the defense mission, and to evaluate whether it is sufficient to fulfill the defense mission or a change in budget constraint or structure content is required.

IMPORTANT ISSUES IN DEFENSE PLANNING

CONSISTENCY BETWEEN DEFENSE FUNDING AND
DEFENSE SPENDING PLANS
The annual defense budget for 2000 was US$2.9 billion, or 5.8 percent of central government total expenditure.[6] Operational costs represent US$2.0 billion, including costs involved in peacekeeping missions, and investments constitute US$0.9 billion.[7]

The fundamental challenge to Norwegian defense planning during the 1990s was the gap between defense funding and requirements consistent with a balanced defense. Since 1985, defense budgets have shown a steady decline compared to general central government spending. In 1985, 8 percent of central government spending was used for defense. In 2000, that share dropped to 5.8 percent. The defense budget share of gross domestic product (GDP) has dropped from 3.1 percent to 1.9 percent between 1990 to 2000. During the 1990s, this budget development was close to the average for NATO. For 2000, the average for NATO is 2.2 percent, and new member nations are asked to allocate more than 2 percent of their GDP to defense. To fulfill the stated ambition in the new long-term defense plan, a substantial increase in defense funding over time is required. However, the current political landscape in the *Storting* with minority governments is likely to continue, which makes it extremely difficult to give high priority to the defense sector at the expense of other government sectors.

In the 1990s, the financial gap has both a funding and a cost side. First, the *Storting* has approved defense plans assuming a funding level significantly higher than the actual budgets appropriated by the same *Storting*. In the case of the Defense Commission of 1990, 0 percent growth budget was assumed, while the actual defense budgets for the following planning period (1994–98) showed about a 1 percent real annual decrease on average.

Second, the costs of implementing the plans have been underestimated significantly. Subsequent costing of the recommended defense structure plans after Defense Commission 1990 and White Paper No. 22 (1997–98) showed that the initial estimates were at least 20 percent to 30 percent too low. The main reason for this is a strong tendency to add elements to the force structure after final cost calculations have been made. This happens in both the political decision-making and the military implementation process.

The lack of ability to come to grips with the growing gap between defense funding and defense spending has had several adverse effects. Defense has had to reduce investments by delaying materiel projects and reducing materiel procurements in a far from optimal way, and it has reduced activities such as training and exercises, patrolling, flying hours, and so on. These measures, not foreseen, and their consequences from both a long- and short-term perspective have been adverse.

TIME HORIZON FOR PLANNING

In a period marked by large uncertainties, long-term plans are difficult to establish. Still, important consequences of choices can be seen fully only in a long-term perspective. One four-year period is far too short to capture the full extent of economic and structural consequences, and an eight-year period would not be sufficient to include important structural issues. For example, replacement of the Norwegian F-16 after 2010 would call for a major share of total defense investment for a longer period. One should notice that, in implementing plans, uncertainty about the long-term perspective could be used to justify delaying critical investments or decisions when funding requirements are not met. Such a focused short-term perspective would not be able to capture and prevent gradually accumulating structural imbalances.

Generally, a longer-term perspective should be used for defense planning, even if uncertainties make it difficult. Planning is not about once and forever establishing "the correct way," but about working with concrete alternatives to make sure that the various consequences of alternative decisions can be made explicit, taking into account the present uncertainty.

IMPLEMENTATION OF DEFENSE REFORMS

The Norwegian experience of the 1990s demonstrates the complexity of and many challenges involved in reshaping military organizations to best respond to a multidimensional and uncertain set of future requirements. Faced with such challenges, large organizations, including the military, often demonstrate a remarkably strong tendency to resist change and preserve their old structure far beyond the limits of its realm of validity.

Successful implementation of defense reforms rests on a number of conditions. First, the leadership and the defense organization itself must accept the need for change, and the new course must be established and accepted. In the Norwegian case, the initiative for change shifted from the political side in the early 1990s, and the Defense Commission 1990, to the military side in 2000. The over-ripped challenges caused by the double imbalance finally had the effect of ensuring acceptance of change as such. But the extent of the reforms required was not conducive to anchoring the conclusions, especially when it came to the need for comprehensive cuts in defense jobs throughout Norway. Still, the *Storting* has supported the recommendations presented, with some adjustments.

Second, funding to implement changes must be provided. As mentioned above, a fundamental problem has been the "financial gap" that developed during the 1990s. Also, the new long-term defense plan lacks a firm commitment from the *Storting* on future funding levels.[8] To ensure momentum in the restructuring and funding for high-priority projects, the MOD and the CHOD would have to establish additional priorities to achieve optimal exploitation of resources. If not, a substantial risk would exist concerning allocating funding to areas not sustainable over the longer term, and the implementation of recommended (costly) reforms. A critical side of this issue is the need for additional "fresh money" to make changes happen, especially within a shorter-term perspective. Substantial funding is required to cover new construction, salaries and overtime payments, consulting services, etc. If such funding had to come from the existing organization, the transformation process normally would be delayed.

Third, the tempo in implementing changes has to be quick to avoid reforms coming to a halt. However, quick tempo in reforms can cause internal organizational problems as well as problems between defense and society. For the 1990s, the White Paper No. 16 (1992–93) described a cut of about 6,100 defense employees, but only two thousand jobs actually were cut. Consequently, the goal of cutting operating costs by 1 percent annually was never met. Instead, there has been a substantial increase in operating costs and a drop in activity level since 1995. This problem has been acknowledged on both the military and political side, and, as a consequence, a more concentrated period for change has been set.

LESSONS TO BE LEARNED

A successful defense transformation process rests on full realization that the overarching key choices that have to be made in reforming defense are political in nature. These choices rest on a number of uncertain assumptions, the most prominent of them being security development, level of defense funding and defense component cost escalation, and technological development of defense and society. The strain between the wish for a stable and optimal long-term vision for defense and the many uncertain and partly conflicting assumptions and goals creates several dilemmas. Since the time constant for defense changes is long, a long-term perspective is definitely necessary for good guidance.

The degree of challenge in reforming defense is more closely linked to limited future defense funding than to the relevant defense task spectrum. The more constrained future defense funding becomes, the more pressing the priority problem will be. Especially for smaller nations, the questions soon turn into the "either-or" type. Substantial cuts in operating costs could free funds for investments. However, Norwegian defense has managed to implement only partially planned manning reductions and cuts in operating costs during the 1990s, and, contrary to plans, actually experienced an increase in operating costs since 1995. Basing decisions about future materiel investments on dubious assumptions of extensive and quick reductions in operating costs is not recommended. Adding shrinking budgets on top of this further aggravates this problem. The lesson: Don't spend money that is not highly likely to become available.

A plan for reshaping defense forces needs to be based on three fundamental considerations: First, a direction or vision for developing defense must be established. This vision has to be viewed in a longer-term perspective to capture the consequences of decisions or lack thereof, and to achieve a sufficient degree of freedom from shorter-term constraints of the existing defense structure in developing alternative solutions. Typically, defense components have twenty to thirty years' operating time, and the lead times for significant structural changes are typically five to ten years.

Second, and closely integrated with the first consideration, is the need for planning consistency among overall defense ambitions, structural development, and defense funding. Lack of such consistency will lead unavoidably to capability gaps from either insufficient funding or investing in wrong capabilities.

Third, one should recognize the need for strong political and military commitment to implementation of defense plans. This consideration can be especially challenging when substantial downsizing and/or reshaping of defense forces is required. Under such circumstances, some actors influenced by the changes are likely to take every opportunity to delay implementation, pending a new and more favorable decision. As a result, the transformation process from the current defense structure to a new one could come to a halt, leaving only fragments of the total force structure to be implemented at a very high cost.

ENDNOTES

1. Bill No. 45 to the *Storting* (2000–2001). The *Storting* is the Norwegian Parliament.

2. The Defense Commission of 1990 was established by the *Storting* to advise on the future of the armed forces.

3. White Paper No. 38 to the *Storting* (1998–1999).

4. Pugh, *The Procurement Nexus: Underlying Causes in Cost Escalation*, UK-MOD, 1992.

5. The size of the age group is about twenty-seven thousand (1999).

6. US$1 = 8.81NOK, as used in the IISS Military Balance 2000.

7. Investments include procurement of materiel (US$0.65 billion, or 22 percent of total defense spending) and investments in buildings and construction (US$0.25 billion).

8. The *Storting* is to debate long-term defense funding in its 2002 session.

CHAPTER TWENTY

Defense Reform in Postsocialist States: The Experience of Latvia

Jan Arveds Trapans

DEFENSE REFORM: OBJECTIVES

The objectives of defense reform in Latvia can be considered under the following headings: The first is democracy, establishing democratic, civilian control over the armed forces and the security sector through constitution and laws. The second is the ability of civilians and the military to define the goals of their reform, that is, a new vision of defense and security for a newly independent state. The third is their ability to attain those goals. Since 1991, Latvia no longer has been in the Soviet world and is intent on returning to the Western community of nations—politically, economically, and socially. Politically, Latvia has restored a democratic, parliamentary system of government, and, economically, it is bringing back a free-market system. These endeavors shape the progress of defense reform.

Thus, Latvia's defense reform objectives are not different from those of the other new democracies. But the Latvian situation, the point of origin for its efforts, is different from those of other Central European countries. When Latvia regained independence and the Soviet Army withdrew, according to a North Atlantic Treaty Organization (NATO) Parliamentary Assembly Report, "[All] that was left behind consisted of twenty-six sunken submarines and ships leaking acid, oil, and phosphorous. On this foundation Latvia began building its armed forces." The military infrastructure was in ruins, and equipment and logistical support were almost nonexistent. Latvia had to build everything from the beginning, and that demanded resources and time.

As a newly sovereign state, however, Latvia did not inherit a large bloc of former Warsaw Pact forces. It did not have to reduce a massive military force structure or restructure redundant defense industries, deprived of domestic markets, as many other transition states have had to do. The political and security objectives Latvia has sought since 1991 actually extend beyond the confines of what is implied by the word, "reform." In some ways, Latvia was in a less advantageous situation than other transition states; in other ways, it was in a better one.

Other postsocialist states have a different armed forces structure, a different regional security environment, and their own particular historical and cultural milieu. Nonetheless, although the obstacles each new government in Central Europe has had to overcome are different—some higher and others lower—all of the transition countries share some common features. Politically, these countries had to change from undemocratic, bureaucratic regimes to parliamentary political systems. Economically, they needed to transform state-directed economies to free-market ones. The political and economic past has left a deep, similar imprint that influences security sector reform down to the present day. Every new democracy was burdened by the heritage of an authoritarian culture. Within this framework of change "from the East to the West," the following specific reform areas are investigated: The first is the political process, establishing democratic, civilian control over the armed forces. The second is the emergence of a civilian defense community, particularly its capability to develop defense policy and plans. The third is the military, how professional soldiers adapted to a new political, economic, and social environment. Fourth is economy and resource management. Last are the new risks, the need for crisis management, and intelligence reform.

When Latvia regained its independence, there was a definite lack of national governmental capacity in defense affairs. There was (and to some extent, still is) a shortage of civilians with comprehensive knowledge of defense policy formulation and planning. This difficulty affects all Central European societies. The civilians involved in defense management initially had little or no experience in democratic, free-market systems. For Latvia, a central problem of defense reform was that radical political changes came hand in hand with radical economic changes. The political-economic combination affected defense affairs more than any other political area. Establishing democratic political control has been an important first step, but only the first step. When a postsocialist state moves away from a socialist economy and enters the free market, it fundamentally changes its economic approach to defense planning and resource management.

Latvian reforms, however, have not proceeded in isolation; they have a strong regional, or Baltic, component. One aspect of the Baltic approach to creating efficient and effective armed forces is close defense cooperation as a force multiplier, and the three nations—Latvia, Lithuania, and Estonia—have collaborated closely since they regained independence. The first major project was the Baltic Peacekeeping Battalion or BALTBAT, proposed in a meeting of Baltic defense chiefs in 1993. This peacekeeping battalion has allowed the Baltic nations to contribute to international peace and visibly reenter the international community. The chiefs also hoped that the Battalion would encourage defense interoperability among the three nations. Thus, from the outset the Battalion had both political and defense aims. It proved to be the first link in a mesh of regional security arrangements, and, in 1995, the Baltic Defense Ministers signed an agreement identifying more specific areas of cooperation. This led to a Baltic Naval Squadron—BALTRON; a Baltic Air-Surveillance Network—BALTNET; and a Baltic Defense College (BALTDEFCOL). NATO membership also requires interoperable staff procedures, communications systems, similar tactics, leadership principles, and a shared military ethos in member countries. English-language training also has high priority. All three countries are developing the same command, control, and information systems, logistics, resource management, and training concepts.

Latvia's defense policy includes as one of its goals to join NATO. The Partnership for Peace (PfP) is a major assistance platform designed to bring Central Europe closer to the Atlantic Alliance. Western experts identify readiness primarily in terms of interoperability at both the highest political-military levels of decision making and military operational and tactical levels. However, these are the requirements for working with NATO. No Western country that has joined the Alliance has had to refashion its military establishment to the extent that candidates like Latvia are required to do. Moreover, during the 1990s, NATO altered its structure and missions. The major changes are a Combined Joint Task Force concept for ad hoc coalitions established among NATO and non-NATO members to handle out-of-area conflicts, a new Strategic Concept with new non-Article V missions of crisis management through force projection, and a very exacting Membership Action Plan. These changes have required substantial planning efforts and revisions from Latvia's defense officials. They have had to perform a complicated maneuver of national defense building coupled with regional and international requirements.

There also is "the West"—governments, institutions, programs and advisers—arriving in the Baltic. Western institutions have exerted strong influence on defense reform, and Latvia has encountered "the entry of the West" on a broad front. Those countries involved represent Western governments, institutions, and programs such as the European Union (EU), the Organization for Security and Cooperation in Europe (OSCE), independent foundations, centers, and academia. Conferences, workshops, and seminars on security affairs frequently take place at Baltic capitals, and local and external experts, advice, projects, and information are ubiquitous. The working agenda extends beyond security, but defense, foreign, and security sector reform affairs have been the major concerns.

PROGRESS, CHALLENGES, AND OBSTACLES

DEMOCRACY AND DEFENSE

The fundamentals of democratic control exist in three areas. First, the military can have no influence on domestic politics, acting as an autonomous organization to safeguard its powers and privileges. Second, it cannot exert influence over external or foreign policy. Third, it has to accept democratic control over defense policy. This means that governments propose and parliaments confirm the defense budget, force structure, procurement, and related matters. Constitutions and laws provide the framework for democratic civilian-military relations. Establishing democratic control has to be considered from two aspects. First is the aspect of legislation, which provides the essentials of democratic control. Second is the aspect of laws as instruments for a fundamental reform of the entire security sector.

The first question in this chapter is the adequacy of Latvia's constitutions and laws in establishing a political framework for democratic civilian-military relations. A constitution must provide a clear hierarchy of civilian control over the military. This involves defining the authority of the head of the state (the President), the head of the government (the Prime Minister), the senior civilian responsible for military affairs (the Defense Minister), and the military establishment as a whole (that is, General Staff or similar bodies), with civilian officials of a government having guiding roles. Second, there has to be control through oversight, which is the function of the Parliament. The Defense Ministry has to respond to parliamentary demands, and the military has to acquit itself as a politically neutral body, with no attempts to exploit political parties to solicit support.

Latvia reintroduced the Constitution of 1922, without fundamental changes, which has been a solid foundation for democratic control. In retrospect, the decision to restore the old Constitution was an appropriate choice. The President, as the head of state with limited political powers, is the nominal commander of the armed forces in peacetime and appoints a military wartime commander. The President can declare war only following a decision by the Parliament but can initiate necessary defense measures without consultation in the event of aggression. Parliament, whose committees consider legislation concerning defense and security, approves the budget in a transparent process, decides on the size and structure of the armed forces, approves the peacetime military commander of the armed forces, and decides on participation in international missions. Some additional legislation was required to clarify the details of civilian-military relations. However, the important factor, provided by Latvia's Constitution, is the clear and distinct lines of democratic control.

It is not enough for the Constitution to declare that there is "democratic control" over the armed forces. It must be made completely clear which political entity—the President, the Cabinet (that is, the Defense Minister), or the Parliament—possesses which political powers for control. If there is any ambiguity, if the armed forces do not have a clear chain of command, there will be political confusion. The new political establishments of Central Europe have encountered recurrent problems in establishing constitutional and legal control. In some countries, particularly the South East European ones, there is an assumption that once a President has been elected democratically, that suffices to establish democratic control. At times, Defense Ministers have used their political office as a basis for personal power. But the most frequently encountered problem is that imprecise constitutional provisions for civilian structure of control over the armed forces have led to conflicting interpretations by Presidents and Prime Ministers of their political prerogatives. This has led to political contests or rivalries among the President, the government (that is, Defense or Prime Ministers), and the Parliament. Latvia has avoided this dilemma.

A NEW NATIONAL SECURITY STRATEGY

Every new democracy requires a new security strategy; it ranks in terms of political importance immediately after the Constitution and laws on the armed forces. The national security strategy, or National Security Concept, as it is called in Latvia, states the vision a nation has of its security and indicates the general objectives for the planned defense reform. Latvia had to take a new approach to its national security: Security strategies no longer can be developed by the military, because this approach disregards democratic control of the armed forces.

Security concepts have to be assessed from three aspects, the first of which is process. Civilians should develop these concepts, but the military has to provide its expertise. The second is content: The civilian authorities have to identify realistic national requirements, establish objectives, summarize the missions of the armed and security forces, and indicate how they should be structured to attain the missions. A new national security concept should include a threat and risk analysis, assessing short- and long-term danger. The third is the security concept's function as a policy document. A concept should provide definite objectives and guide the practical work of developing defense and security in the short, medium, and long terms. If it does not, it is only a public statement without any policy significance.

A national security concept is a summary, a concise document, developed by civilians with assistance from the military. Each state develops its national security concept differently; there is no blueprint for postsocialist countries to follow. However, all concepts have important essentials in common. The contemporary national security concept is a characteristic Western approach to security affairs, developed in its present form during the last several decades. In democratic societies, strategy essentially is a relationship between political and military concerns. National security concepts establish a country's security posture by balancing its foreign policy objectives, economic resources, and security requirements. Moreover, security is no longer a national concern; it involves international cooperation, even for countries that are not members of such institutions as the North Atlantic Treaty Organization (NATO). Western governments acknowledge the need of the citizens, and society as a whole, to know and approve what security demands. Therefore, a national security concept is known to the public and, usually, approved by the Parliament.

Latvia's security concept, a seven-page document, states that the country's national security objectives are to protect the nation's sovereignty, territorial integrity, democratic form of government, market economy, national identity, and human rights. Latvia assumes a defensive defense posture, and its armed forces will be small, formed into brigades and battalions, armed with light weapons, and well trained. Latvia intends to join NATO at some point. A threat to one Baltic state would be considered a threat to all three, and cooperation among the Baltic states would lead to integration into European and transatlantic structures. The security concept underlines the importance of civilian control over the military. It lists probable external threats and recognizes there also are new security risks that cannot be met solely with military means. The concept has been revised because Latvia's security environment has altered; the last version was issued in 1997.

The International Defense Advisory Board to the Baltic States (comprising senior, retired Western soldiers and diplomats) concluded that the concept had been developed via a democratic process. The government—largely civilians in the Defense Ministry, with appropriate military expertise—had done the basic work. The concept was discussed and amended by the cabinet. As a public document, it was known to society and discussed in the media. It was debated and voted on by the Parliament. It does not have the force of law (security concepts should not be promulgated as laws), but it was a policy document, although it stood above party politics.

A NEW DEFENSE COMMUNITY

Defense reform requires reformers. The new democracies have lacked national governmental capacity, people with overall competence in defense policy formulation and planning. Western experts have dealt with democratic control, with attention directed primarily to constitutional and legal aspects, or political control. Presumably, once the armed forces were placed under control—civilian, democratic, and parliamentary—a fundamental settlement would be in place.

Constitutional and legal regulations, however, no matter how well constructed, do not bestow the necessary expertise on policy makers. The fact that constitutions establish the basic rules for national armed forces, and that parliaments have enacted well-considered legislation does not provide the defense reform expertise needed from the military, civilian policy makers, or civil servants. Without competence in the Defense

Ministry, Parliament, and other parts of the government, without a civil service that can meet the military on equal ground, legal acts are not enough to establish effective civil-military relations in the everyday work of defense affairs.

In countries with democratic systems and free-market economies, civilians have a major policy role in defense planning. Furthermore, over the decades, the civilian sphere of activities in military affairs has increased. Contemporary defense planning is complicated and involves long-term economic analyses. It also is international in nature, and overlaps with foreign policy, as in the case of EU, PfP, and NATO. Various ministries—such as foreign and finance—parliamentary committees, and presidential offices require expert staffs with considerable expertise in defense affairs. Latvia's objective was to develop a body of civilians skilled in defense management, but this has been a slow, laborious process.

There are few parliamentarians in any country today—in mature or new democracies—who have sufficient knowledge to deal with defense affairs on their own. This is no reflection on their abilities. In Western countries, every parliamentarian has a private staff, and entire research staffs work for every parliament as a whole. These expert civil servants have the knowledge, skills, and tools to support elected representatives so they can hold defense officials and the military accountable. Parliaments in transition countries do not have such resources; however, staff expertise is essential, and educating civilians in defense affairs is a primary requirement.

When Latvia regained its independence, it had no Defense Ministry; once one was established, it had to be staffed with inexperienced workers. It took time to develop the full range of mechanisms and procedures for the conduct of government business, which the nations of Western Europe have had the opportunity to build and refine over the last half-century and more. However, Latvia did not inherit a large, stodgy, Warsaw Pact defense bureaucracy. There were advantages as well as disadvantages to this situation. There were few defense officials, and they were relatively young. Western observers have commented on this characteristic, where enormous weight rests on the shoulders of a small group of admirable young men and women who struggle to keep abreast of the problems in hand.

From the start, Latvia's Defense Ministry recognized the need for civilian education to develop civil servants skilled in defense management.

The educational system did not provide instruction in security and defense affairs, so Western institutions and schools were used to educate civilians and the military. The problem was that the great majority of the Western schools accept the military, but offer relatively few opportunities for civilians. Nonetheless, by the second half of the 1990s, Latvia had a Defense Ministry with officials functioning with growing confidence and effectiveness to establish their roles and positions vis-à-vis the armed forces and their headquarters. To increase their number, the Baltic Defense College (BALTDEFCOL) has developed a special course for civilians (and some additional, concise training seminars). However, they cover only part of the immediate need, and the Defense Ministry is striving to expand civilian education.

Everyday working relationships in civil-military relations measure the extent to which armed forces are integrated into governmental functions with the required level professional efficiency and effectiveness. Professional soldiers who have spent their careers in authoritarian systems usually regard democratic control and parliamentary oversight as detrimental to military efficiency. On the one hand, they look on civilians as intruders in a sphere of authority formerly reserved for the military. On the other, civilians in the new democracies have had little experience in defense planning and management, and they have to attain a certain level of defense expertise. Their lack of competence is one of the hidden shoals on which defense reform could founder. Civilians have to demonstrate to the military that the latter's needs are understood and its difficulties appreciated. These requirements are important and can be overlooked easily.

REFORM AND MILITARY PROFESSIONALISM

In contemporary democracies, soldiers have moved across the demarcation line that once separated military and nonmilitary responsibilities. A professional officer has to participate in administrative work, help prepare documents for the Cabinet, is involved in developing the budget, and could appear before a parliamentary committee. Because of the EU, NATO, and PfP, contemporary military professionalism requires knowledge of international organizations, interagency stratagems, and the procedures of multinational bureaucracies. Contemporary Western governments conduct their defense and security affairs using an overlapping civilian-military "defense community." Therefore, the military, like civilians, requires a new set of political, managerial, and international skills.

A review of the political relationship of soldiers and civilians in Central Europe shows that the professional military has not been a direct threat to the new democratic political systems. Professional soldiers have not attempted to undermine or overthrow emerging political systems, but they have slowed down the pace of defense reform. According to Western military experts observing reform in Latvia, the progress of modernization in all areas was hampered by the existence of a large number of mid-level, older men, who lie like an impermeable "permafrost," lodged between the leaders at the top, who want to speed up modernization, and those below, who actively desire it.

Latvia required a new type of a professional military officer. New defense requirements, a parliamentary political system, and a democratic society determine the specifics of professionalism, which can be summed up as follows: Latvian armed forces are small, with regular and reserve components. Politically, officers have to recognize that they belong to a democratic society. All of them need a combination of military and civilian skills, including knowledge of the democratic controls placed on the military. Militarily, they conduct operations as platoon, company, and battalion commanders. This emphasizes unit tactics and communications. At all levels of command, this requires delegation of command responsibilities, initiative, individual leadership abilities, and good relations between officers and enlisted men—characteristics that had not been important in the Soviet military.

Company and battalion commanders needed the ability to work with their Baltic counterparts and be good administrators of defense resources in line with relevant legal provisions and procedures. Senior officers serving at higher headquarters, senior staff positions, or at international institutions are expected to be military commanders, military diplomats, and military policy makers. The value of the professional noncommissioned officers (NCOs) who serve in Western armies also has been recognized in, and Latvia is preparing to train its own NCO cadre.

Latvia's National Defense Academy has undergone several reorganizations. The latest one, in 1999, changed the entry requirements; the Academy accepts university graduates who have to pass exacting examinations. The fundamental idea behind this reform is to have a highly educated class of officers who think of themselves as an integral part of Latvian society as a whole. The cadets receive an intensive, one-year education and are expected to understand of the role of the armed forces in a democratic society. They develop technical soldierly skills combined with moral standards, intellectual qualities, and good communications with soldiers in the unit.

Field grade officers are educated at the Baltic Defense College in Estonia. Students there are expected to understand of the role of armed forces in a democratic society. Based on mission-oriented command in a regional environment, students learn the operational art, the advantages and limitations of modern military technology, national defense plans, and planning related to a nation's economic and social resources. Instruction covers strategy, staff duties, and logistics, and graduates are prepared to serve as chiefs of staff at the infantry brigade level and in planning positions in Defense Ministries, General Staff positions, and international duties.

ECONOMY AND DEFENSE RESOURCE MANAGEMENT

National economy and defense are more closely related than other areas of government operations. Defense plans have to be linked closely with available economic and demographic resources. In every postsocialist country, there has been a severe shortage of resources, in terms of personnel or materiel, for defense. Latvia, in particular, has been keenly aware of this. Its economy is small, and so is its population; therefore, a careful approach to its defense resource management is imperative.

There is more to economy and defense than the amount of money available; because there is a free-market approach to defense economics, closely bound to the democratic, political one. Western defense ministries, for example, start defense planning with a budget approximation, estimating how much they will get and prioritizing expenditures on the basis of updated risk and threat assessments. Those who have been involved in this combined resource and force planning know that it is a demanding business with long-range horizons and complex analyses. As the new democracies moved haltingly toward a free market economy, defense requirements had to be estimated for input to the government's budget, stated in money terms, sent to Parliament for approval, and, after the "political masters" make their decisions, translated from money terms to support for personnel, weapons, equipment, supplies, training, and so forth.

After many decades of a command economy, the former socialist countries do not have well-functioning methods of defense management.

The difficulty extends beyond the lack of trained accountants and effective accounting procedures, as has been suggested. Nor does it suffice to proclaim that democratic parliamentary committees are, or should be, in charge of defense appropriations. The Defense Ministries of the new democracies have to implement novel, comprehensive, and effective planning, management, and budget systems. This is difficult because it also requires converting the mentality of the professional military. Professional officers wish to retain the existing force structures, while they modernize weapons and improve conditions for soldiers. However, they continue to think in the planning terms they have known and used for years. As a result, they have pushed for the resources for a traditional defense vision while refusing to accept that economic realities and fundamental political and social and changes inevitably demand top-to-bottom reform.

During the 1990s, resources available for defense declined everywhere. In Latvia, the shortage was particularly acute. Latvia's armed forces, small as they were, lived with "survival budgets" that sufficed only to keep the defense establishment on an even keel. "Whilst accepting that there are always competing demands for scarce resources and that the decisions on how these resources are allocated is a political one, to be decided on the cabinet level," wrote the International Defense Advisory Board, "we nevertheless judge that the low proportion of GNP [gross national product] allocated to defense in all the Baltic States has been historically such as to . . . frustrate internal military development."[1]

Throughout most of the 1990s, Latvia's defense needs had severe budget shortfalls. At the outset, the country had to extricate itself from the rubble of a collapsed Soviet economic structure. The government's annual budget was small, and social needs claimed a large share of what was on hand. Because there was no reliable inflow of government revenues and, therefore, no dependable projection for expenditures, money available to various ministries could be delayed or reduced at short notice. The Defense Ministry probably suffered more than other ministries.

The speed with which Latvia can build its armed forces depends in large part on the level of spending, measured as a percentage of gross domestic product (GDP), as well as the overall rate of economic growth—so concluded a group of Western defense experts. Once Latvia's economy began to generate sufficient resources for defense needs, the defense community—civilians and the military—had to develop rational and effective economic planning to complement the military side of planning. Just as they had to reorient themselves to working in a democratic political environment, they had to adapt themselves to defense planning in a free-market economy. Latvia's Defense Ministry had to have a new, comprehensive planning system.

Latvia has introduced a planning, programming, and budgeting system (PPBS). It is a comprehensive approach, encompassing short-, medium-, and long-term defense management. It is also a complex system, needs time to assimilate, and requires educating Defense Ministry civilians and military. It requires expertise in defense economics from the staff in ministerial, presidential, and parliamentary offices. Latvia is not the only country to introduce PPBS; however, it is one of the few that have succeeded succeeded. The Defense Ministry acquired a team of external experts and spent two years developing the system and educating the staff how to use it. PPBS is not an easy system to implement, but its successful introduction is easy to evaluate: It either works well or not at all.

NEW RISKS, CRISIS MANAGEMENT

The post-Cold War environment is affected by new, well-known risks. There are economic ones, including social unrest following implosion of a country's economy; economic damage caused by regional conflict, like the blocking of the Danube to commercial navigation; ethnic hostility, often exacerbated by religion, which can generate strife or separatism; insecure and inefficient borders that allow illegal migration and smuggling and disrupt good relations; organized crime, which today is a great threat to the viability of many states with serious international consequences; and corruption, which multiplies the effects of several of the threats above and undermines democracy and development of a market economy. Finally, there is terrorism. Identifying new risks and developing structures and methods for national and regional crisis management should be high on the security reform agenda.

The less adequate provision a government makes to meet the new risks, by developing an effective crisis management capability and investing in the right type and quality of security forces—intelligence, border guards, police, and army—the more serious the danger the risks could pose. Risk assessment is carried out largely (though not exclusively) by a country's intelligence services, its first line of defense. In the altering security circumstances, a government has to redefine intelligence, orienting it toward the new security risks. The National Security Concept summarizes the new risks. There also should be a requirements and priorities directive, provided by a high-level government agency, such as a National Security Council or a Parliamentary intelligence oversight committee. Without such a directive, there could be no list of all possible risks and threats, prioritization, an analysis of probability, or, therefore, no adequate preparation to meet them.

In fragile political, economic, and social situations, a crisis is a dangerous event that emerges suddenly and can threaten the lives of a considerable part of the population—the social structure, the political system, or the territorial integrity of a country. Persistent, long-term objectionable practices, like smuggling, need not be designated "crises" by themselves, although, in conjunction with other factors, they could contribute to development of a crisis situation. Crisis management is the means to counter a sudden buildup of a dangerous situation in a country or its immediate vicinity. Therefore, security reform requires management that recognizes, controls, and eliminates crises in their incipient stages. The aim is early containment. In this sense, the definition of crisis management differs from that of Western institutions like NATO, which deal with crises through force projection, that is, after they have been raging for a considerable amount of time.

Crises can be analyzed with scenarios. A scenario developed some years ago for a possible Baltic crisis affecting Latvia, in summary, is as follows: A Chernobyl-type nuclear catastrophe occurs in a location where the borders of three countries join. A frontier area is disputed by two of the counties. Panicked masses of inhabitants flee back and forth across the borders. One country mobilizes its reserve components. Reportedly, the border guards of another country fire shots over the frontier. A cloud of nuclear waste is drifting toward Scandinavia. All counties involved send messages to NATO, EU, and other institutions requesting assistance, but they do not specify clearly what aid is needed. All this takes place within twenty-four hours, starting as a major catastrophe and escalating rapidly, with population flights, cross-border incidents, mobilization, and responses on the national, regional, and international levels.

The concept of crisis management has been introduced only recently in the new democracies. Methods for dealing with new risks are still being developed. A government might have to decide on emergency measures, declare curfews, use the military for emergency tasks, and even prepare for mobilization. Crisis management must provide for the safety of all branches of government and their ability to continue functioning; it must ensure secure communications and be able to provide information to its own population and foreign governments.

On the national level, crisis management should be developed with three requirements in mind. The first is the capability to collect and analyze information about what risks and threats could emerge and how rapidly. The second is the management structure and the method of response. The third requirement is legal: A government might have to implement emergency measures. Civil rights of a society might have to be curtailed temporarily, so there should be definite provisions for declaring crisis conditions, and a clear understanding that the government must declare when a crisis is over. The ways and means of implementing such measures, and knowing when they should begin and when they must end, should be clearly understood. The structure, methods, and procedures of crisis management should be defined in a set of guidelines for government officials, civil servants, and the military.

LESSONS LEARNED

GENERAL LESSONS LEARNED

The major lessons learned from ten years of Latvian defense reforms can be recapitulated under some general headings—constitutional and legal reforms, the need for a new defense community, requirements for changing military professionalism, economy and resource management, and dealing with new security risks through crisis management.

Constitutional and legal reforms must establish a clear, firm chain of command over the armed forces. The military establishments in the new democracies have accepted civilian control. Presidents and Prime Ministers (sometimes the Defense Minister) have contested each other for control of the military. Latvia, fortunately, escaped this dilemma by adopting its Constitution of 1922. In other countries, awkward and ambiguous constitutional provisions have led to civilian struggles for command over the military that, as a consequence, sometimes have drawn the military into the political arena.

Much attention has been given to the issue of democratic, and parliamentary, control of armed forces. But a neglected aspect of democratic control is the issue of whether a competent civilian defense community can implement a defense policy and direct the course of military reform. The fact is that Central and Eastern European countries have not yet been able to develop a body of civilian expertise in defense issues. Constitutional or legal reforms will not establish democratic control over the armed forces by themselves without a sustained education effort, directed toward civilians as well as the military. Education must consider economic as well as political changes.

In most countries, the armed forces have not been reformed but "downsized," that is, shrunk in size, with smaller bodies, but still top-heavy. Economically, however, it will be impossible for any new democracy to sustain a military establishment of the present size for any considerable amount of time. The armed forces would live like patients on economic life-support systems, until they decay and die. They might collapse a few years sooner or later, but their collapse is unavoidable. Throughout much of the 1990s, Latvia (like the other two Baltic states) provided their armed forces with "survival budgets" to keep them afloat. The result was not survival, but a decline and possible implosion of a small defense establishment. Presently, however, it is funded adequately.

The new democracies require armed forces with professional abilities and qualities that respond to new political, military, and regional security realities. Politically, the professional military has to adjust itself to performing its duties in a democratic system. The armed forces will have different missions, a changed force structure, and new regional security responsibilities. It is not sufficient to decrease the number of soldiers and the number of weapons, live with a survival budget, and call it "reform." A drastic reduction of the armed forces, particularly of the officer corps, will be difficult for the professional military to accept, but it is absolutely necessary.

SPECIFIC LESSONS LEARNED

A New Defense Community: The Civilians   Like the military, civilians in the new defense community need education and training; however, the military has received most of these benefits. NATO has been the most active institution in providing defense education programs. NATO schools are designed for the military, although some civilians are admitted to them. The PfP program, essentially, is the annual NATO military exercise program, although some "in the sprit of PfP" events have included civilian participants. Finally, Western nations have tended to focus on only one element of defense reform in the new democracies—the establishment of political, government, and parliamentary control over defense policy.

Although Western institutions and governments have provided education programs to the military and civilians in the new democracies, the great majority of them have been directed toward the military, with relatively few opportunities for civilians. There have been some exceptions, and some institutions have developed excellent security education and management programs. Therefore, Latvia's Defense Ministries has developed education and training for defense administration and resource management, a critical need.

Military Professionalism   The decisive factor in a new type of armed forces will be its officer corps. Latvia's approach to professional military education recognized that it had to meet three conditions. First, Latvia's security environment was completely new, and the education system had to respond to it. Second, Latvia was a democratic country, and education for democracy was a part of military education. Third, Latvian officers had to be prepared for international and regional (Baltic) requirements. Military professionalism is acquired through education, training, and experience. In Latvia's situation, education was the most influential factor; training and experience would follow. An objective method for promoting officers is a central requirement in reforming the armed forces.

The new democracies claim the present military education systems are good and prepare officers of high professional caliber. This may very well be true; however, the real question is not whether high-level education is provided, but whether it is appropriate. The content could be entirely outmoded. Here, some lessons can be learned from the Latvian experience. The National Defense Academy education was fundamentally changed not once but twice, so that it provided all the requisite military skills and political qualities for officers serving in the armed forces of a small, democratic county.

Career Development: Military and Civilian   Without a career development system for military and civilians, Defense Ministers will never be able to institutionalize reform, because they will not be able to identify officers with the qualities needed to create a new kind of army, or put them into positions where they can transform words into action. An objective method of promoting officers is a central requirement in reforming the armed forces. As far as defense reform in the new democracies is concerned, the most important feature of a personnel management system is that it should deliver the right sort of officer or civilian expert the new force structure requires.

Latvia's Defense Ministry is introducing new methods of career management for professional soldiers, with explicit and open procedures, based on established standards of qualifications and achievement. A soldier's career has assignments to command and staff duty and studies at the Baltic Defense College or Western military schools. An impartial board of military and civilian representatives evaluates qualifications and makes recommendations. A similar method is being implemented for civilians. The value of professional NCOs who serve in Western armies was recognized as well, and the Defense Ministry opened a training school for them in 2001.

Economy and Defense Resource Management   Budget shortfalls have overshadowed the need to introduce an entirely new method of defense economics in terms of a money economy. It replaces defense planning of a command economy, which starts with resources: steel, oil, and manpower. Resource management, moreover, extends beyond funding, that is, whether the Defense Ministry gets what it wants from the Parliament or not. Defense planning is a long-term affair. Latvia's Defense Ministry conducts it with short-, medium-, and long-term planning—with one-, four-, and twelve-year horizons. It is linked inextricably to resource management over the same period. Furthermore, resource management must provide a careful assessment of projected needs, contain a method of establishing priorities, and provide all of the information requested by Parliament. In this area, the planning, programming, and budgeting system was the solution.

Defense and Security   Until recently, defense preparedness for an external military threat provided security. National security no longer can be calculated with military strength figures. These risks are not military in the sense that they can be countered or eliminated by national armed forces. In present conditions, the initial response to the new risks and threats would come from police and paramilitary forces. Therefore, governments have to shift resources to strengthening police, paramilitary forces, border guards, enhanced intelligence capabilities, and customs controls.

This does not mean that regular armed forces for conventional operations are no longer significant. Their force structures have to be reduced, but conventional, external threats cannot be ignored, although possible military conflict could occur on a smaller scale. If a state ignores the readiness of its armed forces to the extent that their capability is greatly degraded, small, paramilitary formations operating in another state can emerge as an external threat. However, investment in internal security could increase at the expense of the armed forces. Given a shortage of funds, it is essential that a security effort directed against new risks be designed with clear objectives and a coordinated structure from the start.

Crisis Management   The new security risks not only have to be identified; each country needs to develop a crisis management capability that can counter a sudden crisis situation before international institutions decide to act. This is a problematic area. Western governments and institutions have developed methods and techniques for crisis management; however, to them, crises occur not in their own counties (with the exception of large-scale natural disasters or the completely unexpected terrorist attack in the United States) and are dealt with through force projection. The new democracies have not yet developed structures and methods for encountering a range of possible crisis situations.

A study of crisis management preparations in Latvia (and the Baltic states) revealed serious shortcomings. The study revealed a lack of effective coordination, which could have serious adverse effects if the system were put under strain, through either the heightening of external risk or a major civil emergency. Latvia needed to construct, embed, and practice on a regular basis the mechanisms required for efficient functioning of government in times of crisis or emergency. Management mechanisms were inadequate, or needed to be constructed from the ground up.

ENDNOTE

1. International Defense Advisory Board, *Final Report*, February 1999, p. 6.

CHAPTER TWENTY-ONE

Defense Reform in the Czech Republic

Marie Vlachova

DESCRIPTION OF THE REFORM

HISTORICAL BACKGROUND

In modern history, the fate of the Czech nation has always been decided by politicians, not armed forces. Czech soldiers have seldom fought for "their cause," one they could identify fully with. The existence of Czechoslovakia's prewar military, charged with guaranteeing national sovereignty, was too short-lived, ending ingloriously when the political representation decided to demobilize before the country's occupation by the Nazis. The First Republic tradition was not sufficient to overcome widespread antimilitary sentiments—personified by the infamous Czech literary character, "Soldier Shweik"—that originated in the Austro-Hungarian Empire. During the communist era, most people could not identify with a fight against imperialism, designated by the communist regime as the main reason for compulsory service in the military. The fact that the military stayed away from public resistance to the 1968 occupation of Czechoslovakia by Warsaw Pact forces only exacerbated the common perception that it was no more than an obedient instrument of the Soviet Union's power politics. Doubts about the necessity for a military continued to exist within Czech society, even after the collapse of communism. After November 1989, the armed forces drifted for a short time to the public's and politicians' center of attention, but when it became apparent that the military would not intervene in the political processes, the focus of both the population and the new political representation shifted toward political, economic, and social issues.

The First Steps of Defense Reform after the Velvet Revolution in 1989 The most important steps necessary to move the armed forces to the control of a new, pluralistic political surveillance have been described by Anton Bebler as a separation of the military from the Communist Party; its depoliticization; placement of the military under parliamentary, governmental, presidential, and public control; and creation of channels through which the military can express its interests.[1] It was necessary to build new ties between the military's civilian command and executive levels. In comparison to other postcommunist countries, depoliticization of the Czech military was relatively fast. The passage in the Constitution specifying the leading role of the Communist Party was removed in 1990. The military's Political Administration Center, political departments in individual corps, and political positions were abolished. Professional soldiers and conscripts were barred from participating in any political activity, a measure intended to eliminate the Communist Party's influence on the armed forces and to ensure that the military would remain apolitical after the political system stabilized. Thus, the basic conditions for establishment of democratic control of the armed forces were created relatively quickly. An important step that strengthened the national character of the military was a peaceful departure of Soviet troops from the country's territory in 1992 and the nonviolent division of the Czechoslovak federation and its federal military in January 1993.[2] The powers to manage and control the armed forces were transferred gradually to the political representatives defined in the Czech Constitution, that is, the President, government, Parliament, civilian judiciary, and Supreme Audit Office. With only one exception, every Minister of Defense since 1990 has been a civilian. The incumbent Minister, Jaroslav Tvrdik, is a former soldier.

From the Division of the Czechoslovak Federation to the Madrid Summit—Orientation to National Defense   After the creation of the Czech Republic, both politicians and the public began to pay substantially more attention. For the second time in their modern history, Czechs had the national military as a guarantee of state sovereignty. Establishment of the first Rapid Deployment Brigade, devised according to Western armies' pattern, contributed to increased prestige of the military as well as information about the successful deployment of a small contingent of Czech specialists in chemical protection in the Gulf War in 1990–91. According to opinion polls, public trust in the military doubled (from 30 percent to 60 percent), but that trust proved to be short-lived. Generally, before the Madrid Summit, the armed forces were of little interest to society, and most of the processes connected with defense reform took place inconspicuously, within a small group of politicians.

Among these processes, regular participation of Czech units in peacekeeping operations in the former Yugoslavia was the most important.[3] Various reasons have prompted Czech politicians to decide to accept their share of responsibility for United Nations (UN) peacekeeping missions. This participation played a decisive role in efforts to incorporate the Czech Republic into Euro-Atlantic structures. Moreover, from geographic and cultural standpoints, the Czech Republic considers the former Yugoslavia a relatively close region with a long tradition of friendly relations and a similar history. In the culturally and historically analogous environment of the former Yugoslavia, Czech soldiers have exhibited a sizeable degree of adaptability. Peacekeeping missions have provided Czech soldiers with an opportunity to test their military and political skills, abilities, and knowledge, while allowing to help resolve regional conflicts. During the former totalitarian regime, most Czech soldiers acquired the ability to remain apolitical, which they have transferred to current social and political conditions. Furthermore, economic renewal, to which the peacekeeping corps contributes, could result in the reopening of traditional commercial contacts between the Czech Republic and the nations of the former Yugoslavia.

The Ministry of Defense began to prepare new defense and military legislation, but the huge amount of political, economic, and social legislative work to be done has postponed legislation. Decision making in defense was restricted primarily to irregular meetings of the Prime Minister, Minister of Finance, Minister of Defense, and Minister of Interior Affairs. The State Security Council was only a consultative body of the President and did not play a substantial part in decision making. Work on basic strategic documents (Security Policy, Security Strategy) began in Ministry of Foreign Affairs, but only the *White Book on Defense of the Czech Republic* had been issued by 1997.

The NATO Accession—An Engine of All Transformation Processes Accession of the Czech Republic to NATO was a very important incentive that accelerated and deepened all-important processes in the area of defense. The country has completed reorganization of its armed forces and adopted fundamental laws that define various aspects concerning the military and national security, forming a very solid legislative framework of democratic control.[4] Civilian politicians and military experts have improved their knowledge of security and defense issues, and, society generally has begun to pay closer attention to military issues and democratic control of the military. Slowly but surely, the Czech public's rather negative perception of the armed forces began to improve. Czech military and civilian experts working within NATO have introduced Western norms and standards into the military. Furthermore, pressure to prepare personnel for additional positions within the Atlantic Alliance has motivated the Ministry of Defense to improve language and professional training for both civilians and military professionals.[5]

The military has taken an active part in preparations for the Czech Republic's accession to NATO. It worked on preparation of basic documents and adaptation to NATO standards, gaining a prestige and certain authority with respect to international politics and security. This testifies to relatively good military expertise and good relations between political representatives and military professionals in this area. Tension was created only when soldiers had to transform politicians' rather unrealistic concepts into more practical form, for example, during debates about the possibility of deploying Czech peacekeepers in the Kosovo Force (KFOR) mission.

Czech membership in NATO has intensified and improved ties between the armed forces and political representation. In connection with NATO membership, soldiers have become the bearers and executors of political integration interests, taking active part in international efforts aimed at ensuring European security. Active participation in peacekeeping missions has resulted in an expansion of the areas where democratic principles of control are applied. In preparing new legislation both politicians, especially parliamentarians, and military representatives had to cooperate closely, and they gradually shed their prejudices—about "incompetent politicians" and military "old guards."

The Czech Republic was accepted into NATO, based on a political decision, in which the true preparedness of the Czech armed forces was not of vital importance. Whatever doubts this decision could raise, it is quite clear that the Czech armed forces would not have reached their present state of transformation if it had not been for the accession. The military stepped out of the shadow of societal and political neglect, the transformation processes became more transparent, and the true state of achievement more evident, especially after the Kosovo war, when the insufficiency of European armed forces, including fresh newcomers, became more apparent.

The Radical Reform of the Czech Armed Forces   Two years of membership in NATO had crucial meaning for the armed forces; they revealed all of the existing defense system's weaknesses. A comprehensive analysis of the present state of the armed forces concluded that

> although the existing defense potential of the Armed Forces of the Czech Republic is considerable, due to scattered resources and low efficiency of spending, their operational capabilities do not fully match the requirements and nature of operations, which the Czech military can be expected to participate in. The operational capabilities of the Armed Forces of the Czech Republic is further reduced by an inadequate structure of personnel, where organizational elements supporting command and control are over-inflated at the expense of combat units.[6] Organizational structures do not match requirements arising from the collective defense concept of the Alliance. The efficiency of the command and control system is low. Furthermore, it is burdened with a lot of red tape, and cannot thus focus its attention on conceptual work. There are difficulties and problems in the acquisition system and in the use of funds allocated for defense purposes. All these factors have an adverse impact on training, the executive part of human resources management, executive logistic support, peacetime recruitment and mobilization reinforcement etc. The resulting combat value neither matches the costs, nor meets the requirements for a modern military prepared to cooperate with allies.[7]

Until the NATO summit in 1997, where the decision about the first wave of enlargement was made, the Czech Republic was oriented to national defense and adapted its structure and weaponry to territorial defense. NATO membership marked a new strategic situation, the consequences of which were not defined comprehensively and clearly in the main strategic documents. The prevailing idea, that the Czech Republic could accept the tasks of collective defense while fulfilling the demands of national defense at the same time, proved totally unrealistic in terms of resources, both human and economic. Limited resources led to the Czech Republic's inability to cope with new tasks, especially during the Kosovo war. There was a lack of balance between the elite cadres, which are used for international missions, and the rest of the armed forces, which focuses on territorial defense. Concentration on the elite units deployed in foreign missions abroad has resulted in neglect of the bulk of the armed forces in such areas as training and equipment. Czech armed forces have assigned 80 percent of their capacity to NATO, pledging that units allocated to the alliance will meet NATO standards within a specific period of time. This goal cannot be achieved if the current training, building, and funding of military units remain unchanged. The goals and mission of the armed forces must be redefined to emphasize collective defense, and how the Czech Republic can contribute to it.

The new security situation of the Czech Republic must be reflected in a change of the armed forces' tasks, substantial reduction of personnel and armaments, abolition of conscription, and a different approach to basic operating principles. The main objective of reform is to build a downsized and highly mobile military with modern armaments that will be fully compatible with other NATO forces by 2010. The armed forces must be able to fulfill defense-related tasks of the twenty-first century alongside the Czech Republic's allies, assume specific assignments as part of NATO, and rely on collective defense of Czech territory.

CHALLENGES AND PROBLEMS

The past decade of defense reform revealed the complexity of transforming a totalitarian military into one that is part of a democratic state. The steps taken and results achieved comprise the basic measures every armed force with the same goals will have to undergo. What were the major problems encountered by the Czech Republic in transforming its armed forces?

RELATIONS BETWEEN POLITICIANS AND SOLDIERS

The need to cleanse the military of the influence of communists brought an influx of civilians to the Ministry of Defense, most of them with little or no knowledge about defense and military issues. Moreover, the political leadership was prejudiced against the "old guard" and did not trust their expertise in military affairs. Such a situation created a gap between politicians and soldiers that resulted in many prospective young officers seeking better conditions in civilian companies. Others backed off and left responsibility for decision-making to civilian management. Communication between the Ministry of Defense and the General Staff has been inadequate, and the division of powers has been unclear in many areas. These burdens of mutual distrust, "buck passing," evasion of responsibility for decision making, and the unwillingness of policy makers and executors to share responsibility—the former lacking expertise and the latter, power—became evident in the unpleasant "hour of truth" when the Czech Republic's inability to fulfill its NATO tasks became the subject of the allies' sharp criticism.

THE ARMED FORCES AT THE MARGIN OF THE SOCIETY

Defense issues never played a substantial role in domestic policy; the elite political, economic, and other groups, as well as the public, were more interested in economic, political, and social transformation, preferring to leave defense decision making to a small group of governmental and parliamentary politicians. Defense policy has not been considered as a prestigious and career-building area, and the best people devoted themselves to the political sphere instead. Nine different Defense Ministers in ten years can serve as the best illustration of this weakness of top-level policy. Government and parliamentary decision making was handled mainly in an ad hoc manner and lacked the continuity necessary to formulate reasonable, realistic, long-term prospective policy. Looking back, many old-fashioned defense-related decisions have drawn off a substantial portion of funds from the military budget and continue to do so.[8]

LIMITED CIVILIAN COMPETENCE ON SECURITY, DEFENSE, AND MILITARY ISSUES

Incompetence, discontinuity in thinking and decision making, looking for fast and easy solutions, attempts to implement various Western models without considering their compatibility with domestic environment—all of these factors can be ascribed to a complete lack of self-reflection in defense and military transformation. An analytical overview and precise decision making can be offered by independent expertise, that is, by a broad strategic community, involved in defense issues, but not necessarily bound to a political party or interest group. Such a community has been developing gradually in the Czech Republic, but its power and potential are still too limited to play a substantial role in defense policy. Politicians and ministerial officials recognized the importance of strategic community only recently. Generally, such a situation is the result of too narrow an understanding of democratic control of armed forces, which is limited to state institutions and excludes the vast range of public, nongovernmental, and other groups able and willing to contribute to formulating a reasonable and realistic defense policy. The Czech case illustrates that democratic control that functions only on paper creates a system that exacerbates flaws, prevents change, and hampers full integration of new members into NATO.

CABINET DECISION MAKING

Decision making in security and defense has been restricted to a narrow circle of government politicians. The President, as the High Commander of the Armed Forces under the Czech Constitution, does have some controlling powers.[9] Nonetheless, control of the armed forces is in the hands of Parliament, which must endorse all defense-related decisions made by the President. Only in exceptional situations, when Parliament cannot be convened, can the President order a military operation without that body's approval. In addition, the President's influence over the government appointments, including Minister of Defense, depends on the Prime Minister's consent. The President's influence over the armed forces is in the hands of the State Security Council, the government's consultative body, whose tasks are determined by legislation. The Council, which coordinates activities of all state authorities responsible for national defense, has a long tradition in the Czech Republic.[10]

After November 1989, the right to appoint the Council chairman was transferred to the President, who named the Prime Minister to this position. When the Czech Republic was created in 1993, the Council was not included in the Act on Abolition of the Federation, which allowed transfer of powers of the Federal Assembly, the government, and the courts to the government authorities of the newly founded country. Even subsequent legislative transfers of federal power did not include the Council. Thus, legally, the Council ceased to exist at the same time as the Czechoslovak federation. Important defense issues were discussed during meetings of so-called economic ministers. Although President Vaclav Havel appointed new members in 1993, the Council's existence had no legal grounds and was nothing more than the President's consultative body. A new constitutional law on national security, passed in 1998, placed the Council under the control of the government; however, its responsibilities were defined only vaguely. Further, under the new law, the government is responsible for appointing Council members.[11] Only in 1999, in connection with approval of new defense and military legislation, was the Council's work intensified. In addition to drafting new laws, the Council discussed deployment of the armed forced as part of NATO's military action during the Kosovo crisis. The constitutional Act on Security of the Czech Republic defines the State Security Council as an authority consisting of the Prime Minister and other government members whose structure is decided by the government. The Council's responsibility is to draft measures aimed at ensuring security of the Czech Republic to the extent specified by the government. The President can participate in Council meetings and is entitled to request reports about activities carried out by the Council. The Council has three permanent committees as well as the Interdepartmental Crisis Staff, which, as its name implies, is responsible for handling crises.[12]

UNCLEAR GOALS AND MISSIONS OF THE ARMED FORCES

The first national security concept was written in 1991 (The Military Doctrine), but it has never been accepted as an official document, although it has been used for internal ministerial concepts. In 1995, the *White Book on Defense* was published, representing a pre-NATO-membership level of defense thinking. It grew out of the necessity to adapt the organizational structure of the armed forces to the new strategic context after division of the Czechoslovak federation. The document strongly espoused NATO membership, based on its territorial defense advantages, and supported a conscript military, while gradually increasing the proportion of its professional corps. The *White Book* exhibited two major flaws, and neglect of these areas later became a source of problems.

- The military transformation plan, programs, and concept were not realistic in terms of the state's human and economic resources. The totalitarian idea that the state is obliged to give the military as much money as it needs (or asks for) was evidently behind this superficial approach. The fact that, in the face of a free labor market, recruitment conditions have changed completely would demand new methods and large investment only occurred very slowly to an old-fashioned recruiting system inherited from the past regime.

- The *White Book* devoted one chapter to civil control of armed forces. Controlling powers were assigned exclusively to state institutions: Parliament, the President, government, and the Supreme Audit Office responsible for controlling the military budget and property. Such a concept is problematic, since democratic control cannot be narrowed to civilian control, which is not necessarily democratic, as evident during the communist regime. The concept excluded other democratic control players, such as the media, nongovernmental organizations, conscripts, the public, etc. Moreover, this concept assumed that the military is the main initiator of control by and contacts with nonstate players.

The Security Policy of the Czech Republic, written by the Ministry of Foreign Affairs and published in 1997, incorporates the concept of an international dimension of national security when defining primary threat and security risks. *Security Strategy of the Czech Republic* and *Military Strategy of the Czech Republic*, issued in spring 1999 and approved by the Czech government as basic national documents for dealing with security and defense issues, have brought a certain shift in the narrow perception of democratic control. Standard democratic control of the military has become a matter of national interest. In addition to foreign policy, other important aspects, such as economic development, social stability, progress of democracy, and protection of human rights, were mentioned. These do not mean the role of the armed forces should be weakened. Rather, new elements can be introduced while traditional tasks, which consist of individual and collective defense, are preserved. However, neither *Security Strategy* nor *Military Strategy of the Czech Republic* defines these new elements thoroughly, and the new dimension of democratic control exists in a declaratory form only. Definition of ways to achieve these goals from the point of view of country's economic and human resources is lacking. In the amendment to the National Strategy (January 2001), the new definition of missions and goals of the armed forces appeared in connection with NATO's Strategic Concept for the twenty-first century, but, again, this definition does not take into account the country's resources. In addition, the role of a broader security community has not been addressed.

PLANNING AND BUDGETING

In 1999, the government decided to increase the proportion of military expenditures by 0.1 percent of the gross domestic product (GDP) every year, up to a limit of 2.2 percent. An American planning, programming, and budgeting system was introduced into the Czech military in the latter half of the 1990s. This system never worked as expected, and it finally crumbled. Among the reasons for the system's breakdown was long-term dependence of the military budget on the whims of the state budget, and the lack of clear political goals and missions ruling military investments. The planning was done on the basis of an annual budget, which resulted in an inability to control the financial flow at the ministerial level. This gave extensive authority to middle executive management in the financial section of the Defense Ministry and strengthened the power of the ministerial bureaucracy. Parliamentary control of the budget—the main criterion of democratic control of the armed forces—has been executed properly only on a macro level.

THE STRENGTH OF OLD THINKING

The strength of old thinking inherited from the communist regime appeared to be much more powerful than expected at the beginning of transformation. Eliminating the "old guard" mentality—which dates from a time when military careers were straightforward, membership in a military pact meant awaiting orders from Moscow, and all decisions were made collectively with no need for independent thinking or personal initiative—may prove to be the most difficult obstacle to defense reform. The legacy of the old system continues to have a strong negative impact. Clear rules of career and promotion do not exist or are not implemented fully, creating opportunities for those individuals who remain in positions of sufficient influence to thwart any change that could jeopardize their easy and comfortable lives.

CONCLUSIONS

DEFENSE REFORM IS A LONG-DISTANCE RUN

Defense reform is an extremely complex process demanding not only a change in the structure of the armed forces so they fit into the country's strategic environment, but also adaptation to the new needs that emerged after the end of the Cold War and, particularly, after the Kosovo war (a general trend toward professionalization of militaries, reductions in military personnel, changes in military vocations due to new types of missions, changing values among the younger generation, marginalization of the armed forces, new technologies of war and weaponry, etc.). Undoubtedly, the need to cope with global terrorism will bring still more tasks. Unambiguous, clear, well-argued, and analytically based goals and mission for the armed forces—shaped with a long-term perspective, but precisely defining the single steps necessary to achieve them—play a very important role in defense reform. Strategic documents do not have legislative power, but as a basis for political consensus, they can unify the endeavors of those responsible for reform. Clear and realistic goals and mission for the armed forces are the best way to reach both political and societal consensus on reform.

MISSIONS MUST MATCH TO RESOURCES

The goals and mission of the armed forces should be bound to domestic possibilities; they should always issue from the country's tangible human, economic, and intellectual resources. Any unrealistic, declarative, or blurring determination of what is to be done opens the door to various interest groups following narrow concerns, to bureaucracy and buck passing, and to those who are not able or willing to accept the changes necessary for successful reform.

CONTINUITY IS A CONDITION SINE QUA NON

Defense reform is not a task to be fulfilled by one political force authorized by a general election. This raises the question of how to ensure continuity in the process. The broader strategic community can be helpful if politicians listen to its members and consider them as counterparts working for the common good. Constant analytical, critical, and independent reflection of what has been done also helps to avoid mistakes. Executive staff of state defense departments and other institutions responsible for defense should not be changed with every freshly appointed minister of defense. They are not political bodies, even if they work for ministers appointed to the post by a political party. Executive staff represent important expertise, knowledge, and experience gained through fulfilling the single steps of defense reform. Their expertise and unique knowledge should be available for any politician in charge of defense, regardless his or her political affiliation.

TRANSPARENCY

Transparency in everything not covered by intelligence service rules is another important condition. Transparency is achieved mainly by:

- defense and military legislation;
- regular media coverage of the reform processes;
- an independent strategic community;
- a clear career and promotion system for military personnel, based on qualification and service performance; and
- a clear chain of command and management of the armed forces.

INTELLECTUAL TRANSFORMATION

Creating a new generation of soldiers and civilians seems to be the only way to overcome the heritage of "old guard" thinking. Success of reform depends on those who have personal experience with Western military standards, who understand the tasks of twenty-first-century defense missions, and who have enough strength to follow them. In the Czech Republic, the reform step toward radical change of military goals, structures, and format has been taken by people with personal experience from NATO armed forces. It was this experience that led them to understand the causes of inertia in the Czech defense and military system built during the last decade.

Appendix

Landmarks of Reform

1990

The first Czech military contingent was deployed beyond the territory of the state (a special chemical unit of 169 troops was deployed to the Persian Gulf).

1991

The first civilian was appointed Minister of Defense (Lubos Dobrovsky).

The last Soviet troops withdrew from the territory of the Czech Republic (the troops had occupied Czechoslovak territory beginning in 1968, after the Prague Spring, when the country was occupied by Warsaw Pact troops).

1992

The first Czech unit was deployed in a peacekeeping operation (an infantry battalion was assigned to the UN-led UNPROFOR mission in Republika Srbska Krajina).

1 January 1993

The Czech Republic was established as one of the two successor states of the Czech and Slovak Federated Republic.

1993

The first Rapid Deployment Brigades were created according to Western patterns.

1994–96

The Ministry of Defense was reorganized; the troops were reconstructed; and the military's Soviet division system was changed to a brigade one, fitting more into Western patterns.

1995

The *White Book on Defense of the Czech Republic*, the first comprehensive national security document, was issued.

1997

The *Security Policy of the Czech Republic*, written by the Ministry of Foreign Affairs, was published.

1998

Its duty during huge floods in Moravia (eastern part of the country) proved the military to be the only organization capable of a rescue operation, a turning point of unfavorable public opinion toward the military.

1998–99

The Czech Parliament passed a set of security, defense, and military laws.

June 1998

The National Security Council was established as a working body of the Government of the Czech Republic.

1999

Security Strategy of the Czech Republic and *Military Strategy of the Czech Republic*, prepared by Ministry of Foreign Affairs and Ministry of Defense, were issued, representing the most fundamental national security documents.

March 12, 1999

The Czech Republic, Hungary, and Poland became members of NATO.

2001

The National Strategy was amended according to the tasks of the NATO Strategic Concept for the twenty-first century.

August 2001

The government approved radical reform of the Czech armed forces, aiming for full compatibility with NATO, with a shift from a conscript military to all-volunteer forces by 2007.

ENDNOTES

1. A. Bebler, "The Evaluation of Civil-Military Relations in Central and Eastern Europe," *NATO Review*, No. 4 (1994): 28.

2. The Czech Republic is headed by the President, who is elected by parliament for a period of five years. The President is also the Commander-in-Chief of the Armed Forces of the Czech Republic. The Parliament of the Czech Republic consists of two chambers—the House of Deputies and the Senate. The House of Deputies has two hundred members; their tenure is four years. The Senate consists of eighty-one senators, whose tenure is six years. One-third of the senators are elected every two years. The government is the highest executive body of state administration. It is nominated and recalled by the President of the Republic and is accountable to the Parliament of the Czech Republic.

3. Beginning in 1992, the Czech Armed Forces took part in UNPROFOR, UNCRO, UNPREDEP, IFOR, SFOR I a SFOR II, UNTAES a KFOR.

4. Constitutional Act on Security of the Czech Republic, No. 110/1998 Coll., which defines the terms, "state of emergency" and "state of danger to the state"; Act on the Extent of Military Duty and Military Administrative Authorities (Defense Act), No. 218/1999 Coll.; Act on the Armed Forces of the Czech Republic, No. 219/1999 Coll., which defines the rights and duties of state authorities in respect to the armed forces and the military's tasks; Act on Compulsory or Substitute Military Duty, Army Manoeuvres and Some Legal Issues concerning Reservists, No. 220/1999 Coll.; Act on Professional Soldiers, No. 221/1999 Coll., which defines various aspects of professional military service; Act on Ensuring Defense of the Czech Republic, No. 222/1999 Coll., which defines the duties of state authorities, territorial administrative units, organizations, and individuals in securing national defense.

5. In 1999, the number of soldiers who had graduated from a foreign academic institution exceeded one thousand.

6. Units directly subordinate to the Ministry of Defense and the General Staff account for just 22 percent of the total personnel in the defense sector.

7. *Analysis of Required Capabilities, Target Structures, and Composition of the Armed Forces of the Czech Republic*, Prague: Ministry of Defense of the Czech Republic, August 2001, p. 1.

8. Examples include the purchase of L-159 light attack aircraft, upgrading of the T-72 Main Battle Tank, etc.

9. For example, the President appoints the Chief of General Staff, who is nominated by the government after prior discussion in the Parliament, appoints and recalls the Chief of the Presidential Military Office, and approves basic military decorations.

10. In 1926, the Interministerial Institute for National Defense Matters was established in pre-war Czechoslovakia. When the country faced Nazi invasion in 1939, the Supreme State Defense Council was founded and given extensive powers. After World War II (1945), the government instituted the Military Council; however, this body was abolished when the Communist Party came to power. Established in 1969, the State Defense Council was completely under the control of the Communist Party and was intended to help strengthen the communist regime in the country.

11. Council members must be members of the government.

12. Committee for Defense Planning coordinates plans aimed at securing national defense; Committee for Civilian Emergency Planning coordinates plans aimed at interior security, defense of the population, and protection of the economy and defines detailed requirements for civilian resources necessary for national security; Committee for Coordination of the Foreign Security Policy is responsible for interior coordination of foreign security policy.

CHAPTER TWENTY-TWO

Defense Reform in the Netherlands

Peter M. E. Volten

PLANNING FOR THE UNKNOWN

Before describing the reform measures taken by the Netherlands during the 1990s, it might be useful to remember the circumstances under which the restructuring of the armed forces has taken place. The developments in Europe after 1989 succeeded each other in an extremely rapid pace: the collapse of communist rule and the Warsaw Pact, the implosion of the Soviet Union, civil war in Yugoslavia, and so on. Everybody was taken by surprise. Although it was crystal clear that the armed forces had to be reformed, few had a clue how to do it. The need for a new set of political and strategic objectives was imminent, but the direction of change was not immediately self-evident. Had territorial defense become a thing of the past, or should one take into account a revival of a military threat from the East? Should the European member states take full responsibility in the Yugoslav crisis, or could they still count on American leadership? These and many other questions had a direct bearing on the reform at hand.

The reform and restructuring of the armed forces has been a process that was undertaken basically by the member states individually rather than in a coordinated way. In doing so, the states followed a prudent, step-by-step approach. The North Atlantic Treaty Organization (NATO) produced a number of communiqués and documents addressing the new political-military circumstances, but these could not be considered to be a new strategy providing planning guidelines. NATO's New Strategic Concept only appeared in 1999. Time and again, individual states and organizations like the United Nations (UN), NATO, the European Union (EU), and the Organization for Security and Cooperation in

Europe (OSCE) had gone through new experiences, in both relations among themselves and responding to surprising and challenging events.

Each military action on the ground—Gulf War, Bosnia, Kosovo, and Macedonia—presented challenges and lessons for what now is called security structures reform (SSR). September 11 is the most recent, dramatic event that again asks the question: What kind of security forces do we need in the face of these varying and often unknown challenges?

Evidently, the changes introduced over time have not been flawless, in the Netherlands or anywhere else, and mistakes have been made. The prudent and trial-and-error approaches have not always proven to be effective, nor have they resulted in the "right" solution in the sense that the defense organizations and armed forces were preparing and implementing reform in both an efficient way and in response to political demands. If these two criteria—prudence and trial-and-error—are viewed as essential for professionalization of the defense organization and armed forces, then reform of these institutions is far from complete. These criteria are not reflected fully in the SSR process, at least in the Netherlands. Put differently, the professional armed forces do not reflect fully the new political-strategic demands or the capacity to execute them efficiently.

The following brief review of defense reform in the Netherlands lays out some of the major decisions taken over the past decade. This, in turn, serves as the basis for a critical evaluation to reveal a number of shortcomings, possibly even mistakes in light of the evolved and current security requirements, as I personally see them. This sort of "lessons learned" approach then might offer some useful suggestions for countries just embarking on SSR, in particular because they are now facing generic and basic decisions that, once taken and implemented, are difficult to change again.*

THE RESTRUCTURING OF THE ARMED FORCES IN THE 1990s

The first Minister of Defense after the Cold War, Relus ter Beek, presented the Netherlands *Defense White Paper* in 1993. His task was not only to restructure the armed forces and to reform the defense institutions,

---

*To avoid distracting the reader's attention from the main and substantive issues at stake, this chapter does not present too many facts and figures about the forces. Instead, some quantitative indicators are provided to illustrate the order of magnitude of change and focus on the effects in terms of qualitative factors, that is, the degree of professionalization, combat-readiness, proficiency, flexibility, and sustainability.

but, as elsewhere, to find significant savings in the defense budget, the so-called peace dividend. Ter Beek found a politically ingenuous way out: He abolished the conscript system, thereby cutting the army in half, from some sixty-five thousand men to about thirty thousand men in peacetime. This measure was by far the most substantial change for the Dutch armed forces, especially for the army. The consequences for the navy and air force were negligible, since both services used less than 10 percent conscripts to fill their ranks. Even though Ter Beek himself was in favor of a conscript army, he soon discovered that a vast majority in parliament would support creation of an all-volunteer army. He changed his mind accordingly. Thus, Ter Beek was able to find political consensus and satisfy his Minister of Finance—and party leader—Wim Kok simultaneously. The reductions did not mean that combat units of the army and their equipment were cut in half automatically across the board. A significant number of units were held in stock for mobilization in wartime. Also, the plans to deploy a fully combat-ready air-mobile brigade armed with Apache helicopters, designed to be the showpiece and multimission unit of the army, survived the reductions. Still, the army organization was basically halved.

Meanwhile, the new peace support operations (PSO) missions were moving to the front burner, and Ter Beek's successor, Joris Voorhoeve, was known as a staunch supporter of humanitarian operations. Parliament had backed the decision fully to send a battalion to Bosnia to take part in UNPROFOR and stayed at Srebrenica until the terrible events in July 1995 forced it to return to the Netherlands. This very difficult mission had to be fulfilled, however, at a time when the army was involved with its most drastic reorganization in its history, which certainly hampered preparations for the peacekeeping mission and complicated its execution. In fact, the army was under siege both in The Hague and in Srebrenica. Quarrels with the Ministry of Defense and mistrust vis-à-vis the defense organization, including the defense staff and the other services in competition for scarce resources, turned into sour relations, misconceptions, and poor communications between the army and the home front. Financially, organizationally, and operationally, the army went through difficult years, ending in the morally painful and still traumatic July 11 experience in Bosnia.

As a consequence of the draconian financial measures taken for army restructuring, the navy and air force could be left largely untouched. The navy's surface fleet was reduced somewhat to a total of fourteen frigates, but the four modern submarines and thirteen Orion reconnaissance aircraft were held in service, while the Marine corps was not touched at all. The air force saw its number of F-16 fighter aircraft reduced to 108 operational aircraft and the total inventory reduced from 192 to a planned 122. The air defense units and Hawk and Patriot missiles were left intact. There were reductions in overall manpower strength, but not as drastic by far as in the case of the army.

The budget cuts obviously were not helping financing of the inevitable costs of reorganizing large and complex organizations. Moreover, the services are inclined, if not determined, to maintain the largest possible forces and to equip them well and with modern weapons systems. All of this is expensive. But more reductions were to follow the cuts of the first defense review. The government that came to power in 1998 decided to save 6.5 billion guilders (roughly US$3 billion) through 2010. The new minister, Frank de Grave, had to find 375 million guilders a year through 2001, that is, the first US$1.5 billion. Before sending a new *White Paper* to parliament, De Grave launched a nationwide strategic discussion by submitting the *Main Guidelines Document* in 1999. This rather elaborate work (consisting of more than fifty pages) proposed reducing the number of frigates to fourteen and the number of Orions to ten. There were four new frigates foreseen for the future, and the marines were to be reinforced by a third battalion (three hundred men). plus a new amphibious transport ship and twenty armed personnel carriers for PSO. The army would have to slash about half of the 330 main battle tanks, down to 180. One battalion of each of the three mechanized divisions was planned to be (almost) combat-ready, which would require some five hundred extra men, and the engineers group was to be expanded with three hundred additional men. The air force would have to give up one squadron (eighteen aircraft) of F-16 fighters.

The debate that followed resulted in a range of suggestions and proposals from many different sources. The most pertinent criticism concerned the combat-readiness of the army at the rather low personnel level and, indeed, De Grave agreed to expand the number of army personnel by twenty-one hundred positions, more than nine hundred more than was proposed originally. Moreover, according to the *White Paper 2000*, the army units would be strengthened by an additional six combat-ready infantry companies, bringing the total number of combat-ready companies to twenty-four out of the total of fifty-three companies of the Dutch First Division (with three mechanized brigades). This would enhance the capacity for longer-term PSO. Nonetheless, that part of the army that could be mobilized remained significant (more than 50 percent), and doubts persisted about the official objective of deploying two battalions at any time for PSO, by now a practically uncontested priority for Dutch political parties. Parliament amended the *White Paper* proposals by refusing to scrap the squadron F-16 fighters; it maintained their operational strength at 108. Their inherent flexibility in different missions was recognized and had shown its utility in Kosovo, in particular. Yet, on the whole, the *White Paper* survived as it was presented to parliament. Adjustments from the 1993 *White Paper* were neither drastic nor fundamental. With the exception of the change in size and primary mission of the army, the two reviews since the end of the Cold War have not led to a significant restructuring of the armed forces. Numbers have been reduced certainly. For example, the total inventory of F-16 in 1991 was 192, and the navy still had given up twelve minesweepers and other smaller vessels since. In that sense all three services were cut, on average, by some 30 percent to 40 percent. These measures arguably can be called restructuring, but not structural reform.

SHORTCOMINGS IN REFORMING DEFENSE AS PART OF THE SECURITY SECTOR

A remarkable discrepancy between the objectives and the concrete elaboration of the plans occurred in the *Main Guidelines Document* of 1999. Whereas the first chapter, written by the Ministry of Foreign Affairs, tried to identify new threats and ensuing missions for the armed forces, the contribution of the Ministry of Defense to the remainder of the document conspicuously lacked feedback about those observations. This disconnect between the political analysis and the proposed restructuring of military means did not go unnoticed during the "strategic discussion" in the media and the many meetings held on the subject, but was not redressed in the *White Paper 2000*. In other words, the end-means relationship in strategy and force planning was neglected. Whereas the security situation in Europe had changed dramatically, and was recognized as such, the ingrained inclination of doing business as usual had not been overcome. Loyalty to the existing organization and means prevailed. The services in fact had written in stone their preferences in the *Main Guidelines Document*. The battle for their share of the budget pie had taken place behind the doors of the ministry, and the others involved were urged not to reopen the case and to respect the compromise reached. The Ministry of Foreign Affairs—or the Prime Minister's office, for that matter—has forgone a top-down, politically driven procedure in rearranging the structure of the armed forces. In addition, and not surprising, little was done to adjust the mind-set of military planners regarding the need for new expertise, training, education, responsibilities in nonterritorial defense, and the like. The plans reflected the structures as they were before, and the means (units, inventory) were defended as before. The strategic demands of the new security situation in Europe were recognized in part, but not acknowledged fully. The mismatch between ends and means, inevitable after the drastic changes since 1989, was maintained, if not aggravated.

A decoupling, in a Clausewitzian sense, of the political and military strategic unity of thought and practice is probably the worst that can happen for the resulting armed forces structure. Preventing this from happening is the primary and urgent responsibility of the political leadership, broadly defined as the government and parliament. Leaving reform to the armed forces themselves is asking for the impossible to happen, however. Marginal and cumulative change might be possible, but reform is forgone. Reform needs leadership and knowledge and perseverance. The half-hearted approach to defense reform in the Netherlands is easy to explain and is not much different from what happened in other countries. But the consequences are significant and, in the end, are undermining the very purpose of maintaining a robust defense. If political demands, whether explicitly formulated or not, are not reflected in the organization's capabilities, and not efficiently translated into structures and, eventually, successful actions on the ground, public support and, consequentially, political support, will erode.

The Dutch case provides a number of examples of this fundamental disconnect between the political and military "partners" in strategy and the negative effects on their capacity to contribute to security policy. First and probably most important, the fact is that individual states continue to plan their defense efforts unilaterally rather in a concerted, let alone integrated, way. Even though it is unthinkable that the Dutch forces would ever act on their own rather than being part of an international coalition in a military mission, planning and prioritization of the Dutch forces are organized from the beginning to the end in a national context. However, no single nation can provide for all necessary military means in the ever growing spectrum of possible missions and specialization.

The North Atlantic Treaty Organization (NATO) has been slow in coming forward with a new strategy, but its member states should have taken into account at least an alliance-wide assessment of their own making. Moreover, if forced in the absence of a NATO document, a self-assessment should be made in bilateral cooperation with the most directly involved allies. The Netherlands did not do so. The *Main Guidelines Document* did not wait for allied recommendations and, worse, continued to pursue the existing acquisition program. For example, no one ever questioned the wisdom of putting an air-mobile brigade with armed helicopters in the field, a concept born out of Cold War considerations. Other financial commitments were not frozen or reviewed, thus constraining the options of reform. During the 1990s, billions of guilders were planned or reserved for frigates, amphibious ships, upgraded tanks, infantry transport vehicles, Fokker 50 transport planes, and, for a more distant future, the F-16's successor. The acquisition program kept its own momentum; a pause for reconsidering existing Cold War-rooted plans was not imposed.

An important footnote must be added here: Bilateral agreements have alleviated the lack of integrated planning in NATO. For example, the German and Dutch armies have managed to establish a German-Dutch corps that is more than the sum of the two individual forces. In this case, the cooperation was not a simple putting together of two national divisions with their own, different assets. The degree of integration justifies the name of army corps. By the same token, the Dutch decision to support the German air force and to pay for providing airlift facilities when needed rather than acquire its own—so far nonexistent—capability is a sensible way of making means meet ends. Cooperation between the Dutch and Belgian navies and between the Dutch and British marines also should be noted and welcomed. Yet, this cooperation with regional partners is born out of financial necessity and is not derived from a political-strategic concept, whether nationally or internationally inspired. The existing cooperation is certainly more than ad hoc arrangements, but it is much less far-reaching and less promising than conceptually based measures could be.

Second, threat-based planning has become more and more difficult since the end of the Cold War—witness the surprise of the Yugoslav crisis in 1991 and, more recently, the assault on the World Trade Center. It is said that we may ask too much from the political leadership of foreign affairs, long-term planners, or NATO headquarters in that respect.

However, the Netherlands is too small a country with too limited military means to cover the wide range of possible threats and deploy forces required for each and every scenario. (And even the United States needs allies to complement its huge forces for a major operation.) No matter how difficult it may be, priorities must be set. If alliance guidance for international or regional cooperation is insufficient or lacking, there is no other way than national prioritization, but one that is based on an internationally oriented analysis. Whatever the value of this national analysis of European security objectives, choices must be made and should not be driven solely by competition for limited resources or by costly reparations of experiences on-the-job of new military missions.

The lessons that could be learned from the Dutch experience in Srebrenica come to mind. Limitations of a human, cultural, organizational, or traditional nature should be recognized and put squarely before the responsible authorities, both political and military. Strengths and weaknesses should be singled out and respected in future planning. If the Dutch army proves to be unfit to face the villainous practices of men like Ratko Mladic or "irregular warfare," then this should be recognized in considering possible, future missions and should lead to a thorough overhaul of training and education. This is a crucial qualitative, human aspect of reform that has been neglected too much in the Netherlands and to which we turn later. Leadership, self-confidence, morale, team spirit, and other similar qualities are fully part of reform, even though they are less visible than the military planners' typical activity of preparing for physical output. In both areas, however, guidance is a prerequisite for reform. Even in their most cherished area of professionalism, the armed forces should not be allowed to revert to so-called capability-based planning, giving them a free hand in covering the needs for practically any mission. It sounds attractive and suggests a flexible military capability. The political leadership would choose from a variety of means after the political objectives of the mission have been clarified. This is utterly misleading, however, and cannot be realized in a world of limited and ever decreasing real defense expenditures.

In the Netherlands, the overall defense budget has been reduced by some 40 percent since the end of the Cold War. Nonetheless, the armed services have stuck to their basic organization (although the army was curtailed somewhat, as mentioned earlier) and mission. At the same time, they have argued that the present military means serve a wide range of options to choose from. There are reasons to doubt that assertion, however.

The army has not been tested since Srebrenica and is now fulfilling its peacekeeping missions in the former Yugoslavia satisfactorily, although with great difficulty because of its limited capacity for sustained action. Yet, the limited resources are stretched over many possible, rather than probable and/or prioritized scenarios. Whether the army should receive priority assignments in view of present and future requirements is something that needs serious political attention, but that goes beyond the subject of this paper. If, however, a decision would be made in that direction, then the other services will have to share the pie more generously than has been the case so far.

The navy and air force, though, have never been pushed to review their Cold War capabilities and still have the same force structure in place. The navy has become somewhat smaller, but not different; its assets still reflect its former task of antisubmarine warfare in the campaign to secure the sea lines of communication between the United States and Europe. One need not to be too cynical to ask where and what kind of submarine threat the Dutch navy is supposed to counter. Moreover, ten Orions and four submarines are not going to make a difference, given the generous Cold War "endowment" of the Western Alliance to the navies. The United States deploys more than a thousand Orions, and cooperation with the Americans should be self-evident, freeing considerable funds from the Dutch navy. Conventional submarines have been taken out of service completely by the United Kingdom, and one wonders why the Dutch navy has not done the same. If out-of-area missions are the most likely tasks to perform in the future, it seems that transportation and power projection by a surface fleet and very capable marines are clear priorities. Looking for "virtual" submarines from airplanes and hunting them down with submarines in one-to-one shoot-outs is the dream of heroic, albeit retired sailors. But the Dutch parliament has never addressed the question in this way, nor has it questioned the extent to which Cold War assets have continued to serve different, present-day purposes. Thus, the Netherlands is spending (if not wasting) money on capabilities that are at least of doubtful utility and are, without any doubt, superfluous if one takes into account the total allied inventory.

The same is partly true for the air force. Point air defense, provided by the Hawk and Patriot missile units, was essential at the time in light of the so-called strategic air offensive of the Soviet Union. There is no such threat nowadays. Air defense is carried out by NATO's significant numbers of aircraft, including the capable and strong Dutch force.

Breakthroughs in air defense by fighters are no longer a concern, as they were in the Cold War. Lines of communication are no longer threatened. The worries regarding a ballistic missile threat from rogue states are of a different order and deserve attention, but the Dutch Patriots are unable to deal with that problem, if it were ever to arise. Nonetheless, the air force spends more than one-third of its budget on maintaining the Patriot air defense units.

Third, limited financial resources do force most countries to take stringent measures and practice austerity, and this is the case in the Netherlands as well. Even though the Netherlands still spends almost 14 billion guilders (about US$6 billion) annually on defense, its purchasing power in real terms has diminished by roughly 40 percent. The proportion of gross national product (GNP) allocated to defense has declined from almost 3 percent to around 1.8 percent. As a result, the Dutch armed forces have been forced to stretch their resources, immensely in some areas. The result has been that combat units and platforms have had to be reduced in size, making the relative share of overhead and other noncombat services ever greater. The real combat power output has been made a victim of the wish to keep existing tasks and structures in place. The overall effort has become a fragmented one, leaving combat units and platforms struggling to be immediately ready and ready for a prolonged period. For example, the Dutch air-mobile brigade has been assigned a priority target in defense plans and an "elite" unit within the army. It has never been ready as a unit, but, instead, has been dispersed over the armed forces for a range of—separate—activities in various localities. Or, parts of the air-mobile brigade have been used for missions that should have been assigned to far less capital-intensive parts of the army; in another case, Apache helicopters were sent to Eritrea to support a peacekeeping operation, but were put out of range of the peacekeepers. In essence, parliament used them as showpieces in an attempt to justify these air-mobile assets. In reality, the mission in Eritrea was confined completely to peacekeeping, and the armed helicopters would have been employed only in a sudden exit strategy had been needed. Not surprising, unit cohesion and group building have suffered from taking on too many tasks with only limited manpower capacity. From its inception, the air-mobile brigade has suffered a shortage of men; at present, less than 60 percent of this combat-ready brigade is actually manned. The same holds for other parts of the army, such as the (infantry) units involved in peace-keeping in the former Yugoslavia. The army is stretched to the limit to maintain required numbers in the field, because, among other things, the actual number of men available for combat operations is limited within the organization. Overhead is taking its toll, and redundant staffs of the services exacerbate the problem.

The situation is most difficult for the army, which comprises many different arms and branches. Furthermore, the army faces serious problems in enlisting enough short-term (contract) noncommissioned officers (NCOs) and soldiers and keeping career officers in the ranks. The past decade's strong Dutch economy has complicated the problem of filling the units further. Labor shortages and attractive jobs in the civilian sphere have contributed to the current small proportion of less than 70 percent of available army positions occupied. The number of vacancies in the less attractive and man-intensive parts, like infantry or artillery, is still higher and has reached such alarming levels that the immediate availability, sustainability, and proficiency of the existing units are at risk. At the moment, the ratio of temporary contracts to career—life— contracts is 40 percent:60 percent, but should become 60 percent:40 percent, leading to improved availability and sustainability. This means, however, that some ten thousand men with career contracts must be replaced by men with short-term contracts, a tall order, even under the best circumstances. Implementation of this policy is made even more difficult by the relatively large number of senior officers and the higher retirement age of (now foreseen as fifty-eight instead of fifty-five). As a consequence of army personnel rejuvenation, a significant number of older officers and NCOs will have to leave, at considerable social and economic cost. To illustrate, at the moment, there are as many officers and NCOs as there are soldiers and others in the lower ranks, so the thirty-six army generals would "command" only some six hundred men each, if total manpower were divided among them.

The navy and air force face some of these problems as well, but to a far lesser degree. The navy still has quite a respectable surface fleet that can be run efficiently, although retaining experienced career officers is a serious concern. As to the four submarines and ten Orion aircraft, their role in present-day operations and their contribution to the overall allied inventory is not only of dubious relevance, but the size of these branches also raises doubts about their cost-effectiveness. Their presence clearly reflects the navy's resistance to change. Reinforcement of the marine corps, on the other hand, reflects the importance attached to this flexible and capable arm for a range of present-day missions.

Parliament has insisted on maintaining 108 operational F-16 fighters, in particular because of their proven usefulness and operational capability during the air campaign in Kosovo. At the same time, there has been no thorough review of the need to keep all of the Patriot air defense missiles. Point air defense is in search of a clearly defined mission. The arguably successful assistance against Iraq's Scud attacks in Israel during the Gulf War can hardly serve as the rationale for maintaining this weapons system in such great numbers. The not yet substantiated possibility of upgrading the Patriot for antiballistic missile defense is a totally different line of argument and partly misses the point, since it cannot justify the significant expenditures on operation and maintenance during the past twelve years since the end of the Cold War. Every system can claim some utility, but that cannot be a reason to retain it. In light of the budget restraints and need for investments and reinforcements elsewhere in the armed forces, a cost-benefit analysis is likely to lead to other decisions. In this case, the Dutch contribution to international operations can be made in a more efficient and useful way than by keeping the Patriot missiles—literally—in store. Of course, this would mean a 30 percent to 40 percent reduction of the air force, something no service would agree with, not to mention the resistance this concept would meet in quarters of personnel management.

It should be noted that the air force has not embarked on a new course in airlift capability. The Dutch and Germans have chosen to cooperate in this field and to build and maintain a robust German force of some seventy to eighty Airbus transport planes, partly financed by the Dutch. The Netherlands is entitled to call on the *Luftwaffe* to provide airlift "service" whenever needed. In this way, the German burden is relieved while the Dutch air force can forgo expensive investments as well as the relatively high operations and maintenance cost for the limited force it would mount anyway.

CHALLENGES FOR A NEW PROFESSIONAL ARMED FORCES IN A NEW INTERNATIONAL ENVIRONMENT

Reform is obviously not simply a matter of adjustment to a reduced defense budget and restructuring forces to the new missions that have emerged during the past decade. Nor is the professionalization of the armed forces fulfilled by the introduction of an all-volunteer force. There is nothing new in the fact that the professional soldier executes the demands of the political leadership, nor is the requirement to do so efficiently and effectively. And the fact that a professional organization must reflect these requirements is something the military has been asked to do only since the end of the Cold War.

What *is* new concerns the international context and its bearing on political-military relations and, as a corollary, on the demands of professionalism. Today's professional soldier in Europe faces a very different environment in which he must perform. He also faces a changed relationship with his political masters, meaning that he is called to carry out his duties in an international setting for an internationally defined purpose. Reform of personal and human aspects of defense policy is not always as visible as changes in personnel structures and numbers, but it is an essential part of the overall reform. The military *métier* has changed, as has the relationship between the professional soldier and other actors; the positions of both the political masters and the "parties" engaged in operations have undergone significant change. A brief elaboration on these aspects and on the way the actors involved have been able and willing to adapt themselves to the new circumstances seems useful for our understanding of the subject at hand. One could argue that investment in "human capital development" is at least as important as any other part of the reform and possibly even more important for countries in transition from an inherited system to a democratic style and mind-set.

For the military, professional loyalty to the cause of maintaining and restoring national security has shifted increasingly to international duties and missions, away from the traditional, national oath of allegiance of the military officer. Peace support activities in the name of a loose international community or on behalf of organizations like the UN and the OSCE, and since the 11th of September the combat against international terrorism, have become the business of the professional soldier rather than territorial defense. Identifying themselves with their national security duties is no longer self-evident for soldiers serving at distant and unfamiliar places for rather ideational purposes.

At the same time, both political and military leaders have been slow to recognize the need to adjust the military institution to the new circumstances. The international duties of the military are bound to determine the professional status and judgment of military performance. Professionalism, according to Samuel Huntington, consisting of expertise, social responsibilities, and international esprit de corps or corporateness, must follow. Expertise today includes such new skills as peacekeeping, policing, playing the role of a diplomat and international legal authority, even nation building. Social responsibilities today include providing security in so-called out-of-area regions where neither affinity with the territory nor shared values and identity with the locals is self-evident, to put it mildly. International esprit de corps today requires a fundamentally reviewed system of education, career planning, promotion, and internalization of group culture.

Professionalism cannot be left simply to the military. Political purpose guides military professionalism and often seems to contradict it. The military has to take into account the societal and international changes arriving from social forces, ideologies, and institutions. The last of these—institutions—ultimately define the outcome of civil-military relations, and these have to be addressed actively, not passively, in our rapidly changing political environment. For example, as NATO changes and its mission changes, the role of the military is bound to evolve as well.

All the same, to a large extent we are stuck with the strategic thinking dominant during the Cold War. Educational institutions train our young officers for largely outdated or less than probable missions, and these young men are reluctant to engage in roles and missions that do not represent the "real stuff." Here again, choices must be made. For example, if one believes "The military are not trained for peacekeeping support, but they are the only ones who can do it," then we have to either change the military and their training or find others to do the job. Defense diplomacy in a remote village in Kosovo requires a different type of soldier from one who would deter and hold back the Soviets in Germany.

In practice, the Dutch military have been learning on the job in Bosnia and Kosovo and may again in Afghanistan, partly because political leadership—government and parliament—did not develop strategic guidance, and partly because military leadership did not think through strategic developments. New conflicts, whether ethnic cleansing, civil war, or asymmetrical warfare, were imposed rather than prepared for. Too often, all this was left to the military professionals who, in turn, hung on to their current assets and their common idiosyncratic, somewhat guarded approach vis-à-vis politics and society.

Political and institutional influence on "the military way" is self-evident and, in the long run, of overriding importance for political-military relations. The point is that it should be made explicit, in particular the changed nature of that imperative. Today, the "sociopolitical imperative" has increasingly become an internationally defined imperative. As a consequence, military professionalism can no longer be understood strictly in terms of national security. The concepts of threat, national security, or balance of military power have receded into the background. The international "sociopolitical imperative," embodied in an admittedly vague notion of international community, requires a wide range of capabilities that go beyond traditional needs. The post-Cold War military has become diplomat and civil servant as much as operational officer in regular forces; his responsibilities are extended to protecting "strangers" and helping to establish democratic values and the rule of law; and the military has to share his distinct corporateness with foreign officers, civilians, international organizations, and nongovernmental organizations (NGOs) in the field. Decoupling military professionalism from this new international "societal imperative" is not only unwelcome, in the end it is senseless: It will undermine military professionalism, lead to a waste of resources, and erode public support.

The primacy of politics has assumed ever more pronounced leadership of the civilian side in both setting objectives and managing the process of strategy. The autonomy the military enjoyed during the Cold War in designing force structures as a unilateral response to unequivocal threats is a thing of the past, or should be. Political leadership in determining and enabling military professionalism and in striking a new balance in civil-military relations is in high demand. In concrete terms, ministries of foreign affairs should set priorities and make some tough choices about how the security forces—in a broad sense—could and should be used to further foreign policy in the EU or NATO framework. In the Netherlands, we were lacking such strategic insight and political guidance, as is shown above. The Ministry of Foreign Affairs or parliament did not guide. Thus, one cannot merely blame the military for poor performances if the strategy, conceptual work, and political purpose are not in place. The position of the professionals and the armed forces is dependent on a transparent and coherent policy to a far greater degree than during the clear and feared confrontation between East and West. In the end, the legitimization of our defense budgets depends on the trust and belief our societies have in the common political-military "strategic soundness" and ability to implement it accordingly.

At the same time, as we have seen, the Ministry of Defense and the armed forces have been slow to adapt. Military education at the academies reflects much of the Cold War curriculum; diplomatic and leadership skills, crucial in local confrontations in peacekeeping missions, are badly needed; little is done to make the officer aware of his contribution to a new world and operating in strange cultures; recruitment and retention policy is taking on disastrous proportions; and too little attention has been paid to the fact that the officer is not only a servant of his nation, but also a defender of the perspective of the "world citizen," human rights, and international law.

Here we also are pointing at the need for "civilianization" of military education and training. Civil professionals and institutions in the Netherlands have not been involved sufficiently in reform of the military curriculum; education and training have been pretty well guarded as part of the traditional prerogative of the professional soldier. There is, for example, no cooperation with universities—except in technical matters with the University of Delft—on relevant nonmilitary sciences and skills. One could think of history, international relations, civil-military relations, security studies, defense diplomacy, and so on. In this respect, the disaster the Dutch battalion experienced in Srebrenica should have been a clear and alarming warning. Yet, its commander has never shown any awareness of what happened, not even before the International Court in The Hague. He was promoted routinely to full colonel in the army. Of course, this commander and his colleagues were educated and trained during the Cold War. The curriculum had not changed, or if it had, not sufficiently, because there had been no real pressure from the political side to do so. The lesson to be learned is that human capital development has become a priority concern, and it should be reflected in the curriculum of the young cadets and, with even greater urgency, be taught as part of higher military education.

Suggestions to Take into Account in Reforming Armed Forces in Transition

The foregoing is a critical review of the Dutch reform or restructuring of defense and the armed forces. The shortcomings as well as progress made can be described in many different ways, and their presentation here certainly can be challenged. Reform of large organizations is a complex and time-consuming process that travels along a bumpy road. Some might argue that the Netherlands did not do so badly at all and rightfully point to modest achievements in other member states of NATO. After all, the Netherlands is still a member state that ranks somewhere in the middle in terms of defense spending, meaning other member states are doing less. By the same token, the Netherlands has made a number of meaningful decisions and has restructured (part of) its forces in accordance with the new political and military-operational requirements in Europe.

No country can or should serve as "the" example for defense reform. Each country has its own peculiarities and historic, economic, and cultural legacies. Yet, the experience of a decade of reform and restructuring in the Netherlands suggests at least the following points worth considering for the process of change, in general.

First, defense reform takes place in an international context to a far greater degree now than in the past. Habits of national planning, rooted in the practice of centuries rather than decades, remain strong and threaten to distort analytical clarity and thoroughness. The impact of the internationalization of security—rather than merely defense—policy is present everywhere and should be recognized as such. Whether one speaks about missions, acquisition, professionalism, or military education, the issues at stake cannot be approached properly but in the broader (political, economic, social, legal), international context. Except for the United States, no member state of NATO is likely to operate unilaterally in military missions. However, unilateral, national planning and its negative effects on operational output are looming large and, as a matter of fact, NATO has been plagued by a renationalization of defense planning under the financial constraints imposed during the past decade.

Second, thinking and conceptualizing in terms of international, pan-European security are not the same as reforming all European or NATO armed forces in a single "master plan." In many cases, regional cooperation by comparing national assets and seeking mutually enforcing output is more realistic and manageable, as evidenced by Dutch-German and Dutch-British bilateral efforts. States aspiring to NATO membership very well could embark on regional cooperation keeping the broader, international perspective in mind.

Third, reform should be concept-driven rather than means-driven, and this process should be directed in a top-down approach. Political leaders and the central planning authorities at the Ministry of Defense should guide that process. They should not direct and command the services in detail or micromanage, but should leave them considerable freedom to implement reform. The main point is that respect for the professional organization does not lead to the freedom to reform itself.

There should be a clear division of rights and responsibilities in the processes of security reform and force restructuring, respectively.

Fourth, loyalty to the existing practices, forces, and military means should not lead to a self-propelling momentum in planning and planning procedures. Changing security requirements should serve as a constant source of critical scrutiny and review. Acquisition of weapons and systems might be postponed or cancelled, if so required. Decoupling the end/means rationale might—and probably does—lead to modern or large forces (or both), but it does not lead to a necessary and efficient force structure.

Finally, the quality of the armed forces cannot always be inferred from what one sees: organization charts of the forces, modern weaponry, or impressive parades. The forces might be largely hollow, the weaponry obsolete for the tasks at hand, and the parade a façade hiding professional incompetence. Less visible, albeit of paramount importance, is the human factor and the personnel's ability to lead the forces, use the weaponry, and "parade" in action. It is commonplace that acquisition and operation of the forces assume priority in the planning process; personnel policy too often comes at the end. Yet, human capital development is essential in a demanding and rapidly changing security environment. Education, training, recruitment, retention, career planning, promotion patterns, esprit de corps, trust in the organization, public support, and respect all ultimately define professionalism and, thus, the professional soldier who must face dangerous and unknown situations in full confidence and awareness. In reforming security structures, personnel reform might turn out to be the toughest—and most costly—hurdle.

About the Contributors

CHRISTIAN CATRINA is Deputy Head in the area of security and defense policy of the General Secretariat of the Swiss Federal Department of Defense, Civil Protection and Sports. He has been involved in the reform of both Swiss security policy and the Swiss armed forces. Before joining the Swiss Department of Defense, Dr. Catrina was Research Associate at the United Nations Institute for Disarmament Research. He has also been a consultant to a United Nations expert group on the transfer of conventional armaments.

ANDREW COTTEY is Jean Monnet Chair in European Political Integration in the Department of Government, University College Cork, and a lecturer in the Department of Peace Studies, University of Bradford. He has previously been a Research Associate at the International Institute for Strategic Studies, a NATO Research Fellow and worked for the EastWest Institute, Saferworld, and the British American Security Information Council. His publications include *Democratic Control of the Military in Post-Communist Europe* (2001), *Subregional Cooperation in the New Europe* (1998), and *East-Central Europe After the Cold War* (1995).

CHRIS DONNELLY is Special Adviser for Central and Eastern European Affairs to the Secretary General of NATO, Lord Robertson, having served three former Secretary Generals in the same function. Prior to his joining NATO in 1989 he was for 20 years at the Royal Military Academy, Sandhurst, initially as an instructor in Russian and Soviet studies, and from 1973 as a member of the Soviet Studies Research Centre, which body he headed from 1979 until 1989. Born in Rochdale, Lancashire, UK, Chris Donnelly graduated from Manchester University in 1969. He has published numerous articles on Russian and Soviet military and political issues. He is the author of *Red Banner—the Soviet Military System in Peace and War* [1988]. From 1970 to 1993 he served as a reserve officer in the British Territorial Army. His current major interest is in the reform of defense and security establishments in Central and Eastern European countries following the end of the Cold War, and the development of collaboration between Eastern and Western defense establishments.

ALAIN FAUPIN has completed a 40-year military career in which he served in many operational, staff, education, and foreign service positions before retiring with the rank of Major General. A graduate of St Cyr Military Academy he held several assignments with cavalry and light armor with the French Foreign Legion in the Sahara, Algeria, and Southern France, as well as different command and staff positions in Germany during the seventies and eighties. He also served successively as assistant military attaché in Washington, head of the French Army General Staff Intelligence and International Relations Directorate (1987–91), military attaché in Washington, head of the French Delegation to the United Nations Military Staff Committee, and Deputy Director, Strategic Affairs, in 1994–1996. General Faupin retired in 1999 as Assistant Chief of Staff for International Relations (J5). Since then he has been a professor at the George C. Marshall Center, before joining DCAF as a senior fellow in the spring 2002. He has published many articles in the military, strategic, and national media.

DENNIS M. GORMLEY is a Senior Fellow at the International Institute for Strategic Studies in London. He served for 20 years with Pacific-Sierra Research as a senior vice president. Mr. Gormley received a B.A. and M.A. in history from the University of Connecticut and was commissioned a Second Lieutenant in the U.S. Army, serving on active duty from 1966 to 1969. He is the author, most recently, of *Dealing with the Threat of Cruise Missiles* (Oxford University Press for IISS, 2001).

ANATOLIY GRYTSENKO has served as President of the Olexander Razumkov Ukrainian Centre for Economic & Political Studies, one of the most influential nongovernmental think tanks in Ukraine, since December 1999. Following a 25-year career in Ukraine's Air Force, Colonel Grytsenko finished his military career as head of the Analytical Service in the National Security & Defence Council of Ukraine. Dr. Grytsenko is a member of the Public Advisory Council on Domestic Policy Issues under the President of Ukraine.

ISTVÁN GYARMATI is Senior Vice President for Programs at the EastWest Institute in New York. Prior to joining EWI in 1999, Ambassador Gyarmati enjoyed an extraordinary career in the Hungarian Foreign Service, where his postings included Deputy Head of the Hungarian Delegation to the Follow-up meeting of the CSCE, to the mandate talks of the CFE, to the CFE and SCBM Negotiations in Vienna (1987–1990); as Head of the Hungarian Delegation to the Follow-up Meeting of the CSCE and to the CFE and CSBM Negotiations in Vienna (1990–1992); Head of Hungarian Delegation to the Preparatory Meeting of the CSCE in Georgia (1991); Head of the Hungarian Delegation to the Preparatory Meeting of the CSCE Summit in Helsinki (1994); Chairman of the Senior Council of the OSCE to Moldova, Nagorno-Karabakh, and Chechnya; Personal Representative of the Chairman-in-Office of the OSCE to the Negotiations on Confidence and Security-building Measures in Bosnia and Herzegovina (1995–96); and Chief Advisor to the Minister of Foreign Affairs on Security Policy (1999). From 1996–99 Ambassador Gyarmati was Hungary's Under-Secretary of Defense for Policy. He has also served as Chairman of the Missile Technology Control Regime (1998–99) and as Chairman of States-Parties of the Organization for the Prohibition of Chemical Weapons. Ambassador Gyarmati graduated from the Faculty of Diplomacy at the Budapest University of Economics in 1974 and earned his Ph.D. in political science in 1977. He is the author of numerous publications on European security, conflict management and Hungarian defence issues.

LJUBICA JELUŠIČ is an associate professor of polemology, military sociology, and peace studies, and Head of Defense Studies at the Faculty of Social Sciences, University of Ljubljana. Her research interests are civil-military relations, restructuring of armed forces, defense conversion, conflict resolution, military profession, military legitimacy, and relations between Slovenia and NATO. Her recent publications include: *Defence Restructuring and Conversion: Sociocultural Aspects* (ed. with J. Selby), (2000); *European Defence Restructuring: Military and Public View* (ed. with P. Manigart), (2001).

ALI KARAOSMANOĞLU is Chairman of the Department of International Relations at Bilkent University. He holds a Doctorate in International Law from the University of Lausanne (1970). He has been a Fellow at the Hague Academy of International Law, a Fulbright Fellow, and a NATO Fellow. He was a visiting scholar at Stanford University in 1980–

81, and at Princeton University. He has been member of Turkish Delegations to various intergovernmental conferences, including the UN Conference on the Law of the Sea. Dr. Karaosmanoğlu has researched and published on security affairs, foreign policy, and peacekeeping operations. His articles have appeared in such journals as *Foreign Affairs*, *Europa Archiv*, *Politique Etrangère*, *Security Dialogue*, *International Defense Review*, and *Journal of International Affairs*.

Andrzej Karkoszka has served as the Head of the Think Tank at the Geneva Center for the Democratization of Armed Forces since October 2000. Prior to that he spent two and a half years as a professor in the Defense and Security Studies Department at the Marshall Center in Garmisch-Partenkirchen, Germany. Before coming to the Marshall Center he worked in 1991–92 as an expert in the Chancellery of the President of Poland and, from 1992 until 1998 in the Polish Ministry of National Defense, where he served as a Director of Strategic Studies, later International Security, Department and, from 1995 until the end of 1997, as Secretary of State-First Deputy Minister of National Defense. In the latter capacity he was Chairman of the Military Reform Commission at the Ministry in 1996 and a deputy Chairman of the Polish Team for NATO accession negotiations in 1997. Dr. Karkoszka received his Ph.D. in political science from the Polish Institute of International Affairs in 1977. He is the author of several publications on arms control, disarmament, verification, European security, and NATO enlargement.

George Katsirdakis has been a member of the Defence Planning and Operations Division of the NATO International Staff since December 1986. In NATO he has worked in the Defence Policy Section, where he was mainly involved in arms control work (support of the CFE negotiations) from 1986 to 1990 and defense cooperation since early 1991. When Parnership for Peace (PfP) was launched by NATO he was directly involved and worked mainly in PfP implementation and PfP policy issues. In March 1995 he moved to the Defence Partnership and Cooperation Section. Currently, he is the Deputy Director of the Defence Partnership and Cooperation Directorate in the Defence Planning and Operations Division of NATO's International Staff.

Mika Kerttunen is a Major (GS) in the Department of Strategic and Defence Studies at Finland's National Defence College. After graduating from the Finnish Miltary Academy as a Major (GS) he started his service in the Jaeger Brigade in 1986. He has studied at the general staff officer course in Helsinki in 1993–95, and served since at the Department of Strategic and Defence Studies, National Defence College, teaching Strategy and International Relations. He is also a graduate of the Norwegian Armed Forces Defence College. When writing the article on the Finnish defense reforms Major Kerttunen was on study leave to complete his post-graduate studies at the University of Helsinki. His special interests cover Nordic security policies and weapons of mass destruction.

ERIC V. LARSON is a Senior Policy Analyst at RAND, Santa Monica, California, USA, with two decades of experience in national security, defense and foreign affairs, and technology policy. After graduating from the University of Michigan in 1980 (A.B. with Distinction in political science), he worked at the White House Office of Planning and Evaluation (1981–83), the National Security Council Staff's crisis management center (1983–87), and the Institute for Defence Analyses (1987–89). He joined RAND in 1989 as a Fellow in the RAND Graduate School (RGS), received two Distinctions in the 1991 RGS qualifying examinations, spent a term as Visiting Student at St. Antony's College, Oxford University, United Kingdom, and, in 1995, received his M.Phil. and Ph.D. in policy analysis with a specialization in national security studies from the RAND Graduate School. His research interests include defense planning, homeland security, public opinion and media issues related to foreign and defense affairs, and innovation and technology.

ZOLTÁN MARTINUSZ is the Executive Director of the ATLANTICA Center for Defense Policy Research and Advisory Services. He previously served as Deputy State Secretary for Defense Policy in the Hungarian Ministry of Defense from 1999 to 2001. Prior to that he held different positions in the Ministry of Defense—including Director for Defense Policy and Director for NATO Affairs—and in the Ministry of Foreign Affairs. He was a member of the Hungarian team negotiating Hungary's NATO accession in 1997.

MARGARITA MATHIOPOULOS is Partner and Managing Director of the EAG European Advisory Group GmbH Germany and Founder and Executive Director of the Potsdam Center for Transatlantic Security and Military Affairs at the University of Potsdam, where she also holds a professorship in International Security Policy. During 2000–01, Prof. Dr. Mathiopoulos was appointed by the Greek Minster of Defence to chair an International Commission of defense experts to review the Greek Strategic Defense Requirements 2000–2015. She has published extensively on U.S.-European relations and transatlantic security, defense, and military issues.

LIVIU MUREŞAN is the Founder and Executive President of EURISC Foundation—European Institute for Risk, Security and Communication Management in Bucharest. Since 1990 he has served as Senior Advisor to the Romanian Prime Minister, leader of the majority in the Romanian Parliament, Deputy Director of the National Defense College (the first civilian to be appointed to a command position in the Romanian Army after 1990), Senior Advisor to the Minister of Interior, project director of the Regional Centre for Combatting Transborder Crime in Bucharest, and as visiting Professor at the Academy for Economic Studies in Bucharest.

KARLIS NERETNIEKS is the president of the Swedish National Defence college in Stockholm and holds the rank of Major General. The college has the responsability to educate middle ranking and senior military officers for staff positions and higher command postions. It also has the task to educate senior civil servants in areas as security policy, crisis management, etc. Before he took up his present position in 1998, MG Neretnieks has held positions as chief of operations in the Central Joint Command and commander of a mechanized brigade.

ANDRUS ÖÖVEL is currently working as a Senior Fellow for Geneva Center for Democratic Control of Armed Forces. From 1990–93 Mr. Öövel served as Commander of the Estonian Border Guard, the first paramilitary organization in re-independent Estonia. He was elected to the Estonian Parliament in 1995 and served between 1995 and 1999 as the Minister of Defence. Mr. Öövel participated in the establishment of the Estonian law enforcement system in the Ministry of Interior and the defense system in course of his work in the Ministry of Defence. Mr. Öövel graduated from the Law Faculty, Tartu University, Estonia, in 1985. He also holds an MSc in Global Security from Royal Military College of Science & Cranfield University, Shrivenham, UK. His hobby is mountaineering.

JONNY M OTTERLEI is a chief scientist at the Norwegian Defence Research Establishment (FFI) with over ten years of experience in providing analytical support to Norwegian long-term defense planning. He teaches operational analysis at the Military Academy in Norway and, for six months, provided analytical support to KFOR headquarters in Kosovo. A former Fulbright scholar, he graduated as a physicist from the Norwegian University of Science and Technology and holds a master's degree in Engineering-Economic Systems from Stanford University.

MARC REMILLARD heads the Outreach & Projects Department at the Geneva Centre for Democratic Control of Armed Forces (DCAF). His academic background includes a bachelor's degree in Political Science and a master's degree in International Relations from Indiana University of Pennsylvania, in the United States. His work experience includes three years in investment banking in London, three years in the United States Army, one year with the OSCE Parliamentary Assembly, and two and a half years with the OSCE Mission to Bosnia & Herzegovina as a Politico-Military Advisor. Mr. Remillard joined DCAF in August 2001. He has published articles on political barriers to security cooperation in Bosnia and Herzegovina, and on political, military, and economic challenges to security in that country.

JAN ARVEDS TRAPANS is a Senior Fellow at the Geneva Centre for the Democratic Control of Armed Forces (DCAF). Dr. Trapans previously served as Latvia's Minister of Defence (1994–95) and as Latvia's Ambassador to NATO (1995–97). Previously, he was a senior executive at Radio Free Europe-Radio Liberty (1981–94). Dr. Trapans also worked in the United States Department of the Army on the civilian staff of the Commanding General of the U.S. Sixth Army and Deputy Chief of Staff for Operations (1971–80). Other previous appointments include: Ambassador in Residence at the Centre for European Security Studies in the Netherlands (1999–2000), as Senior Visiting Fellow at the Institute for Security Studies of the Western European Union (1998), and Assistant Professor of International Relations at California State University, San Francisco (1996–70). Dr. Trapans holds a B.A. from Stanford University (1960) and an M.A. (1962) and Ph.D. (1976) from the University of California at Berkeley.

SCOTT VESEL joined the EastWest Institute in July 1999 as Chief of Staff and became Deputy Director of the Security and Governance Program in January 2001. He has published articles on NATO enlargement, American perspectives on European integration, and the work of Richard Ullman. He holds a B.A. from Yale University (1995) and an M.P.A. in international relations from the Woodrow Wilson School at Princeton University (1999).

434 • About the Contributors

Marie Vlachová is a military sociologist and has served as Head of Research Department of the Ministry of Defence of the Czech Republic since 1995. She is currently on secondment to Center for Democratic Control of Armed Forces (DCAF) in Geneva. From 1999–2001 she was the Czech delegate to the NATO Committee on Women in Armed Forces. She also served as President of ERGOMAS (European Research Group on Military and Society) for the period of 1998–2000. She is particularly interested in security and defense reform of Central European countries and she is coordinating the DCAF Working Group on Military and Society.

Peter M.E. Volten is Professor in International Relations and Organisations at the University of Groningen and Director of the Centre for European Security Studies, also in Groningen, the Netherlands. The Centre's main activity is currently the project on National Security Education in Eastern and Central Europe. Professor Volten joined the Institute for EastWest Studies in 1989 as Director of Research and became Senior Vice President for Programs and Policy in 1990, responsible for the substantive work of the Institute's research program, conferences, and symposia. He previously served concurrently as Professor of the History of War at the University of Utrecht and Director of Studies and Strategic Planning for the Ministry of Defense of the Netherlands. He is a member of the Advisory Council for Peace & Security.

Theodor H. Winkler is Director, Geneva Centre for the Democratic Control of Armed Forces (DCAF) and Representative of the Department of Defence, Civil Protection and Sports (DDPS) for the Geneva Centres, ISN, and the "Maison de la paix." Previously Ambassador Winkler held a range of positions within the DDPS, including Deputy Head of Security and Defence Policy (1998–2000), Head of International Security Policy (1995–98), Representative of the Chief of Staff for Politico-Military Affairs (1985–95) and Political Analyst (1981–85). He has also served as Chairman of the Interdepartmental Permanent PfP Office (1996–2000) and as Director a.i. of the Geneva Centre for Security Policy (1995–96). He earned his Ph.D. in Political Science from the Geneva Graduate Institute of International Studies in 1981. Ambassador Winkler is the author of several books on arms control, nuclear proliferation, and international security issues as well as several dozen articles on international security issues.

www.ingramcontent.com/pod-product-compliance
Lightning Source LLC
Chambersburg PA
CBHW032337280326
41935CB00008B/361